RENDEZVOUS WITH INJUSTICE

HOW A **FAMILY** SURVIVED HELL
AFTER BLOWING THE WHISTLE ON
THE 1MDB FINANCIAL SCANDAL

LAURA JUSTO - XAVIER JUSTO

Foreword by **Mahathir Mohamad**
former Prime Minister of Malaysia

rendezvouswithinjustice.com

Editing and publishing services
Kenny Hodgart & Johan Nylander
@HodgartKenny | johannylander.asia

Cover design
Darren Hayward | darrenhayward.design

Layout and formatting
Pankaj Runthala | manuscript2ebook.com

Additional editing
Lucy Cotillon

Back cover photo
Jose Jordan

Disclaimer: This is a work of non-fiction. The events and experiences detailed herein are all true and have been faithfully rendered as the authors remember them to the best of their abilities. Some names and identities have been changed to protect the privacy of those individuals. All dialogue is as close an approximation as possible to actual conversations that took place, to the best of the authors' recollection.

ISBN (paperback): 978-84-09-46001-4
ISBN (e-book): 978-84-09-47052-5

Laura Justo and Xavier Justo
Published in Spain

For more information, documents and images, please visit:
rendezvouswithinjustice.com
Support our cause: gogetfunding.com/justo-family

"A real-life horror story, grippingly and movingly written, that deserves to be read by anyone opposed to corruption. Laura Justo's battle to save her husband from languishing in a barbaric Thai prison is nothing short of heroic."

— Clare Rewcastle Brown,
author of 'The Sarawak Report: The Inside Story of the 1MDB Exposé'

"An astonishing first-hand and no-frills account of both human greed and human resilience at its boldest. A must-read for bankers, lawyers, journalists and anyone curious to discover the inside story of one of the largest financial scandals ever. Rendezvous with Injustice is also a beautiful love story."

— Florence de Changy,
author of 'The Disappearing Act: The Impossible case of MH370'

"A riveting tale of love, betrayal, greed and fraud that takes the reader from London high-life to a Thai jail via Venezuela and Cannes. Honoré de Balzac wrote in the 19th Century that behind every great fortune lies a great crime. Laura and Xaxier Justo's story shows that sentiment is just as true today."

— Randeep Ramesh,
The Guardian

"A captivating first-hand account from the whistleblower in the world's largest corruption case. All persons faced with the prospect of taking on a role in a corrupt enterprise should read this book to make them understand the likely cost to their life."

— Daniel Eriksson,
CEO of Transparency International

"By any definition, Xavier Justo is heroic, and his compelling story is one of courage and perseverance in the face of threats and intimidation by those hoping to prevent him from telling it."

— John Kucera,
former US federal prosecutor

"The story of a financial scandal and a story of love, the book also goes much deeper, showing that what's normal and acceptable should never be let out of sight. It has all the potential of a blockbuster movie."

— Eelco Fiole,
Adjunct Professor of Finance Ethics, University of Neuchâtel

"Justo paid a huge price for saving Malaysia from the world's largest kleptocracy."

— Tong Kooi Ong,
Chairman of The Edge Media Group

Foreword

IN 2018, I had the opportunity to hear a direct account of Xavier Justo's painful experiences after he was incarcerated in 2015 for so-called "crimes" related to the 1Malaysia Development Berhad's investments in PetroSaudi.

Justo suffered while the real perpetrators walked freely along the corridors of power, unashamed and confident that their unfettered power would never be challenged and would ensure their crimes would go unpunished.

Mention of 1MDB in fact never fails to conjure negative connotations of greed, lust, lies, corruption and a total absence of moral values.

As courtrooms around the world have since unraveled, 1MDB was used to misappropriate Malaysian state funds on a colossal scale. The United States Department of Justice described it as "one of the world's greatest financial scandals."

Beyond the despicable acts perpetrated and the eye-watering sums of money stolen lies another facet to the story, however: the victimization of individuals.

These individuals include people who dared to blow the whistle on what was happening. Justo was among them.

I first heard Justo's name in news reports concerning 1MDB. Much of the coverage pinned blame on him for allegedly leaking information and for trying to blackmail his former employer. Luckily when I became Prime Minister I had the chance to meet Justo and hear his side of the story. By then he had already been released from an 18-month prison sentence in Thailand.

I am much saddened by the fact that in the pursuit of covering up crimes, vulnerable individuals should be victimized and subjected to injustice. Families are made to suffer and are broken up.

It is worse when the perpetrators of crimes are in positions of authority. All too often, they have no qualms about abusing the powers vested in them to escape justice and cause others to suffer.

Modernity and the advancement of technology should make us more civil to one another. Unfortunately they have turned some of us into barbarians whose only motivations are greed and lust. What a contradiction.

I do hope that Justo's experience can serve as a lesson for anyone who cares about combating corruption. His story, as documented in this book, should serve as a reminder that in our midst there are monsters who will look for any opportunity to increase their own wealth and power.

When faced with such monsters, we can either stand up to them and slay them, or we can retreat to our comfort zones, ignore them and continue with our lives as best we can.

Of course, the second option only serves to allow these monsters to commit their crimes with impunity — and at some point our lives will be affected anyway.

Obviously, Justo chose the first option, and today we are hopeful that his efforts can help to bring about justice in the biggest case of financial fraud the world has ever seen.

I wish Justo and his family all the very best.

— Mahathir Mohamad,
former Prime Minister of Malaysia

Introduction

MILLIONS OF WORDS have been published, in thousands of articles, about the undoing of the 1 Malaysia Development Berhad — a national wealth fund, better known simply as 1MDB, that from 2009 was used effectively as the personal piggy bank of a cast of unscrupulous individuals operating both in Malaysia and internationally. Less focus has been given to how the scandal came to light, and about how a Swiss family suffered unforeseen and shocking consequences for exposing it.

Since 2015, the full extent of the corruption involved in what ranks as one of the most colossal swindles in history has become gradually clearer, like the digital image of a vast tapestry slowly depixelating. Few outside Malaysia would have known or cared about the fund's existence before reports began to emerge of billions of dollars vanishing from its accounts and allegations arose that the money had been used to enrich Najib Razak, the country's then Prime Minister, and to fund the playboy lifestyle in the United States of 1MDB's Gatsby-like alleged mastermind, Jho Low. But when a financial scandal involves such purportedly unethical characters — not to mention a modern-day Marie Antoinette figure in Najib's wife, Rosmah Mansor, the complicity of private bankers, the bankrolling of a blockbuster Martin Scorsese movie ("The Wolf of Wall Street") about venality in the world of finance, and the attentions of investigators across Asia, Europe and the United States — the world tends to pay attention.

It is now believed that a total of around $4.5 billion was embezzled from 1MDB, while a Malaysian government report has put the fund's outstanding debts at $7.8 billion. But what did it take for these numbers to see the light of public exposure? How did the scam's conspirators manage to pull the wool over the eyes of banks, regulators and auditors only to have the details splashed all over the world's media and for the US Department of Justice to spend years hunting down their misappropriated assets?

It's clear from investigations in Malaysia that questions were being asked by certain executives at 1MDB — primarily about the lack of transparency in its accounts — from the company's earliest days. Suspicions were also rife among the nation's independent media that something was awry. However, the pivotal moment in the fate of 1MDB came in early 2015, when members of this small faction of independent publishers and journalists met with Xavier Andre Justo... and he found himself faced with a choice: whether or not to give them the evidence they said they needed to expose the fraud being perpetrated on the Malaysian people.

Around the time of 1MDB's inception, Justo had worked in London for PetroSaudi, "an oil services and production company" which had loose ties to the Saudi royal family and is thought to have leveraged those associations to win exploration contracts in Latin America and elsewhere. It so happened that PetroSaudi's owners also knew the mysterious Jho Low — well enough, at least, to help him divert a major tranche of 1MDB cash out of Malaysia in a scheme involving a supposed 1MDB-PetroSaudi joint venture. Justo didn't know any of this while he was working for PetroSaudi, but after leaving the company in acrimonious circumstances, in the summer of 2011 he came into possession of a copy of its network server, a piece of hardware that contained thousands of files pointing to fraud on an eye-popping scale. Initially he sat on it; however, in 2015, after he had met a British journalist named Clare Rewcastle Brown and some well-connected Malaysians who were able to put his evidence in context for him, everything changed — and he opted to give them the PetroSaudi data they wanted without asking for recompense. In doing so, he set off events that were to have untold repercussions not only for those incriminated and for Malaysia, but for himself and his family, too.

If the PetroSaudi-1MDB arrangement involved manipulation and deception, aspects of what came next are perhaps even more grievous.

In *Rendezvous with Injustice*, you will discover details of this scandal-of-the-century drama which have been somewhat less widely rehearsed than the tales of Jho Low's excesses. These include claims of some jaw-droppingly ruthless actions taken by PetroSaudi's Patrick Mahony and Tarek Obaid, and by others including a former police officer who seemingly masqueraded as a current Scotland Yard detective: actions whose consequences Xavier and Laura Justo are living with to this day.

A story, in part, about their devotion to one another through adversity — this book offers a powerful testimony to Xavier's resilience and Laura's indomitable courage in the face of intimidation and kangaroo justice. It also takes a clear-eyed view of what it means to be a whistleblower, and refuses to shrink from describing the difficulties inherent in "doing the right thing" when the people you're blowing the whistle on seem capable of going to any lengths — aided and abetted by expensive lawyers and PR hitmen — to protect themselves. As Laura writes, the book contains all the elements of an outlandish thriller novel: "Billions stolen from a country that badly needed the money by its own prime minister and a small band of crooks; drugs, decadence and gangster-like behavior; twisted lawyers; the scapegoating of an innocent man; and at the center of it all, me, a young mother alone with her child and living in fear."

The book's lengthy gestation can be explained in part by the slow pace of justice in the various jurisdictions in which 1MDB's activities have come under legal scrutiny. The Justos are still awaiting the outcome of a Swiss investigation following a complaint they filed against Obaid and Mahony in 2017. Xavier is also the subject of a separate investigation in Switzerland over allegations, which he strongly denies, of industrial espionage in relation to the PetroSaudi data he handed to journalists in 2015.

In August 2022, Najib Razak — who was ousted from office in 2018 — began a 12-year prison sentence in Malaysia after losing his final appeal against conviction on seven counts of abuse of power, money laundering and criminal breach of trust. The following month, Rosmah was also found guilty of corruption and sentenced to 10 years in jail, although she has appealed her conviction and remained free on bail at time of writing. Earlier in 2022, the former Goldman Sachs banker Roger Ng was convicted by a US jury on charges of helping to embezzle and launder billions of dollars from 1MBD and bribery of foreign officials. Tim Leissner, who had been Ng's boss, pleaded guilty to similar charges in 2018, and in 2020 Goldman paid nearly $3bn in fines.

Lawsuits have also been filed in Malaysia and the United States against Jho Low; in Malaysia against some 1MDB officials; and in Malaysia, as well as Switzerland, against Obaid and Mahony. Most of those implicated deny any wrongdoing, while some — including Jho Low — are fugitives. Whether the individuals accused of putting Xavier and Laura Justo through the worst experience of their lives will ever stand trial remains an open question.

— Kenny Hodgart, Editor
January 2023

Table of Contents

Prologue

Xavier

A LAST MOMENT OF FREEDOM

MONDAY, 22 JUNE 2015. It's 6am on Koh Samui, a small island in the Gulf of Thailand famous for its stunning beaches and exclusive resorts, and I'm ready to set off on a 100-kilometer bike ride. Early mornings are the best time to go out: it's still reasonably cool and the island is asleep. I've had my breakfast and our dogs have been fed too.

I get on my Cervelo P5, a bike designed specifically for triathlons — those who know it will appreciate why — and head out for three hours of sweet suffering.

At the age of almost 50, I've just learned to love sport. Having a beautiful wife and an eight-month-old baby motivates you to stay in shape, but that's only part of it. With time and training, fitness has become an addiction: being physically sore and mentally tough are my daily pleasure.

The triathlete community of Koh Samui has also been a huge motivating factor, and I'll be forever grateful to my friends Laurent, Alex, Billy, Stephen and others for pushing me and sharing my toils and personal triumphs. This kind of training strengthens the body and hardens the soul — two things that will undeniably help me during the 547 days of pain and suffering that I'm about to recount to you in this book.

I've signed up for an Ironman triathlon — in November, in Australia — and right now I'm in the preparation phase. Next week I have an intensive training regime planned on the Thai island of Phuket, which happens to be one of the biggest triathlon centers in the world. To be honest, my old friends in Geneva would hardly believe this version of me. I was never a sportsman; I'd always preferred simply to watch football or Formula 1 from the safety of my sofa, equipped only with the remote control.

After returning from my bike ride, I have a three-kilometer swim scheduled, and then I plan to spend the remainder of the day resting and waiting for a visit from the Thai Immigration Department about the annual renewal of my work permit. My wife Laura and I are building a resort in Koh Samui and it's almost finished. The project has taken a long time and cost us a lot of money, but we're confident the results are going to be magnificent.

Laura and our little boy Xander are currently in Geneva visiting family on holiday and I'm due to join them in a fortnight's time to celebrate Laura's birthday. I call Laura in the afternoon to say hello and talk to my son. The conversation is brief. I tell her I'll call her back in an hour or so once the immigration officers leave.

All told, I'm feeling great. In fact, I feel like I'm the master of my world. I have a dream life, an incredible wife and an extraordinary son. I've achieved everything I ever wanted to.

Around 3pm, our cleaning lady, Pon, calls my attention. I look out the window and am surprised to see about ten cars and 20 people standing outside our house. The military took power in Thailand about a year ago in a coup d'état, and my first thought is that the new government must have tightened controls for obtaining work permits.

I walk out of the front door and an officer approaches me and says hello. I reach out to shake his hand, but instead — out of nowhere —

another man comes up to me, grabs my arms and handcuffs me. I'm in utter shock.

They push me back into the house and tell me they're police. They then hand me a document written in Thai and tell me to sign it. My first confused thought is how exactly they expect me to do so with my hands cuffed behind my back.

Another ten or so policemen make their way into the house, all dressed in civilian clothes. If they hadn't shown their badges, they could all easily have passed for local *tuk-tuk* drivers. None of them seem to speak English. I ask Pon to try to translate what they are talking about, but they tell her to be quiet.

The handcuffs are very tight, and I start yelling. The guy in charge orders another officer to put new handcuffs on me, this time with my hands in front of me. The officer puts these new cuffs around my wrists so tightly that I start bleeding quite profusely — at which point they at least have the decency to put on looser-fitting ones. (Pon will keep the bloodied set of handcuffs and show them to Laura when she returns to Thailand in August.)

Before turning the place upside down, the officers next look for the electric switches to turn the power off on our security cameras so that nothing is recorded. They search the house for at least two hours, taking computers, tablets, phones and other items.

Finally, one of them speaks to me in pretty good English. I figure he'd acted dumb just to put more stress on me. He tells me he is an officer of the Crime Suppression Division (CSD) of the Royal Thai Police, and that his name is Pongsawai. This man will play a huge part in what's coming for me.

After searching every corner of the house, they put me in the back seat of one of the cars and tell me they're taking me to the police station in Nathon, the nearest town.

I have no way of guessing it but this will in fact be the last time I see our house. My arrest signals the end of our dream life in Thailand — and the beginning of a long nightmare. Never again will I see this beautiful island where Laura and I got married, nor our Thai friends, nor even the pets and animals we've grown so attached to (all save for our dog Veggie, who will have the dubious honor of continuing to share in our tribulations). By extension, I will not see the completion of the resort project in which we have invested so much time and money.

I'm told I must go to the station to fill in some papers, and that they want me to sign a document stating that I am guilty of blackmail. Blackmail? This is all news to me. I refuse, naturally, and tell them I want to speak with my lawyer. To my astonishment, I'm not allowed to call one. I start to feel increasingly bewildered.

The person in charge of the Nathon police post tells me he can bring in some lawyers he knows. Since I have no other options, I accept his offer. These lawyers will later turn out to be small-time crooks, as is often the case in the legal profession in Thailand.

The lawyers arrive, a man and a woman, both in their 40s. They look friendly and are very nice to me. They read the documents to me, in Thai, and tell me I'm only accused of a minor offense — in fact, they're 100 percent sure I will be released on bail in Bangkok. Since the supposed offense is said to have been committed in the capital city, that's where I'll have to go to sort things out. In the Thai documents I can see names that are familiar to me — "PetroSaudi" and "Patrick Mahony" — but I can't understand the connection to any crime I could possibly have committed.

The lawyers ask me for money — for their fees and for my release. I naively give them my Thai credit card and the codes they need to use it… which turns out to be a big mistake, as they subsequently empty my account.

I'm to be taken to Bangkok in the morning, which means spending the night locked up in a cell — it feels more like a cage — outside the station. It's filled with cockroaches, bugs and rubbish.

Pon comes to see me together with Rot, the construction foreman we've been employing. They bring me food and drink, because when you're arrested here you get nothing from your jailers. Pon starts crying and Rot offers to give me money for my bail: a sum of about $10,000, his entire fortune. I'm moved by their kindness. I decline his generous offer and thank them both.

I ask the duty manager at the police station if I can call my wife, but he refuses. Rot knows him, however, and the manager reluctantly allows me to talk to Laura through speakerphone on Rot's phone. I explain the situation to her as calmly as I can. I try to reassure her that everything is under control — I tell her not to worry, that it's a minor offense. I'll go up to Bangkok the next day to pay the bail, I say, then I'll come back to Koh Samui on the evening flight.

She is crying. She is in shock. I reassure her again. I am 100 percent convinced I will be back the following day — because I haven't done anything wrong. It's all a mistake.

HOW CAN YOU go from being on the top of the world one moment to the depths of hell the next? What events and decisions shape your path? To understand how this all came about, how we ended up in this nightmare situation, I'll have to start from the beginning.

Prologue

Laura

FAREWELL TO THE CAREFREE LIFE

IT'S THE BEGINNING of June 2015 and I'm on holiday in Geneva, together with my son Xander. He was born in Thailand, so it's a chance to introduce him to all of my friends and relatives back home in Switzerland. Xavier is preparing for an Ironman race in Australia and is staying in Koh Samui to train.

I'm having a great holiday and enjoying seeing all my friends and family again. I have missed them enormously. I spend lots of time by Lake Leman in Geneva, where I indulge in one of my greatest passions: wake-surfing. I'm often to be found at Le Reposoir, a small harbor, where I hang out at the wake-surfing club there, EasyWake. My dad also has a little boat, and we love to take it out on the lake to go swimming. I even introduce Xander to water sports, which he loves.

We spend time too in our little secret garden at my parents' home in Grand-Saconnex. It's where I grew up and where they still live, and it's the best place I know to have a barbecue.

We go for walks in the forest and by the lake. I also go with my mother to visit some flea markets — her passion. I am filled with happiness, love, friendship and a sense of safety. Surrounded by my family for the holidays, I feel like I'm living a dream life. I couldn't be happier.

We miss Xavier, though, and he misses us very much. I feel like going back early to be with him, and I tell him I can change my tickets and shorten my stay in Geneva. But he says to wait: he'll be coming to join us in just a few short weeks.

In mid-June, I meet a friend of Xavier's. This guy happens to know a certain Tarek Obaid — a friend and former employer of Xavier's. He tells me he has heard from someone that Xavier should be careful, because Tarek is "planning something against him."

I call Xavier on Skype to warn him, but he jokingly brushes off the warning. Instead, he makes fun of me by pretending to be under arrest as we speak. He doesn't take me seriously.

Two days later, on 22 June, I speak to Xavier briefly on the phone early in the morning — but when I try to reach him later he doesn't answer. I feel increasingly uneasy, and I begin to fear something has happened to him. I tell my mum that I think maybe he has had an accident, but in reality I suspect it's something else. In the early afternoon, as I am walking with Xander and my mum in the park of the Château de Pentes in Geneva, not far from my parents' house, I receive a call from a Thai number.

I pick up and I hear Xavier on the other end: "My love," I burst out. "Are you alright?" He answers me: "Darling, don't worry... but I am in detention at the police station on Koh Samui." It's hard to hear him, and he tells me it's Pon, our cleaning lady, who is holding the mobile phone — because he is in a cell.

I feel myself trembling. From my meeting with Xavier's friend, I have a pretty good notion of why he is there. He quickly explains to me that Tarek and his business associate Patrick Mahony have filed a complaint against him in Thailand, but adds that everything will be sorted out very quickly. He says he'll go to Bangkok the following day with the police to get bail, and that everything will be fine.

I'm scared and I'm crying. Little do I know that this is just the beginning of the hardest and longest period of suffering that I could ever have imagined.

Chapter 1

Xavier

GROWING UP IN A CITY OF APPEARANCES

I WAS BORN in 1966 to Spanish parents in Geneva, and grew up in Les Pâquis, a working-class neighborhood of the city.

My school class was made up of ten Spaniards, ten Italians and a few Swiss: a real mix, and one in which we all felt integrated. There was no violence, no racism. It was also a time when children could be left outside playing and having fun until 10pm in the summer. The playground or the park were our adventure grounds. My friends and I weren't glued to screens like many kids today. (I'm not saying things were better or worse, just that different generations enjoy life in different ways.)

My parents had come to Switzerland in the early 1960s. My father, Andres, was a bus driver and my mother, Maïté, a cleaner. Like most of my friends, we didn't have a lot of money, but it was a happy childhood.

The only holidays I took, with my parents and my younger sister Rocio, were to visit our family in Spain. My mother was — and still is — the authentic Mediterranean mother: her children are her main reason for living. To this day, she worries when I catch a cold in winter, and knits me scarves so that I will stay warm.

My father was a great human being with a big sense of humor. He was strict — but he taught me the real values of life.

Coming from this modest background would — for a time in my later life — make me feel a little embarrassed and insecure, however. This was especially the case at the beginning of my financial career, as the people I worked with all came from much wealthier families. Talking about my origins at times seemed humiliating. But soon enough I replaced this embarrassment with a strong desire to succeed, and a great pride in my background.

I was never very motivated by school. I always preferred the company of friends and playing with a ball to bothering with teachers and pencils. I would just do what was necessary in class to make sure I passed my exams at the end of the year — without honors, but certainly without failure.

After high school, I spent four years at the Ecole Supérieure de Commerce, a business school in Geneva. On graduating, in 1987, I had a one-year internship at the bank UBS, also in Geneva. This was my first real contact with the banking world, and I began to be fascinated by the ins and outs of how a financial institution works, something that would occupy my interest for many years to come.

Before throwing myself into a finance career, however, I first took time off and went backpacking across Australia for six months, partly to discover the country and partly to discover myself. This experience of traveling was a magical one, and something I will certainly recommend my son to do when he is old enough.

Back in Geneva, I put applications in at a few job agencies and it didn't take long for interested banks to come back to me. Out of several job offers, I chose to start working for The Banque Scandinave en Suisse, in Geneva. I already had a good relationship with the head of the department involved, and she told me that, somewhat unusually for the industry, I would be working with five women. I felt lucky and some 30 years later I still have strong friendships with many of my colleagues from that time.

By the age of 25, I had already been promoted twice and found I could move comfortably in a world of international finance and wealth, an environment that was the complete opposite of the one I grew up in. I now found myself becoming friends with people who went to private schools, who went on holiday to the Caribbean and other exotic places, and who had led a life quite different to what I was used to. I felt a desire to be part of that and decided I would do anything I could in my professional life to achieve that goal.

In terms of the work, I was dealing with both professional and private investors, which made for some diversity. It wasn't a creative or artistic job where I would be driven by passion, but I was involved in one of the most important spheres of life for any human being — money.

The job was therefore personally satisfying, and it paid well. Of course, it wasn't only the money that motivated me, but for sure it's more fun to go on holiday in paradise or to drive a nice car than to be stuck on a gloomy camp site (much as I loved going camping with my parents when I was a boy).

I changed banks in the mid-1990s to boost my career and was appointed deputy manager at the Banque de Financement et D'Investissement. I was 29 and felt proud and happy about what I'd achieved. Unfortunately, I was unable to share this moment with my lifelong idol: my father. He had died the year before, and it would take me some time to realize how important and influential he had been to me. A few days before he passed away, he said something that I will remember for the rest of my life: "Don't do what I did; don't destroy yourself at work. Enjoy the time you have on this earth, and do things right." I would only understand much later how wise these words were.

I spent three years working in this small bank, but my desire to progress hadn't deserted me. Staying as an employee meant waiting for years before taking on more responsibility and I just felt I didn't have the time — so I decided to leave. It was not in my nature to sit back and just earn a good living.

Consequently, in 1998, quite against the advice of most of my relatives, I became one of the founding partners of an asset-management company named Fininfor et Associés. I was only 32 years old.

Before I joined, the company consisted only of my friend Roger Palma and a secretary. In time it would grow, and when I left in 2009 it had seven employees. I found the work rewarding and it slowly became second nature; the more time you spend doing something, the better you become at it, after all. We managed capital for French and Spanish clients, and at the time Switzerland still enjoyed a level of absolute banking secrecy that would only start to crumble in the 2000s (partly thanks to the American private banker Bradley Birkenfeld, like me a whistleblower who was destined to spend time in jail. In fact, Birkenfeld's revelations exposing the criminal activities of Swiss banks would mark the end for many asset management firms like mine. But this was all far off in the future when Fininfor started out…)

I got on well with Roger, seeing him in some ways as the older brother I never had. The only problem — I came to realize — was that he was going through a mid-life crisis, one that would create personal and professional headaches for both of us. He had a tendency towards the unconventional, and although I asked him not to, he started to invest our money in a number of ventures away from finance.

In retrospect, I know I should have forbidden him, but it was difficult as he was my friend as well as my partner and that strong bond stopped me from putting my foot down.

During those seven years of running a wealth management business, my life and my lifestyle changed. For one thing, I was lucky enough to be able to buy a beautiful flat in the old town of Geneva, one that had belonged to a former client and friend.

I also got married at the end of the 1990s to a young woman I had met in one of the banks I had worked in before starting my own firm. Settled in our new home, the standard life of a Geneva banker awaited me. Life was good, and my friends — not only financiers but people from all manner of professions, from insurers to real estate brokers to graphic designers — were interesting and diverse. We would play football and other sports every week. We were thirty-somethings who didn't want to grow old.

ONE SUMMER'S DAY at the end of the 90s, I was playing basketball with one of my best friends. He in turn had brought and introduced to me another of his closest friends: Tarek Obaid. This meeting would mark my life.

Tarek, a Saudi national, was in his early 20s, cultured, funny and so different from the people I usually hung out with. He came from a good family and had been to good schools, but his refusal to conform made him attractive to me. In time, his refusal to adhere to the conformity of Geneva would bring us closer. Perhaps recognizing that we were both different from others, we became the best of friends.

It was around this time that I also became increasingly disillusioned with my professional life. Even though I was doing well, I didn't find it fulfilling anymore. Yes, I had succeeded beyond my teenage expectations. I had a big house and a nice sports car, and I was able to travel to many countries. But I was bored.

In 2004, I divorced, and at almost 40 years old I found myself single — without children but with plenty of money.

Accordingly, I started to live the life of a single man, a party life that I had never experienced or envisioned before. I bought a Ferrari and became part-owner of a bar and a nightclub. Every single man's dream, right?

Meanwhile, my working life remained much the same: boring but financially rewarding. Living in Geneva and being in finance conditions you to take it for granted that you can have money without doing much work. Owning a second home in the mountains or by the sea is de rigueur, and so is having at least two cars, one of which should naturally be a sports car.

I'm not about to criticize this lifestyle but I will say that when you experience losing it all and having nothing, you realize — or at least I have realized — that the real riches in life are in the people around you: in love and friendship.

Back in the 2000s, after two years of living this bachelor life that was increasingly filled with artifice, it began to dawn on me that I was moving away from my real values and the things that really mattered to me in life.

By contrast, Tarek's night-time habits were slowly starting to take over his life and I tried to tell him to stop, or at least to control himself. Unfortunately, many of his friends would in different ways encourage him or take advantage of his predicament.

Something he once said to me lingers still in my mind: "I don't have any real friends except you; I buy my other friends because then at least I know why they're there." I always knew he meant it. Today, I would guess he doesn't have many real friends but still surrounds himself with people who enjoy the pleasures that can be bought with the money he has at his disposal.

Patrick Mahony, who I also met at that time, was one of Tarek's few childhood friends. At the beginning, we got along fine. Patrick projected an image of himself almost as the likable suitor trying to impress a prospective father-in-law — the perfect gentleman. Physically, he was quite small, but people found him good-looking and he was able to take advantage.

When we met, he was working for one of the UK's largest investment management firms, Ashmore Group. He had been educated at exclusive private schools and had the easy confidence you would expect from a guy from that background. He was also a sharp businessman and a great speaker — assets that would serve him well in the career that awaited him in white collar crime. It was only much later that I would see him in his true light: that of a sick and immoral man. He shared the same vices as Tarek.

Their appetite for satisfying these vices is what gradually separated me from both men, while bringing them closer together. Excessive use of substances increasingly made them lose all common sense and become detached from reality. It was like they genuinely felt themselves to be Masters of the Universe.

Of the characters around him that I met at that time, the only ones who could have remained close to Tarek in the longer term were those he would pay for various services. One was Aziz, the guy he would always count on for whatever he needed to fuel his partying. Another was Raphael, who he called his "stooge." (Tarek would go so far as to say in public that having a Jew as a "slave" was, for a Saudi, the ultimate sign of success.) There was also Pierre, a psychiatrist, who — in exchange for "some gifts from Tarek" — would prescribe any kind of medication he was asked to. (For the record, this Pierre, who also happened to be a very old friend of mine, would later jettison our friendship when he chose Tarek's gifts over supporting my wife in her battles on my behalf.)

Another of Tarek's childhood friends was Samir, who worked at the Mayo Clinic, a non-profit research hospital in the United States to which Tarek would later donate $10 million (perhaps the only benevolent gesture made by anyone connected with the financial scandal you'll read about in this book, even if Tarek's aim was simply to make himself look good in the process.)

And then there was Prince Turki, one of the sons of the former King of Saudi Arabia. Turki bin Abdullah Al Saud was introduced to me by Tarek as his friend — although seeing them together I soon realized their relationship was more like one of boss and subordinate, Tarek being undoubtedly the subordinate.

Tarek essentially wanted to use the Al Saud name to further his business interests. Prince Turki, who would later be among 11 princes detained by his cousin Mohammad bin Salman in a much-publicized 2017 power grab in Riyadh, seemed friendly and well-educated, but he was really not interested in the details of his business dealings with Tarek — as would become painfully clear as time went on. Rather, he just wanted access to money that wasn't tied in with his family. I am sure that if he had bothered to look at what Tarek was using his name to achieve, he would have learned that here was a man who would go to any lengths simply to get rich and thought twice about their association. But he did not.

It is relevant to state that Tarek and his family really had no money of their own at this time. Tarek's father had died, leaving almost nothing behind, and for a while myself and some others were making payments from time to time to help support the family. After becoming wealthy in the dishonorable way I will relate, however, he would gradually distance himself from those of us who had helped him, almost as though he was desperate that his background and time of penury be erased.

In the early 2000s, Tarek and Prince Turki did some business that would blow up into a financial scandal involving Barclays Bank — a small-scale scandal but one that showed just how far Tarek was willing to go to make money. Barclays was owed a large amount of money on a Saudi government back loan. Tarek used Turki's influence in the Kingdom to secure its repayment… and in exchange Tarek and Turki were paid a few million dollars. Having the Al-Saud name caught up in an investigation into this kind of activity — and mentioned in the international press — was not something that was welcomed in Riyadh.

Also in the early 2000s, Tarek set up a company with a brilliant name: PetroSaudi. Unfortunately, that would be its only praise-worthy quality. This so-called oil services and production company rented a small office on the premises of Fininfor and shared one of our secretaries. Tarek was a co-shareholder along with one other individual: Prince Turki.

The thing to note about PetroSaudi, however, is that it had no assets and in fact no real business. Instead, it existed to exploit and abuse the Saudi name and the cachet attached to it. It would eventually succeed — but illegally, as you will discover.

On a more positive note from those years, in 2008 a new employee joined our company, hired by Roger. This extraordinary woman is today my wife, Laura, without whom I could not have found the resolve to write this book. Her love, courage and boundless devotion are what have ultimately kept me alive. My story is therefore a tribute to her. In these pages, you will discover for yourself her extraordinary personality.

One day, before we began our relationship but knowing that cars were her passion, I lent Laura my Porsche. The following day, she returned it — but she'd had a small accident. She was upset and embarrassed about it, and for the first time I realized her personality was different to that of others I had known in the financial community: she was humbler, more honest, and to me more interesting. From that moment on, I could no longer look at her just as an employee, although in the beginning we kept our interactions private, as we didn't want our co-workers to know anything.

What neither of us could predict at the time is that we were about to begin an incredible odyssey of the kind that few couples will ever experience — an odyssey that would both test us and make us stronger, and which is still ongoing.

As alluded to, I was still bored stiff in my professional life. Early on in our relationship, however, Laura and I went on holiday to Thailand. We had an amazing time together and when we got back I told her I wanted this to be my last year in Geneva. I wanted to live elsewhere and do other things, and I asked her if she would be willing to go and live with me in Asia for a while. She didn't hesitate for a second.

Our departure for Asia was planned for September 2009. We used the time we had left in Geneva to settle up on a few things and embark on our new adventure without "baggage." This included selling my shares in Fininfor — a good time to sell, as it turns out, as the end of banking secrecy had truly arrived, heralding some bad consequences for asset managers in Switzerland. (My friends who have continued in the sector say it is now unrecognizable from the profession I knew in the 1990s and 2000s.)

I was 42 years old, and Laura only 21. Some people close to me said either that she was too young for me or that I was too old for her. I simply knew that she was my better half. The truth is that she was more mature than those 21 years and I felt younger than my 42. I loved her, and love does not count difference in years.

We were leaving with open minds as to what this new life would bring us, and with no more than a suitcase each. We had sold everything — cars, watches and other belongings — and put together all our savings and the proceeds from the sale of my shares. All in all we were more than comfortably well-off. Our aim was not simply to live off our capital, however, but to find some new activity to keep us occupied. We didn't want to work in the boring world of finance anymore, that much was clear.

Things didn't pan out quite as we intended.

A few weeks before our departure, Tarek told me — to my great surprise — that he was now in business with some Malaysians and was about to do a $2 billion deal with them. He also asked me if I knew anyone who could value PetroSaudi for more than that sum.

Besides my activities as an asset manager at Fininfor, I had also been acting as a director of various PetroSaudi companies (of which there were several, spread across various countries). PetroSaudi — meaning Tarek — had tried to monetize the firm's name to conduct oil business in South America, mainly in Argentina. Patrick's employer, Ashmore, had granted the company a loan that was meant to help it get a foothold there. The attempt failed — but it transpires this was just the starting point for Patrick and Tarek in their efforts to turn PetroSaudi into a cash cow.

Thanks to my directorships, I knew for a fact that PetroSaudi had almost no assets and was virtually worthless. Nobody could possibly evaluate it for what they were asking.

(Turns out I was wrong: they found a guy. But this is for a later chapter…)

In brief, I told Tarek I didn't know anyone capable of valuing an empty shell at $2 billion. And with that, Laura and I set off for Thailand, with plans for further adventures in Vietnam, Cambodia and Laos.

After leaving, however, I remained in contact with Tarek. I had a few remaining business ties with some PetroSaudi companies, and ending all of these took some time.

Then, one day, I opened my inbox to find he had sent me a press release stating that a Malaysian state fund, 1MDB, had invested $2 billion in a joint venture with PetroSaudi — a venture in which PetroSaudi was committed to contributing an equal amount. I was astonished, but he had obviously landed something of a coup.

By February 2010, we were staying awhile in the Krabi region of Thailand, and by coincidence met up with some mutual friends of Tarek's and mine. We happened to be with them when I received another message from Tarek. This time he was asking me to come and join him in London — to work for PetroSaudi.

He wanted me to oversee the group's operations, especially its activities in Venezuela. I declined. Better if we just stay friends, I thought. But Tarek persevered, asking me a second time. This time I hesitated… and after discussing things with Laura, we finally decided I should accept. Why not? We settled on the idea of spending two or three years in London and then returning to Asia.

It was another new beginning for us, and a return to Europe — with consequences that no one could have foreseen. Andy Warhol said that "In the future, everyone will be world-famous for 15 minutes." I would have happily kept my time to come in the spotlight that short.

Chapter 2

Laura

YOUNG AND ADVENTUROUS

I WAS BORN in Geneva, in 1987. My parents, Walter and Kate, had met in the 1970s, in London, where my mother had moved from her native Scotland to find work. My dad had left La Chaux-de-Fonds, a small town in the canton of Neuchâtel in Switzerland, to do the same.

They fell in love, got married and moved to Geneva, where my dad worked as an electrician. My mother was always there for my little brother William and I and would wait until we were old enough to resume her work with antiques, her lifelong passion.

William was my best friend, and always will be.

Our youth was marked by walks in the mountains in Haute-Savoie, an Alpine region in Southeastern France, where our parents rented a small chalet at the foot of the mountains. No video games and no television there — because there was no electricity. We spent our holidays in the open air, building huts and playing in the old barns with our friends from the village. In the winters, our parents took us skiing and tobogganing, and at weekends we'd often go to our grandparents' house in La Chaux-de-Fonds.

We were not rich but I had a golden childhood. My parents educated me in love, respect, tolerance and justice, and gave me values that I am proud of and that today I pass on to my son.

I graduated from the Ecole Supérieure de Commerce, the same business school Xavier had studied at, in 2006. During my studies, I also earned money indulging one of my greatest passions — cars. Two days a week, I worked at Dream Car Racing, a racing accessories shop in Geneva. I will never forget those years: sharing my passion for cars with customers all day, and heading out with my colleagues at noon for lunch and even more car talk.

During the four weeks of the Geneva Motor Show, we would set up and take down our show booth all by ourselves, as we were a small shop. The laughter, the evenings spent taking apart catalytic converters on VW Beetles to replace old parts, or fitting new nitrous oxide engines onto vehicles... To me it wasn't a job: I felt like I was doing what I loved most. I felt at home.

Granted, it wasn't always easy. At the beginning I had to fight for my place in this 99.9 percent male environment — and on top of that I was only 16 when I started. With time, however, I managed to gain respect, and even protection from my colleagues if anyone wrongly thought I was there for pure decoration. Eventually, my colleagues became like a second family, and even clients became friends. One of the latter, Phil, is one of my best friends to this day.

After graduation, I was out to enjoy my independence and freedom, and I landed a job at a financial institution in Geneva. My role was to oversee the opening of off-shore companies and then follow up on various administrative and banking matters pertaining to them. I was also in charge of supervising letters of credit, and following containers of goods for our customers. The work was interesting enough, but the working atmosphere made me want to hang myself every day. I felt full of life and much too young to be bothered with this kind of job or anything much like it, so at the end of November 2007 I left. I was ready for a new adventure.

I was soon living every young person's dream: I was just 21 years old, single, had my good friends and family, and a diploma in my pocket. I also had my driving license, a little sports car that I had bought with all my savings, and a flat in Geneva that I rented. Around this time, I also landed an interview for a new job at an asset management company, Fininfor. This interview would change my life forever.

I was nervous beforehand, and I knew I would have to give it my best shot. As soon as I arrived at the office, however, I had a good feeling: the place just seemed to have a calming, *zen*-like atmosphere. I was received by one of the directors, Mr Roger Palma. The interview went well, and I remember thinking that I would find the job interesting.

Roger asked me to wait awhile then returned to tell me that I was hired — if I wanted the job. I couldn't believe it! I replied with a big "Yes!" A short time later, I was celebrating the good news with my friends and family. I was so happy and couldn't wait to start.

Monday, 7 January 2008, right after the Christmas holidays, was my first day at the office and I felt full of energy for this new adventure. In a meeting with the woman I was about to replace, she walked me through the most important tasks I would be responsible for. Amongst other things, I was to be in charge of the admin for another company that was domiciled at the Fininfor office. The company was called PetroSaudi — and it had no employees.

She also introduced me to the rest of the team, all of whom seemed very friendly. Then, all of a sudden, a tall, dark-haired man entered the room: a strikingly impressive, breathtakingly handsome man who seemed to me to exude class. He approached me with a big smile. "Nice to meet you, I'm Xavier Justo." I introduced myself in return, embarrassed and a little shy. He told me that if I needed anything his office was just across the corridor, to the right of mine. Only then did I realize he was the other director of the company.

I quickly became part of the office milieu and routine, and I enjoyed the work very much. As part of my job, I was in charge of the administration of both Fininfor and PetroSaudi, a company owned by a man named Tarek Obaid, but this last activity didn't take up much of my time.

It wasn't long before I met Tarek for the first time. He and Xavier got on very well, and were close friends. Some time later, I also met a man named Patrick Mahony, a friend of Tarek's who was also connected to PetroSaudi and who would often come to the office.

TWO MONTHS after my start at Fininfor, a special connection was born between Xavier and I — and it was through talking about his Porsche that I had the chance to get to know him.

As mentioned before, sports cars were (and remain) one of my passions, so when we started talking about cars, it lit a spark. And when he offered to lend me his Porsche, I jumped at the chance.

From that time on, we started going out for drinks on the sly at weekends and texting regularly. As our connection blossomed, we urged one another to be discreet, but that wasn't easy as we were always laughing together. Then, after a few weeks, Xavier asked me to go with him to Porto, Portugal, for an extended weekend. I was so happy. We had a wonderful time and never stopped talking and having fun. It was when we came back from this trip that I knew, deep down, that I had real feelings for him. He made me laugh, he was interesting and cultured, and I felt safe with him when he held me.

The following months were an amazing time. The summer of 2008 passed and we became more and more attached to each other. But because of the circumstances at work we were not officially together, and this was starting to bother me. I wanted more.

At the beginning of December I felt I had to put Xavier on the spot — the situation was becoming too difficult and I didn't want to suffer, so I told him that it was either official or we would stop seeing each other. I felt sick to my stomach as I said it but I had to do it. After talking things over, he told me that he loved me and believed he had found his other half. I was only 21 and he was now 42, but it felt so right.

Days before Christmas, we finally announced the good news to everyone, and were able to enjoy a wonderful holiday season together — as lovers, officially! We both knew there was something incredibly strong between us.

In January of 2009, Xavier suggested we go on holiday to Thailand. Before flying out, I introduced him to my parents and my brother and they loved him right from the start. We left in mid-February and had a magical holiday, spending a few days in Bangkok and then traveling on to Koh Samet, a wild jewel in the Gulf of Thailand. It felt so good just being there. The people were just unbelievably friendly, everything we ate was delicious, and the island's dreamy landscapes exuded a serenity you'll never find elsewhere.

Back in Geneva, months went by, and I could feel that Xavier was no longer happy at work after the freedom he'd experienced during our holiday. One evening, out of the blue, he suggested that we leave — that we drop everything and settle in Thailand. I was a bit scared to go to the other side of the world, and I knew that I'd see less of my friends, my parents and my brother, who were and are my whole life. But still: I didn't hesitate.

We left Geneva to begin our great new adventure in the summer of 2009. We wanted to explore more of Thailand to begin with and so we traveled around from north to south, east to west, looking for a place where we would like to base ourselves. We also visited Laos, Vietnam,

Cambodia and Singapore, but after several months of adventuring, we decided we would settle in Koh Samui. It was a lively place — and developed, certainly — but without the extremes that you might find in other parts of Thailand. Our dream was to open a hotel.

Before settling in Koh Samui, we were spending a few weeks in Krabi when, one day, Xavier received a message from Tarek offering him a job as a director of PetroSaudi, to be based in London. Xavier turned him down as we had exciting plans — but Tarek kept insisting he reconsider. They were close friends and Tarek can be very persuasive. Amongst other enticements, he promised Xavier some very attractive living and working conditions.

We talked about what to do for a long time and — after weighing it all up — we thought to ourselves "let's give it a go." Thailand would still be there for us later on — and, after all, London is a beautiful city, full of life. I had always dreamed of living there. Xavier was going to work with one of his best friends, in a job that seemed interesting and exciting.

So, then: goodbye Thailand. We were off to the UK, on a different adventure to the one we had envisaged.

Chapter 3

Xavier

RICH THIEVES

I ARRIVED IN London in March 2010, and Laura joined me a few weeks later.

The only discussion I'd had with Tarek before agreeing to go and work with him was about my salary. He knew I was not all about the money, but I had put our Asia dream on hold to join him and I needed to have some vision of where it would get me.

He promised me an annual salary of £400,000 (roughly $600,000 at that time) plus a bonus that would take me up to about £1m a year. With typical naivety, perhaps, I didn't sign a contract with him. After all, he was my friend first and foremost, and his word would suffice. Or so I thought.

On arriving in London I stayed in a hotel at my own expense to begin with while I looked for a flat. Tarek found me one that was two minutes' walk from PetroSaudi's new — but unfinished — office. It was right bang on Berkeley Square, Mayfair, but even so the rental was eye-watering: over £10,000 a month for 60 square meters (650sqft). I was horrified at the price but Tarek assured me it was normal for the area, and that PetroSaudi would pick up the cost anyway. This turned out to be one of his many lies.

The dusty temporary office housed five other employees besides myself. Its dilapidated state surprised me, but I was constantly assured the new place would be luxurious. I was introduced to everyone as the company's No. 3 behind Tarek and Patrick, and told I would be co-ordinating everything from London.

Most of the staff worked part-time, including the personal secretary of a renowned British business executive named Rick Haythornthwaite. At the time, he was the chairman of Mastercard — and the public face of PetroSaudi in London. His role was really to give PetroSaudi an image of respectability. He was in his mid-50s, elegant and very British — and was being paid a fortune. (Interestingly enough, at the time of writing, his stint at PetroSaudi is magically missing from his LinkedIn profile and Wikipedia entry.)

When I first met Rick, his first question to me was whether the arrangement with the Malaysians was legal or not. I told him I hadn't been there for the deal so unfortunately I couldn't certify anything, but added that I had come to London to work for PetroSaudi on the assumption that it was indeed legal.

Some time later we moved into our new offices, at 1 Curzon Street. It had room for 30 people but there were still only seven or eight of us. The main activity keeping employees busy was a contract with PDVSA, a Venezuelan state-owned oil company.

At Curzon Street, we were joined by a new lawyer, Tim Buckland, who had previously worked for the prestigious American law firm White & Case in London, in which capacity he had handled the legal aspects of the 1MDB deal. In hindsight, it's perfectly clear why the company would hire the lawyer who had helped to set those arrangements in motion — but we'll come to that.

In addition, I brought on board "S.T.," the IT expert from my old company in Geneva, to install network and computer hardware for us. He performed these installations with the assistance of a firm called

Ocean, who sent a guy named Svapnil. (This information, about the IT installation, is important… because as you will discover, PetroSaudi later attempted to pass me off as an IT manager. An absurd idea, given that I had, and still have, very limited computing knowledge — at least not enough to be able to access all of PetroSaudi's data, as Tarek and Patrick were to claim.)

Around this time, I was also made — along with his lawyer — a director of Tarek's new real estate companies in Geneva. Tarek had invested some of the money received from Malaysia in these companies. Their management was entrusted to his brother Karim, along with an associate from outside the family. Just like in mafia movies, however, Tarek would not accept people giving instructions to his brother — and I ended up having to go to Geneva several times to settle conflicts.

On a number of occasions, I asked Tarek and Patrick about the state of the PetroSaudi group's finances, but I never received any convincing answers. The details of the 1MDB deal were, by and large, not open to PetroSaudi employees. Only Tarek and Patrick knew them and they never showed me anything. In fact, even the group accountant didn't have proper access to the figures. It was unbelievable that in an operation worth almost $2 billion, there were no compliance officers, no auditors and next to no controls of any kind. Tarek, Patrick, the lawyers and the tax specialists kept their scheme in a closed circle, with no knowledge filtering out to PetroSaudi staff.

I knew very well how easy it would have been for Tarek's favorite bank in Geneva, JP Morgan, to check on his situation at that time. He'd had next to no money, and his American Express card was regularly blocked — but suddenly, and I know this because he showed me statements, they were receiving more than $100 million into his personal account. Geneva is like a small village where other people know your business. JP Morgan could easily have looked into the scam, but they preferred to take the money and their commission and be satisfied with whatever story Tarek and company told them.

According to some press reports at the time, and the PetroSaudi employees I spoke to about it, the money came from a 1MDB-PetroSaudi joint venture. The Malaysians brought cash to the table and — at least on paper — PetroSaudi brought assets. All of which brings us back to 2009, when Tarek and Patrick were looking for someone who could value the company at more than $2 billion.

Patrick, without giving me any figures, explained to me that PetroSaudi had acquired a so-called Farm-in Agreement — a contractual arrangement commonly deployed at the development stage of oil exploration projects. I would later realize that such an agreement does not amount to possession of any real asset, and is in fact nothing more than a lease on an oil field, with some benefits. In short, you don't possess anything — it's as if you presented a lease on a flat thinking it could get you a loan from a bank.

I would also later learn that the person who valued PetroSaudi for more than $3 billion — $1billion more than they were originally asking — was a man named Ed Morse, a former business associate of Patrick's who had been a senior official in the US State Department and chief energy economist at Lehman Brothers, amongst other things. He charged $50,000, but PetroSaudi paid him $100,000 to thank him for his work, an evaluation done in a few days without checks on who owned the oil fields or anyone going to inspect them. (This evaluation would remain secret for a long time; in fact, it would only come to light once I learned the facts of the 1MDB-PetroSaudi swindle and subsequently decided to blow the whistle on it.)

It seems that since the Malaysians were desperate to find a partner to help siphon off their money, they were happy enough with PetroSaudi's Farm-In contract, which was in Turkmenistan. These oil fields, which PetroSaudi would present as its own, were in fact in an area disputed by Turkmenistan and Azerbaijan and not awarded to either party for years to come. (This dispute was public, and I am surprised no journalist ever picked up on its bearing on the deal, which of course suited PetroSaudi and 1MDB.)

I was to meet twice with one of the main characters in the 1MDB-PetroSaudi deception: Jho Low. The first time was in London at Nobu restaurant, and the second was in Cannes, on the famous Princess Mariana yacht. At Tarek's request I could never talk to him about the PetroSaudi deal or Malaysia, but Tarek and Patrick themselves told me several times that Jho Low was the money maker for Malaysian Prime Minister Najib Razak and his wife, Rosmah Mansor.

Jho Low never struck me as a great financier or businessman; he was simply very close to Malaysia's wealth fund — a fund that, as we were to discover, Najib, Jho Low himself, Tarek and Patrick were using as their personal piggy bank.

Alongside the greed of my own employers, Jho Low's closeness to the Prime Minister and his wife, combined with his knowledge of various financial stratagems, would be the key element in this scandal. Money would be splashed everywhere, in astonishing quantities and at astonishing speed.

The Princess Mariana was rented in my name because Tarek did not want his own to appear on any documents, fearing he would somehow be exposed. The cost was €375,000 per week, even before additional expenses — which were considerable. How easy it is to have a good time with money that isn't yours. For the record, Paris Hilton, the American socialite with whom Jho Low became quite synonymous, was on board during his visit.

JP Morgan's Swiss bankers were also no strangers to partying on the yacht, I hasten to add. Would it be a stretch to wonder if these good times helped them to turn a blind eye to the massive influx of money into Tarek's and Patrick's accounts?

IT WAS COMMON for the yacht-owning community to visit each other's yachts. I remember on one occasion some young Saudis, apparently with the sole aim of provoking Tarek, repeatedly playing a song on the loudspeakers by the rapper Travie McCoy. The song's lyrics: "I wanna be a billionaire, so fucking bad." This showed how much everyone knew about Tarek's greed and desperate hunger for riches.

All through this time, Tarek and Patrick spent lavishly and without scruple. In fact, I couldn't keep track of all the expensive dinners, the bottles of wine costing more than $10,000, the jets rented to fly around the world, the staggering hotel bills. PetroSaudi would hire a private jet and fly from London to Ghana, then on to Venezuela and back to London; not even first-class on a commercial flight was good enough, it seemed. Tarek and Patrick both bought houses in London, and Patrick a chalet in Switzerland.

Tarek even finally managed to get himself a credit card — this one from a bank in Dubai. It was, of course, prestigious and exclusive, and had a small diamond on the surface of the card. The vanity was just staggering.

The connections between Tarek and the Malaysian Prime Minister were to deepen, too. At one point Tarek boasted, after coming off a telephone call, that Najib wanted him to become his son-in-law by marrying his daughter.

Tarek and Patrick also invested in other businesses, including — through a friend — private schools in Switzerland and the UK. Owning educational tools financed by stolen money: what a great example for the youth of today.

Another company Tarek invested in was Palantir, an American business specializing in espionage. His shares would be seized a few years later as part of the capture of $1.5 billion in dirty money from Malaysia that was laundered in the USA. At time of writing, Palantir is worth some $15 billion, which means that the $2 million Tarek invested would today be worth a few tens of millions.

Tarek even created, and attached the names of his parents to, a foundation: The Essam and Dalal Obaid Foundation, or EDOF. Set up in association with CNN, and still going today, its purpose is officially humanitarian, but the main reason it was brought into existence was to improve Tarek's public image.

In meetings with various business partners, Patrick's and Tarek's speeches were well rehearsed. The aim was to make even employees of PetroSaudi like myself believe the company was an unofficial instrument of the Saudi Kingdom, with the understanding that of course the royal family couldn't be publicly involved even if somehow their money was on the scales. Most of these interlocutors were fooled; others saw through the deception but were more interested in the money than the legality of the business and were therefore happy to comply.

One of Patrick's revealing phrases when we would consult lawyers on PetroSaudi business was: "The law is a raw material that can be bought and sold." I would see some years later that he held dearly to this view of justice.

In Venezuela, we were received as representatives of the Saudi Kingdom without question, although I would later realize that another incentive for the Venezuelans to work with us was because Patrick seemed to have all the solutions to help them be as corrupt as possible.

The company's first activity in the country, before I joined the office in London, was operating a ship that PetroSaudi had purchased for about $150 million. It was about 30 years old and I always refused to get on board, as it seemed to me a near-wreck. Having this boat, however, meant that we could enjoy a contract with PDVSA, and get about $500,000 a day from them for providing our services, which consisted of drilling wells at the bottom of the sea according to their instructions. Given the state of the boat, this drilling was barely effective, but we were paid handsomely nevertheless — as indeed were some PDVSA executives, according to Patrick. He told me that in order to get the first contract, he had paid $1 million into the account of a PDVSA executive, Jose Luis Parada, at the end of a lunch in Panama with Mr Parada and his family. He told me this was a normal way of doing things. Everything, it seemed, was done in the open and the word "corruption" was never mentioned.

I remember a trip to Ghana with Patrick, where we were trying to work with the country's government to get concessions on oil fields. We were escorted around for two days without any result, and Patrick became extremely angry. He told me PetroSaudi had paid more than $1 million to intermediaries to get concrete results.

Later, the Venezuelans offered us a second contract — on the condition that we bring a second drillship to Venezuela. That's when I really started to realize that a lot of things were just not above board. The second boat cost $250 million, and I thought PetroSaudi had the liquidity for the purchase… but according to Patrick and Tarek it didn't. The coffers were empty, they said. When I asked what had happened to the Malaysian money, they refused to discuss figures. They would say only that the sums mentioned "in the media" were not a reflection of reality.

On one occasion I saw some papers lying around the office Tarek and Patrick used. They aroused my curiosity and suspicions, but when I asked about them again there was no real discussion. They just went on about "the Malaysians" — as if that explained everything.

I was in fact a director and signatory on all PetroSaudi accounts… except for those relating to the supposed joint venture with 1MDB. For those, my employers wanted as few people involved as possible; not even their supposed friend could know the details.

We began researching other ways of financing the second boat, and the purchase was ultimately sealed through a deal with a Norwegian company that specialized in these kinds of contracts. During discussions with this firm, Patrick and Rick Haythornthwaite made PetroSaudi sound as though it was absolutely a Saudi state company, something that — as indicated — I would witness Patrick doing time after time.

On clinching the deal, the Norwegians came to London for a big dinner, followed by drinks at a famous cabaret club, Stringfellows, where you had to pay half-naked dancers with fake notes that you bought on the way in. I strongly refused to take part. Leaving the place later in the evening, I remember thinking the world was becoming crazier and crazier.

I actually have a precise memory of the signing of the deal for this famous boat, the PetroSaudi Saturn. We were in the London offices of White & Case, the law firm that had structured the deal with 1MDB, and had to sign more than 2,000 pages of documents to finalize the purchase.

At the end of this exercise, I had a severe cramp in my hand, and when I returned two days later for additional signatures, one of the lawyers in the office confided to me that she would never forget me. Apparently she had spent 24 hours simply writing my name by hand next to the signatures I had made. A funny job for a lawyer, I thought.

With the purchase of the second vessel, the Venezuelans were ready with a new contract giving PetroSaudi $1.3 billion over a period of seven years, via PDVSA. Again, the work involved the ship drilling wells at the bottom of the sea wherever PDVSA wanted them.

I actually felt quite proud of us having won this business — because it would give work to a few hundred Venezuelans. And considering the state of the country, that's at least one good thing we were able to do with 1MDB's money. To begin with at least, I was blissfully unaware of the extent of the benefits PetroSaudi gave PDVSA executives and officials in exchange for us being awarded the contract.

I made the first trip to negotiate the matter with Patrick. However, he would go alone to certain meetings to "arrange things" — as he put it — with certain managers, none of whose names I ever learned. He told me PetroSaudi was to receive about $50 million in "mobilization fees" and that a good part of this cash would be for payments to PDVSA executives, a normal procedure according to him. Turns out that when you pitch up with a boat to work with PDVSA in Venezuela, PDVSA pays you an amount to get you started working… but apparently the cash is meant for paying kickbacks to key people involved in the deal.

(Incidentally, PDVSA's head of production, the aforementioned Mr Parada, would later make headlines when he was arrested on corruption charges — and then escaped from prison and fled the country.)

I myself had to go back to Venezuela several times in order to address various administrative problems, and one thing I can say is that the whole PDVSA operation symbolized a society in decay. Nothing worked.

During my visits, I got to meet most of the PDVSA group executives and some Venezuelan ministers, none of whom seemed to know the reality of what PetroSaudi actually was. They just wanted Saudi Arabia to invest money in their country. It's my belief that the corruption was driven by two or three leaders within PDVSA, while the government ministers seemed earnest about wanting to do something that benefited the country. As I am Spanish and share a common language with them, our relations were friendly and our meetings would often end with a glass of whiskey.

At some point, PDVSA fell behind with its payments and owed us more than $100million. If they didn't pay us, PetroSaudi was going to have big problems. Once our debt reached $120million, it would be necessary to notify our partners and activate letters of credit in our favor.

If our golden contract in Venezuela ended, so too would disappear PetroSaudi's only ostensibly legal activity and the jobs of all our employees in the country. This was out of the question for me. Some of them had become my friends, and their livelihoods mattered to me. I had to get the matter resolved, so I spent three weeks there and also brought Laura with me.

It worked. In meetings with PDVSA middlemen, Laura's charm — combined with my persistence — got us paid.

Our weekends during this trip were spent with the family of Gerardo Pantin, one of Patrick's intermediaries, on their family boat in the Los

Roques archipelago. It was certainly one of the most beautiful places I had ever seen and stands out as one of the few happy memories I have of our whole Venezuelan experience.

Venezuela is a beautiful country, full of incredibly friendly people, but it's also dangerous. You might get killed for an iPhone. I could only move around in an armored car and had to be constantly protected by bodyguards. I have fond memories of the politicians I met there and can't imagine all of them were corrupt. I actually believe many of them truly had faith in the Bolivarian revolution — a movement for hardline socialism that was led by Venezuelan President Hugo Chávez — and the omnipotence of the regime to be able to solve the country's problems.

The Pantin family were among those well-compensated by Patrick. Years later, indeed, the press would report that Gerardo's company had, over the years, billed PDVSA for more than $1 billion in relation to various oil industry services. He went into exile in Miami, where according to reports he has tried to grow his wealth by investing in real estate.

I would also learn after my departure that the contracts we'd negotiated were completely crazy. As mentioned, we were paid at least $500,000 per day for our services — but this was regardless of the results of our drilling activities, or even the resources we expended.

BACK IN LONDON, meanwhile, Laura was enjoying herself and had made a group of friends with whom she went out regularly. They would go dancing together. She was also studying international business at a school near our flat. We felt happy living in this beautiful city.

Trouble was brewing, however. My first salary was late — and instead of the £400,000 a year Tarek had promised me, it had been knocked down to £240,000. What's more, they said the flat — which I had been paying for anyway — was no longer part of my package.

When he told me about these changes, I didn't say anything. I still considered him as a friend and I've never been money-driven — my Achilles heel, according to most of my relatives.

During my entire time in London — 13 months — I would in fact only receive five months of salary, and I had to pay all my travel expenses, except for flights, myself. After the first few months, I received a $1 million bonus, but a large part of that cash would go towards paying Tarek's own expenses. For example, I paid for various private medical check-ups and procedures both for him and his girlfriend, along with fees for a private investigator he hired. (Tarek loves and has always loved employing detectives to keep tabs on people close to him. As you will discover, I later found out more about how this worked when I became a target myself.)

The few times we talked about money, he told me I would get the missing salary payments later and that my year-end bonus would be very large — several million dollars, he insisted.

I was the only employee in the PetroSaudi group with the right to sign payments of more than $1 million. If I had only been interested in money, I would have helped myself to at least my salary, but it was not in my nature to help myself to other people's money.

As interesting as the work was, life with Tarek and Patrick became the opposite of what I had expected. They spent an increasing amount of their time partying wildly, and I wondered how their wives and girlfriends could accept their absences. Patrick's answer would be: "I'm a good father and I stay home until noon to look after my family." Tarek would simply respond: "My girlfriend has nothing to say; I'm a Saudi and Saudis do business at night."

I met these two women, Patrick's wife and Tarek's girlfriend, several times in London. They were interesting and decent women, but I found it hard to look them in the eye. Tarek had over $100 million in his accounts. That meant he had the freedom to indulge his vices and perversions. No limits, no boundaries.

Thanks to Tarek's brother Nawaf being a Middle East specialist for CNN, meanwhile, the Obaid family (through their EDOF foundation) contributed to the CNN Freedom Project, a humanitarian media campaign whose advertising on the network made me want to vomit every time I saw it. Here was a guy who I knew to have used his ill-gotten wealth to exploit young women: on one occasion, he was even called in by the vice squad in Geneva to discuss his sexual proclivities as part of an investigation into a bar which they subsequently closed down. And yet now here he was purporting to fund the fight against human trafficking. My God, the irony.

Tarek's other brother, Karim, asked me to keep an eye on his lifestyle in London. I told him I was doing my best, but that as I didn't share his vices and never saw him much outside the office, I had little influence.

I lived a peaceful life with Laura in our flat. We both loved being in London — our walks in the parks with our dog, having friends over at weekends, dining out. We found the city pleasant, and only the weather bothered us from time to time. I simply steered clear of Tarek's and Patrick's crazy nocturnal goings on, and although I didn't approve of what they got up to ultimately I wasn't their father.

I clearly remember, however, that Patrick brought one of his 'friends,' a certain Stéphanie, to a business dinner, introducing her as a friend of someone else in our group. I told him it wasn't a clever move at a restaurant — the Cipriani — that was next to the PetroSaudi offices and where everybody knew us. Patrick told me that with the money she had cost him, he didn't care. He told me he was sponsoring her horse-riding career: apparently she was an outstanding rider in France, as I was able to verify online.

Not participating in Tarek's and Patrick's degeneracy allowed me to distance myself from them, and I don't regret it. I would occasionally try to reason with Tarek, but to no avail. Seeing your friend destroy himself in this way can be painful.

On one occasion, I went to the Mayo Clinic in the US with him. He was in his element, truly believing that he might be suffering from every possible disease under the sun. Of course, they didn't find anything (although it should have been clear enough to them that his head was sick because of his lifestyle).

Afterwards, we flew by private jet to Las Vegas, where Prince Turki was waiting. Over the next three days, he and Tarek lost everything they could at blackjack. One of the managers of the Encore casino actually told me that they could have won from time to time, if they'd only played logically. Some people find pleasure in losing and not in winning. Odd but true.

That experience in Vegas actually shocked me. At the hotel's private pool were dozens of young women just waiting to be "chosen." It was like they were fish in a kitchen aquarium, waiting to be caught and plated. As ever, I declined to participate, and for two reasons. The first was that I've never enjoyed these kinds of "entertainments," because I respect women too much not to realize that this is not a job they choose by vocation. And secondly, I reasoned that sharing in their vices would have given Tarek and Patrick all the more power over me.

It is often said that money makes you crazy. I don't know if this is true. What I have seen is that too much money makes it possible to indulge in perversions and fantasies — expensive alcohol, private jets, yachts, escort girls and drugs on demand. It takes courage not to sink into degeneracy or avoid being surrounded by malign influences. Unfortunately for my friends, neither of them had any courage and the only company they kept was that of profiteers and parasites.

I should point out that I never told Laura everything about how far Tarek and Patrick were drifting. She had already noticed their strange behavior and party lifestyles but she knew that I was not like them, and that I didn't go out with them at night, so we tended not to talk about it. We were happy and that was the main thing.

Inevitably, however, there came an episode that would mark the end of my friendship with Tarek and precipitate our departure from London.

I was supposed to join Tarek and Patrick in New York to meet with some Venezuelans, but — for the first time in my life — I missed the plane. It was raining like crazy in London, meaning I couldn't get a taxi fast enough and missed the flight by a few minutes. Tarek got immediately upset and started treating me the way he treated the parasites he had surrounded himself with — by insulting me. The difference was that I was not one of his stooges, however, and he knew it.

I offered him my resignation the next day, but he refused it. This was in December 2010, and I suddenly felt like I was at war with him, a feeling that would persist until I finally left in April 2011. The reason things dragged on for so long was that I kept finding excuses for Tarek and his weaknesses and illness. At heart, I still had a friendship with him and during all these years I had regarded him as a little brother.

During this time, however, our relationship grew cold and distant, our correspondence purely official. I told myself it would return to normal in time but I had no desire to go to New York, where he remained for several weeks after our disagreement.

On one last trip to Geneva on PetroSaudi business, I noticed the same person sitting near my table two days in a row and felt sure I was being followed. It had no effect on me: I knew all too well of Tarek's need to know everything about everyone around him, but I wasn't scared of him.

One evening in April, he wrote me an email to blame me for having made him invest money in my former company in Geneva. I replied immediately, telling him the whole truth, point by point. I had never made him invest in anything. On the contrary, I had always protected him and advised him against making many investments that I felt would come back to bite him. He had in fact invested money in my company at the request of my former partner, who acted most of the time without telling me.

Tarek's response was a stream of insults. In turn, I emailed him my resignation, copying other PetroSaudi officials.

In the days that followed, he called me dozens of times, left messages of apology, wrote me emails asking for my forgiveness and pleading that we were all brothers. But my mind was made up — I couldn't take it anymore.

I also knew for a fact there were at least two reasons he couldn't bear me to leave. The first was down to his character: he couldn't stand to be left out or rejected. And the second was that I was one of the only people who knew everything about his life.

He even resorted to having his relatives call me, but nothing would do — the vase had overflowed, as the French idiom goes, and my decision was final.

When Tarek finally accepted it, he appointed Patrick to finalize the steps for my departure. Patrick asked me to think of a figure for my severance pay, and I came up with a simple calculation that took into account all the years of support I had given to Tarek and his family, my years of work for PetroSaudi, my unpaid salary, and Tarek's promises of millions.

If I'd counted everything I had paid for him and his family since 1999, all the work I'd put in for him over the years, the amount would have been astronomical. The figure I came up with of $6.5 million might still seem excessive to many people, but in light of the years of service I had given him I did not think it unreasonable. I am happy to explain this again, because it is an important element in my story.

I come from a modest family, as described in Chapter 1. My father was a bus driver, my mother a cleaning lady — but I had spent my entire professional career working in finance in Geneva, where bonuses running into the millions were commonplace. For the biggest professional footballers, $6.5 million would be a few weeks' income, and nobody is really shocked about that. Executives at large companies also earn much more, even when their companies are losing money. So whatever judgment you might make of my claim may or may not be justified, but it's your personal view. I leave it up to you to make up your own mind.

Patrick called me the day after I submitted my claim and confirmed that Tarek had agreed to it — and that his lawyer would prepare the contract.

I discussed with Laura what we were going to do next, and we decided we would return to Geneva for a few weeks.

Patrick arranged to meet me at the Connaught Hotel, next to our flat. We had a drink, then Patrick called Tarek in my presence. When he hung up, he told me Tarek wanted to pay me $5 million — nothing more. I accepted on the spot without saying anything, because at that moment I realized for the first time that this was the end of 20 years of friendship. I was upset and I even shed a few tears. We parted ways and Patrick told me I would receive their severance contract to sign very soon.

The next day, however, he called me back to tell me that Tarek and his lawyer now only wanted to pay me $4 million. "Take it or leave it," Patrick said, adding that Tarek's lawyer was ready to wage war if I refused.

I never wanted conflict between us, and in fact I was deeply unhappy with the whole turn of events. With regret and a heavy heart, I accepted. Of course I should never have caved, but they abused my position of weakness and sadness to make me give in.

Laura left for Geneva a few days before me, as I had PetroSaudi papers to sign annulling my involvement with clients.

Then, the day before I was due to leave, Patrick called me again while I was in a taxi. He warned me I would be followed in Geneva as Tarek wanted to know if I was dealing with any lawyers. Again I recognized his obsessive nature.

These were my last moments of life among the world's proverbial 1 percent in income terms. There were some good times to be remembered, but in the end I couldn't escape the overwhelming realization that the world's richest embodied such misery and loneliness that I could only be better off outside their club.

Chapter 4

XAVIER

LIFE CHANGES

WHEN I ARRIVED in Geneva at the beginning of April 2011, I still had Patrick's words in mind that I would be followed. Indeed, when my sister picked me up at the airport and we were walking to the parking lot, we suddenly came face to face with two men standing next to her car, one of whom was writing down the plate number. What a bunch of amateurs. They didn't look too pleased with themselves when they realized we had caught them in the act.

The $4 million we'd agreed on was paid into my account right away, and I thought this would be the end of my relations and misadventures with Tarek, PetroSaudi et al. What a mistake. It was in fact just the beginning of another, much more painful, episode of my life.

Laura and I decided to go to Greece for a few weeks to recharge our batteries. We planned to go back to Asia in the autumn, but first we wanted to enjoy a summer in Europe with our loved ones before another big departure.

In June, I contacted S.T., PetroSaudi's IT guy. As mentioned in the last chapter, I actually met S.T. when I first joined Fininfor as a partner, in 1998, and he had served as our IT expert there. He was my friend and

I told him I needed his help, so we arranged to meet one morning at the Café Lyrique. Over coffee, I asked him if he could give me a copy of the PetroSaudi data. I explained to him that I needed it to protect myself in case of any problems in the future. The amounts of money that had passed through PetroSaudi in the 1MDB deal were huge, and I wanted to be able to prove — if one day it became necessary — that there were certain activities I'd had nothing to do with.

To my surprise, he already had a hard drive with him — and handed it over to me. He must have known I was going to ask him for it, and his own suspicions of what was going on at PetroSaudi probably matched mine.

He told me the drive was a complete copy of the PetroSaudi server. He also told me he had deleted all the data from that server, at Tarek's request, and all that remained of it was the copy I now had in my possession and one that he had given to Tarek. I didn't ask, but I suspect he also kept a copy for himself. He explained to me that the drive contained a colossal 90 gigabytes of data altogether. A few days later, I had to get back in touch with him to ask how to actually read it, as I had no knowledge of how this stuff worked.

During our meeting at the café, I stressed to him that I would never reveal to anyone that he had given me the drive, and that it would remain a secret between us. Later on, I am sorry to say, I betrayed this promise. As I will relate, however, this was not to protect myself — nor even for financial reasons, as others have alleged — but rather for reasons of morality and justice.

My betrayal of S.T.'s trust would occur because new facts came to light, changing the whole picture of what we were dealing with. In essence, we would learn that Tarek, Patrick and others had used PetroSaudi to steal billions of dollars from the people of Malaysia— money that belonged to that nation and its future; money that was not supposed to be spent on yachts, private jets, wild parties and other frivolities.

Yes, I broke my word. And in a way, I am proud of it… even if the price was high.

The next time I would meet S.T. would be six years later — at the Federal Prosecutor's office in Bern.

IN SEPTEMBER 2011, Laura and I finally returned to Koh Samui, the beautiful Thai island that had enchanted us during our trip two years earlier.

Koh Samui is about an hour's flight from Bangkok. Compared to Phuket and other tourist destinations, it's not as populated and doesn't have the same crazy nightlife scene that is found in many parts of the country.

We started to look for our dream house and plan our new life, firmly believing we could put everything to do with PetroSaudi behind us and that it would have no more impact on our lives.

We looked at a lot of houses, none of which we were truly infatuated by, until one day we found a very charming property on the south of the island. It was close to the water and had beautiful views both of the sea and the jungle. On the downside, it was not very big and needed a lot of refurbishing, but we decided to make an offer on the condition that we could get the piece of land next to it. Our dream was to build a larger property that we could transform into a resort hotel.

Buying a property in Thailand requires a Thai as the majority owner, and we asked a Thai friend from Geneva to come in with us on the purchase. Our resort-building venture had begun, and would prove to be full of surprises.

As the project took shape, many of our friends and relatives came down to visit us, which meant that in the first year we only had about three months to ourselves. But what a beautiful place to welcome friends — so gorgeous and quiet.

Laura and I came to know our new corner of the world little by little, and made several new friends, many of whom we remain close with to this day.

Laurent, a friend from Brittany, ran a computer and multimedia company nearby. He installed IT systems on our entire property and would later introduce me to triathlons. A Dutch couple we befriended, Brenda and Wilfriend, had lived on the island for a few years and would later host our wedding in their hotel. Wilfried introduced us to Thai boxing, which we started practicing every week.

We also decided to learn Thai. Laura stuck with it and learned to read, write and speak the language. For my part, I gave up after one lesson.

We got ourselves three dogs. First we acquired a Rhodesian Ridgeback, a real sweetheart of a dog that would prove to be a constant ally through our coming ordeals. There was also a Jack Russell that we bought in a pet shop where he had sadly been kept in a tiny cage, and a French Mastiff that we found in the north of Thailand.

In addition, we assembled four parrots and eight cats. Luckily we love animals and had plenty of space to make them part of our home.

Our days were filled with work at the resort and hosting a steady stream of visitors. Life was peaceful and healthy, a world away from the hustle and bustle of London, although we also kept up with friends and family by going back and forth to Switzerland a couple of times a year.

Around this time, I was invited to the Singapore Grand Prix by a friend. I have always been interested in Formula 1 and my friend worked in the business, which meant I had the privilege of being given the VIP treatment, with access to exclusive hospitality and trackside events. It was at one of these events that I met some well-connected Malaysians who became very interested when I told them about my career at PetroSaudi and my knowledge of 1MDB. To this day, I remain convinced that it was through this meeting that my name would be connected to a certain British journalist who will be introduced later.

On one trip back to Geneva, I met some of the friends I had in common with Tarek and learned his side of the story from them regarding my departure from PetroSaudi. His version of events? He had fired me, I had been doing a bad job… and other baseless nonsense.

I didn't care, and attributed his smears to his frustration at me leaving him. And besides, as much as I was happy to be in Geneva, I looked forward to going back to Thailand. That's where I really wanted to be.

At the same time as the construction work on our resort was going on, Laura and I decided to set up a company to import and operate solariums. Strange idea, you might say: Who needs a solarium in Thailand? Well, it might seem far-fetched but in fact Koh Samui gets quite a lot of cloud and a long rainy season that can make it hard for holidaymakers to get a tan. We therefore had lots of interest in our venture, especially from hotels, and we quickly racked up enough pre-orders to launch our little operation.

After making some inquiries, we found a company in China that could make the solariums for us, and we made some plans to visit the factory to check everything out. After a whole day spent waiting at the Chinese Embassy in Bangkok, however, we were told our visas could not be issued the same day. Visas on the spot were only for Thais, apparently; ours would need a few days longer.

At that stage, we decided it might be better to use a third party, so we commissioned a logistics company in Bangkok that had experience of working in China.

We paid 30 percent of the cost of the booths — more than $30,000 — upfront, with the rest to be paid on delivery after customs clearance. It then took several weeks before they left China for Bangkok… and in fact we would never set eyes on them. Without the logistics company noticing, they were wrongly labeled as "electric beds" by the manufacturer and seized by Thai customs on arrival.

We got some of our money back, and then quickly did our best to forget about the whole project. We also found ourselves beginning to have some sympathy with the general opinion of our foreign friends living in Thailand: not doing business in Thailand was the key to tranquility.

As the construction of the resort continued, we learned a bit more about what our foreign friends meant. The headaches that come with trying to build in Thailand really have to be experienced to be believed. Indeed, if I have gray hairs today, I think most of them probably come from that time rather than from the nightmare I was to experience later.

One of the most shocking things to us was the complete lack of safety standards in the construction industry — and the risks taken for monthly salaries of about $300 a month were frightening. In standard contracts, there was no compensation for workers who had accidents. For Europeans like Laura and I, this was hard to bear.

With many of those we employed, via our contractor, we insisted on doubling their expected salaries. We also settled debts and paid for schooling for some of their children. We tried to treat our workers with the kindness and humanity they showed us — and we found our modest financial support repaid in close friendships, many of which continue to this day.

On one occasion, one of the team was electrocuted on the job. His heart stopped beating for a few minutes, and he was only saved due to the persistence of the site manager, who massaged his chest for several minutes.

When he came round, I offered to take him to the hospital immediately — but he refused. Instead, he asked me for a glass of whisky and a cigarette. The poor man drank the glass in one gulp, smoked the cigarette and took the afternoon off. He came back to work the next day — after all, there was no paid sick leave in his contract.

The construction was progressing little by little, but the problems came thick and fast. One day, it was discovered that no gaps had been created for windows, so an entire wall had to be taken down. Another time, a toilet paper holder was fixed to a wall... three meters away from the toilet. There was even a towel rack fitted directly under a shower head. Most of the issues were small, but there was always something. I learned that problems often originated because the workers themselves lived in housing that was very basic and they didn't know how things should be done.

None of this detracted, I hasten to add, from the kindness and goodness shown to us by the workforce and the wider community. On many occasions, people went out of their way to help us, and without asking for money. I remember once my car broke down right in the middle of a tropical storm. Out of nowhere, four Thais came to help us. Then, realizing we needed a new battery, off they went on their scooters to buy one while we took shelter. This kind of unquestioning assistance would be highly unlikely in Switzerland — or other places in Europe — where we have lost our sense of solidarity. In rural Thailand, solidarity is key to survival. I still feel warmly about our Thai friends and employees in my mind and in my heart.

Meanwhile, Laura and I bought a boat. Many beaches on the island are overcrowded, but off Koh Samui is an archipelago with about ten wild and mostly uninhabited islands. These islands became our refuge and the place where we took the people who came to visit us. We thought we could also use the boat to entertain future resort guests.

I wanted to get a Thai license to drive the boat, and because I had already had boats in Geneva, the exam was simple. Basically, they just asked if I knew how to operate a boat. I showed them my Swiss license, written in French, and that was enough for them to give me a Thai license — in return for a small contribution to the marine employees benevolent fund.

We also became very close to Denis, who we knew from Geneva. He was now living in Bangkok and we started seeing each other often. He had previously worked for the UN, but now wanted to develop a high-quality organic tea brand. We were interested in his project, and we invested some money in his company, meanwhile becoming the best of friends. He would also later be incredibly supportive during my time in prison. He has a place in my heart that can never be supplanted.

In February 2012 I felt ready to ask Laura to marry me, but I decided Valentine's Day was a little too clichéd. Instead, I proposed the day after. On Valentine's Day itself I did nothing; in fact, I acted distant and didn't even bother to buy her flowers — which irritated her. I had my surprise in store, however.

When she awoke the following day, she was in a terrible mood. While we were still in bed, however, I told her that there was a beast moving under her pillow, and when she looked under it she found my outstretched arm holding a ring. I asked her to marry me, and she said yes. We were engaged!

Later the same day I had a check-up at the Koh Samui hospital and the scale read 99.7 kilos. I was horrified: that was 15 kilos more than I had ever weighed. I made a promise to Laura and to myself that for our wedding — on 15 February, 2013 — I would weigh 85 kilos and spare no effort in hitting that target.

I started on an intensive work-out regime right away. I was out of shape and had a hard time to begin with, but I had set myself a challenge. With time and persistence, I would reach my goal, largely thanks to eating better food and a year of doing sport.

Patrick Mahony came to Thailand around this time and asked me to see him in Bangkok. We met at the Mandarin Oriental. He was again accompanied by Stéphanie, the beautiful young blonde woman he had once brought to the Cipriani restaurant during a dinner with some PetroSaudi executives in London. He said he had come to meet with executives of

PTT — the Petroleum Authority of Thailand, today renamed PTT Public Company Limited — to try to do business with them.

During our meeting, Patrick told me that Tarek intended to pay me — at some point — the $2.5 million he still owed me out of the original $6.5 million severance we'd agreed. He asked me to give Tarek some more time and said that maybe I could work with them again on some Venezuelan business. Of course, I didn't believe a word of what he was saying; Patrick is a good orator but his words no longer held any water for me.

THE DATE OF the wedding was getting closer. Nearly 100 guests would be there, with about half of them coming from Switzerland or abroad. Some stayed at the house with us and others were spread out in hotels nearby.

The days leading up to the main event were filled with parties and lunches by the pool — all of which passed in a haze of bliss and sunshine. When the big day arrived, however, it rained like crazy all morning.

I had spent my last night as a bachelor at our Dutch friends' resort — where the wedding was also to take place. The ceremony was scheduled for 3pm, and the organizers were meant to come in a few hours beforehand to set up the tables, music, flowers and everything else.

By 11am, the rain was still pouring down and none of the catering staff had arrived. I started to panic. I called the organizer, who told me that some of the workers who were supposed to be there couldn't make it, and that she was now looking for replacements. I was really worried but I didn't dare call Laura. And it was still raining...

Around noon, the rain stopped, and the workers arrived to fix everything. I could finally breathe.

The guests arrived, and everyone settled down as we waited for the bride to enter with her father. But she was taking her time, which seemed strange. We were all sitting there sweating in the hot sun.

We later discovered that Laura's father, emotional because of the occasion no doubt, had taken a wrong turn somewhere in his car and called Laura's entourage to figure out how to get back on the right road. She had been on the phone frantically trying to work out his location.

Luckily, they all finally pulled up in the right place and the music we'd planned for the bride-to-be's entrance started playing: "Samba Pa Ti," by Santana. And suddenly there she was, looking so beautiful. In fact everything was beautiful. I felt so emotional I started to cry.

Everything went well, and everyone who came to share the day with us was happy. It was a simple ceremony, but filled with warmth, joy and friendship.

One dark moment left an impression, though. One of the guests, a mutual friend of mine and Tarek's — the previously mentioned Aziz — told me Tarek had offered to pay him $20,000 to create some "havoc" at our wedding. For a moment, I was mad with rage. It was typical of Tarek: he simply couldn't bear for others to be happy.

The guests left over the next few days, and we slowly went back to our routines: supervising the resort's construction, and (for me) sport and fitness.

Our friend Laurent had got me hooked on triathlons. I found that I loved getting up at 5am to put in two hours of cycling then go for a run. It became almost like a drug that I needed every day. I found a trainer who was based in Phuket — a man named Jurgen Zack, who was a triathlon legend — and told him about my dream of doing an Ironman, which involves 3.8km in the water and 180km on a bike, followed by a marathon run. He told me it was doable if I put in the time and put my mind to it.

The more I trained the more I discovered that I had deep reserves of mental strength. That was good news if I should ever truly need them (which it turned out I would...). I did a few small triathlons, and felt I was in the best shape of my life.

Between July and October 2013, and following the discovery of Tarek trying to disturb our wedding, I had some email exchanges with Patrick and asked him to pay me the balance of what PetroSaudi had said I would be paid — $2.5 million. I insisted that they had abused my position of weakness not to pay me what had been agreed on in 2011, but that our verbal agreement was legally binding. Patrick asked to meet me again to discuss the matter.

We met at the Shangri-La Hotel in Bangkok in October, and I reiterated my position. Patrick asked me if I happened to have documents from PetroSaudi that could show any potential wrongdoings on its part. In response, I provided him with an Excel file that contained screenshots of various documents, including bank transfers — although I had been deliberately careful in selecting these not to give the game away that I now possessed a copy of the entire server.

My conversation with Patrick during this meeting would later be used by PetroSaudi to cook up a complaint against me — an allegation of blackmail, which I had apparently committed on Thai territory. When it came, it was a truly treacherous move.

BACK ON KOH SAMUI, life was good. The resort was nearing completion and it felt to us like we'd left PetroSaudi in the rearview mirror.

And then, in January 2014, things got even better: Laura told me she was pregnant. I was going to be a father!

That wasn't the only major event affecting our family in this period, though. In May 2014 I received a call from an English journalist named Clare Rewcastle Brown, who said she wanted to meet me to talk about PetroSaudi, 1MDB and corruption in Malaysia. We arranged to meet in

Bangkok in June. This encounter would change my life, and that of my family, forever.

Clare started off by telling me all about Malaysia, a country close to her heart, and the corruption that prevailed there. She clearly had a strong character and sense of justice, and she reminded me a little of my wife — which is perhaps the main reason we got along so well from the outset.

The meeting went well. I immediately felt an attachment to this courageous woman and her fight, and I did not hesitate to show her some of the documents in my possession.

(Besides those relevant to Malaysian dealings with PetroSaudi, incidentally, these files also happened to include emails regarding payments made to the former British Prime Minister Tony Blair, whom PetroSaudi had hired as a consultant to help "unlock situations" for them in new markets, primarily China. That Clare is related through marriage to Blair's successor as prime minister and putative rival, Gordon Brown, will no doubt give some added piquancy to this detail, at least for British readers.)

Clare asked me what I wanted in return for handing the documents over in their entirety. I thought for a moment. I told her I wasn't holding out for riches but that I had to protect myself and my family from any trouble that might ensue. What I wanted, I said, was the equivalent of the money PetroSaudi owed me, nothing more. Of course, as I have related, that meant $2.5 million — in other words, a lot of money.

I have been asked many times to explain this request, and why I asked for money instead of just handing over the documents without monetary compensation.

My answer has never changed. I thought it was likely that handing the documents to a journalist would bring me trouble, and that I would need money to defend myself or settle any difficulties. Naturally, I could barely imagine what these might be and what would actually happen. I wasn't out to get rich from simply leaking documents — I was never that kind of person, and if I was I could have contacted Jho Low or others close to Najib Razak to get a better price for my silence. After all, the data I had proved they were all corrupt. This thought never crossed my mind, however.

Future events would show that money wasn't my motivation in exposing this scandal. Despite the attacks and the accusations I've experienced over the years, I have always remained true to my values.

Clare told me she would look into finding a buyer for the file and keep me informed. Weeks and months went by, however, and I didn't hear back from her; and nor did I try to reach her. I had other things on my mind — after all, Laura was about to give birth to our child.

My son, Xander, was born in Koh Samui Hospital on October 3. At the age of 48, I was a father.

As with most first-time parents, I couldn't have anticipated what it would do to me in terms of the emotion and the feeling that life now has a meaning and a purpose. I was the happiest man alive.

My mother and my in-laws came to visit us on Koh Samui in the following days. What a joy it was to bring our son into our home, and to share these moments as parents.

The months went by, and I watched Xander grow day by day. There could be no better feeling than this new love.

At the same time, I continued training for the Ironman event in Australia. I had become a true athlete, and our son did his bit for my training routine by sleeping well. He wasn't even bothered by any of the construction work at the resort. He was — and is — an amazing kid.

Then, in February 2015, Clare contacted me and asked me to go to Singapore to meet with some people who were interested in the PetroSaudi data. This meeting was to change everything.

I flew to Singapore in the second week of February to meet with Clare and two others: Tong Kooi Ong, the owner and chairman of the Edge Media Group, and Ho Kay Tat, its CEO. We talked for hours, and Kooi

Ong and Kay Tat explained what they already knew about the mechanisms of corruption involving 1MDB in Malaysia. They knew what was going on alright; they just didn't have the evidence.

I showed them some documents and immediately they realized the evidence they needed was right there in front of them. They asked me what I wanted in return, and I told them what PetroSaudi owed me — although instead of $2.5 million, I asked for $2 million.

Kooi Ong agreed and asked how I wanted to be paid. I told him I hadn't expected things to proceed so fast. I didn't want to keep too much money in Thailand as I was not a citizen there, and the only bank account I had in Switzerland was with BSI, where Tarek Obaid also banked, so I didn't want the money to be transferred there either.

In response, he offered to give me a guarantee: a painting worth several million dollars, by Claude Monet. I told him I couldn't keep a painting of that value in my house in Thailand — I would be too afraid of the cleaning lady damaging it. I looked him in the eye and told him we had to trust each other as gentlemen. I was convinced of his honesty and integrity. I also told him that if he didn't want to pay me that would be fine too, and that I recognized this was not a question of money but of morality.

I saw them a few days later, again in Singapore. They'd had problems accessing the data on the hard drive, and I showed them how to do it. It wasn't difficult, but there were so many files — over 220,000 emails — that it took a long time to navigate the folders.

From this point on, I became committed to the Malaysian cause. I had discovered from Kooi Ong, Kay Tat and Clare how Najib's government was plundering the Malaysian people. If my documents could expose this predatory, kleptocratic activity, I would be proud of myself. I realized that ethically I couldn't insist on being paid for the documents — laying bare the wrong that had been done was more important.

In a sense, our meetings in Singapore were like finding the key to a puzzle. The vastness of what was on the hard drive — the huge number of files, 90 percent of which were not relevant to the scam, and the fact that the emails were written in four different languages — meant that sifting through its contents was a painstaking enterprise. Unless, that is, you had a good idea of what you were looking for. Clare and the Malaysians had that knowledge and understanding. My evidence was the proof they had been searching for.

Clare's first article, headlined "The Heist of the Century," was published at the end of February, on her blog, Sarawak Report, and it was explosive. I thought from our discussions that she would write about the scandal bit by bit, but she blew it all up at once. It created an earthquake.

I was slightly worried, but at the same time I felt we were protected on our island in Thailand. This feeling of safety would turn out to be a big mistake — perhaps my biggest.

I started to follow closely what was happening in Malaysia, and the political implications of the data I had passed on. The scandal was growing day by day and I wondered when Najib Razak's corrupt government would fall. There were rumors of resignations and arrests — but nothing decisive happened. There were also huge demonstrations involving hundreds of thousands of protesters, but still the Prime Minister held on to power.

A friend from the bank in Geneva where Tarek and I both held accounts called me one weekend and told me that he had met with Tarek — and that my old friend was planning something against me. He thought Tarek intended to somehow block my money in Switzerland.

Again, I didn't feel too worried about what Tarek could or would do. I felt safe in Thailand and knew I hadn't committed any crimes. But I was underestimating the power of money. They had stolen billions, and they would go to considerable lengths to protect that stolen money.

In May, I transferred most of the money I had in Switzerland to Laura's account in Thailand. I thought that by doing this we would be out of Tarek's reach.

At the beginning of June, Laura left with Xander for Geneva, for the summer holidays. I accompanied them to Bangkok, and we shed a few tears as they departed. A month apart wouldn't be so bad, would it?

There is a saying that I heard a long time ago: "When time stops, it becomes a place." Time was about to stop — and I would arrive at my new place.

Chapter 5

Laura

AND THEN THERE WERE THREE

WE MOVED TO Koh Samui in September 2011. The house and the land we chose were beautiful; even if the place needed some work, it was perfect for our planned resort. And Xavier had another surprise, too: he adopted a dog, a Rhodesian ridgeback, who we named Veggie. She was adorable — and is still with us today.

We bought an extra plot of land next to the house and started building. We hired local contractors, led by a man named Rot. His wife, Modeing, and mother-in-law, Pon, would also help us, the latter in a sort of "housekeeping" role. They were all very kind and true, and friendships were easily and quickly established.

I decided to take Thai lessons. Xavier was supposed to do them with me but it turned out to be not his thing, so all the lessons we'd bought — a total of 300 hours — were transferred to my account. I studied for two hours every morning and after a while started to make good progress.

We also both decided to take up sports. I had always liked and practiced fighting sports, so I chose MMA with a Dutch guy who soon became one of our best friends. Wilfried lived 20 minutes away from us, at a resort by the sea, and gave his lessons from home. He and his wife

Brenda, and their two children, were a lovely family. We trained several times a week and I got myself in great shape.

My brother William and my parents came over on holiday and were mesmerized by the place. We spent an incredible month together, then my brother decided to take three months off work to visit us for longer before traveling around Asia with one of his friends.

With the construction work, plus regular visits from friends and family, as well as my Thai classes and our training, we were busy but happy. I also took a voluntary job in a local school. I taught English to children aged between two and eight years old, and gave them swimming lessons in the school's small pool. I felt a real connection with the children — they were all extremely adorable — and they helped me improve my Thai. Having good Thai friends as well as expat friends also helped in that regard, and we really started to become part of this amazing community. It felt like paradise.

The months rolled past and I distinctly remember February of 2012 — specifically a couple of dates in the middle of the month. I'm not crazy about February 14, Valentine's Day — it's a very commercialized event — but it's nice to have a little kiss and some recognition from your partner, isn't it? To my surprise, Xavier hardly spoke to me. In fact, more than that, he ignored me! All of which made me a little cranky. Had I done something to offend him? Had we had a disagreement that I'd forgotten about? That evening, we went to bed without even saying "good night." Very strange indeed!

The next morning, I woke up next to a different Xavier. "Good morning my love," he announced. What was going on? I barely had time to notice I was smiling again, and I still had my eyes half-closed, when he said dramatically: "I think there's a beast under the pillow!"

I started and opened my eyes in a panic. I lifted the pillow… and discovered his outstretched arm. In his hand, he held a ring. I was shocked! Xavier looked at me and asked if I would become his wife. I immediately burst into tears… and of course told him that yes I would. It was absolutely the best moment of my life.

We hastened to announce the news to our relatives. First Maïté, Xavier's mum, and my parents — as well as my brother, who already knew about it because Xavier had told him about his intentions. They were all so happy for us. I also called my friends Mel, Nina, Bea, Louis and Phil. We started thinking about how to get everyone together for the wedding and decided we would hold it exactly a year to the day from our engagement. By then, the resort would surely be almost finished.

Wilfried offered to let us use his house by the sea for the ceremony and said some of our guests could stay with him. We had so much to prepare that we enlisted a wedding planner to help with decorations and flowers, setting up tables, catering, all the official documents, and so on. We decided the celebrations would last from 1-17 February 2013, giving our guests coming from Switzerland the chance to spend a couple of weeks on holiday with us in Koh Samui. The RSVPs quickly came flooding back — everyone was on board.

Following our engagement, Xavier decided to take on a new challenge to get into shape for the wedding: he started triathlon training. Xavier never does things by halves, however, so the goal he set himself was to compete in an Ironman. He bought and shipped over "a Ferrari of a bike" from my godfather, Yvan, who had a bike shop in Geneva, and signed himself up to be coached by an Ironman champion, Jurgen Zach, who worked in Phuket and who also prepared a special diet for Xavier to follow. After a few months, almost every day he was out riding 100km on his bike in the morning, followed by a 3km swim in the sea and sometimes a 20km run to finish things off. Ahead of our wedding, he lost some 15 kilos — and with my MMA training working wonders too, we were both in the best shape of our lives.

Just in case we ever started feeling lazy, however, our household was also growing. We took in two more dogs — a French Mastiff, Pablo, and a crazy Jack Russell named Jambo. But that wasn't all: seeing that we loved animals, our Thai construction workers kept bringing us stray kittens, and we ended up adopting eight of them over the course of a year. Meanwhile, at a market in Bangkok, we bought two parrots — which resulted in farcical scenes as we drove them home to Koh Samui. One of the birds, whom we named Tequila, soon managed to tear a hole in her box and I had to practically sit on top of it to stop her from escaping. We then stopped at a supermarket on the way to the ferry and bought two plastic cat cages. Moving the parrots into the cages was a struggle in itself, however — we managed it but they screamed the whole time, louder than sirens.

The new year came around and everything seemed to be in order for the wedding and for our guests arriving. I went to Geneva to pick up my wedding dress, my parents' gift to me, and I will never forget how my mum looked at me during the fitting. She was very moved.

Our family and friends all seemed to arrive in Koh Samui at once, and the following days and evenings were incredible. Everyone got along like one big family. It was a case of non-stop laughter and activity: we had barbecues at home, visits to great local restaurants and trips to different beaches, including a day at the famous Nikki Beach Club. It all felt like one big non-stop party.

The evening before the wedding, we organized a dinner at Larder, a restaurant that belonged to one of our friends. Afterwards, we went out separately for our final evening before tying the knot: Xavier with his friends and me with mine.

The night before the big day, I slept poorly because I was so excited. In the morning, my bridesmaids helped me to get ready, then we had lunch together with my parents. Everyone did their best to try and calm me down, because it was raining like crazy — and we hadn't arranged for any tents at the wedding site.

It was finally time to leave for the ceremony — we had a mini-bus waiting to transport me along with my mum and my bridesmaids. On the way, however, someone called to say that my dad, who was driving to the venue with some friends, had taken a wrong turn and got lost. We stopped — me in my wedding dress next to a field of buffalo — to try and find out what was happening. After all, I was supposed to go in with Dad after everyone else had arrived.

Eventually we heard that he had found the right way and would be there soon, so we got back on the road. By the time we arrived, of course, everyone was already sitting down — waiting and ready for our big moment. And, thank God, Dad was there too. When he saw me arrive in my dress, he started crying. It was going to be an emotional day.

The organizer told me we were ready to start. Our music — Santana's "Samba Pa Ti," the most beautiful piece of guitar music in the world — started playing. My friends and bridesmaids came forward one by one, and I walked down the aisle with my dad on my arm.

At the end of the aisle, surrounded by all our best friends, and on a terrace overlooking seas that blended with the colors of the sky, stood my husband-to-be, my Xavier. The flowers, the light, the happy faces around us: everything was perfect. We looked at each other and tears of absolute happiness flowed on our cheeks. It was even more beautiful and vivid than I had imagined in my wildest dreams. The ceremony moved absolutely everyone and we said "yes" in voices trembling with happiness and emotion, then kissed — a strong and tender kiss — as the sun set slowly on a magical scene.

An elephant arrived for us on the beach, and we got up on it for a short ride along the seashore. The remainder of the evening then opened with our wedding dance — which we performed to "I've Had the Time of My Life" from the movie Dirty Dancing. (We had taken dance lessons for it and I have to say that while Xavier is good at most things, dancing is not one of them. In the end, we didn't dare to do the lift in the air that you see in the film, because I didn't want to lose my teeth on my wedding day!)

Everyone danced and celebrated like our lives depended on it — we were all crazy with joy and laughter. We cut the wedding cake, watched the fireworks and released traditional Thai "lucky balloons," lanterns that fly up into the sky and are supposed to bring good luck. It was magical — we all watched as the black sky filled with little lanterns that went up into the stars. By about 2 o'clock in the morning, we didn't have the energy to stand up anymore. All the emotions and the party had exhausted us, and everyone went home with warm hearts from an unforgettable day.

The following days were full of goodbyes. The holidays were over, the time for our friends and family to leave us had arrived... and I was suddenly Mrs Laura Justo Winkler.

WE STILL HAD visits from friends in the following months, but we resumed our daily rhythm, and we were happy with the life we were building. Unfortunately, Xavier still received upsetting fragments of news from Geneva. It was always Tarek: he was annoyed at Xavier for leaving the way he did, and he couldn't bear the fact that he could no longer control Xavier. The way he saw it, no one should be able to turn their back on him.

We learned that he was telling lies about Xavier — bad-mouthing him behind his back and trying to ruin some of the business that Xavier might be able to do in Geneva from Thailand. Xavier also got very angry when he found out that Tarek had tried to pay a friend they had in common, Aziz, to mess up our wedding. That felt like the final straw!

The year passed quickly and just after we had celebrated our first wedding anniversary, early one morning I found out the most beautiful news of my life — I was pregnant! When I told Xavier, he was overjoyed and told me he knew it was going to be a boy. The wonderful news was confirmed at the hospital in Koh Samui, and we rushed home to tell our closest friends and family. Right away I could already see myself with our little baby. My God, we were going to be parents!

The weeks passed and after three months of pregnancy I decided to go to Geneva to show my swollen belly before I could no longer travel. I was also looking forward to having a baby shower with my friends. My family treated me like a princess.

When I got back to Koh Samui, almost four months pregnant, I told myself I should do some sport every day, and try not to go overboard with food. I didn't want to gain more than 11 or 12 kilos. Since I was throwing up due to morning sickness as often as three times a day, that shouldn't have been too difficult — or so I thought. I was wrong. I ate healthily, but in fairly large quantities. As the months passed, however, I became sicker and sicker and found I had less and less strength to do any exercise. My weight ballooned.

On 1 October, by which time I was 24 kilos heavier and having difficulty walking, I had contractions and spent the day in hospital. They sent me home in the evening because they didn't think I was ready to give birth. I thought I could feel things coming on — but I had almost four weeks to go before my due date.

The next day, I felt unwell all day... and the contractions started again. My water broke at around 10pm. We rushed to the hospital.

On 3 October, at 8.16am, our little angel — Xander — was born. Xavier told me right away that he was perfect — and it was true, he *was* perfect. We both gushed with tears of happiness and pride. It was really the best day of our lives. We had been blessed.

Our life as new parents was wonderful. We adapted immediately to our new rhythm and enjoyed every moment of just being around Xander. We felt like we were flying on a cloud of love and well-being.

AROUND THIS TIME, Xavier was contacted again by Clare Rewcastle Brown, a journalist he had met a few months earlier in Bangkok. She was fighting corruption in Malaysia and thought Xavier could help her out with some information. He agreed to fly to Singapore and meet some people who were interested in what he knew or had seen at PetroSaudi in relation to Malaysia. I told him several times to be careful — because we were not alone anymore. We had become parents!

I told Xavier I felt anxious, even though I couldn't really express why. His reply was always the same: "Don't worry."

The meeting in Singapore, arranged by Clare, was with two Malaysians who ran a newspaper in Kuala Lumpur. When Xavier returned the next day, he told me the story was even bigger than he had thought. When he had finished explaining everything, I was stunned.

This was huge! If the stories were true, Tarek and Patrick had been involved in the theft of billions of dollars, with the help of the Prime Minister of Malaysia and other accomplices. Xavier told me he had left the Malaysians with a hard drive containing a copy of PetroSaudi's server, but that nothing would be exposed by Clare or the Malaysians just yet.

He was wrong. A few weeks later, Clare came out with a bombshell article — all based on the documents Xavier had given her and the two Malaysian journalists. She had blown the cover on one of the biggest financial crimes in history.

At this point, I told Xavier that things had gone too far. He was a bit surprised, because Clare had promised to publish her articles little by little and not blow everything up right away. Still, he told me we weren't at risk.

"What do you want them to do?" he asked me. "What is written is the truth, and anyway we are safe in Thailand, so don't worry."

That was a real error of judgment. The truth — when you expose powerful criminals — has a price. A high one.

Chapter 6

XAVIER

A DIFFERENT KIND OF PRISONER

CROUCHED IN MY cell — or should I say *cage*? — at the Koh Samui Police Station, as 22 June gave way to 23 June, sleep would not come. The cell was dirty, swarming with mosquitoes, and located next to a road, along which scooters and motorbikes raced all through the night.

I was picked up early in the morning and escorted to the airport by five police officers, along with the police chief Colonel Pongsawai, who told me everything was going to be fine. We were the last to board the plane, and I asked to put a sweater over my handcuffs so the other passengers wouldn't see them. It was a small airport, and I believed I would be returning the following day.

The flight took an hour, and again we were the last ones to get off. I don't think anyone had noticed that I was handcuffed. We walked through the long corridors of Suvarnabhumi Airport, and in the distance I noticed a small group of about ten people who seemed to be military or high-ranking police officers. Some were in commando uniforms and were heavily armed. As we approached them, it didn't cross my mind for a single moment that they were there for me.

But sure enough, they were. Without taking their eyes off me for a second, they ordered me into a waiting vehicle. We then crossed the city in a motorcade at unbelievable speed, sirens howling, and arrived in no time at the headquarters of the Crime Suppression Division, a powerful unit under Thailand's Central Investigation Bureau that happens to be responsible for investigating organized crime, serious fraud, electoral crimes, and so on.

My lawyers from Koh Samui were waiting for me. The person in charge of the investigation told me I would have an appointment in court the next day, and that I would have to sleep in a cell at a local police station overnight. My lawyers assured me this was normal, and that I had nothing to worry about. They seemed confident I'd be quickly released on bail.

I stayed in the office for an hour, discussing my predicament with them. An officer then arrived to take me to the station. He was about my age, kind and attentive, and didn't handcuff me. On the way, I asked him for a cigarette even though it had been two years since I'd stopped smoking. He stopped at a gas station to buy a pack, which he shared with me, and he bought me a coffee, too. We sat on a sidewalk, and he asked me not to run away. He was too old to chase after me, he said. I thanked him for the cigarettes and the coffee, and we chatted for a bit before heading back on the road. To this day I wonder what would have happened if I had just run away and taken refuge at the Swiss Embassy.

We arrived at a seedy police station in town where I was thrown into an overcrowded cell. For company, I had an assortment of desperate-looking characters: alcoholics, drug addicts, others who just seemed to be mentally ill. I huddled in a corner and waited for the night to pass. There was no water, no food, and no mattress. Clinging to the belief that I would be back in Koh Samui the next day, however, I acted as if everything was fine.

The next morning, the same friendly police officer picked me up and took me back to the CSD building, where I was left to wait for several hours alone in an office. Eventually he returned — only this time dressed in combat gear and carrying an automatic weapon. He led me into a van and drove me to court.

On arrival, I was escorted to the office of the Chief of Police and told to wait again, this time in the company of four commando police officers, all of whom carried shotguns. I was given a bowl of rice, but I felt so burdened by the stress of the situation, being handcuffed and persistently watched, that I couldn't eat.

My lawyers from Koh Samui came and again assured me that the application for bail would go smoothly. They stressed that I was accused of having committed a minor offense, namely "attempted blackmail," and that they had offered the court bail of about $10,000 — which they had already taken from my bank account. I remained confident about a positive outcome.

The Chief of Police arrived — a tall man with copious military decorations pinned to his uniform. He told me, in decent English, that there was an officer from Scotland Yard waiting to see me. A well-dressed European man then entered the room, introducing himself as Paul Finnigan. He explained to me that there was an ongoing international investigation involving Thailand, Malaysia and the UK, and that I needed to collaborate with him in order to exonerate myself.

He said this was my one window of opportunity to walk away with a slap on the wrists — but that I needed to cooperate with him, sign what he asked me to sign, say what he told me to say and plead guilty to what he wanted me to. He was extremely insistent and seemed very sure of himself. His tone of voice and body language pressed home a sense of authority.

Still, I was skeptical, and resisted his demands. I had done nothing wrong and pleading guilty was out of the question. His response was that bail would be denied, now and in the future. He was strongly adamant that my best option was to plead guilty… but still I held my ground. I knew I was innocent, and innocent people don't plead guilty. Once he had finally grasped my unwavering refusal to comply, he notified the Chief of Police that I could be sent to prison. I was taken to the basement where a worn-out bus — occupied by about 20 other men — awaited me.

Officers attached chains to my feet and made me get on the bus. It was evening by now and we drove for about an hour through dark streets. I had no idea where we were or where we were going. All the other prisoners were Thai, many of them very young, and we were all in chains.

The bus stopped and we shuffled out in our chains. They took us to the back of a poorly lit building where we were handed light brown uniforms that had a horrible smell to them. Clearly they hadn't been washed for a long time. We were made to strip naked, lift up our testicles and lean forward so that they could check whether we were carrying any concealed objects. We put on the vile prison outfits and were taken to yet another dimly lit building. It was 8pm.

Next we were taken to a canteen — staffed by prisoners — and had aluminum plates and plastic spoons shoved in our hands. The food, rice and fish, looked completely inedible, and the putrid smell coming from the fish was revolting. I only managed to eat a spoonful of rice. (During the entire time I would spend in prison, this was the only meal I ever ate in the canteen. I soon found out you could buy food at the prison's small on-site shop. You needed money — which I was often short of because of the infrequency of the visits I was allowed to receive. But I never gave in; I would rather have gone hungry than eat what they served in the canteen.)

After "dinner," we were taken to shower at the back of the building. The showers consisted of a plastic pipe, pierced with holes, under which you had to stand and wait for a trickle of water to come out. There was no soap.

Afterwards, we had to put the same stinky prison outfits back on and were taken en masse to cell number 13. Another prisoner informed us we were to sleep there for the first night, and that we would be assigned to our final cells the next morning. Cell 13 also happened to be used as a dormitory for the sick and lame, and as I looked around I saw a mentally handicapped prisoner, a sick elderly man, and another with a missing leg. We were given blankets that smelled of damp and mold. I later learned that these were only washed once or twice a month.

I couldn't sleep for a second. All the lights stayed on and I just lay there on the tiled floor. Throughout my entire period of incarceration, I would in fact never have the pleasure of sleeping with the lights off. Only once, when there was a power outage, did I enjoy 15 minutes of pleasant, peaceful darkness... before the generator rebooted.

At six o'clock in the morning, all the cells were opened. As day broke, I came to realize that my nightmare had truly begun; now, I belonged to *them*.

WE WERE TAKEN to a courtyard, where all of the prisoners in our part of the jail had to line up — more than 700 of us. The building was filthy, there were holes everywhere in the concrete flooring, and none of the shrubs in the courtyard had any leaves on them. Everywhere you looked, there was cat feces. The cats were there to chase the mice — and there were a lot of mice.

My name was called, along with those of the 20 others who had arrived with me the previous evening. We were taken to a small room where they cut our hair. Instead of scissors, they used what I have seen people use to shear sheep. Two minutes later, my head was completely shaved.

Afterwards, they took us to another room to have pictures taken of our faces, and of our tattoos. I have some tattoos, and it was explained to me in very basic English that if I got any new ones in prison, I would have six months added on to my sentence.

They wanted me to sign documents, but I refused — because they were all written in Thai. They left us in the courtyard again, and I suddenly felt incredibly alone. I was terrified; nothing I had ever experienced before had prepared me for this shock. Everything about the place was wretched — for example, the toilets. These were outdoors and consisted of nothing more than a line of holes on a bench perched over a small gutter, along which ran the foulest-smelling water. I restricted myself to going to the bathroom every two or three days — I tried to last for as long as my body would allow.

I only saw two other Europeans but I didn't talk to them. I was still trying to grasp what was happening to me. I simply spent the first hours of my prison nightmare paralyzed in a corner of the building. At 1pm, we were counted again, and they began to allocate cell numbers to arrivals from the day before. I was assigned to cell 7.

I sat under the only tree in the building until 3pm that day. A few Thai men approached me, explaining that they had seen me on TV the night before. Yet again, I badly needed a cigarette. A young Thai prisoner offered me one of his that he had rolled himself. It tasted horrible but I smoked it anyway. We were counted yet again, and it was time to go back to the cells. Turns out I was sharing cell 7 with around 50 other people. The room was tiny, and I couldn't imagine that we were all expected to sleep there — but again I was wrong. I was given another thick, filthy blanket, and assigned a place to rest.

Some prisoners had stacked several blankets to fashion small makeshift mattresses — but these were the gang leaders of the prison. Everyone else was almost literally piled on top of each other, making it just about impossible to lie down. In the cell there was also a tank, which had one bowl for inmates to use to splash water over themselves. The water was only filled once a day, and often it was empty. Besides washing in it, we had to use it to brush our teeth. Some of my cell-mates also used it to relieve themselves in, and some even masturbated into it — in full view of everyone else.

I soon discovered that it was impossible to sleep. With all the lights on, it was brighter than broad daylight. This was supposed to prevent violence, sexual violence in particular. For the first time in my life I was terrified — almost in total panic. My heart beat so hard I thought I was going to have a heart attack.

AT 6 A.M EVERY day, we were taken out of the cells, counted in the yard, and herded to the showers.

It was on my first such visit that I witnessed one of the most shocking things I had ever seen in my entire life. Some inmates had inserted artificial nodules or marbles into their penises. I learned that this is a common practice in Thailand, where men implant solid, spherical objects, in the form of beads, into the shaft of the penis, to make it look bigger.

During my time in prison, I even saw the procedure being carried out. Inmates would open the "glans" of the penis with a mirror, insert the desired objects, then treat themselves with antibiotics to avoid infection. What horror, what hell, as far as I was concerned.

I felt so lost during the first few days that I would fumble for my mobile phone in the morning — the habits of a free man don't vanish immediately. On my second day, I went to the prison library but was told by the inmate in charge that books were only available to those who had spent at least two weeks in prison. Then, around noon, I was called on the loudspeaker and told that I had a visitor. I was elated — I didn't know who it was but thought that someone must be coming to get me out.

I was escorted to the prison's visiting facility, which consisted of just a handful of booths serving all 7,000 inmates. Prisoners and their visitors were separated by glass screens and conversed via old-style telephone handsets. The place was overcrowded, full of people shouting and pushing each other. I was taken to one end of the room and found the two lawyers from Koh Samui waiting for me. Again — incredibly — they told me not to worry because the offense I had committed was minor. They said they had made a second request for release on bail and assured me I would be out of prison in two days.

They said they would take more money from my account — "for the bail procedure." I later found out they were taking plenty of money for themselves, but there was nothing I could say, nothing I could do. They also deposited some money into my prisoner account, for basic necessities such as soap, a toothbrush, drinking water, basic food and other commodities that were sold from the small prison shop, which was run by inmates. I left the meeting feeling reassured, even overjoyed; I would be getting out soon!

I spent the next day doing nothing. I tried to isolate myself as much as possible, but I was approached and asked to join a workshop where everyone sat on the floor assembling electrical outlets. It was unbearably hot in the room and incredibly dirty, so I quickly conjured up a lie, explaining that the Swiss Embassy had an agreement with the prison and that it was illegal for Swiss inmates to work. After that they left me alone.

I also had a brief visit from the Swiss consul — and I could tell straight away that he considered me a common criminal. He told me the embassy had had dozens of requests for interviews with me from newspapers. I told him not to do anything — that I would be getting out on bail soon.

That afternoon, I was approached by a French prisoner named Karim. He was the first person to help me adjust to life on the "inside," which he did by explaining how the prison and its rules worked. He was in jail for using fake credit cards, a common enough crime in Thailand. He offered me food and drink, and bought me cigarettes. He was incredibly kind and knew the environment well. He explained that the prison was really managed by the inmates, as there were only about 100 employees for all 7,000 of us. Everything was therefore administered by selected prisoners under the orders of a few dozen employees.

Karim also explained that in the building certain activities were controlled by small prison mafias — who were best obeyed. I began to see how everything had its own corrupt rules. I couldn't buy things in the store if I didn't buy cigarettes from certain prisoners; I couldn't wash my things if I didn't pay the prisoner in charge; I couldn't get a haircut without offering some form of payment; and so on and so forth. It was all racketeering.

Karim also told me that a certain group would ask me to clean either the toilets or the prisoners' clothes. He warned me not to comply if I didn't want to become their "slave," or be constantly targeted. Karim was used to the prison and the way it operated and he allowed me to discover a world unknown to me. Without his help, I would've had to face many more problems.

Other lessons he taught me were never to show weakness and never to trust anyone. To show fear was to expose yourself to others. I often felt the weight of stress and anxiety in prison, but following Karim's advice I never showed it. In fact, I never showed any of my feelings. One of the purposes of prison is to strip you of your humanity and reduce you to a number. You have to manage around that; to avoid confrontation and becoming the target of violence, you have to succeed in being forgettable, but at the same time assert yourself and show your strength. I owe my ability to adapt to that world and survive to Karim's counsel, aspects of my own character, and the love I have for my wife and son. I very soon came to understand that prison in Thailand is not an institution to rehabilitate criminals, but a cash cow for the guards and a dumping ground for the judicial system.

That same day, I also witnessed a fight — or rather an act of mob violence. A group of 20 prisoners beat up another inmate, kicking him in the face until he fainted. Two prisoners then continued to attack him, jumping on his head. The inmate's jaw became detached from his head and as he lay in a pool of his own blood I was sure that he was dead.

Two guards arrived but the crowd had already dispersed. They took the inmate away and I never saw him again.

ANOTHER NIGHT IN our overcrowded cell. I was exhausted but it was impossible to sleep, not with the legs of other inmates stretched out over my own. The stench of urine and excrement that filled up the room was unbearable.

The next morning, as Karim had anticipated, a group of about ten prisoners took me aside and asked me to clean the toilets. I refused — and the leader of the group punched me in the mouth, breaking my tooth. Gripped by a rage, I grabbed his head and smashed it against the wall. He cursed me, spitting out blood, but the group dispersed. The officer in charge walked over, acting as though nothing had happened, and the day went on.

My mouth was in a lot of pain, and I requested to see the prison doctor. One of the officers explained that I would have to pay 10,000 baht ($290) for a short appointment… or wait two months to see a dentist. I wasn't surprised, but I was angry all the same. I refused to comply and left.

On my third day in prison, I had another morning visitor — this time my friend Denis, who now ran a business in Thailand but whom I had known since the early 2000s in Geneva. I cannot describe the joy it brought me to see a familiar face, and I was so happy to receive news from Laura. We were given only 15 minutes together — the standard time for all prisoners, except for those who bribed the guards in charge of the visiting room. But the visit cheered me up.

Denis also informed me that my lawyers were outside and waiting to see me. I only spoke to them for three minutes that day — but it was enough for them to explain that my application for bail had been denied again. Again, they persuaded me to stay confident, telling me they had support from the judges in Bangkok for a third request.

Dejected, I headed back to my unit; but once more I heard my name being called on the loudspeaker. I was told I had yet another visitor, however, this time instead of being taken to the visiting room I was escorted by two guards to the prison governor's office.

As I entered, I recognised Colonel Pongsawai, who had arrested me in Koh Samui, and Paul Finnigan, the detective from Scotland Yard. The room was air-conditioned and pleasantly cool, and they offered me a cup of coffee and a cake. Paul told me again about the ongoing international investigation, and repeated his plea for my co-operation. This would include signing confessions which he would dictate. He told me I would have to do everything according to his instructions.

I explained once again that I could not and would not confess to crimes I had not committed. His response turned into a threat: he warned me that I could either accept what was on offer and be home before Christmas, or refuse and spend the next nine to ten years of my life in cell number 7, which he described as the worst prison cell in Thailand. He also told me that all of my requests for bail would be refused. I asked for a cigarette and said I needed time to think it over. My mind was racing; the thought of spending years in that hellhole terrified me.

Tormented by the reality of the situation I found myself in, aching for my freedom and to be back with my wife and son, I decided I had no choice but to accept Paul's proposal. He said he would return the next day — and informed me that Patrick Mahony was now waiting for me in the visiting room.

Before I knew what was happening, I was face to face with Patrick — a man I'd hoped never to see again. He was there with Dave Thomas, a private investigator whom Tarek had used in London. Patrick explained that in future he would visit me in the same office as Paul had done, but that he first needed to make sure I had agreed to co-operate.

The next morning, I was again escorted to the prison governor's office. This time I met with Colonel Pongsawai, Paul and Patrick all at once. Patrick was elated about my decision to collaborate, and said I had made the right choice. He told me that if I complied with their demands and instructions, I would be back in Geneva for Christmas, and added that Tarek would take care of my family's security and financial well-being.

Patrick also explained that Paul would contact Laura, who was still in Geneva, to inform her of my decision to co-operate. He cautioned that there were security concerns that meant it was too dangerous for her to come back to Thailand. If I followed through with my commitment to work with them, however, he would arrange a call with her for me. I couldn't stop thinking about her and my son: I was prepared to do anything to see them again.

The next day, Paul and I began writing depositions in which I accused myself of a number of different crimes. I was forced to scrupulously follow their script — I had to confess that I had stolen the data, that I had worked with journalists and the Malaysian political opposition, and that the files in the hard drive I had given them had been manipulated. I also had to stress that PetroSaudi was a good company, whose dealings with 1MDB were legitimate and entirely legal. I had no other options; I simply had to do as he demanded.

Paul came every day, and we wrote and re-wrote the statement several times until he was satisfied with it. The purpose of my collaboration was to throw doubt on everything that had come out in the press about the 1MDB-Petrosaudi scandal, and to cast it as fabrication and a manipulation tactic by Malaysian opposition figures operating in league with journalists.

Inevitably, they insisted I denounce both Clare Rewcastle Brown and the people in charge of *The Edge* newspaper. But they also had me comment on the involvement of others I didn't know, including individuals named Kamal Sidiqqi and Sufi Youssuf. According to Patrick and Paul, these two were close to Mahathir Mohamad, a former Prime Minister of Malaysia and Najib Razak's main political opponent.

Interestingly, Patrick and Paul never asked how I had actually obtained the data; instead they simply ordered me to write that I had hacked into Tarek's and Patrick's computers in the London office and stolen it.

I would come to understand when I got out of prison that by asking me to confess to this theft, they were trying to render the evidence on the drive inadmissible in a court trial. They had thought of everything — or almost everything.

To this day, I still wonder how Patrick and Tarek thought they would get away with it all. They embezzled $1.5 billion of the money they received from Malaysia, more than 80 percent of the total sum. Their sense of impunity continues to astound me. They must have thought Najib Razak would continue to be re-elected, and that the whole operation would just fade away over time.

During one of his visits, Patrick confided to me that Tarek was co-ordinating matters with Malaysia and Najib, and that everything also had to be done in co-operation with "the English authorities." He said I had no reason to doubt their promises to me and even insisted I would be given a new official identity once I was released from prison.

He also explained to me that PetroSaudi had paid back a "loan" from Malaysia in a complex arrangement in which 1MDB appeared to recover $2.32 billion from the PetroSaudi deal in the form of "units" in a Cayman Islands fund that were essentially promissory notes. (The "promise" of payment would never have to be fulfilled, of course.) A broker had agreed to value these units for an amount equal to the PetroSaudi debt plus interest, and a bank had put the units — showing the "fake" amounts — on the bank statements of 1MDB. As a result, Patrick was able to assert that all of PetroSaudi's "debt" had been repaid and 1MDB was able to say it had made a profit. It sounded to me like a world of financial make-believe.

After several days of "collaboration," I was moved from cell 7 to cell 11, which was apparently reserved for political figures, businessmen and other "VIPs," all of whom paid to be housed there. There were only 15 of us — instead of the 50 in cell 7 — and there were two shower-toilet facilities. I met a former minister, a former senator, a young man from a good Thai family who had killed an Australian in a fight, a businessman from a wealthy Thai family, and an older inmate who was in prison for having committed lèse-majesté. Some of them spoke English, which helped reduce my feelings of isolation and loneliness.

The conditions in my new cell were more bearable than what I'd experienced up until now, but they were still bad. There were no newspapers for the prisoners, just one TV channel in Thai which only broadcast programmes approved by the ruling military junta, and we all still slept on the floor. The only difference was that there was a little more space between us. Where I slept, there were two young prisoners on either side of me. One of the VIPs told me that these were my bodyguards. I was surprised at this and thought he was joking, but perhaps PetroSaudi and Scotland Yard actually wanted to protect me. I later came to perceive them as spies, however — they followed me everywhere, even into the shower. They would watch my every move, and try to prevent any of the Europeans in the prison from approaching me. They effectively isolated me from the other inmates; I was under permanent surveillance.

After some time, one of the officers told me I would have to spend my days alone in a cage so that I could be more easily monitored. I simply refused to listen and decided to wait for all the prisoners to gather for the morning roll call. With everyone present, I began to loudly exclaim that I wished to see the Swiss consul and the person in charge of my investigation, and that until then I would be going on a hunger strike.

I was met with deafening silence. Nobody moved; all the inmates just stood there staring at me. I continued to shout in English, until after a few minutes the director of the unit came to inform me that there had been a mistake and that I would not be put in isolation after all. This incident showed me that I held a certain power.

Despite the presence of my "bodyguards," over time I was able to make friendships with a number of European, African and South American inmates who arrived in the prison. I shared my food with them and gave them advice, and I tried to help the newcomers as I had been helped in the beginning. Solidarity is key to survival in prison.

I soon came to discover that each type of foreign prisoner tended to be associated with particular crimes. The Eastern Europeans were mostly in the business of counterfeit credit cards, African inmates were often involved with counterfeit money, and many South Americans had stolen jewelry from Thai homes. I met a South American man who was a former gangster in Colombia. He explained, nonchalantly, that his speciality had been to kidnap people from rival gangs and take them to a veterinary practice to be castrated. For some of my companions, theft and violence were just normal activities.

I also discovered that my height and weight worked to my advantage. The Thai prisoners on average measured around 1.70 meters tall and weighed about 60 kilos, while I was 1.90m and weighed 90kg. This helped me seem more dominant to other inmates, while my tattoos made others perceive me as more threatening.

The days passed and 16 July arrived — Laura's birthday. I spent it in a deep depression, wishing I could be back with her. The thought of missing my son's birthday on 3 October also made me very upset, but I comforted myself by thinking that I'd make up for it all over Christmas, and that we'd have the best Christmas ever.

PAUL AND COLONEL Pongsawai made me stop working with my lawyers from Koh Samui. It seemed that both the Thai police and PetroSaudi wanted to be involved in all legal proceedings and wanted to know about everything I was doing or saying.

Pongsawai also asked me for all of my email passwords, "in order to remove elements that could hinder the investigation." In addition, they rewrote WhatsApp conservations that I had kept in paper form and which had been seized in the police raid: I had printed these out, and they used the printouts as the basis for creating a fictional correspondence between myself, Clare and Kay Tat. References to Najib Razak or Jho Low were removed.

As promised, Paul arranged a call with Laura in the days following the start of my co-operation. I cannot express the extent of the emotion — the overwhelming joy and happiness I felt — when talking to her. For the few minutes that we spoke, I felt free. I told her to work with Paul and Patrick, and that everything would end soon if she did.

Paul, Patrick and Pongsawai said my trial would be up soon. They explained that the sentence would be six months at a maximum and repeated that I would be home before Christmas. Paul sent me photos of Laura and Xander, suggesting I write them a letter which he would give them when he saw them in Geneva.

I missed my wife terribly, and felt incredibly lonely without her. But I couldn't show weakness. I had seen what was done to the weak in prison. They were used as slaves, either to work menial jobs or to massage the guards as they sat idly in their chairs. I therefore never expressed any emotion in front of the guards or the other inmates, even when things were at their worst. The only times I cried were when Laura visited — in fact, I cried each time I saw her. I am not ashamed of that; if anything, I'm proud of it.

Patrick told me during one of his visits in July that PetroSaudi had hired a top Swiss lawyer to defend me and handle the press. He said he had also arranged an interview with a journalist who was close to Najib Razak's party and wrote for *The Straits Times*, a Singaporean daily broadsheet newspaper. Paul gave me a list of questions and their pre-prepared answers a day before the interview. I was again being forced to confess to the crimes I was charged with and clear PetroSaudi of any wrongdoing. Incidentally, the reporter involved would receive a "Journalist of the Year" award for his article about me, and was later promoted to be head of the paper's Washington bureau.

At the beginning of August, Paul and Patrick visited me again to inform me that my new Swiss lawyers would arrive the next day. When I met with Marc Henzelin and Sandrine Giroud from the Lalive law firm, I found the former to be arrogant, overconfident, and conceited. He did not seem very interested in my case and told me to plead guilty. I saw him a couple more times in the days following, and he left before my trial took place. As I would later learn from Laura, Mr Henzelin was very much involved in orchestrating a press campaign against me and in favor of PetroSaudi. The objective was to clear PetroSaudi of any responsibility and portray me as a thief and a criminal. He was effectively being employed to destroy my image and my name.

Everything had happened so quickly. PetroSaudi, Patrick and Paul had first made me confess to crimes I was innocent of. Then, ably assisted by Mr Henzelin, they forced me to give interviews with journalists where I again had to incriminate myself and vindicate PetroSaudi. All of this happened in the space of a few weeks and I was defenseless against their onslaught. They brought me news, letters and pictures from my family, they had good relations with the prison's governor, and they were friends with the police. Everything they did and said seemed so convincing.

I suppose I had developed some kind of Stockholm Syndrome. I later came to better understand my captors' motives, which were to put out the fire that was raging outside. Unfortunately for me, their manipulations were just getting started.

Chapter 7

Laura

CAUGHT IN A WEB

ON 22 JUNE 2015, as I ended my phone call with Xavier, I could hear my mother in the background asking me what was going on. She had panic in her voice. I couldn't think of anything else to say other than that Xavier was being detained because of immigration issues. I couldn't tell her the truth — partly because I didn't know exactly what was going on myself but mainly because I didn't want her to panic any more than she already was. In fact, I couldn't talk to anyone.

I didn't sleep that night. The next morning, I had a call from Rot, the foreman on our resort project. Xavier was on the line. He told me he was being taken to a police station in Bangkok to apply for release on bail, and that he would call me back soon. I was in shock — although the worst was to come later when I heard from some lawyer who was supposedly helping Xavier that he was in fact being taken to a *prison* in Bangkok.

As the day progressed, I discovered the extent of what was going on by reading articles from local Thai media saying that Xavier had been arrested. I was terrified — I didn't know how he was, what state he was in. I felt numb and desperate. I couldn't even respond to the wailing cries of my son.

The next day, there were articles in the Swiss newspapers, and in international media too. My friends called and came to visit me and I broke down in tears; I was so shaken up. I couldn't stop thinking about how people we knew must now believe my husband to be a thief and a blackmailer. What was written in the articles about him stealing the PetroSaudi data made me sick. He was portrayed as a gangster, a criminal who only cared about money.

I tried to calm down, but my desperation quickly turned to rage against Tarek and Patrick, the real criminals. I wanted to get back at them for what they had done. I immediately contacted Clare Rewcastle Brown, sending her an email with the subject "URGENT JUSTO." She called back a few hours later and said she would fly from London to see me the next day.

Clare arrived on 27 June, and it was the first time I had met her in person. I could immediately feel that she was determined, compassionate, and had a strong sense of justice. We got along very well. I could tell she was a fighter — and she stressed that we needed to fight, and that they had no right to have arrested Xavier because he hadn't committed any crimes. She wrote an article headlined "It's All Lies About Xavier" and published it on her blog, Sarawak Report. I was very happy with it.

I'd started casting around for a lawyer when the phone rang. On the other end was an Englishman, judging from his accent. He asked if I was Laura Justo. "Trust me," he said. "I am here to help you. I was with Xavier just a moment ago."

This gave me hope, although he didn't elaborate on the details of his contact with my husband. I had tears in my eyes. He said he was from Scotland Yard, and that he was out to help Xavier and I. "You have to trust me," he said again. "My name is Paul Scott. I'll try to call you back and put you through to Xavier. He'll explain everything for you."

After he'd hung up, Clare asked me what was going on and I explained what Paul had said. "How can Scotland Yard be there?" she wondered.

"Why are they involved?" Before leaving, she told me she would do some investigating. I knew I could count on her.

The next day, Paul called me back. I was trembling, praying for him to put Xavier on. And then I heard a voice on the other end of the phone: "My love?"

I burst into tears. It felt so good to hear his voice. I heard him crying too. He said that Paul was our ally, and that I had to do everything he asked. I couldn't understand what was happening.

Xavier explained that I must go to BSI bank in Geneva and search in his safe for a hard drive and a computer. He told me that he was going to plead guilty to the charges, and that Paul would help us. He spoke about an international investigation involving Thailand, Malaysia, and the UK. It was important, he said, that I give the hard drive and the computer from the safe to Paul. Echoing Paul, he also told me I had to stop talking to Clare.

We didn't have much time on the phone. Biting back tears, I told him I would do what he had asked. I had no choice.

I went to the bank with my mother, who waited for me outside. When I opened the safe, I found two hard drives, a laptop computer and a bag of USB sticks. I put everything in a secure place and waited for Paul's instructions. He'd said he would come to Geneva to collect the safe's contents.

I had an uneasy feeling about Paul and my instinct told me not to trust him. He called me back later the same day, and I insisted on knowing what was going to happen to my husband once I had handed over the evidence.

"Xavier is facing up to nine years in prison for having this evidence," he replied, coldly. "Nine years. The computer and hard drive are neither your property nor his; they belong to PetroSaudi. Keeping this evidence in your possession is illegal and I have the power to arrest you for it in Switzerland. If you want to help your husband and avoid legal trouble, then I advise you to hand everything over to me."

He told me he would arrive in Geneva on 30 July, early afternoon, and that he expected me to meet him at the airport.

Having listened to Paul's talk of an "international investigation," I searched online and found a report on a Thai news site, where a Thai CSD commander was quoted as saying Britain had dispatched officers to Bangkok to question Xavier over his alleged blackmailing of PetroSaudi.

Two days later, I heard from Paul again, and he put me through to Xavier. We could hardly speak from the emotional intensity of hearing each other's voices. He told me again to trust Paul and repeated that he was from Scotland Yard. He also said something that left me utterly paralyzed: "Patrick came to see me, to help us. Patrick and Paul are going to help us."

Our time on the phone was short. Xavier said he was going to write me a letter and reiterated that I had to trust Patrick and Paul. Our voices quivered when we had to hang up. His parting words, time and again when we had these calls, were "I love you — and tell Xander I love him." I would always reply: "We love you more than anything. It's going to be OK; we are here for you."

When I hung up the phone, I was more confused and angrier than ever. What did Xavier mean that Patrick was helping him? After putting him in jail?! Was this a joke? And how could PetroSaudi have direct contact with Scotland Yard?

It was fast becoming the norm that I had trouble sleeping, and that night was no exception. With the time difference between Thailand and Switzerland I had started getting up at 3am each day to make sure I didn't miss a call or a message from Paul. He was my only line of communication with Xavier.

The next day, 14 July, I received Xavier's first letter, via email from Paul. I burst into tears as soon as I began to read it:

"My love, I miss you so much, I miss you so much. It's so hard without you two. I spend my days thinking about you and Xander....

"They put me in a bigger cell with educated people; it helps with spending the 15 hours in the cell.

"I don't need a lawyer because I'm pleading guilty. It's the only way I'm not going to spend years here and I need to co-operate, which I'm doing to the best of my recollection. Paul spends a lot of time with me, he wants to help us as much as he can. Patrick has been here twice, he's a really good guy. He's going to do everything he can to make sure the sentence is six months and that I get out before then.

"Don't get a lawyer and don't listen to others. Call Paul and Patrick and ask them to explain the situation and the current demands."

I was stunned. The conditions Xavier found himself in were, he said, better than before, but they were still awful. The fact that Patrick had visited him in prison alarmed me, but one thing in particular made me sick to my stomach: Xavier had written that Patrick was a "really good guy." I could tell he was being monitored, and I knew that Paul must be sending copies of the letters to Patrick. But again, what could I do about any of this? I had to refrain from getting a lawyer, as Xavier had asked me not to.

I had written my own letter to Xavier and printed out some photos for him, but of course I had to email them to Paul because no one else was allowed to send him mail. I couldn't think about anything else other than Xavier. I was in a state of ongoing panic.

A few days later, Paul sent me by email attachment another letter from Xavier that had clearly been written under close monitoring. This time it urged me to trust Paul and do what he asked of me. I would later realize — when I gained access to Xavier's prison files and cross-checked the dates — that this letter, dated 24 July, was written on the same day as one of his forced confessions: the *ultimate proof* that Paul was with Xavier, inside the prison, at the time of his confessions.

A DAY LATER Paul messaged me saying he needed Xavier's passport, which was still in Koh Samui. I asked our friend who lived in Bangkok, Denis, to go and collect it. He then had it delivered, at Paul's request, to Detective Inspector Toon at the CSD. Paul's close contacts in the Thai police went a long way to convincing me that he must be from Scotland Yard like he said.

On 30 July, my mother and I went to the airport to meet Paul. I had searched on the internet for Scotland Yard agents under the name of Paul Scott, but had found nothing. Full of anxiety, we waited.

Suddenly a man approached me. "Laura Justo?" he asked. He held out his hand and said: "Nice to meet you, I'm Agent Paul Scott." He was quite tall and had short white hair. He was also in good shape and seemed very confident and sure of himself. From his accent, he was definitely English. I put him at around 55-60 years old.

We sat down at a café next to arrivals, and he asked me straight away for 'the evidence' — the hard drive and the computer. I placed them on the table and he assured me I was doing the right thing. He said it would help Xavier, that I was just giving back what didn't belong to me, and that I didn't want to risk any legal problems by refusing.

In the way he talked, the words he used, his attitude, I felt absolutely sure that he was a police officer. He wrote down the serial numbers of the hard drive and the PC on a notepad, explaining that he didn't have his computer with him just now but that he would put the details in an official receipt from Scotland Yard and send it to me when he got back to his office in London.

Everything seemed legit and official — apart from one detail. When I asked to see his badge, he said didn't have it on him, but promised (falsely, as it turns out) that he would send me a copy of his identification, along with the report of our meeting, as soon as he was back at his office.

After signing the report, he made me sign it too. He congratulated me, and said the material would be given to his colleagues in London.

He also told me he would visit Xavier again soon, and that now that the evidence had been returned, Xavier would soon be released.

The next day, he was back on the phone. He told me he was returning to Thailand to help Xavier and that he would put him on the phone when he was with him. I felt sick with anticipation. I told myself everything was going to be OK, even if I didn't feel it inside.

What Paul didn't know was that when I had gone to empty the safe at the bank, I'd found more than what he was asking for. It contained a PC, two hard drives and some USB sticks, but Paul had never asked me for anything other than the PC and one hard drive, and Xavier had never said anything on the phone about the other stuff. I'd sensed that Xavier had made copies deliberately, and therefore I made the decision to keep them from Paul.

I was scared. When I got back to my parents' house, I hid the other hard drive and the USB sticks where no one would be able to find them, then told my mum where the hiding place was, just in case anything happened. My parents were supportive, but I could see that they were in a state of panic and very worried. I felt guilty for putting them through this.

On 3 August, I received a call from Aziz — the mutual friend of Xavier's and Tarek's who had attended our wedding. His words were kind but I could tell he was far from genuine. He told me he had spoken with Patrick and Tarek and that he knew they were trying to help Xavier. He also knew about Paul.

Aziz said he wanted me to come to his flat: apparently Patrick wanted to talk to me directly but didn't want to risk calling me on my mobile. According to Aziz, we weren't supposed to know that Tarek and Patrick were helping Xavier because if that information got out they wouldn't be able to do anything for him — it wouldn't look right in the press, given that they were the ones who had made the charges against him. The whole story just sounded dodgy, and I could tell that something rotten was going on.

When I arrived at Aziz's place, he picked up one of several phones and called Patrick through a secure app.

I thought to myself that if only Patrick had come in person I would have had the satisfaction of breaking his nose. But I had to restrain myself — again, I had no choice but to listen to him. Aziz spoke to him for five minutes before passing the phone to me. I bit my lip to keep myself from insulting him.

I had always had a bad feeling about Patrick. He seemed uncomfortable speaking to me, and told me straight away that Xavier had taken something that belonged to them, that he had done something wrong and that he and Tarek had been forced to press charges against him.

"Paul is there to help you," he added, "Xavier is doing a great job with Paul. Don't worry, we'll have him out of there in no time."

He told me there was "politics" at play, and that Clare had put Xavier in a lot of trouble. I was not to talk to her anymore. I immediately asked Patrick why they didn't just withdraw the charges. His answer seemed more far-fetched than anything I had heard so far: there was, he said, an international investigation in progress and withdrawing would seem suspicious. Now that the media was over all the story, the only solution was to see the charges through to the end. Patrick stressed, however, that thanks to Xavier's confession, his collaboration, and their contacts in Thailand, "he will be out in a few weeks."

"It's political," he repeated. "You must understand. We've even hired lawyers for Xavier." This was proof, apparently, that he and Tarek were trying to help Xavier. The lawyers, he said, were Marc Henzelin and Sandrine Giroud from the Lalive law firm in Geneva. "They are one of the best law firms. They will contact you and you can go and sign the mandate for Xavier. Don't worry, I'll take care of everything."

My naivety and my despair brought me to believe and obey him — even though I didn't feel it in my heart. In any case, everything was already in motion and I felt I couldn't stop it if I tried. Aziz comforted me and told me to trust them. He said Tarek and Patrick were sorry, and that they really wanted to get Xavier out of prison.

I got home just in time to put my eight-month-old to bed. He was the only one capable of calming me down… but at the same time, when I looked at him, I couldn't think of anything but Xavier, alone in a Thai prison, in horrible conditions, far from me and from his little boy. Every night, I showed Xander photos of his father and told him he would be with us soon. Xander's eyes would flutter and he'd say "papapapa…" Without fail, this brought me to tears.

I wondered how such misfortune could have befallen us. The situation was destroying me; every day was more difficult than the last. I prayed for it to end, for all of us to be together again as a family.

THE NEXT DAY, 4 August, I received an email from Sandrine Giroud. "As you know," she wrote, "our firm is here to represent your husband."

She had scheduled an appointment for me to meet with her and Marc Henzelin at Lalive's offices. My mum came with me. My instant impression of Henzelin was negative: he came across as haughty, dishonest, snobbish and full of himself. He barely spoke to my mother. I already hated him, and I knew the feeling was mutual. Sandrine Giroud seemed to be his apprentice.

I was also introduced to Marc Comina, who was to oversee "public relation matters and the press." He seemed like a jerk, too.

Their goal was to write a long article in Xavier's name that would be published in *Le Temps,* a French-language Swiss daily, and other newspapers they had selected. The purpose would be to help his image as he pleaded guilty, by emphasizing his remorse. This would help him in his trial, they said. The following week, we were all scheduled to meet in

Bangkok so that Xavier could sign over power of attorney and they could outline how they planned to help us.

Everything seemed to be already arranged between PetroSaudi, the lawyers and their PR handler. The meeting, I perceived, was a charade to convince me that a genuine legal defense was being mounted.

Meanwhile, the press was still in a frenzy over Xavier, which made me want to vomit. I had so many journalists calling at my parents' house or trying to acquire my phone number. They acted like vultures; they wouldn't leave us alone.

My mornings were filled with the hope of hearing from Xavier or Paul; in the evenings I would succumb to despair if I'd heard nothing. In between I had to deal with reporters, give constant explanations to friends, talk to my in-laws, reassure my family and allow myself to be comforted by them. Most importantly of all, though, I had to take care of Xander. It made me heartsick to see how he missed his dad.

Patrick was organizing for the Swiss lawyers to go to Thailand, but ahead of their departure I was finally traveling to Bangkok myself — finally, I was to be allowed to see my husband. God, it felt like so long since we had been together.

Patrick and Paul said it was too dangerous for me to go to Thailand alone, so Paul was to accompany me. I was also to be escorted by him to Koh Samui to sort out some paperwork and pick up some things.

I was instructed to meet Paul at Heathrow Airport on 6 August. The business class flights we were put on, and the five-star hotel we were booked to stay at, were all paid for in full by PetroSaudi. What awaited me? I was full of hope and prayed that this was the beginning of the end of our nightmare. But I had a bad feeling.

Chapter 8

Xavier

A BITTERSWEET MOMENT

THE SEVENTH OF August 2015 couldn't fail to be my best day in several weeks. Laura was due to visit!

Since my arrest, Patrick and Paul had convinced me that it was too dangerous for her to come to Bangkok and that she should stay in Switzerland, where she was safe. I had no access to outside information and hardly any visitors. Patrick and Paul had guided me through the entire process, and the last thing I wanted to do was put Laura in danger. Besides, she had to look after our son.

But no matter how hard I tried to convince myself that I was strong enough to make it through until December — when Paul and Patrick had said I would be released — I had no idea how I would achieve this. I was too alone in this hell. I missed my family terribly. I missed Xander. I felt truly empty.

I had only been in detention for six weeks, but I was already trying to count down the weeks until the promised release date. And no matter how much resilience I was able to muster, the reality was that I still had another 20 weeks of misery ahead of me: 20 weeks of filth, abuse and loneliness.

The night before Laura came, I couldn't stop thinking about her visit. A thousand questions ran through my head. How was she? How was Xander? What did she think about all this? Was she safe? What does she do with her days? Did she have moments of happiness, or at least joy? Was Xander aware of my absence?

Before her visit I asked one of the VIP prisoners to lend me an outfit, one that didn't smell of dead rats. Some VIPs had servants who washed their clothes on a daily basis, and their clothes had been bought on the outside to begin with so were therefore much nicer. I shaved as best I could with the only kind of razor available to buy in prison — for safety reasons it hardly cut at all, and of course there was no shaving gel. I even managed to find some cologne. Again, some of the prisoners in my section enjoyed the privilege of having cologne; most of us didn't. The prison generally forbade it because the officers were afraid inmates would use it to get drunk.

I really wanted to look (and smell) my best so that I wouldn't worry Laura; I wanted to show her that I was taking care of myself and that everything was fine despite the circumstances. I was peculiarly anxious: I felt like I was going on a first date and I thought my heart was going to explode with anticipation. It was also not far off 40°C (104 Fahrenheit) and I was covered in sweat, ruining the outfit I'd borrowed.

A guard came to pick me up from our building and took me to the prison governor's office. I walked into the office — and there she was, as beautiful as ever. I cried like I had never done before, not even stopping to look around and notice that Paul was with us in the room. For a moment we were alone in the world, and I was free. We sat down and she showed me pictures of Xander. As she spoke of him, I started to cry again. No-one can imagine the emotion of that moment; there is nothing to which I can compare the intensity.

I told Laura about my life in prison, which of course meant I had to lie to her — she didn't need to know that I was living in a filthy, overcrowded hell, because I didn't want her to worry about me. I told her about the few friendships I had made, and described the more enjoyable moments of a prisoner's daily routine (some of which I had to make up). We still managed to laugh as we recalled happy memories of better times.

I also explained everything that was going on with Patrick and Paul, specifically around the agreement we had so that I would be out in December. I told her there was an international case being managed by Scotland Yard, and that this accounted for the fact that we could meet in the governor's offices and not in the visiting room used by everyone else. And I summarized everything I had been forced to confess and the words that had been put in my mouth — all the lies that seemed to be my only way out of this nightmare.

When our time was up, it felt like our moment of freedom had only lasted five minutes, but in reality an hour had passed. My heart ached for having to leave my wife but despite this I returned to my unit with my spirits lightened. Because of Laura, I felt an obligation to stay positive and to carry on fighting so that I didn't disappoint her or increase her burden. Having an incredible wife and son was a blessing that many in the prison were not so lucky to have. I knew they would be my lifeline during difficult moments to come and prayed for the strength to keep this knowledge in my heart.

Chapter 9

Laura

A YOUNG MOTHER IN A SEA OF CORRUPTION

PAUL AND I arrived in Bangkok at 7am on August 7 and checked in at the large and luxurious St. Regis Hotel. The Swiss lawyers were traveling separately with Patrick a couple of days later. We dropped off our bags and headed straight for the prison. My heart was pounding. We had just landed and I hadn't slept in 24 hours but I wasn't tired; on the contrary, I was so excited to see Xavier again.

Paul told me that he and Patrick had made all the necessary arrangements, and that he had already settled everything with his police contacts in the prison. We were even given a private office for the visit.

This was my very first visit to any kind of prison, and the first time I was going to see Xav since his arrest. When I arrived, I started to realize the kind of hell he was living in. It was horrible — I was sure prisons at home were luxury hotels by comparison. At the entrance I could see trucks of prisoners being unloaded, the inmates handcuffed at the wrists and ankles and bound by chains. It was impossible for them to take more than half a step.

At an office at the entrance we were met by a police inspector from the Crime Suppression Division who will feature heavily in this story, Colonel Pongsawai. Paul gave him our passports, which the inspector photocopied. Two other officers signed the copies for authorization.

We entered a big hall where the visiting area was located and in which hundreds of people, including children, stood around waiting for their names to be called. Dogs, cats and rats roamed around freely. The visiting "rooms" were at the back, inside a rusty cage structure. Visitors could be seen there talking to prisoners on phones, the two sides separated by metal barriers with inset windows. Hellish noises and foul smells ran amok everywhere.

As I took in the scene, I noticed I was being stared at. It hadn't occurred to me before but of course it made sense: you didn't see many foreign women in this place. As a European woman who spoke fluent Thai, I would soon become known as "the White Wolf" — appreciated by some, hated by others.

Two prison officials signed the authorization for my visit, and we were left to wait outside again in front of a big iron door, the same door through which new inmates entered. After a while a guard escorted us inside again, and as we were led past the visiting room in the direction of the prison offices, I could tell that this wasn't a standard visit. I could also feel hundreds of eyes on me as I walked.

En route to the offices, I saw a guard reclining on a chair, while a chained prisoner massaged his feet. It seemed to me grotesque and inhuman.

I was in a state of intense anticipation, however — all I could think of was seeing my husband and holding him in my arms again. We arrived at a small, air-conditioned building and I was told to wait in one of the offices while they went to collect Xavier.

The wait was horrible, but after what seemed like an age I suddenly saw him walk past the window. I got up, the door opened and we looked at each other, automatically bursting into tears as we hugged. For a brief second we forgot everything: we were happy.

After so long apart we had so much to say to one another that it was hard to know where to begin. On the subject of his living conditions, I knew that Xavier was playing down the gravity of the situation to reassure me, to make it hurt less. I knew he was confined in a terrible, chaotic, ruthless place — but still he wanted to reassure me that he was OK. He also told me he'd had to plead guilty because of the international investigation and because it had been the only way — according to Paul and Patrick — that he could avoid spending years of his life locked up.

He added that Paul — who during the entire visit stood two meters away — had spent a lot of time with him writing his confession. And he kept repeating that I shouldn't worry: Patrick and Tarek had planned everything so that he would be out soon and back in Switzerland.

Mobile phones weren't allowed inside the jail but I showed Xavier some photos of Xander that I had printed and that Paul had been allowed to take in with him. On seeing them, Xavier started to cry again: it was incredibly difficult for him to look at pictures of his son, whom he loved and missed so much.

It was clear to me that Xavier was suffering like he had never suffered before. It was horrible and hurt me deeply; everything that had happened was just so unfair, especially because I knew he was innocent.

We stayed in the office for over an hour, but the time flew by so quickly. When we were told the visit was over, we hugged each other tightly and I promised I would return in the coming days with the lawyers, and that hopefully after that I would be able to come back on my own. I also intended to be there for the trial, which was scheduled to take place in the coming days. In the meantime, I had to go to Koh Samui to take care of the resort and our animals, pick up some things, settle some papers, and pay our bills.

I went back to the hotel with Paul. When I got to my room I just collapsed. The situation seemed even worse than I could have imagined. I realized, however, that all I could do was follow the instructions I was given and pray that it would all be over soon.

The next morning, I left for Koh Samui, accompanied by Paul. It was such a shock to be back. I was glad to see the house again but at the same time it was difficult and painful to be home. I barely had time to collect my things and see the animals before we had to leave again.

I hadn't been sure whether I would be able to come back on the same day, so I had only booked a one-way ticket. Paul had done the same. On our way back, therefore, we went to a travel agency that was run by one of my Thai friends in the town of Nathon, a five-minute drive away from the house. My friend booked our tickets and asked for our passports. When Paul handed her his British passport, I looked over and noticed that his name was written as "PAUL FINNIGAN." He had previously introduced himself to me as "Paul Scott." I couldn't believe it. He had given me a fake name! A policeman using a fake name? I became immediately scared.

I decided to confront him. "Your name is Paul Finnigan?" I asked him. "Why didn't you give me your real name? Why did you lie to me? It's because of Patrick and Tarek, right?"

Paul told me to calm down and — with his characteristic, calm self-confidence — assured me he couldn't use his real name on a sensitive mission like this one. He said his identity card was under another name and that now that he knew me he didn't mind me knowing his real name.

My sixth sense told me something didn't add up, even though everything else had indicated this guy was a real policeman. He had entered the prison with the Thai police and had been with Xavier from the beginning. He had put me through to Xavier on the phone — something that was officially forbidden by prison rules, no matter who you were. He had also arranged for Xavier's passport to be sent to Bangkok's chief of police, with whom he was in close and constant collaboration. And he had given me Xavier's letters, which were dated the same day as his confession. Surely only a police officer should have been able to do all that. Moreover, the Swiss lawyers working with PetroSaudi, Henzelin and Giroud, were aware of his presence and his role in the case, and they wouldn't have allowed a fake policeman to be involved, would they? I was not comfortable with the situation at all but I couldn't talk to anyone, and I couldn't ask for help. I was afraid — and Paul knew it.

We flew back to Bangkok on 9 August, and I had a meeting with Patrick that evening. He told me that Paul was there to help us, that everything was under control, and that I had to be careful and follow their instructions if I wanted Xavier to get out of prison soon. I didn't trust any of these people, but my naivety and innocence still made me want to believe them — Paul the police officer, Patrick the savior, Tarek who was so apologetic, and the Swiss lawyers who were now supposedly there to defend Xavier.

The following day, Paul, Patrick, Henzelin, Giroud and I met in the hotel lobby, but it seemed there was an issue with me being allowed to go to the prison with them. Paul ordered me to stay in the hotel and not go anywhere. I didn't understand why and when I insisted on being given answers, he said that if I wanted to see Xavier the next day I would have to co-operate. He couldn't let me and the lawyers into the prison at the same time, he said. Besides, they had to discuss the case.

I was angry at this but he was very insistent. Denis came to visit me and we had lunch together at the hotel restaurant. He listened to me and comforted me, and he agreed that something was wrong. Why hadn't I been allowed to go? It didn't make sense.

I was beside myself. I'd brought one of the spare USB keys from my mum's house in Geneva and I showed it to Denis, who smiled when I told him that even though I was still too afraid to open it, I was pretty sure it contained another copy of the PetroSaudi server. He reassured me that I was wise to have kept it but advised me not to do anything with it for the time being. I resolved to keep it safe so that I could use it as leverage if and when I needed to.

In the afternoon, I sent a message to Paul telling him I wanted to see Xavier. He ordered me once again to stay in the hotel — but I went alone anyway and was admitted for a visit in the regular visiting room, by which time Paul, Patrick and their accomplices were on their way back to the hotel.

I would only find out much later that the real reason for their insistence that I stay in the hotel was because Paul *et al* were with a man they absolutely did not want me to meet. His name, as I would later learn, was David Scholberg and his firm, KBSD, specializes in cybersecurity, "reputation management" and "intelligence-based PR." It would eventually emerge that he had been hired by PetroSaudi to make sure the Swiss lawyers were paid without PetroSaudi's name appearing on the bills — and to handle other aspects of what amounted to a co-ordinated campaign against Xavier's interests.

Scholberg, it turns out, made the trip to Thailand in the company of Patrick, Henzelin and Giroud. (They all traveled in first class, of course — paid for by PetroSaudi.) I would also later learn that he accompanied them on their little excursion to see Xavier at the prison that day, but without introducing himself. He had stood quietly at the back of the room as Henzelin and Giroud spoke to Xavier. Moreover, he even stayed at the St. Regis along with everyone else in our little entourage. During the meetings I had with Paul, Patrick and the lawyers over the course of those four days, however, nobody ever mentioned the presence or existence of this mysterious individual.

And it got worse. After these visits, Paul and Patrick asked me to go back to Geneva because, according to them, the trial wouldn't take place for a while. I therefore returned to Geneva on 14 August — only to learn on arrival that the trial would in fact happen just days later, on 17 August.

As I had just got back, I couldn't immediately leave again as my son needed me. It was hard to avoid the conclusion that they had done everything to ensure Xavier would be alone in court, that we would be separated once again. In fact, it was exactly a repeat of how things had played out when he had been arrested — at which time I conveniently happened to be on holiday in Geneva.

When I arrived back home, I was so excited to see Xander again. My trip was the longest time I had ever been away from him, and I had missed him so much. I held him close and told him that Daddy would be home soon. I could only dream of one thing — for our family to be reunited; for us to be together again, happy.

The promises that Patrick and Paul had made brought me to believe in this hope still. I needed to believe it. But deep down I was beginning to doubt if my dreams about us being together at Christmas had any basis in reality.

Chapter 10

Xavier

MY FOUR-MINUTE TRIAL

AFTER LAURA'S FIRST visit in August, life — or rather, the lack of it — went on.

I saw Patrick, and he told me a Thai lawyer had been taken on to represent me and to be there for my trial. Even if everything was negotiated beforehand, he thought it would be better to have a lawyer present. He also wanted things to look legitimate in case journalists were present and asked questions. I didn't suspect anything awry in that; I was just focused on gaining my freedom.

The day of the trial, 17 August, arrived. The norm for all prisoners going to court, including VIPs and political prisoners, was to leave on the prison bus. There were about 10 of us who had to go to court that day, and all the others were put on the bus — but I was asked to wait. A mini-van then arrived to pick me up and I was escorted to court by four guards.

They attached chains to my feet — once again, it seemed the goal was to try to take away my humanity; but again I was determined they weren't going to succeed. As I got into the back of the van, I told myself: I am much stronger than these people. I have an amazing family, I have great friends, and I'm going home soon.

We drove through Bangkok for 30 minutes, and I got a brief glimpse of life outside: buildings, street vendors, cars. I even managed to take the time to smoke a cigarette given to me by one of the guards. Arriving at the courthouse, the driver stopped for a few minutes and made a call, before we finally got out and entered the courthouse building. As we stepped out, I saw a dozen photographers waiting. One of the guards told me they were there for me and that we'd lingered a while to try to avoid them. Thinking back, it's more likely that PetroSaudi had instructed the guards to make sure I *was* photographed.

I tried to hide from their lenses as we passed them. Inside, I was taken to an upstairs office where Colonel Pongsawai and a "translator" were waiting for me. They had brought this person to translate what was said during the trial, but in reality she hardly spoke any English.

My new lawyer, hired by PetroSaudi, was also there — and didn't speak a word of English. He was also badly dressed; in fact, he looked like anything but a lawyer. Scribbling on the seat of a chair, I signed over power of attorney for him to represent me. This was the only time I would ever see him.

Colonel Pongsawai then told me I wouldn't be appearing in a courtroom but that we would go directly to the judge's office for reasons of practicality. Still under escort by the guards, I was taken up a few floors. The chains dug into my feet so much I could hardly move forward.

The judge, a well-dressed man, was waiting for me in his office, along with his assistant. We entered and he asked us to sit down, all the while avoiding eye-contact with me. Another man entered and spoke into the judge's ear. The translator explained: "Big Boss."

The judge then spoke in Thai and the translator wrote down the numbers six and three in a notebook and showed them to me. My immediate thoughts were that the sentence was six months, but that as I had pleaded guilty this was being whittled down to three… in which case, I would be going home very soon. I felt a surge of elation.

And then the world collapsed around me — I realized that next to the figures the translator had written the word "years." I was being sentenced to three years in prison!

I was hurried out of the office again, and as I passed Colonel Pongsawai, he told me not to worry — that this sentence was "for the press." He told me he would change the papers afterwards with the real sentence, as agreed with Paul and Patrick.

I was stunned but I wanted and needed to believe him. The whole "trial" had lasted only four to five minutes.

I was escorted back out of the court building and immediately found myself confronted by the waiting press pack, who of course already knew my sentence. The chains tied to my ankles weighed a ton; I shuffled but made no comment. I could see the faces of my friends Denis and Billy in the crowd, but I couldn't look at them. I was being taken back to prison, and I was in a state of despair.

I would realize later, upon my eventual release from prison, that my three-year sentence was intended to keep me locked up and silenced until after elections scheduled for May 2018 had taken place in Malaysia. (Unfortunately for the criminals orchestrating this silencing, events beyond the control of their twisted minds would derail this plan... but we'll come to that.)

The rest of my time in prison will be described at best sketchily in this book. I didn't have a calendar or anything to keep a diary in, but I found I could at least count the months. When you are in prison with no occupation, that is one of the only ways to survive — a month at a time. When nothing ever happens and a Monday is as good as a Saturday, counting the days just drives you crazy.

How many days, how many weeks, how many months would I have to stay in this dump? I still had no clear answer.

Chapter 11

LAURA

TWISTED TAPES

WHILE READING THE news on 16 August, I came across an horrific article about Xavier. It was titled "Tout ce qui l'intéressait, c'était d'être payé" ('His only interest was to get paid.') This was without doubt the work of Patrick, who had masterminded a misinformation campaign through the Swiss lawyers Henzelin and Giroud, as well as the PR agent I had been introduced to, Marc Comina.

The article described Xavier as a man who was greedy for money. It said that he had been fired from PetroSaudi because he was bad at his job and that he had been able to steal the data because he had worked for them as an IT guy. I was furious! The whole thing was a pack of lies dictated by PetroSaudi.

The fact that Tarek and Patrick had chosen Xavier's lawyers was one thing, but that this band of crooks could have fabricated this nonsense sickened me. I immediately emailed the Swiss lawyers, but they didn't give me a response — all they did was offer me an appointment to talk. This made sense: people who have things to hide don't leave a paper trail, especially when they're reputable lawyers.

I was so angry and sad. I would later learn, in July 2016, that David Scholberg — who I mentioned in chapter 9 and whose small Geneva-based firm, KBSD, was paid by PetroSaudi, although he was never introduced to me — was also instrumental in mounting this conspiracy against Xavier.

Aziz called me later the same day: he wanted me to come and see him because Patrick apparently needed to talk to me on the phone again. I left Xander with my parents and went to Aziz's flat late in the afternoon.

When I spoke to Patrick, he told me (again) that I had nothing to worry about. He had taken all the necessary steps to get Xavier out quickly; we would be together before Christmas, and after that we could put all of this behind us. Xavier's trial was to take place the next day, and when it was done, Patrick insisted, we would know a release date. He even said he had a way to get Xavier out faster, "through the back door," if it came to it. Everything was under control, he repeated; I mustn't worry.

He then asked me to call Clare. He said he wanted me to record her, and that they would then use the recording to clear themselves of all allegations once and for all. Everything had already been planned out: seemingly Aziz just had to install a recording application on my phone and I would be all set. He also told me to write down some key points that he wanted me to discuss with her.

The aim, he said, was not to have concrete information to use against her, but instead to make her talk about her work, what she knew, and also about Tong Kooi Ong and Ho Kay Tat, the two Malaysian journalists Xavier had met in Singapore. I was also instructed to make sure she criticized Najib Razak.

Patrick said he wanted to know what kind of woman she was, and that he couldn't work out a strategy against her until we got her on tape.

In explaining all of this to me, Patrick patronized me. He assumed I was completely ignorant — that I didn't actually know who Najib Razak was, for instance, or what my husband had really seen and done.

As I spoke to him, I realized the idea that I might have some knowledge of what was going on had never entered his mind. Accordingly, I decided there and then that I would use this to my advantage. If they had known what I knew at that time, and what I had in my possession, they would have seen me as a real danger. It made more sense, therefore, to let Patrick maintain his foolish belief in my ignorance. It was my only asset — not to mention a small but powerful source of satisfaction.

Nevertheless, I knew I had to collaborate with them for the time being. When the call with Patrick ended, Aziz set up the recording application on my phone, ready for my call to Clare.

I felt stressed. I didn't want to do what they had asked of me because I knew Clare was a good person, but really I felt like I had no choice. Patrick had given me his word that this would help Xavier. It would help the real criminals, too, of course, but I ask you this: would you refuse to do something you thought might get your husband or wife out of prison, especially if not doing it might only make things worse for them? I submit that most people would do whatever was most likely to help their family.

I wrote to Clare explaining that I needed to talk to her and she messaged back quickly telling me to call her. When she picked up, I felt ashamed because I knew that what I was doing was wrong. Nevertheless, I looked at my notes and started to ask her about everything Patrick had briefed me on. Aziz stood a few meters away from me, listening. I knew he was watching me intently, ready to submit a full report to Patrick.

Clare responded to all of my questions without suspecting for a second that she was being recorded. After all, she was telling the truth in everything she said — and I knew it.

My sense of shame grew as she talked. Amongst other things, she said Xavier ought to have used the press to defend himself and rebut what PetroSaudi were saying — and that such a defense of his innocence could have swayed the Thai authorities. I didn't say much in response.

It occurred to me that she may have been right, but there was also the possibility that using the press to defend himself would have made things worse. She couldn't know how much PetroSaudi were controlling us.

After about 40 minutes, I had exhausted Patrick's talking points. When I hung up, Aziz said we had to send the recording to Patrick. He tried to send it from my mobile but for some reason he couldn't figure out how to do so because the file was too big. It was late in the day and I had to go and take care of my son and put him to bed. I told Aziz I would find the file and send it to Patrick later on from my computer. He put Patrick on the phone again and I could sense him gloating at the idea of this little victory over Clare.

When I got home, I felt emotional and stressed, both because of what I'd had to do, and because I knew Xavier was due in court the next day. I cried when I saw my Xander again; how I hoped for this nightmare to end soon.

THE NEXT DAY, 17 August, was Xavier's moment of reckoning. Rising at 3am, my stomach ached, but I prayed that Xavier would be sentenced to six months only. He had already been in prison for two months, and I made myself believe that with Patrick's and Tarek's contacts and "strategies" working in his favor, we could be reunited in a month or less.

Denis had gone to the courthouse with our friend Billy, and I messaged or called him every five minutes for updates. My heart pounded as I paced around the flat. By this time, I had woken everyone up with my calls, so I left Xander with my parents and went to my room. How desperately I wished I was there to support my husband.

At 7:19am, Denis sent me a WhatsApp message that read: "Three years."

"This isn't possible," I thought. "It must be a joke." No other messages followed. When I called Denis, he picked up and said: "I'm so sorry, Laura."

There was nothing left in me. I felt like time had stopped and the ground had opened up beneath my feet. My body was shaking and I started to cry; I couldn't even speak. My mum understood that I needed to be left alone, so she took Xander out to the park.

I couldn't believe it — three years! They had promised us a maximum of six months, and now it was three years. I couldn't think; I just felt so sad, so lonely and helpless.

The sentence was in fact six years divided by two, so three years for confessing. But I still didn't know how this could have been calculated, given that we'd been told Xavier's supposed "crime" was a minor one. Now my husband was all alone on the other side of the world and faced having to spend three years in a situation I wouldn't wish on anyone except for the criminals who had made it happen.

I suddenly wanted to just break everything — but I realized I had to be strong. I had no right to feel bad; I had to be there for Xander and Xavier, and crying wasn't going to help them. I'm a fighter, and I wasn't about to give up: I swore to myself I would beat them all, that I would expose them for what they had done.

I quickly wrote a message to Aziz: "You promised he would get out and now it's three years. You bastards."

He replied: "Wait, I'll call Patrick to see." And then: "He just told me that the sentence means nothing."

I replied: "From now on, Clare will be the least of their worries!"

There was nothing left for me now but to defend my family with everything I had. Besides the data and documents I already had, I would keep records of all our communications and gather as much information as I could. However long it might take, I would prove what these criminals had done. They had no idea what was coming to them.

ON 20 AUGUST, Patrick and Tarek sent Paul to see me in Geneva. He was accompanied by Tarek's right-hand man, Dave, who owned a company called "Spy Games" in London. Dave was ex-military, and Tarek used him for all sorts of tricks, mainly spying on people, either in the flesh or via technology. I had seen him several times before at Fininfor; now Patrick was putting him to work too.

I figured they were probably coming to calm me down after the sentencing and to try and deceive me yet again with more stories.

We arranged to meet at the ICC, a hotel next to the airport. When I arrived, they began by explaining that the sentence meant nothing, that Tarek and Patrick were on the case and that Xavier would be out of jail in no time. All he would have to do to ease things along would be to conduct some interviews with newspapers that Tarek and Patrick had chosen for the purpose. This would be organized through the Swiss lawyers — so that their own fingerprints weren't detectable, no doubt.

They then pulled out printed messages from text conversations between Xavier and Clare. These messages were supposedly from Xavier's phone, and had been seized by the police when he was arrested in Koh Samui.

It occurred to me that this was probably a large part of the evidence on which the Thai police had built their case against Xavier. What a joke. Paul didn't say anything about how the messages had been accessed, so I kept quiet, but what none of my tormentors could have known is that I had been next to Xavier when he was messaging Clare and I knew to a certainty that the conversations had been doctored.

I was shocked, but what could I say? Paul and Dave definitely sensed my shock, but I believe they ascribed it to surprise at me discovering what Xavier — as it would have seemed to them — had dragged me into behind my back.

They told me that Tarek and Patrick were going to make these messages public and run a press campaign based on them. Xavier would have to be interviewed and say he had only wanted money and that Clare's objective was to overthrow the Malaysian Prime Minister.

Tarek and Patrick now wanted me to call Clare again and this time have her come to my parents' apartment. There, Dave and Paul would set up hidden cameras and I would talk to her about her conversations with Xavier. They wanted to film her, cut the footage in a way that proved her "agenda" and then make it public to discredit her. "She's an individual who needs to be brought down; she's a threat and a madwoman," they said to me.

As I pretended to agree to what they were asking, I thought: "Oh my god! What else are they going to get us into and make us do?" I had to think of something, and fast. I couldn't call Clare to warn her because I was sure my phone was now bugged. (It was the same for my emails — I was sure they had hacked my hotmail account. How else would they have known my movements, allowing them to have Xavier arrested while I was away in Geneva?) I felt scared but — again — I didn't feel I had any leverage to say no to them.

When I got home, I attended to Xander, but I couldn't stop thinking about what they had asked me to do. What kind of trouble were they going to get me into? I knew Clare was a good woman and hadn't done anything but tell the truth and work to expose one of the biggest financial crimes in history — a scandal that Tarek and Patrick were complicit in.

I realized I couldn't sabotage her the way they wanted me to.

Suddenly, an idea came to me. Paul and Patrick had forbidden me to talk to Clare, so I hadn't written back to her for some time. All I had to do was say that because I had cut her off, Clare no longer wanted to talk to me. I changed her number on my phone, replacing one digit and memorizing the real number, in case I really had to call her at a later date. I then called the altered number several times at different intervals and even wrote a message. I took screenshots and sent them to Paul, saying that it was really strange but Clare wasn't answering me.

He told me to try again the next day, so I did the same thing again. Paul and Patrick became increasingly frustrated, but I explained that she must be angry with me, or that perhaps she knew I was co-operating with them. Luckily, they believed me and finally told me to drop it.

I DECIDED I needed to go back to Thailand to see Xavier. I couldn't leave him there after the sentence he had received. I told Paul, who said he would have to come with me, and that Patrick would also meet us there. (This turned out not to be the case: Patrick was briefly in Bangkok during my visit but I never saw him.)

I left Geneva on 24 August. The following day, I was allowed another private visit to the offices inside the prison. I think that after the sentencing, this was Patrick's way to reassure us and to calm us down.

When Xavier entered the room, I fell apart, and so did he. "It's not possible," he said, "I'll never be able to spend three years here! I won't make it." I knew I couldn't survive either.

He said things that hurt me to hear, such as that if it wasn't for Xander, he would be ready to just give up. How could this be happening to us? I pleaded with him and tried to cheer him up. I told him it was all going to be OK, that we would be there for him always, and that we'd fight and appeal the sentence no matter what.

Paul, who was again present during this visit, insisted they would sort it all out and that everything would be fine. He reiterated that Patrick was adamant the sentence had been a political decision intended for the media's consumption. He also told us it would be changed soon — no small thanks to a letter that PetroSaudi had drafted. He even showed us a copy of this letter, which pleaded for a reduction to the sentence on the grounds that Xavier had been fully co-operative in ways that benefited PetroSaudi. Of course, this gave us hope. Paul said PetroSaudi would sign it and send it to the Swiss lawyers.

Once again, there was nothing we could do but accept the only "help" that was being extended to us. The sentence had been pronounced, the dice had been thrown; for now we had no choice but to continue collaborating with PetroSaudi.

When it was time to leave, Xavier told me he was feeling better, but I knew it wasn't true. I knew he must be desperate, and in a lot of pain. When I got back to my hotel room, I broke down. I couldn't stop crying. I missed my son, and even though I was in the same city as Xavier it felt like we were galaxies apart. I felt so alone and powerless in the face of this whole situation. Nothing had prepared me for it. And yet only I could face it and find a way forward. I had to pull myself together.

ON WEDNESDAY, 26 August, I had to make my visit in the normal prison visiting area, as Paul hadn't managed to set up a private visit. It always felt like he needed to remind me how much we depended on him and Patrick.

I got up at eight o'clock and called the Swiss Embassy. For the communal visiting room the rules were that if I wanted to be with Xavier for any length of time I had to ask them to send a fax to the prison requesting the right to a double visit. This was possible for foreign prisoners, and corresponded to two fifteen minute slots rolled into one.

At 9:30, I arrived at the prison with Paul. I had to get my papers signed by three different officers to be allowed to see Xavier but I was told that this would take some time — because one of the officers whose signature was required wasn't there. (This rule about the signatures applied only to Xavier, I ought to add — other visitors could go and see their relatives simply by presenting ID.) In the meantime, I went to order food for Xavier from the prison shop, so that he had something decent to eat in the afternoon.

At noon, my papers still hadn't been signed, and I went to eat lunch in the canteen next door with Paul. I didn't listen to what he said to me. He annoyed me with his stories about being in the police, so I just smiled at him and nodded as he spoke, thinking all the while about Xavier, who would know full well that I had been waiting for hours.

At 1pm, we were back in the prison — but still there was nobody to sign my papers. I felt sick. It wasn't so much the waiting in 37°C heat that bothered me; it was more seeing all the lazy, corrupt guards and officers sitting around with their feet up. It seemed that all they did all day was eat.

My papers were finally signed at 3pm — but I was made to wait another hour before Xavier finally appeared. We were the only ones in the room, as visiting was officially over, but we only had 15 minutes together instead of the 30 I had applied for.

Xavier was in tears. He was so angry that I had been there since 9:30am. I told him that Patrick had arranged for us to have a private, no-wait visit the next day, and Paul — who was waiting next to the visiting booths — confirmed it. But for now we were separated by metal and glass and had to speak through a lousy old phone. It tore us apart. It was so hard not to be able to touch his hand, to hug him. Afterwards, I went back and locked myself in my hotel room. I couldn't stop thinking about my baby and my Xavier.

In the days that followed, luckily, we were able to have more office visits. It felt good just to be able to see each other in private (or almost in private). On 28 August, however, I was told I would only be allowed another private visit if I handed over the recording of my conversation with Clare, the one that Patrick and Aziz had forced me to make on 16 August.

They had forgotten to pursue me for it but Paul told me Patrick absolutely wanted and needed it. I knew Patrick would go ahead and use it as he saw fit — even though he had promised he wouldn't make it public without my consent.

I said I was afraid of getting into trouble with the law, but Paul responded that he and Patrick guaranteed nothing would happen to me. He repeated that everything was legal. Reluctantly, I sent them the file.

What they didn't realize was that they had just made a huge mistake — they'd given me the impetus to record *them* from now on. They had installed an app on my phone to record conversations, and they'd confirmed to me through Paul, the supposed police officer from Scotland Yard, that it was all legal. More fool them.

MEANWHILE, THE SWISS lawyers had found a new Thai lawyer to handle Xavier's appeal. His name was Khun Worasit, and he seemed quite nice and decent.

This lawyer explained that we could appeal Xavier's sentence. Paul said he was confident we would be successful. To start the ball rolling, there were numerous documents that I would have to prepare, which included having them translated, authenticated and signed.

When I left the prison, I jumped on the back of a scooter taxi and headed for an official translator's office to have various papers translated into Thai. I then had to visit several bureaucratic buildings — the Ministry of Justice, the Department of Correction, the Swiss Embassy, the Courts of Justice — to have everything stamped and authenticated.

In addition, I had to go to the bank to make transfers to our housekeeper Pon, who was taking care of the animals we had had to leave in Koh Samui. I also needed to call our friends in Thailand to see who could go and visit Xavier when I got back to Switzerland. After that, I had to pay some more bills… and finally I found the time to call my parents so that I could see Xander! And that was just day one — most of the next several days were spent in a similar flurry as I scuttled between Thai administrative offices and lawyers, all the while waiting anxiously for any news that Paul and Patrick could give.

On my last day before flying back to Switzerland, I got to spend a full hour with Xavier. It was so hard to leave him, knowing that I wouldn't be able to come back for several weeks. We hugged like it was the last time we'd see each other, not wanting to let go. Every time I left the prison, I felt sick to my stomach for having to leave him in that hellhole.

I returned to Geneva and was not surprised to learn on arrival that — with the help of the Swiss lawyers — Patrick, who was still in Thailand, had already made use of my absence to set up the media interviews Xavier was to give. Of course, I would again be absent and therefore unable to wield any influence on how these interviews were conducted.

Back home, the days were all more or less the same. I had to get up at 3am each morning and call Denis to see if there was anyone to visit Xavier in prison. There were cash transfers to be made — so that Denis could go and top up Xavier's prison account and bribe the guards to allow him to receive reading materials and photos of his son. On top of that, I spoke regularly over the phone with the Thai lawyer about various matters.

Around this time, I also reached out to the Swiss Foreign Affairs Department in Bern to ask them for their assistance — but their response was essentially that there was nothing they could do because Xavier had confessed to committing crimes.

Besides all of this, I had to reassure Xavier's mother and play down the harsh reality of our situation to her. Moreover, having received dozens of phone calls from our friends and relatives asking what was going on, I had to call them all back and lie to them. It was horrible.

Most importantly, though, I needed to be a mother to our son. With everything I was having to juggle and with all the emotions I was feeling, holding myself together for Xander's sake was hard, but I had to be calm in his presence; I couldn't let him feel the sadness that haunted me from morning to night.

I tried to be fun and do lots of things with him, but there was always a distraction: something that needed done quickly, a call to make, an email to write, a payment to send, paperwork to do. If there wasn't a lawyer or an official to deal with, things were blowing up again in the press. Each week brought new anguish, new blows, new disappointments. And my to-do list only grew and grew.

I tried to stay strong, but I really let myself go physically. All I consumed were cigarettes and coffee; I slept five hours a night and I no longer knew what it meant to take care of myself. Everyone started to tell me that I had become too thin, and that I needed to take time for myself. I wanted to say: "I don't even have enough time for my son; how can I take care of myself?" And for all that people were concerned, I couldn't explain what was really going on, because for now it had to remain a secret.

When I saw Xavier's sister, she insisted that we urge the Swiss Embassy to help us, because Xavier had rights. My God, if only she had known a fraction of what I was doing and what Xavier had been forced into doing. If only she could have realized how little power Switzerland had in Thailand, how corrupt the Thai system was and how boxed in we were by the situation.

When confronted, it was better to nod my head and say very little. If anything reached the press about Patrick's and Paul's involvement, not only would they stop "helping" us but it could lead to catastrophic consequences for Xavier and I.

On 30 August, Patrick called to tell me that Xavier had done very well in the media interviews, and that as things were now looking better for PetroSaudi, he would be leaving Bangkok for the time being. He said he had to be careful not to be seen in the vicinity of the prison, as this might seem suspicious. *Seriously?*

He also congratulated me for being so "strong." I could have punched him in the face when I heard that, but instead I pretended to be grateful. In my head, I thanked him for letting me record him, and with a big smile on my face, I thought: "Fuck you."

Patrick told me the plan to get Xavier out was evolving. He was going to come to Geneva later in the week to see Aziz. First and foremost they were going to party because he "needed to clear his head," but he said we would also meet and that he would explain the plan to me. He added that he was too scared to talk about it over the phone.

A few days later, I saw an article headlined "Swiss freeze millions amid investigations of Malaysian fund." It described how authorities in both Switzerland and Malaysia were making inquiries and that 1MDB was suspected of corruption and money laundering. For the first time in a long time, I felt a degree of satisfaction.

I prayed for more to come... but who can predict the future?

ON 4 SEPTEMBER, I had an appointment with Patrick at Geneva's Hotel Président Wilson. He was staying there — and Aziz, who was also there for the meeting, kept telling me he had rented a big suite. They made no secret of the fact that they would be partying afterwards.

Patrick kept telling me that everything Xavier had done was positive for his prospects of gaining freedom. I knew that what they'd made Xavier do helped PetroSaudi more than anyone — but hey, those seemed to be the rules of the game. He said he'd been in Bern all day showing the

Swiss authorities how PetroSaudi had nothing to do with this whole "fake scandal." It sounded like they believed him and his explanation that the only people guilty of anything were Clare and opposition factions out to get Najib Razak.

Suddenly, Marc Henzelin arrived with his girlfriend — apparently by chance because he lived nearby and said he used this exclusive hotel as his "canteen." We all had a drink together and at that moment it struck me that never in my life had I socialized with so many people that I couldn't fathom and couldn't stand. I almost felt like laughing at how ridiculous this meeting was.

Patrick told me they wanted Xavier to file a complaint against Clare, Tong Kooi Ong and Ho Kay Tat in Singapore and that he was looking into how best to do this. On his way out, he also mentioned that following some conversations with important people in Bangkok, he was confident of our appeal against Xavier's sentence being successful.

There was also another plan: once Xavier and Petrosaudi were no longer in the news, Patrick would have him "sneaked out the back door." In other words, a jet would pick him up and simply ship him out of the country and back to Switzerland, where his ordeal would be over.

I found this hard to believe — especially as it was clear he and Aziz were already in party mode. I knew exactly the kind of debauchery they were going to indulge in up in their big suite, while Xavier suffered in a rat-hole and I had to put my son to bed without his daddy all because of them.

On my way home I stopped by to say Happy Birthday to my friend Luis, who was having a celebration at our friend Mel's house, across the street from my parents' place. It felt so good to see my best friends after all the bullshit I'd listened to that day.

On 10 September, I phoned Patrick and told him I wanted to go to Bangkok from 19-25 September. He said neither he nor Paul could travel on those dates but that if I wanted to go alone that would be possible and that he would organize everything for me, including arranging private prison visits.

Finally, Xavier and I would be able to meet without Paul! It seemed too good to be true; and obviously there was a price: Patrick said Marc Henzelin would call me to explain what they needed from Xavier for the complaint.

Thirty minutes later, Henzelin rang me. He said the purpose of this complaint was to assert legal pressure to get back the "stolen" hard drive that Xavier had given to Tong Kooi Ong and Ho Kay Tat, and to force them to reveal who else had been given access to the information on it. There was also the added benefit of helping to discredit them — by turning the focus on those with an agenda against the Malaysian government, people would forget about PetroSaudi, Najib Razak and by extension, Henzelin said, Xavier.

I tried to tell him it wouldn't do any good and that it might even look suspicious because a man in prison in Thailand surely has other things to do than to file a complaint in Singapore. But no, he insisted. He said it was a great idea because it would turn everything on Clare, Kooi Ong and Kay Tat. Ultimately, PetroSaudi was paying for it and had asked for it... so why refuse?

I arrived in Bangkok on 21 September, just in time for Xavier's birthday on 23 September. I couldn't wait to see him and could only think about how hard everything must be for him. In terms of practicalities, we had to discuss the bail application, for which I still needed to get a letter from the police attesting to Xavier's co-operation so far.

Patrick and Paul said they had already put this in motion with Colonel Pongsawai. Once again they had also booked me to stay at the St. Regis Hotel. (Incidentally, Patrick always booked rooms at the St. Regis, but when I was in charge of my own arrangements I stayed at a hotel nearer the prison that was perfectly agreeable but considerably cheaper.)

In addition, they said they had arranged all my visits to the prison. When I arrived for my first visit, however, things didn't go smoothly. One senior official ranted at me for having so many "advantages." I could tell he was making fun of me, but to his great surprise I answered in Thai. At which point he became embarrassed — which didn't help me either. I should have kept my mouth shut. After messaging Paul and Patrick, several hours later I was allowed 30 minutes with Xavier in the regular visiting room.

It wasn't what we'd been promised, but the most important thing was being able to see one another, and to talk, even though we were separated by glass. Our emotions always ran high in these reunions: tears flowed, and we gazed at one another with joy and love.

I explained to Xavier that his new Thai lawyer, Khun Worasit, would file the bail application, and that I was finalizing the translation and preparation of the documents required.

I dared not tell Xavier what was on my mind — that I was afraid that since PetroSaudi had effectively cleared itself in the press, or so they believed, and since Tarek and Patrick had got everything they wanted from Xavier, they were becoming less attentive to us. Communication was decreasing, as were our private visits.

I left with a lighter but still a heavy heart. It hurt enormously that I couldn't do more for Xavier, especially given the atrocious conditions he had to endure, and the fact that he was separated from Xander. I wished I could teleport him to Geneva for five minutes. I needed both of them so much but in a way it felt like I had neither.

When I spoke to Patrick on the phone that evening, he told me had arranged the next day's visit. He blamed the Thais for what had happened and said he was sorry but that everything was now under control.

I asked him again about his promise of getting Xavier released by December, but his answer told me I should stop believing it. He said things were difficult for everyone, and that his own bank accounts had been blocked and his wife's credit card too. He told me he couldn't pay for his children's schooling and that it wasn't a happy time.

This was the first I had heard of this straight from the horse's mouth, so to speak, although as mentioned it had been reported in the press that money linked to 1MDB was being frozen. I was glad it was happening, but still: if I'd had Patrick in front of me right then, I'd have knocked out all of his teeth one by one. I had never known such a manipulator. Did he honestly think I would feel sorry for him? He had put my husband in jail on trumped up charges to clear himself of stealing hundreds of millions of dollars, but after everything he had put my family through, he still thought I should be sympathetic and understanding towards him?

I was boiling with anger but I knew I had to keep my cool — because a loss of control could be costly to Xavier and probably to me too.

After giving me his sob story, Patrick passed me the phone number of Colonel Pongsawai, whom he said I should call regarding my visit to the prison the next day. It turned out to be a good phone call: Pongsawai told me I could see Xavier in a private office for an hour the next morning at 10am.

Amazing. We would be able to hug and hold hands. The feeling of closeness when you have been deprived of it is so strong as to be indescribable. It makes you live the smallest moments together with someone completely differently.

WHEN I AWOKE at 5am the next morning, the first thing on my mind was that today would be a good day. After all, it was Xavier's birthday! I felt so tired but I was excited to see him, to be with him. Come on, get up!

After printing more papers and photos for Xavier in the hotel's business center, by 9.50am I was close to arriving at the prison when

Colonel Pongsawai called to say he would be sending a Sergeant Bird to meet me, and that this sergeant would be a little late.

I smoked a few cigarettes to relieve my stress before Bird arrived at around 10.20am and took me straight to the private office, where I was left to wait again. The seconds passed like hours, or so it seemed, until Xavier eventually appeared and we threw ourselves into each other's arms. For a moment, the world stopped and we were in some happy, parallel dimension where life was normal.

Wishing him a Happy Birthday, I reeled off a long list of friends who had written to wish him well and tell him they were thinking of him. For my gift, I took out from my bra a collection of ten small photos of Xander. Xavier's face showed his joy but also his pain. I told him that it was OK and that he didn't need to say anything; our understanding of each other was stronger than words.

It seemed the officers had forgotten about us. It was noon and through the tinted window of the room we occupied we could see them starting to eat. Of course: it was "kin kaow" (lunchtime), and lunch in Thailand — especially in official places like prisons — is a sacred moment of the day. The world stops turning. We got up to leave but were signaled to stay where we were. Thanks to lunch, we were to be given an extra hour together. What bliss!

It was quiet and we felt completely alone. We kissed tenderly, almost like never before; we wanted each other so much. Suddenly, it felt like the electric tension of our love could have brought down the prison walls.

We laughed and talked and I told him stories from our friends and about Xander's progress. We chatted about our future plans and our dreams for life as a normal family, away from this hell. I promised him that I would get him out of here, come what may, and that I would be there for him always.

In the afternoon, I had an appointment at the Swiss Embassy to have some translated documents certified and legalized. The Bangkok traffic meant I was late, but I got what I needed.

Afterwards, I called Colonel Pongsawai to try and arrange the next day's visit, but there was no answer. The thought of missing a visit made me feel sick to my stomach.

That evening, Denis and his friend and brother came to see me and we went to eat together at the hotel's Italian restaurant. They helped me just to take my mind off things a little, even if 95 percent of the evening's talk was about the problems Xavier and I faced.

When I got to my room at midnight, I was exhausted — but sleep wouldn't come. I couldn't stop thinking. The dangers. The possibilities. The shape of our future. Where? When? How? Would the perpetrators ever pay for the hell we were living in? I felt afraid, and I missed Xander.

I also felt sick when I thought about Xavier sleeping just 5km away from me, on the ground, like a dog. He had done NOTHING to deserve this! The injustice infuriated me, and I was getting myself into a state. So I called my most faithful friend, my "other half" for the first 23 years of my life, my brother William.

He cheered me up almost instantly. My brother is strong and sensitive — and understands me better than anyone else. I always feel so lucky to have him and don't know what I would have done without him. Only he could have calmed me down in that situation, at least enough for me to finally get some sleep.

The next morning, 6am, I felt dead. It had now been 94 days. NINETY-FOUR DAYS. My stomach was in a knot at the thought of not being able to get a hold of Colonel Pongsawai. I simply had to speak to him. I was leaving for Geneva that night, and I couldn't imagine going without seeing Xavier one more time.

I called him at 8am, and then every 15 minutes afterwards. After several attempts, he finally picked up and in a very soft voice told me he was sick. I said I was sorry, to which he replied that things would be difficult today. I begged him, and explained this would be my last visit before going back to Switzerland.

He sighed and told me he would make some calls, then call me back. After hanging up, I paced the room, staring at the seconds ticking away on my watch as if it were a countdown clock connected to a bomb.

The day before, Xavier had asked me to prepare several envelopes containing money to pay some of the guards so that he would be allowed to have books and not have his pictures of Xander confiscated. Even with what Patrick and Tarek were paying for this whole charade of justice, we still had to fork out for the smallest privileges. It seemed Thai officials would take bribes for anything. What a world! What hell! And money wasn't enough, either. Xavier had told me to take in a bottle of whisky for them too.

The more time passed, the more stressed I became. I had tears in my eyes and started praying on the edge of the bed. Please God! I beg you! Please let me see Xavier!

At 9am I called the Colonel back but he didn't pick up. Then, five minutes later my phone rang and it was him. Sergeant Bird would meet me at the prison at 10am, he said. I thanked him as if he had just offered me his kidney. I hung up in tears of joy.

Loaded with bags containing the whisky and the envelopes full of money for the guards, as well as books, magazines and sudoku puzzles for Xavier, I jumped in a taxi. Santa Claus is coming, you immoral people!

On arriving, I met Mike, Xavier's "private guard." (Patrick and Tarek paid this guy ostensibly to protect Xavier's safety but it was obvious that he was there to spy on him and report on who he spoke to.) Mike escorted me up to the offices on the second floor, where the staff — as per usual — stopped what they were doing when they saw me. I was the little *farang* ("foreigner"), the only visitor allowed to come up to their offices, the VIP wife who came bearing small bribes just to make her husband's life a little more bearable.

Thanks to the donations from PetroSaudi, I thought, my husband is the reason each of you has a better salary at the end of each month!

I asked to see Khun Yatavi, the guard Xavier referred to as "the shark" and who seemed to be at the apex of all the rackets. I showed him my bags and told him in Thai that I had some small gifts. He smiled and laughed: "You don't have a gun, I hope?" He put the bags under a desk, his eyes shining like a child's on Christmas Day. As I had his attention, I took the opportunity to ask him whether he had passed on the things I had brought for Xavier the day before.

He said that he had. (If he hadn't, I think I would have taken everything I had just given him back.) I then insisted he pass on the books I had brought to Xavier immediately. My smile told him: "I just paid you handsomely and if you don't give these books to my husband these payments will stop." He promised me everything would be handed over that evening.

I went back outside to where Sergeant Bird was waiting for me. Nothing was ever guaranteed until you had the papers in hand — and he had them. I had been a nervous wreck and was by now swimming in sweat (the prison rules were that you couldn't wear shorts and t-shirt, so I was sweltering in jeans, a shirt and shoes), but I suddenly felt calm and relieved.

Bird escorted me inside, and en route to where I was to meet Xavier we passed through a room full of the prison's top brass. Again, everyone stopped to look. I was getting used to this. Bird then waited with me in our designated office for Xavier to arrive. When he entered, we flew into each other's arms, our smiles all the way to our ears. Once more, we were in heaven, if only for an hour.

We discussed the appeal. We were afraid it wouldn't work but PetroSaudi had advised us to pursue it and we felt we had little option but to continue to collaborate. I couldn't tell Xavier what I really felt — which was that I didn't trust them as far as I could throw them — because I knew he was clinging to the shred of hope that they would come through for us.

He told me about some horrible things he had witnessed: inmates being burned by others, fights, bullying and racketeering. I didn't know what to say about any of it. He told me he would be fine — after all, he was strong, and taller than 99 percent of the other prisoners. But that didn't change anything for me. This place was hellish enough to visit. Thinking about these stories made me scared to death for him. I wanted to vomit.

He gave me a letter he had written for me, and told me to read it on the plane that night. I had no words in response, only tears. I felt as if I had a dagger in me all the time and that it was twisted a little each day, so that I suffered and bled a little bit by bit.

As we parted and hugged one last time, the tears welled again. Xavier told me to come back in a fortnight. He said he would be fine now that he had seen me and that the time would pass quickly. I'm not sure whether he was trying to convince me or himself.

One last "I love you," one last look, and the door closed. Welcome back to reality, Laura.

Before flying home I had to visit Worasit to give him the documents for the appeal. All that was now missing was the letter we had been promised from PetroSaudi, which Patrick and Marc Henzelin had said would make all the difference. I would have to pick it up from Henzelin when I got back to Geneva.

After the meeting with Worasit I barely had enough time to return to the hotel and quickly rush out to buy a few things for Xander before I had to leave for the airport. Shortly before my flight, Patrick messaged saying that he wanted to come to Bangkok but that it was impossible at the moment. I sensed he was just avoiding Xavier after all the broken promises about getting him out of jail.

At the airport, I opened and read Xavier's letter. Tears flowed again. I felt so sad to be leaving him but I had to go and be with my little love. I resolved once more to do everything I could to get my husband back.

I landed in Geneva on the morning of 25 September having hardly slept from excitement at seeing my son. My mum picked me up at the airport accompanied by godmother, Val, who was visiting from Scotland, and I was so happy to see them both. When we arrived at the house, Xander was waiting and jumped into my arms, exclaiming "mamama!" My tears were of pure joy.

It felt really good to be back. My brother came over and joined us for dinner; later on one of my best friends, Mel, also dropped by. We all raised a glass to Xavier. "What are you doing right now?" I thought to myself. It hurt even to think about him sleeping on the ground in that rat-hole prison.

Mel and I went to visit Nina, our other childhood friend, and they both cheered me up. Aside from my parents, my brother and three other friends, they were the only people who had any idea of what was really going on, although in reality no-one could entirely understand the gravity of the situation.

The next day, I looked after Xander while also trying to deal with Henzelin on the phone. According to what I'd been told, he should by now have received the letter written by Tarek and Patrick lobbying for Xavier's sentence to be reduced — but he said he hadn't.

I texted Patrick immediately asking him to send the letter directly to Worasit instead. Patrick insisted that he had already sent it to Henzelin but that he nevertheless would look into the matter. It was becoming clearer to me by the minute that these crooks were working together but against us. It stank, and the stink was becoming harder and harder to ignore.

I also had to prepare for Xander's upcoming first birthday on 3 October — which included asking Yvan, my godfather (and the best pastry chef ever) to make him a cake in the shape of a lion's head. I tried not to think about Xavier missing the occasion. I had to grit my teeth and keep on living so that our little angel would think everything was as it should be for his birthday.

I spoke to Paul later in the day. He said he was busy working on another case, in Spain, but that he would take care of everything. He said he would call Patrick and make sure we got the letter, and that he would also make sure Xavier's "ranking" improved.

The ranking system is a grade given to Thai prisoners, and ranges from excellent down to very good, good, moderate, bad and very bad. When the King of Thailand grants his amnesties to prisoners, reductions to sentences are awarded with reference to these rankings. If you are in the excellent category, you stand to have your sentence reduced by 50 percent; for "very good" prisoners, the reduction is 33 percent, and for "good" ones it's 25 percent. You start at "moderate" once your sentence is finalized and your ranking is reassessed every six months based on whether you've created any problems during your incarceration. Patrick said that if Xavier managed to get his ranking raised up, he could be granted a significant reduction to his sentence.

The next morning, Xander woke me from his cot and I took him into my bed and showed him pictures of his dad. He smiled and reached out to hold my phone. When I said "Look, it's Daddy," he would gaze at me with starry eyes and say "Daddy!" I held him close to me; I needed his comfort so badly.

I followed up with Patrick again about the letter and he said he would put his Thai lawyers in touch with Worasit. As per usual, he said everything would be done according to his instructions and that I wasn't to worry.

Again I had the feeling there was something rotten about this letter, but what could I do? I wasn't the one holding the cards. And I had to keep hoping. Luckily hope isn't something that can be easily extinguished by disappointment.

Chapter 12

Laura

25-HOUR DAYS

AUTUMN 2015. The days were not long enough to do everything I had to do; and yet they felt endless. The nights seemed short and unbearable. Luckily I could count on my parents, my brother and my best friends: Mel, Nina, Phil and Bea. In the evenings, they would often pick me up and we would go and sit in front of the church next to my parents' home.

There, you have a clear view of the lake and the mountains and even though I couldn't think of anything else but Xavier, at least sometimes — looking out at these familiar scenes — I could breathe and be myself. Captivated by the silence and the landscape, for a short while I could forget the feeling of being sunk in a mental abyss.

As Xander's birthday approached, William, my parents, and my close friends all helped me to prepare a party for him. At the same time, I had ongoing communications with Patrick, Paul and the Swiss lawyers, mainly about plans to return to Thailand later in the month. I desperately hoped this would be one of the last trips I would have to make there, and that my days of being torn in two between Xander and Xavier were soon to be over.

The emotional pressure of it all was becoming almost too much to bear, and I didn't know how I would cope if Patrick, Tarek and Paul couldn't keep their promises about getting Xavier home by December. I kept telling myself that everything would be over soon and that we would be reunited, but I couldn't ignore the feeling of a black spot somewhere in my vision of this bright future.

On the day that Xander turned one year old — Saturday, 3 October — Xavier had been in prison for 104 days. I opened my eyes at 6am to the sound of my little ball of love making his little cooing noises and I took him into my bed and covered him with kisses. I had so much love for him… but still I couldn't help crying my eyes out as I held him.

My heart tightened with pain to think of that day only one year before. It was the most beautiful moment of our lives — we had never been so happy as when the doctors put our son on my chest and we watched him take his first feed, snuggled up against me.

Lost in tears, I forced myself to wipe them away and smile for my boy. "Come on, Laura! You're going to celebrate your little angel's birthday and make him happy. Xavier will be here soon and this will all be behind us."

The party that afternoon brought so many of my favorite people together — family and friends came out in force to shower my little rascal with kisses and presents. Of course, he would have been over the moon if only his daddy were there, but the happiness in his cheeks was pure and priceless.

As for me, conversations were difficult because I still couldn't share the things I knew and the way I felt. When people would ask if I had a lawyer for Xavier and I told them it was Marc Henzelin, they would exclaim "Oh, that's good!"... and I would feel like shouting: "You think you know the situation? Everything is a thousand times worse than what you imagine!"

At 4pm, it was time for my godfather Yvan's amazing lion's-head cake. We sang Happy Birthday and I helped Xander to blow out the candles. I made his wish for him, knowing that my wish was what we both wanted. I prayed in my heart that it would come true and that we would soon be celebrating Christmas together as a family.

By Xander's bedtime, I couldn't hold it together anymore. Looking at him in his room, I just broke down in tears and my mum had to hold me and comfort me. Everything just seemed so unfair. Once Xander was off to sleep, Nina came to pick me up and we went outside and sat by the lake. I felt exhausted.

In the following days, I received some interesting information from a good friend of ours, who told me that Tarek had been taken into custody, on an unrelated matter, in China. (This short-lived detention, which had to do with complicated power politics in Saudi Arabia, was documented in detail a couple of years later by *The Washington Post.*)

At the time, it was hard not to feel some flicker of satisfaction, but my real concern was for Xavier. What would happen to him now if PetroSaudi was no longer able to pull strings to get him released?

Knowing what a coward Tarek was, I knew he would be scared to death. In fact, he would be having a heart attack. The thought of him suffering gave me some solace, and in a mischievous mood I wrote to Patrick to ask him if there was anything I could do to help them. He replied that everything was above board, that Tarek's arrest was "political" and that there was nothing to be done.

I prayed that nothing would change in terms of Xavier's prospects but the thought played on my mind that he could be in jail for the full three-year term. Would I take Xander with me and go and live in Koh Samui? I might be permanently scared but I would do what I had to.

I also spoke to Paul about my next trip. I wanted to go to Bangkok on 19 October — with Xander. It was important that he and Xavier see one another. We would then go back and stay in Koh Samui, at least for a while. From there, it would be much easier to go back and forth to Bangkok than it was from Geneva. Not to mention that I had to maintain a home and our pets there, pay the bills and put things in order with the resort — work on which had finished, although we never got round to actually opening it.

I called Denis to tell him all of this and also Laurent, our French friend in Koh Samui. He said he had been to see Xavier and that he looked good but had said I needed to get back to Thailand as soon as possible because he was missing me.

As soon as possible? I bristled at this. Here I was, forced to co-operate and collaborate with vicious crooks and their lawyers whilst juggling being a mum and a thousand other demands. I had to constantly reassure everyone from Xavier's mum to our friends and extended family; I had to deal with the press; and I had to make sure our bills were paid and that our house in Koh Samui and our pets were looked after. All of this while being at the mercy of PetroSaudi as to when I could come and go from Thailand and while having to put a smile on my face because our baby needed me and shouldn't be allowed to see me angry because his daddy wasn't around.

I thought: "Yes, Xavier. I would like to be back as soon as possible, but do you suppose I just click my fingers and turn up in one of the offices in Bangkok Remand Prison? If there's a way I can go faster or do better, I would love to hear it!"

To top things off, my parents' old dog, Scott, who was senile, decided to attack my foot when I was using the bathroom. My mum had to take me to the emergency room and our sad old puppy, who was 13, had to be euthanized. What a day. Could things get any worse?

PAUL MESSAGED ME me on October 7 to say he was in contact with Patrick and waiting for his green light for us to return to Thailand. Patrick later confirmed by WhatsApp that he had arranged for me to visit Xavier with Xander on 22 October.

After breakfast, Xander and I went to the Thai consulate in Geneva to get our visas in order. The lift wasn't working, so I had to tackle six floors on foot with Xander in my arms. I remember telling myself that at some point my luck would have to turn — how could it be otherwise? But then on the way back home, Xander had a screaming fit. The poor kid was teething. I felt I was at the end of my wits.

Once I'd calmed my son down, I spoke again to Denis. He told me Xavier wasn't feeling well and was scared. I got the sense there were things he was keeping to himself.

Later on, there was better news. Worasit told me Xavier was going to apply for bail — and that he now had the letter we needed from PetroSaudi. He said the Swiss lawyers had sent it to him.

According to everything we had been told, this letter would help Xavier get out of jail. Ultimately, however, although it was addressed from Patrick I never actually saw a signed version of it. In hindsight, it was something of a "paper tiger" that didn't help us in any way — but I didn't know that at the time.

I also learned from Worasit that we would have to submit an additional letter from the Swiss Embassy to certify that they wouldn't give Xavier a new passport if he was released on bail — he had to stay in Thailand. Furthermore, he informed me that I would have to write out a cheque to "Bangkok Royal Court" for the sum of 1 million baht (approximately $30,000). I said I would take care of it when I arrived.

Patrick still hadn't confirmed the arrangements for our trip, but he wrote to me saying that he was having a tough time and that they were fighting on all fronts. Amongst other things, Clare had just published an article headlined "Raking in the profits of Malaysia," which mainly described how Patrick had paid the modest sum of £6,150,000 for a house in one of London't most exclusive areas, Notting Hill. Truly, these crooks hadn't wasted a minute before investing their stolen money in luxurious mansions in the world's most conspicuous property market. Patrick seemed to suggest, however, that Clare's article was a net positive because it gave them new grounds to go after her.

I knew I had to think carefully about how I replied — and do so cleverly. I wrote back that I had seen her article and that it was "disgusting," adding that: "I think she suspects that the complaint against her in Singapore came from you indirectly." At the end of my message, I wrote: "Please call me when you have a moment. I just need to know as soon as possible if I can take my son to see his dad or if I need to fly to Koh Samui and leave my son there then go back to see Xavier."

My gambit had the desired effect. Thirty minutes later, Patrick wrote back to ask when exactly I wanted to take Xander to see Xavier. The powers that be had asked for a specific date.

I wanted to cry from joy. Xander and Xavier were finally going to see each other again. I told Patrick I wanted it to happen on 22 October, and a couple of hours later this was confirmed. The only thing that soured my feeling of delight was his request that I send a picture of Xander's passport. The idea that the bastards who had put my husband in prison to cover up their own crimes would demand a photo of his son just for them to be allowed to see one another made me both sick and scared. But once more, what choice did I have?

That wasn't the end of it, though. A short while later, Patrick emailed again: "I wanted you to know that a video has been made. I think it's good but she's going to know that it was her conversation with you. She doesn't need to know how it was recorded. Just don't answer if she calls you."

Attached was a video they had made from the conversation they had forced me to record with Clare. They had cut it with various photos of Clare and of me, including pictures they had obviously found on Facebook of me with Xander.

Suddenly, I was freaking out. Not only had they exploited me to try and discredit this extraordinary woman, but I felt sure it could only land me in trouble.

The video looked cheap and ridiculous. In fact, it looked like a teenager had spliced together some clips with barely a thought to how one related to the next. But somehow the soundbites they had selected, taken out of context and interspersed with a commentary by a male narrator, incriminated Clare by making her seem like she had a political agenda. I was in a state of panic watching it. It seemed these people were even more unbalanced than I had thought.

I told Patrick straight away: "You promised me that you would ask me before doing anything! Clare's going to know that it was me who recorded her. You told me the recording was just to listen to her and see what kind of woman she was."

He replied that they hadn't made it public yet. "That's why I'm sending it to you first. We need to talk about it."

I knew that I had to calm down — I knew they would use it anyway, whether I liked it or not, so I had to play along somehow.

"It's really well done," I lied, adding: "Where do you want to post this video? YouTube? In the newspapers?"

He wrote back: "We want to send it to all the people who are subscribed to [Clare's blog] Sarawak Report first. We got the list of email addresses. Then it will go all over Malaysia, to the media there, and everywhere. Only she will know that it was a conversation with you, no one else."

I told him I wanted to say yes but that I was afraid of getting into trouble. But yet again, what if this really helped Xavier? What if it were the last thing they asked us to do? I demanded to know if Xavier would really be out of jail before the end of the year.

He replied: "From what I understand, even before."

When I saw those words written, hope flooded back. Could they be true? Was it possible that we would be reunited even earlier than we had hoped? Seeing the prospect spelt out in black and white — even by a liar like Patrick — was too much for me to ignore.

In another message, he wrote that "Clare is the cause of all our problems; she must lose all credibility."

He told me they would instruct me on what they needed me to do to help land this blow against her — but the real subtext was clear to me. If I didn't co-operate with their planned campaign, it would be Xavier who would suffer. I felt sure that if I refused to play ball, they would simply let him rot in prison out of revenge.

That evening, Nina organized a meal at her place and several of my good friends showed up. It helped me to take my mind off of things and cheered me up. By midnight, we were all in the mood to go out, so we took a taxi into town and headed to a nightclub. It was exactly what I needed — the sound of the music, the memories of better times, the energy. I was someone who loved to dance and the atmosphere took me away from myself and the hell I had been living for so long.

The next day I had to get everything ready for our trip. We were going back to Koh Samui so I was taking everything: clothes, Xander's little bike, his books and toys. In total we had four 24kg suitcases. As instructed by Patrick, I also had to call Worasit to arrange a meeting with him and Paul.

We were due to leave the following day, 20 October, but Xander must have had other ideas. He was up all night with a sickness bug, meaning neither of us slept a wink. In the morning I looked at my mum and burst into tears. "What should I do?" I asked her. I couldn't make Xander travel with me in this state — but Xavier was waiting for me and there was important paperwork to be finalized with Paul and the lawyer.

My amazing parents decided on the spot that I should leave Xander with them, then go and do what needed to be done. I quickly took him to the pediatrician, who gave us some medicine and said he would be fine in a couple of days. Reassured, I canceled his ticket and then barely had time to drop him at home — and kiss him and my parents goodbye —

before heading to the airport. Xavier would be disappointed not to see his son after all, while I was devastated to leave him and panicked about the trip ahead, the bail application, having to deal with Paul. An hour into the flight — sad, broken and barely having slept a wink for 72 hours — I crashed out.

I landed in Bangkok at 9:30am on 21 October. Paul was waiting for me at the St. Regis, and it turned out he had a room two doors away from mine. I dumped my luggage and headed straight for the bank to make out a cheque for one million baht, for Xavier's bail. Paul accompanied me — he seemed keen not to let me out of his sight. He was also incredibly nosy: at the counter I could sense him looking over my shoulder to take a peek at my bank statements.

I called Worasit and he told us to come over and meet him at the courthouse with the documents we had discussed, as well as the cheque; but when we arrived it was *kin kaow* — lunchtime — and that meant that by the time we got to meet it was already afternoon and too late to go and see Xavier. I felt like screaming.

Back at the hotel, Paul invited me to eat with him. He talked a lot and asked me lots of things about my relationship with Xavier. I feigned politeness but I had a bad feeling in his presence.

The next morning I woke at 6.30am, dog-tired. After calling home and speaking to Xander, I went to the hotel's business center to print some pictures of him for Xavier, and by 9.30 I was in a taxi and on my way to the prison, confident that Patrick and Paul had made the arrangements for my visit. Another mistake: as it turned out, I had to wait almost until noon because apparently one of the inspectors had forgotten I was coming and I had to pester Paul to chase him down.

When I finally got to see Xavier, the disappointment that I hadn't brought Xander was written all over his face. I told him our little man was sick but that I'd go back for him and bring him back to Bangkok in no time. I told him that Scott had bitten my foot and had been put down. We also talked about the bail hearing, which was set for that coming Monday — five days away. He seemed pessimistic, so I tried to gee him up, telling him that Patrick and Paul were confident we'd get bail this time. I said that Xander and I would be there for him when he was released. The 30 minutes we'd been given were over in a flash and I left with a horrible feeling of emptiness.

At the hotel, we — Paul was there, of course — had another meeting with Worasit. He explained to me that if Xavier was granted bail "on lease," he would have to stick around and wait for the result of his appeal, which could take up to a year, and depending on the final verdict might of course involve his returning to prison at some point. In such an eventuality, he added, time spent outside on bail would not be counted as part of the sentence.

Paul could see that I was distraught but I tried to hide the hopelessness I suddenly felt inside me — no, I couldn't give him the satisfaction of seeing me defeated. He told me I shouldn't worry and that he was due to meet a little later with someone very important, a general in the Thai police whom he referred to as "the great Ping Pong." All would be well, he said.

When I returned to my own room, I broke down. I was sobbing, my legs were shaking and I collapsed on the bed. I felt so alone, so lonely and hopeless, cut off from my baby and my husband. How had it come to this?

When I had managed to calm down a little, I called my parents. They put Xander on.... and I burst into tears again. But Mum soothed and comforted me. Xander was getting better, she said. Together, my parents and my son managed to put a smile back on my face and replenish my hope. I felt so lucky to have my family.

Paul called me to say he had finished his meeting with "Ping Pong" and wanted to see me. I met him in the lobby and he said he had good news: under arrangements made by Patrick and Tarek with the authorities, Xavier would almost certainly be released soon. The understanding was that once he got bail, under-the-table arrangements would be made for him to return to Switzerland, where he would be safe. Yet again my spirits soared, as I imagined Xavier walking free of all this, and back into my arms.

I called Worasit thinking I would surprise him — but he already seemed to know, and told me it would all happen for Xavier on Monday in court. To my surprise, he also asked me to bring another 1 million baht, in cash, in addition to the 1 million baht I had already made out a cheque for. This would be to "thank" the judge for Xavier's release, he said.

Unbelievable. I can't say I was shocked, but it did occur to me to wonder why we were having to pay this money when PetroSaudi had supposedly "taken care of everything" and thrown money around at the Thai police and judiciary.

For the hundredth time, however, my instinct to question what was being asked of me had to be suppressed. I really had no choice but to pay up and felt that even raising the subject with Paul or Patrick might have jeopardized things.

I called Denis and explained how things stood. I told him I would visit Xavier with the good news the next day — but he reminded me that the next day was a holiday, so there would be no visits. It also meant there would be no banks open, which meant that if I wanted to get that 1 million in cash I'd have to rush to the bank right away.

Thankfully I made it just in time and got what I needed. An hour or two later, as I put the money in the safe in my hotel room, I felt like some kind of criminal trafficker. It wasn't doing my paranoia any favors. What if PetroSaudi had somehow planned all of this to get me arrested? I needed to stop these thoughts or I'd go crazy. And another thing — I'd been on the move all day without stopping to eat. I needed food or I'd pass out. It felt like I'd been starving myself for weeks.

Paul called again and we met for dinner at the hotel's Italian restaurant. Again, he seemed nosy and inquisitive, as if he was constantly testing me.

I figured he must be making regular reports back to Patrick and Tarek. Of course, I played along: I was the poor little idiot who didn't understand anything about what was happening. I needed them to believe I wasn't a threat to them.

During our meal, a friend called me to say that Patrick, Aziz and Tarek (whose detention in China, it transpires, only lasted a few hours) had been spotted the previous day partying in one of Geneva's plushest hotels. I thought about Patrick's wife, who was pregnant again at the time. What did it take for a woman to turn a blind eye to such debauchery? Was it the luxury house in central London, the chalet near Gstaad, the fleet of luxury cars? Everyone else seemed to know what Patrick did. Could she really be oblivious?

I excused myself from the dinner table and went back to my room, but even there I couldn't escape their tentacles. Patrick messaged to say that on Monday he would be sending a security team to the courthouse for Xavier's and my own safety. He said that if Xavier were released, he would need an escort, because there were Malaysians who might want him dead. Was he trying to scare me? The thought of Xavier being released from jail and ending up in a coffin filled me with terror.

The following day Paul set about briefing me on PetroSaudi's "security" plan. On Google Maps, he showed me the location of a secret safe-place that he said the Thai police would allow us to take Xavier to after his release. From my laptop, he made me print out pictures of the prison, the court and the safe-place — ten pages in total, and four copies, one for each of the security team.

On 25 October, I woke up at 5am. An early morning message from Paul said to meet him at 9am for breakfast and for introductions to the security team.

One of the team was Dave Thomas, who I knew only too well — Tarek's spy and henchman. Of course he would have been there. The other three guys looked exactly like mercenary killers. Paul assured me they were used to "these kinds of missions."

I spent the rest of the day packing things to store at Denis' place until I had returned with Xander and we were able to decamp to Koh Samui. As I did so, my nerves about what would happen in the court the following morning had frayed to the point that I was physically shaking. When I called home I couldn't see my son without bursting into tears. I needed to calm down.

I awoke again at 5am the next day and was in the hotel lounge having breakfast by 6am — coffee was all I could take. The hearing was at 10am and we were supposed to be picked up by a driver just after 7am. At 7.15 the driver called to say he was stuck in traffic. I felt like I was going to explode. Twenty minutes later he finally arrived.

At the courthouse, a huge warren-like building, Worasit was waiting for me. Paul and the security team lingered in the van in the car park while Worasit led me to a waiting room where we sat in silence. I was shaking again; the seconds ticked like hours.

Finally, a door at the back of the room opened and three Thai men — dressed in SWAT gear and armed to the teeth with machine guns — entered. In their midst was Xavier, wearing his brown prison uniform (for some reason, inmates wore blue in jail and brown in court). Another two armed Thais followed him.

I was shocked by the escort, and by the look on Xavier's face. As he came closer, I heard a clanging sound and noticed that he was cuffed both by his feet and his hands, with chains running between each set of cuffs. Hard enough walking with your feet chained, but the chains were too short, meaning he could hardly walk at all. He shuffled.

When he was about two meters away I burst into tears. To this day I have no words to describe the pain I felt at that moment. The guards were kind enough to let us touch hands and hug each other — as well as we could in his chained state, at least. I could feel a numb, unknown ache. I felt anxious, powerless and lost.

Next, we all entered the courtroom. I sat with Worasit opposite the judge's huge desk, while Xavier sat below us on a bench. The judge entered by a small door and everyone stood briefly before being motioned to sit. I clutched my big bag and prayed that it would soon be emptied of its 1 million baht.

When the judge started to speak, my heart sank. My Thai was fluent, but she was speaking judicial Thai. She used legal terms I couldn't understand, she spoke too fast and I could only pick out a few words. It was clear, however, that some of these words were negatives.

Had I heard right? No bail? I looked at the lawyer. "I'm sorry," he said. I couldn't quite understand what had happened but I broke down once more as Xavier turned to me, also in tears, and said "I knew it." Against the rules of the court, we hugged each other again. No, please no. Why?

Almost immediately, Xavier was taken away and as the door closed behind him I was left with Worasit. I felt completely depressed. He explained to me that the decision was "political," that it was all very strange, but that I had to understand that this was a big case and that there were people in high places involved. I couldn't even find words to use to respond. I just wanted to go back to my hotel room and call my mum so that I could see my son.

Outside, Paul was waiting. No, I told him, it didn't work. I was so angry and he knew it. Another empty promise; another of their tricks. Paul and Dave said they were sorry, but they knew not to talk to me. I got back in the van, surrounded by their goons. We drove off in silence.

I really didn't know what to think anymore. Had it all been a charade? Had they really thought Xavier was going to be released? I realized I would have to cool my anger. What if Paul told Patrick and Tarek that I was becoming a threat? Take it down a notch, Laura.

When we arrived back at the hotel, I said I wasn't well and had to go to bed. On the way up to the 42nd floor, I felt worse than I had at court. My head was spinning and I could hardly stand up. When the lift opened, I rushed to my room, scanned my passcard in the door, entered and just started screaming.

Curled on the floor, I screamed and screamed. I felt like I was in a trance. I wished I could have cut my hand off to stop the pain.

After 30 minutes I had calmed down enough to call my mum and tell her the news, but I was too sad to talk to my baby. Afterwards, I finished packing and left for the airport.

All the way back on the plane I felt like I was on another planet. I landed in Geneva on 27 October and rushed home just in time to say goodnight to my parents. I took Xander into my bed and we fell asleep together. My only dreams were of my love thousands of miles away, separated from us, helpless and deprived of all dignity.

Chapter 13

Xavier

PROSPECTS UNAPPEALING

AFTER THE DISAPPOINTMENT of my sentencing in August 2015, I began to regain some composure. After all, I still had visits from Paul and Patrick, who told me that they would do everything necessary to get me out, even "by the back door" as they put it. I believed them — because to have believed otherwise would mean thinking about serving almost three more years in this purgatory.

My visits were becoming more and more controlled, though. Each visitor had to have papers signed by the prison governor to be allowed to come and see me. On several occasions this governor was absent, and my visitors had to leave at the end of the day without having seen me. I had fits on days when I knew that Laura had been waiting there since 8am. Other prisoners had seen her waiting, but then I didn't see her until 3pm. What an injustice, what torture.

I now understood how the prison worked and the vast system of corruption that prevailed there. Its day-to-day running was in the hands of a select group of prisoners, identifiable for the white T-shirts they wore. These inmates were chosen because they were obedient and because they relished having a small degree of privilege and power over others. They operated under the supervision of a hundred or so guards whose job it was to maintain order rather than to enforce the law. Their duties included counting the inmates, escorting them to and from visits, and bringing the guards their food.

To live a better life inside, you had to understand the specific circumstances of each guard. The one who watched over me, Mike, came from the poorest region of Thailand, and for him working in the prison meant he was successful because he didn't have to gather rice in the fields anymore. He spent his days sitting around having food and drinks brought to him by obedient prisoners and being massaged by the prison's ladyboy inmates. (The ladyboys, incidentally, fell into two categories: those who hadn't been operated on and those who'd had their male genitals removed. The latter were kept in isolation to avoid rapes.)

Meanwhile, the guard in overall charge of my unit was just three years away from enjoying his pension; he didn't want any fuss and was happy to continue earning his wage and pocketing a few extras from the various rackets of everyday prison life.

Luckily for me, this guy's number two liked me and would sometimes allow me to stay out of my cell past the 3pm curfew — until 6pm. Hence for those three hours I would feel less like a prisoner: with most of the other prisoners having returned to their cells, there would only be about 50 of us roaming around and enjoying the extra space.

Another guard who showed me kindness was the one in charge of the visiting room — he was friendly to most of the "VIP" prisoners, and often when Laura or another of my visitors came to see me he would allow me a few extra minutes more than he was supposed to. It was a gesture of friendship that I'll never forget.

And then there was Khun Yatavi, the guard who oversaw the foreign prisoners. He had several rackets on the go: he demanded payment from you to bring in or take out mail, but also to see a doctor or dentist when you needed one. He even asked for money to help with routine documentation that the prison required of all inmates, or to "speed up" legal procedures. If you didn't pay him, these bureaucratic formalities would take months. Here was a guy who smiled in your face while holding his knife towards you by the handle. As with any criminal organization, all the money collected from the prisoners would be divided between the guards and those in charge according to their rank.

ONE NIGHT, AN 18-year-old kid from Madagascar arrived at the prison, completely terrified. He had stolen a $1 can of beer from a small supermarket and couldn't understand why he was now being locked up.

He would spend the next month with us before being released — and it was a living hell for him. He simply didn't have the mental strength for this experience. Despite efforts by myself and some others to protect him, he was beaten daily by other young inmates. It was painful to see. In reality he was just a child who had done something stupid. I often think of him and about the mischief my own son might get up to. It is hard for a parent to contemplate the inhumanity of the prison machine.

Also around this time a busload of about 15 prisoners arrived one day. I was told their case was an important one, and that they were all VIPs. These were old men; the youngest was 70 and the oldest over 80, and one even used a wheelchair. Three were sent directly to the infirmary, the oldest of whom died a few days later. Meanwhile six were sent to my already cramped cell and it was hard not to feel pity for them. Some needed constant use of toilet facilities, and this was the wrong place for that.

They had been convicted in a case that was by now more than 12 years old and had links to the former Prime Minister of Thailand, Thaksin Shinawatra, the enemy of the country's military government. They had each been sentenced to between 12 and 18 years in prison. I found them to be pleasant and educated, and as a former banker I discovered we shared some common interests.

It still pains me to think of these men being jailed for so long in such inhumane conditions. It seemed to me that their real crimes were simply to have worked for authorities which had been deposed of.

Meanwhile, my appeal procedure was launched. Our new lawyer, Khun Worasit — although paid by PetroSaudi — seemed earnest and capable, but he was not optimistic about the sentence being reduced, as he said this could only come about through us presenting new facts or evidence.

Patrick gave him a letter from PetroSaudi, sent via Marc Henzelin. It said I had co-operated well with the police and that I had not caused PetroSaudi significant damage. Worasit's view, however, was that this letter did not present any new information and was therefore worthless. One of the senior guards in the prison said he agreed.

At the same time there was talk about the possibility of an amnesty for the King's birthday — but to benefit from such an amnesty, your sentence has to be final. In my case I was appealing, so if an amnesty came before my appeal had been decided I wouldn't be eligible for it.

Patrick and Paul came to visit me at the end of August. They told me Henzelin and Giroud would be coming to see me soon — and that Marc Comina, a PR guy, would be helping them to prepare me for an appointment with journalists chosen by PetroSaudi. Mr Comina would instruct me on how to talk to the press in order to be convincing, they said. (For this task, we were to discover later from Lalive's case files, he would receive almost 30,000 Swiss francs from PetroSaudi.)

Patrick also told me Henzelin would have me sign power of attorney to a lawyer in Singapore to bring a case against Clare Rewcastle Brown and the people from *The Edge* newspaper in Malaysia.

My meeting with Henzelin, Giroud and Comina involved another guy who didn't introduce himself and who I took at first to be Henzelin's driver or assistant. Much later, I learned that this mystery man was David Scholberg, another PR guy whose company — KBDS — PetroSaudi was apparently using.

Following their tutorials, I was interviewed (with Henzelin present) by two Swiss journalists. I had to incriminate myself, admit that I had stolen the data, and make various accusations against Clare, Tong Kooi Ong, Ho Kay Tat and the Malaysian opposition. I also had to attest that PetroSaudi was an excellent company and that money had been my only motivation.

I got the impression that the journalist from the *Tages Anzeiger* newspaper didn't believe a word of it, but I had to follow the script. When the journalist asked me how I could afford to pay such prestigious lawyers, I gave the answer Henzelin had rehearsed with me — that even though I was in prison, my finances were in order. If the journalists had had any idea how much PetroSaudi was paying for all of this, their stories might have been different.

As planned, Henzelin also arranged for me to file a complaint against Clare, Kooi Ong and Kay Tat, essentially demanding the return of the hard drive I had given them. I didn't fully understand the objective, but Patrick insisted it must be done — and besides, PetroSaudi were paying for it. In terms of the outcome, I would discover later that it didn't go any further than garnering some negative media coverage of its targets. Perhaps that was the real intention.

On a brighter note, on the day of my birthday — 23 September — I was allowed a special visit from Laura. We were able to meet in one of the prison offices, unsupervised by Paul, and the guards kindly left us alone for a while. Finally I was able to enjoy some moments of absolute happiness. I almost convinced myself I would be leaving with her, but the dream only lasted two hours.

The other inmates in my cell also put their heads together and made me a birthday cake. I didn't feel like celebrating but I knew they meant well and that they wanted to share the moment with me and help me to forget the reality of my situation. The cake was close to being inedible but I appreciated the gesture and almost shed a tear. I missed my wife and son so much.

Chapter 14

Laura

WAR LOOMS

ON 29 OCTOBER, I had a meeting with Gilles Crettol, a lawyer Xavier knew. It had nothing to do with the case — Xavier had opened a Hong Kong-based consulting company in Geneva several years before and I needed to close it. To be truthful, I wasn't looking forward to talking to another lawyer but Xavier said he was very nice.

He was right. Crettol turned out to be a very gentle individual — tall and charming — and we got on well from the beginning. He told me that like everyone else, he had read about Xavier's case; but he said he couldn't understand it, and that the sentence was insane, even if Xavier had in fact been guilty of blackmail. He said something should be done about it. I told him it was more complicated than it looked.

He asked me how Xavier was doing. I was touched, which might sound stupid but none of the bastards I had been dealing with on my husband's case ever bothered to ask that simple question. Finally, someone human! Crettol told me that if I needed anything, we could meet again to talk.

At that moment, I felt like telling him everything. I don't know why but I just trusted him and the desire to share everything about our situation burned on my tongue. I decided against taking the risk, but my instinct about Crettol proved to be right: months later he would prove to be one of the main actors in exposing the conspiracy against Xavier.

The same evening, I had an appointment with Patrick at their regular "party palace," the President Wilson Hotel. He was accompanied by Dave and was all sweetness and charm. The purpose was to try to convince me that it was time to release the video of my conversation with Clare.

I told him I was scared, that I was all alone in the world with my infant son, and that I didn't want to take a political stand that would put us in danger. "It's probably illegal... You've completely modified it. Seriously, Patrick... I don't think I can do this and Xavier doesn't want me involved. He says it's too dangerous."

Suddenly, he changed. Dr Jekyll became Mr Hyde. His look frightened me. He insisted everything about the video was legal and that PetroSaudi's lawyers would protect me. Then he looked me right in the eye and played his joker card: "You know, if you do this, Xavier will be able to get out even faster than the end of the year. They told me... this video, it will help everyone enormously! Xavier, you, us!"

He added: "You don't care about that bitch anyway. What is she going to do?"

His tone was insistent and his request became a demand. This video *had* to be released to the media.

Then came the carrot. He said that he would be going to Bangkok on Monday or Tuesday and that we should meet with Xavier, he and I together, and talk. He would organize everything, as usual. He said he would also arrange for Xander to visit Xavier with me if we wanted it.

I felt like I was being blackmailed, but what could I do? I told him I would sleep on it. When I left them at 11pm, Aziz had just arrived. He was already high — the excited look, like that of a child waiting for his Christmas presents, could be read a mile away.

"Enjoy yourself," I said to him sarcastically and he burst out giggling. "Thanks," he grinned and went up in the lift with Patrick and Dave.

At home, I could hardly sleep. My fear about releasing the video was because I knew it was wrong. Clare hadn't done anything. And what consequences might I face? But then, equally, what consequences would there be for Xavier if I refused to co-operate? What if this really were a chance to save him? If I could be certain of that, then I surely wouldn't hesitate to act.

The next morning I was up at 5:30am to fly back to Thailand — this time not only with Xander but also, thank God, my mum. Neither she nor I will ever forget this flight, because it was easily the worst of our lives. Xander's stomach hurt, and probably his ears too, and for a child who rarely cried he gave it his all for some nine hours out of the 12 we were in the air. Arriving in Bangkok on Saturday, 31 October, we were all simply exhausted. What a trip.

We tried to rest up over the weekend but I was too excited about Xander and Xavier finally getting to see each other again after five months. Just the thought of it made me shudder.

MONDAY, 2 NOVEMBER 2015 is a day that Xavier and I will never forget.

Before setting off for the prison, I spoke to Colonel Pongsawai, who confirmed our appointment and said Patrick had arranged everything. He said he would meet us there.

When we arrived at the jail at 9:45am it was already 32 degrees and Xander was hot and tired, although thankfully too young to realize where we were. My head was spinning as we settled down to wait for the Colonel — outside, where we had no shelter from the sun. Every scooter that passed, I prayed it would be him.

The more time that passed, the more nervous I became. At 11am, I tried to call Pongsawai but there was no answer. Xander wouldn't be able to handle much more waiting — he'd already been up for seven hours — and my own patience was fading fast.

At 11.15am the colonel called back to say he would be sending his colleague. Inspector Toon would arrive in 20 minutes, he said.

At 11:40, Toon pulled up and went to the prison director's office to sign the papers. He then escorted us to the office where I normally met with Xavier, and told Xander and I to wait there. My heart was beating at 200 miles per hour.

When Xavier finally entered, the feeling between the three of us was just incredibly intense. Seeing his dad, Xander smiled and held out his arms. Finally together, we just wept — neither of us could speak. I watched Xavier looking at Xander with so much love and so much joy, but with so much pain at the same time. The happiness between us tore us apart as much as it warmed our hearts.

Conscious of time, we came to our senses. Leaving Xander to play at moving the office chairs around, I told Xavier that Patrick had asked me to go public with PetroSaudi's video of Clare. He asked me how I felt and I had to be honest — I was scared and knew it was wrong, but I would do what they asked if he thought it would help us. I told him Patrick wanted to come and talk to us about it, although I left out the details about how they were pressuring me as I didn't want him to panic.

Xavier got angry and said he didn't want me to be involved in this. He said it was out of the question for me to put myself in the media. He was disappointed, sad and angry. We both suspected these tactics from PetroSaudi were a front and that the plan was to keep Xavier in prison for as long as possible.

He also told me he thought he should cancel his second appeal for bail. If he applied for it and had to wait for the process to play out, he wouldn't be eligible for either a reduction to his sentence or release under amnesty from the King. He said all the talk was of an amnesty very soon

— although no-one could be quite sure of it actually happening, not even the lawyers.

Unfortunately, we couldn't stay for the full hour. Xander was at the end of his tether — too hot and tired. Xavier took him in his arms once more and hugged him tightly. It was the hug of a dad who doesn't know when he will see his son again.

In the taxi back to the hotel, Xander fell asleep in my arms, leaving me to my thoughts. My sixth sense was telling me not to talk to the media or release the video. I was convinced that Tarek and his team of crooks were taking us for a ride and just wanted to keep Xavier compliant for as long as possible.

I resolved therefore that I should stand my ground: When we met with Patrick I would confront him and tell him that we couldn't meet their demands. I knew that I would have to be tactful — any wrong moves and Xavier could pay the price. But I also had to be prepared to fight for our real interests. If they released the recording without my agreement or if Xavier was punished in any way over it, that would be a signal that it was time to blow the whole thing up. I would go to the press not to release their doctored recording but to expose them as the bunch of crooks they were. I would nail them all.

In the meantime, I asked Patrick nicely if he could arrange another visit with Xander. I calculated that he would agree because he and Tarek were desperate for me to do their bidding with the video, and I was right. He said he would organize it; but then he added that he was feeling "down" after coming out of a meeting with the Swiss prosecutor that had gone very badly.

He explained to me later on the phone that the prosecutor's office had "pissed us off" and "will continue to piss us off for the time being." He said the Swiss authorities were suddenly asking questions about PetroSaudi's dealings with 1MDB because they didn't want to be accused of doing nothing.

He was adamant that the Swiss "have nothing." I felt like saying to him that if he was right it would be because he and Tarek had destroyed the evidence. Everything about what they had done disgusted me more and more.

Meanwhile, the picture grew worse and worse. Worasit called me to say that he couldn't continue representing Xavier until he was paid. He asked me to pass this message to Patrick. I couldn't believe it! Worasit had been selected by Patrick and Tarek without any say-so from Xavier or me, and he was meant to be paid through Henzelin.

When I called Patrick about this, he said he would call Henzelin and sort it out, then call me back.

This time I was ready for him. I decided I would use the app Aziz had installed on my phone and record what he said. I felt nervous about it. What if it made a sound that would make him suspicious? But I didn't have any moral qualms — Paul and Patrick had themselves insisted it was legal when they made me use it to record Clare.

I still remember being on the rooftop bar at my hotel — where I often went to get some air and to make phone calls — and praying that everything would go well. Part of me wanted to just delete the app, but a stronger urge told me I had to try to get Patrick to talk. I wanted him to tell me that PetroSaudi were pulling all of the strings in Xavier's case — on everything from prison visits to the legal process — in collaboration with both the Thai and Malaysian authorities, and that it was all to clear their own name.

If I could get him to admit to these things, I would be able to expose them to the world — and save Xavier.

AS I PACED up and down, my phone began to ring. My stomach hurt, but I took a deep breath... and told myself to act as naturally as possible. If I pushed Patrick too hard, he would be on to me.

His first words were to ask me very nicely how I was doing. I wanted to slap him in the face.

We kicked off on the subject of the second bail application. I explained to him that Xavier thought he shouldn't apply for bail anymore — because it could jeopardize his chances of getting an amnesty. But he didn't like that idea. "If Xavier does that, it will suddenly look weird." Yes, weird for you, I thought to myself.

I said that if he got out on bail and then his appeal failed he would simply have to go back to prison at some point to finish his sentence. "No, not at all," Patrick countered. "Once he's out, he's out."

What did he mean? Was he seriously proposing that Xavier be smuggled out of Thailand?

"I'm going to organize a visit for the three of us together with Xavier because we need to talk about this video which is going to be in the media," he said. "The media are not in our favor because of Clare; she is very aggressive with her articles. I have to be careful when I come to Bangkok and we see each other at the prison because there are people watching. I have to see how to do it right without being seen."

I asked him why the Swiss authorities were on PetroSaudi's back? He replied: "As I told you, the Swiss have nothing, you know, but they are just afraid of being accused of doing nothing and that's precisely because of these fucking media who are pissing us off and who are not at all in our favor."

He added: "The Swiss told me they are just going to stay quiet and say they are watching things, and then when it calms they will unblock things. The prosecutor admitted it: they are scared to death of the media and they are just afraid of being accused of doing nothing."

If this was true, then the Swiss were complicit in corruption, I thought. If Patrick was lying, then it was just more manipulation.

"But just one question," I said, as innocently as I could. "Why don't you sue Clare in England if she writes crap about you?"

His answer made me want to burst out laughing. "No, pfff, the thing is that she managed to get police protection because she said she was being followed by Malaysians. She's manipulating everyone, that bitch! Now we are preparing something to attack her, but in the traditional media. We have to see exactly where, when and how because there are still things coming out in Malaysia."

He went on: "We know who she works with in Malaysia. I'll tell you our strategy but I'm going to ask you again to do something in the media. We need to get this conversation out there, we need people to see this video that we made."

In as soft a voice as I could muster, I tried to make him understand why I didn't want to comply. "If I do what you are asking me to do, I'm taking part in a huge political affair. I'm afraid of the repercussions. I'll never be able to find a job in Geneva, I'll be attacked and I'm alone with my son… so just imagine [how it will be for] Xavier!"

He replied firmly: "You'll get a job, and as far as the media is concerned, you'll be the biggest victim in all of this! You have a bitch who manipulated your husband; you can say it's us if you want but in the end it's because of [Clare] that he's in prison. Don't worry, the media will spin this as Clare not giving a shit about your welfare or Xavier's!"

He proceeded to rant about how I would be portrayed in the media as a victim — and that Xavier would be too.

I wanted to scream back at him, to cry with rage. Did he seriously think I was dumb enough not to see how he was trying to manipulate me? What a monster! Every word out of his mouth reeked of lies and manipulation. It was pathetic. He must really have been used to being surrounded by stupid people. What scared me the most, however, was that it all came so naturally to him.

I jumped in: "We would need to know exactly, me and Xavier, we would need to see that his sentence would be reduced, so that he can get out [earlier] as you said."

Patrick, referring to Najib Razak: "I told you the other night who is the ultimate person who can control this. I have to go and have a meeting with him very soon. There are lots of options, Laura. This guy is scared to death that all of a sudden Xavier will come out and say 'no, I said all this to get out but there are really bad things that have been done.'"

Me: "But if Xavier asks me about his release in December, what do I tell him? [Do] I tell him that he can forget it or that there is still hope?"

Patrick: "We just really need to get this thing out. This guy [Najib] keeps stressing, it's his political career that's in the shit. This guy is in trouble and... and he's only thinking about that, nothing else."

Me: "Yes I know, but Xavier... What do I say to him?"

Patrick got really angry at this stage, and raised his voice: "Like I told you, the only way I can show him that you're willing to be part of this and be part of the team is if you're willing to put yourself in the media! Literally. And if you are willing to speak out against this! To show that there is a conspiracy against him and that you are ready to denounce it!"

Me.... desperate, scared, angry: "But will there be guarantees behind it?"

Patrick raised his voice again: "Of what?"

Me: "If I do this then will we have guarantees that Xavier can get out earlier?"

Patrick's anger went up another notch: "Listen! For the moment this guy doesn't see you as people who are willing to help him. I told you that the other day. All I can say to you right now is that you can help the situation or not help the situation."

If he had been in front of me, I think I would have killed the scumbag. What he was essentially telling me was that if I didn't do what he told me to, Xavier had no chance of getting out. And he knew that I was powerless against this, because he and his co-conspirators were in control of everything. He was manipulating me, 100 percent. The only thing that wasn't clear was whether he knew I knew it — and that uncertainty was my only source of leverage.

Me: "Patrick, you told me the other day that Xavier could be out by December. You promised me and you promised him..."

This made him freak out: "I didn't promise you; I just told you I'm going to do everything I can! And I'm still in the shit! Every day I live in this shit! Ok?!?! We all live in this shit! I don't like that he's in jail and you're all alone with your baby and I feel for you, but I'm still in a lot of shit, there's a lot of people who are in shit. THERE'S THE PRIME MINISTER OF A COUNTRY WHO'S IN THIS SHIT! BECAUSE HE'S BEEN PUT IN THIS SHIT!"

At that moment I prayed that my phone had recorded what he had just said, because I knew that his words would be worth their weight in gold. He had just made a clear reference to Najib and the 1MDB mess.

My voice trembled as I answered: "Yes, but there's no one in jail in the meantime! Only Xavier is in jail!"

I went on: "Patrick, during the trial, on the day of the trial, you told me, you promised me, that it would never be three years. That it all meant nothing! You told me, 'I promise you Laura, it doesn't mean anything!'"

Patrick yelled: "YES! And I keep telling you that, but there is a difference between three years and three months!"

You manipulative fucker! I was shaking with rage. I couldn't take it anymore! I was doing everything I could to keep calm but I was welling up with tears.

I replied: "You told me 'by December he'll be out the back door for sure!'"

Patrick: "Yes, I can get him out through the back door but I didn't promise you December. I'm going to do everything I can to get him out as soon as possible but in the meantime we're still in trouble because of the media and only because of the media!"

And again he played his ace card, the one that he knew would leave me out of options: "You want to help your husband? Then help me in the media."

I replied that they had promised Xavier after his last interview that there would be no more calls for him to exonerate PetroSaudi and denounce Clare.

"But I'm not asking Xavier anything," he retorted. "I'm asking you! With the recording you made."

I couldn't believe it. Now he was trying to say that I "made" this recording. "YOU ASKED ME TO DO IT," I said.

Patrick: "YES! I asked you to make a recording! I told you one day we would need to use it and that day is today."

Me: "No, you told me it was to listen to Clare, and then you went behind my back and made a video with it."

I asked him to tell me who had already seen the video, to which he responded "only people I trust 100 percent."

Me: "I know you're in trouble but ..."

He cut me off: "I've got Malaysians, I've got Thais, I've got you, I've got Xavier, I've got my wife, I've got my children, I've got everyone who pisses me off every day and asks me when it's all going to be over? I didn't start all of this!"

Honestly? That Xavier and I "pissed him off" I could understand, but his wife and children? How can you talk like that about your family? Especially to someone who isn't a friend.

He went on: "I have appointments with prosecutors, media, lawyers. I do this all day long, 24 hours a day, and I can't think of anything else.

OK? You are part of a situation. You can help or not; I don't want to force you to do anything."

Patrick again: "There are two sides and you have to show which side you are on…"

Me: "Look, you made Xavier look like shit in the media. Nobody believes him anymore; there are even friends of ours who believed what was written. I don't think he could have helped you more than that. He did everything for you."

Patrick: "Yes, he did something, but what I'm asking for is from you. That's totally different."

I told him again that I needed guarantees. That I wouldn't let go of this infuriated him. "Who got us into this shit?" he demanded.

The discussion went round and round and round, neither of us giving ground. It was obvious that he wasn't used to being challenged on his dirty tricks.

In one exchange he told me that he had done nothing but help me and that I could stop working with him if I wanted to — and go and talk to the media. He then moved on to how much he was suffering.

Patrick: "It's not about the money, it's about my whole future, my life; I can't do any more deals anywhere because of all this…. Everything has been taken away from me; I have nothing at the moment. Do you think I'm living the good life? I borrow left and right to pay my bills, to pay for my children's schools! I borrow!"

In a haughty, ironic tone, I replied: "But this situation is temporary; you haven't done anything, have you? So this situation will soon be resolved… right? You'll be cleared? If you didn't do anything then there's no reason for you to be punished for something you didn't do?"

Amazingly, he didn't catch my scorn. "Exactly!" he said, and rallied back to his earlier bullshit. "And if it continues to persist, it is because of the media. So do you want to help with the media or not? It's up to you.

But in the meantime I can't come [to Bangkok] because I have papers to prepare for the prosecutor, so I advise you to go and talk to Xavier."

I told him that Xavier insisted on seeing him before we made a final decision on the video. At which point he accused me of treating him "like shit." I replied that if I were treating him like shit, he would know about it.

I also put it to him that he wouldn't put his own wife through something like this, to which he replied: "Yes, 100 percent. If it would help me, of course I would." I suddenly had a sense of how lucky I was to have a husband that cared about and wanted to protect his family — and who wasn't a coward and a lowlife.

I then pointed out that not only would it be my face in the media but Xander's — because he was in the video too. I said: "You could have blurred his face or cut him out of it." He reluctantly said he would ask the video people to remove it… and then veered off into another hateful rant about Clare: "We have to keep undermining her and then it's the other people around her that we're going to start attacking — the whole group that she's part of. She barks, that's all! She's a dog, that woman, that's it! She barks! She can't do anything to you except write nasty things about you, so you don't have to be afraid to get on her bad side. You're a poor victim who's been manipulated by a cunt and has her husband in jail and that's it!"

I realized I had to try to take things down a notch or two. I said that before agreeing I would have to know exactly what they wanted me to do and that we would have to discuss it together with Xavier. He assured me that this would happen, and that in the meantime he had organized visits for me for the next two days. "As soon as I have more information," he added, "I'll take a plane and we can meet, the three of us."

As we hung up, my heart was beating a mile a minute and my hands were sweaty as I fumbled with my phone to check whether the app had worked.

On the homescreen, I found Patrick's number displayed on a file. I pressed play on it and there before me were the full 27 minutes, 45 seconds of our conversation, beginning with "Yes Laura, this is Patrick..."

Alone in the dark on the roof of the hotel, listening back to his voice, a smile spread across my face. I couldn't remember feeling this good in a long time. Looking up at the sky, I thought: "I've got you, you bastard!"

I knew this recording was priceless. He had talked about Najib Razak and how they were connected. He'd admitted that he had personally managed pretty much everything to do with Xavier's incarceration, right down to bribing the guards. He'd acknowledged manipulating the media to suit PetroSaudi's interests and discredit others, including Xavier. And he'd admitted to paying Xavier's lawyers in Switzerland and Thailand. He'd even suggested that the Swiss authorities would be easy to fob off, saying the prosecutor would "unblock things" and that they were only making inquiries because they were afraid to be accused of doing nothing.

I also had proof that they had forced me to record Clare, had altered that recording and now were trying to force me to use it to clear their name in the press.

In short, I now had my own leverage. If they failed to do what they had promised, I had evidence up my sleeve that they were entrenched in guilt. For me, this would be a new chapter — I swore again to myself that I would keep gathering whatever evidence I could.

If Patrick thought he could keep manipulating me like he was used to manipulating everyone else, he would have a rude awakening some day. I'm not everyone else: I'm a fighter and a go-getter, the daughter of a Scotswoman and a Swiss sailor, a free spirit with a sixth sense that rarely fails me. How stupid they must be to think that I would keep quiet no matter what.

THE NEXT DAY, unfortunately, I was unable to take Xander to see Xavier as I'd planned to because he wasn't feeling well.

When I got to the jail, Xavier told me he'd decided he wanted to cancel the bail application. I cried when I heard him say it, because it was a big gamble, but I trusted his judgment on the matter. He had his ear to the ground inside the prison on the subject of amnesties.

As ever, I left him with a heavy heart — but lighter than usual, because this time I wasn't leaving Thailand. I would only be in Koh Samui, an hour's flight away. The thought of us being closer in distance was reassuring.

Xander, my mum and I arrived back on the island on 5 November. It felt good to be back there and to see our pets and the house, but it was strange too. The place felt empty without Xavier, and I was still lonely and lost.

I didn't have much time to think about that, however, as reality soon took over. The resort needed to be repaired due to a lack of maintenance; the internet wasn't working; the car wouldn't start; and the pool was dirty. Xander's mattress smelt of damp, so I had to buy another one. The only time I got a break was when I put him to bed at night.

In the evenings, I would sit on the terrace, look at the sea and ask myself a thousand questions. Are we okay? Will we make it? Will we ever be able to live like we used to? How did it come to this?

On 6 November, I got a call from Worasit, who said Xavier had been forced to go to court for a bail hearing. I instantly felt panicked. How could this be? But it got worse. The lawyer said the bail had been granted — but that Xavier had refused it! I felt like collapsing.

I couldn't understand what was happening. Why had Xavier done this? I knew we'd decided to cancel his application… but he could have been about to walk out of jail. It almost felt worse than the day he was sentenced. I wanted to strangle him! If he had been released, couldn't we have somehow escaped from Thailand?

I called my friend Alan and explained what had happened. He comforted me and told me Xavier probably had good reasons for refusing bail (as it turns out, he did, and explained them to Denis, who later explained them to me). I felt like I was at the end of my rope, but you have to keep going, and being told "It's going to be OK" was about all I had left to cling to.

The following day, I learned from the Thai and Malaysian newspapers that a Malaysian delegation planned to come and interrogate Xavier. This made me more afraid, as it seemed a fair bet he would have to repeat more lies against himself.

I decided there and then that the time had come to ask the Swiss Embassy to provide Xavier with protection. They seemed to have no idea what was going on — and that had to change.

I asked Patrick who these Malaysians were, but Patrick told me not to worry and that there would be no "interrogation." He added that he would be coming to Bangkok to meet Xavier and I, but that I shouldn't mention anything to Worasit or anyone else because he wanted to be discreet. He said the Swiss prosecutor had asked to see him again but that he would come after that.

He offered to arrange a visit for me to see Xavier on Monday, 23 November, and suggested he and I meet that evening. "I will then arrange a visit for the three of us on the Tuesday and an interview with the press for you in the following days."

He asked me if I wanted him to make a reservation for me at the St. Regis, but I told him I would book elsewhere.

ON 23 NOVEMBER, I left home at the break of dawn to catch a 7am flight to Bangkok, and went straight to the prison from the airport.

Patrick had said my 9am office appointment was confirmed, but yet again I had to wait for hours. Nobody could help me and Colonel Pongsawai wouldn't answer his phone. Finally, after spending the whole day waiting outside in a heatwave — without eating, and having begged a thousand times to speak to one of the prison chiefs — I was granted an appointment in the visiting room.

Sweating, exhausted and with my stomach hurting from hunger and anxiety, I waited for Xavier to appear. When he did, he was livid. He grabbed at the phone and begged to know what was happening. Our hands clung to the glass, aching to touch. He said he'd been informed that I'd been waiting since 9am. I told him we couldn't waste time — that it was enough simply that we were together now. We only had 20 minutes.

For Xavier, there was nothing to discuss. He simply didn't want me involved — even if it somehow helped him, he didn't want me all over the news. I told him Patrick wanted to come and talk to us both the next day.

I tried to summarize everything that was going on, but in doing so I realized just how little he knew about how he had been thrust into the spotlight internationally. He had no access to newspapers or world news, so he couldn't follow events closely. (Admittedly, this was perhaps a blessing in disguise.)

Our time was ticking away, so I changed the subject and gave him an update on Xander's latest exploits. That got a smile out of him and we laughed for a few seconds, Xavier's hand again placed against mine though the glass. A final, tearful "I love you" and the guard stepped forward to escort him back to his cell. Our eyes followed each other with kisses as he left the room.

Back at my hotel room, I started to psych myself up for my conversation with Patrick that evening by listening to one of my favorite rock songs, "Highway to Hell." I steeled myself to dig my heels in over the Clare video and to continue to push for him to honor his promises to have Xavier released before the end of the year. After all, up until now he had done everything they had asked of him: from co-operating with the lawyers they had appointed to filing the complaint against Clare, Kay Tat and Kooi Ong.

When we met at the St. Regis, Patrick was all smiles. "How are you?" he gushed. I felt like spitting in his face. I tried to make conversation, commenting on the beauty of the hotel. "Yes, you should see the suites," he said. Nice to be able to afford all of life's luxuries on the backs of those Malaysians you stole from, I thought.

We sat on the terrace. No-one else was around and the atmosphere was tense. He started telling me why he thought there hadn't been an office visit that day but it was bullshit and I barely listened. Next, he stressed that he and Tarek and Paul were all "here" for us. It seemed that he was on a charm offensive. "How is your son?" he asked. "I've seen the photos; he's really sweet." Of course he had seen the photos, because everything I gave to Xavier in prison had to be analyzed and vetted by him.

On his third glass of wine, he started telling me about his wife, Alejandra, who was pregnant with their third child. He asked me if I'd had any "blues" after giving birth and I said no, I'd been lucky — everything had gone well, apart from me putting on 25 kilos in weight.

When I mentioned that, he looked at me and commented: "But that's not possible. You must do a lot of sport, then?" It made me uncomfortable, and I felt more uncomfortable as he went on.

"My wife, she had the baby blues," he said. "It was terrible; she's never been such a pain in the ass."

His tone was incredibly degrading; he disgusted me. "Right now, for the third one, she's huge. She's never been so fat. Look at her chest!"

He proceeded to show me a picture of his wife's breasts, veiled in a white pregnancy bra, her face out of the frame. I couldn't believe it. How could he have so little respect for the mother of his children? Not for the first time, I took comfort in knowing that — horrible though my life currently was — my husband was opposite in every way to Patrick. His obnoxiousness almost cheered me up.

Having made his cack-handed attempt to relax us both, he then went on the attack, telling me that he had a journalist lined up for me to talk to who would cast Xavier and I as victims of a conspiracy. He said the video with Clare would be released at the same time and would "go viral."

My reaction was far from calm. I looked him in the eye and reminded him that I hadn't agreed to anything — and that there had to be a discussion with Xavier before I spoke to anyone from the press. "Go and see what state he's in," I added. "The prison is inhuman. And now, I tell you, I'm willing to do this but only if I have guarantees that Xavier will get out like you promised us."

Moving in closer to him, so that he couldn't avoid my glare, I repeated: "I WANT GUARANTEES THIS TIME!"

He responded by pushing his face even closer to mine, 30cm now separating us, and raised his voice higher than mine. "You think I'm stupid? You think you can make me give you guarantees? It doesn't work like that, OK?"

Me: "It will work like that, Patrick. Or it won't at all!" I was shaking more and more, torn between fear and anger.

"Listen to me," he yelled. "As you have seen, we are in charge here. Your husband — I decide when he comes out, OK? I can get him out tomorrow or in 100 years if I want to. So you do as you like but I advise you to collaborate, OK?" And with that, he squeezed my arm on the table. It hurt.

I was stunned, shocked. I knew he was crazy and of unsound mind, but I didn't think he was violent. I could have spat in his face, gouged his eyes out, strangled him. I wanted to scream for help but nothing came out. Deep inside, I was numb. I pulled my hand away and looked him straight in the eye. He could see my rage and despair as I started to cry, my voice and hands shaking.

I could tell from his reaction that he realized he had lost control — but that he regretted it only because he had squandered his own sense of being in command.

As I fumbled for words, he was the first to speak. "Look, I really don't want to get angry… so we'll go and see Xavier tomorrow and we'll talk and find a solution, but you know the only way to help him is to release this video and for you to do this interview."

To take the sting out of the situation, I told him "OK," and excused myself to go to the bathroom.

Staring into the bathroom mirror, I slapped myself, and dried my tears. My wrist still hurt, and I was struggling to stop shaking. I knew I had to regain my composure: Xavier's whole future was at stake. A deep breath, and I returned to face my tormentor again.

Back at the table, Patrick proceeded to ask me if I partied often. Was he for real? I had a one-year-old baby and my husband was in jail, but yes, sure, I partied. I said nothing. He then explained that with all the pressure he was under he liked to take his mind off things. "I have a guy here who has *stuff* to party with; do you want to take your mind off things?"

Suddenly, he thrust one of his three mobile phones into my hand. "Here, call him for me, and ask him to come here." I looked down and the phone was ringing. What the hell was this? Was he trying to set me up so that I would end up in prison too? Had he gone mad? He was clearly drunk.

I panicked. I stood up and put the phone to my ear, then took a few steps away from the table, making sure to hang up as I did so. I then pretended to wait for a few moments, before handing him the phone back. "No answer," I said.

I told him it was time for me to get going, that I was exhausted. We said goodnight cordially enough but I really wanted to get away from him as quickly as I could. What a sick guy.

Back in my room, his words and everything that had just happened ran through my head. I felt too shocked and distraught to sleep and lay awake for most of the night.

THE NEXT MORNING, Patrick messaged to say he had to go and visit some people "in high places" to sort things out, and that I should wait for him at his hotel. By about midday I'd had enough waiting and messaged him back demanding to know what was happening.

Some time later, he replied: "I'm eating with one of the police chiefs. They explained to me why you couldn't see [Xavier] the other day but I'm going to sort it out now. I don't know how long it will take; I'll let you know."

I knew it would now be too late to go and see Xavier that day, which left me feeling wretched and depressed. By the time Patrick finally showed up at the hotel, it was 6pm, and he had clearly enjoyed his afternoon. He was drunk, and possibly high.

Immediately, he told me to follow him and said he wanted to show me some documents in his room. When we got to his floor, he pushed open the door to reveal an apartment that must have measured 250 square meters, complete with a panoramic view of Bangkok. I had stayed in nice rooms in some nice hotels with Xavier, but this was on another level. Who needs that amount of space? And on a so-called business trip where he was supposed to be helping Xavier?

It felt like a trap, and true to form Patrick announced to me that a freelance reporter was about to arrive downstairs. He said I had to talk to her — and tell her the same things Xavier had said in the newspapers. Simple: that Xavier had been tricked by Clare, Kooi Ong and Kay Tat into stealing the data; that they had promised him money; but that in actual fact there was nothing to incriminate PetroSaudi. "She's here for you, so go ahead; we'll sort this out and we can all move on, OK?"

I should have known better. He'd had it all planned! I felt crushed and my stomach hurt. He had backed me into a corner; once more, I felt my options shrinking.

He led me back down to the bar, where the journalist was waiting. Introducing herself as Christine Jackmann, she said she had read our story and was here to help us. She seemed sincere but I still didn't trust her.

She tried to break the ice by telling me she had an idea of what I was experiencing, because her boyfriend had been wrongly imprisoned in Egypt. Patrick had left us and I took my courage in both hands: I told her she didn't know everything that was going on. It was vague, but she seemed curious.

I continued, saying she could have no idea of the truth of the matter because what had come out in the press was false and everything was much bigger than it seemed. I added that I was scared because I was now alone with my one-year-old son in Koh Samui. People knew where I lived and I couldn't take any chances, given the circumstances.

She said she understood what I was saying, but I got the sense that she had been manipulated by Patrick. Perhaps he had promised her some kind of exclusive based on his made-up lies.

I left things there and she gave me her email address in case I changed my mind and wanted to talk some more. (As it happens, I followed up later that evening just to repeat what I'd said earlier: that I felt it was too risky for me to talk.)

The next morning, when I went to meet Patrick in the lobby of the St. Regis, he said he had ordered the hotel limousine to take us to the prison. (In fact, he paid for it to wait around for him the entire day just so that he could cool down in the air-conditioning.)

On the way over, he was in one of his chatty moods. He told me again that his wife was a pain in the ass and always asking when this whole business would be over. He then told me about his father, who had apparently abandoned him when he was a child and rebuilt his life in Asia with a Malaysian woman. He then returned to the well-worn theme of how stupid and dangerous Clare was. He added that everything would work out soon and that when it did we'd put it all behind us and be friends.

I couldn't help but wonder if he had been taking drugs to be capable of saying such things. He truly lived in another dimension.

When we arrived at the prison, he told me to wait downstairs and went straight up to the prison governor's office. Twenty minutes later he came back down, looking angry. The governor wasn't around and his deputy couldn't do anything for us. Patrick's face was like that of a spoilt brat throwing a fit when he doesn't get his way. I wanted to see Xavier right away but seeing Patrick in this state almost made me happy.

Patrick decided we should try our luck with one of the other chiefs. I accompanied him and he asked me to speak to the guy in Thai. I asked about the visit that was supposed to have been organized for us but he said couldn't help, which just made Patrick even angrier. He proceeded to pace around the guy's office making calls and complaining about the heat. It was noon, so everyone had stopped for *kin kaow*. I felt like rolling on the floor laughing.

I suggested we go and get some lunch at the only place close by — a canteen run by some female prisoners close to the end of their sentences. I will let you imagine the kind of place it was; they served decent street food, but suffice to say Patrick was extremely uncomfortable there. He looked almost afraid, and disgusted to be outside of his five-star bubble.

At 1.30pm we returned to the prison. Patrick called Pongsawai and told him he had better sort things out because he wouldn't wait around all afternoon. At about 2pm the deputy warden came to pick us up and escort us not to an office but to the visiting room.

The situation felt beyond bizarre. Here I was waiting to speak to my husband whilst sitting with the man who had put him behind bars to clear his own name. It was hard to imagine anything worse.

Xavier came straight out and told Patrick I couldn't be a part of their little games — he wanted me kept out of it.

Patrick was less of his usual cocky self when talking to Xavier; perhaps he knew that if we weren't separated by glass and steel, Xavier would have knocked his teeth out. He immediately said he understood Xavier's feelings and that they would find another solution. How strange that he should just climb down, I thought. Knowing how desperate Patrick had been for me to speak to the press, something didn't feel right. He knew that I had stalled for time the day before with the journalist at the St. Regis. What did he have planned next?

Patrick told Xavier not to worry, that he was there for us and that he would get Xavier out soon; and then he left us alone. We didn't have much time, so I quickly told Xavier that I would take care of all the paperwork in relation to something else we had been discussing: his application for a transfer to Switzerland. If accepted, he would finish part of his sentence there, probably in something approaching a five-star hotel compared to this shithole. As ever, we parted with tears in our eyes.

Outside, Patrick was waiting by the exit. He didn't look at all happy, although I was sure he'd enjoyed being a witness to our suffering. He told me we had to go and collect the evidence the police had seized from Koh Samui when Xavier was arrested, and ordered the limo driver to take us downtown, to the headquarters of the Crime Suppression Division.

Inside the building, it was clear he knew his way around only too well, and listening to the chatter around the place I worked out that he was known to all of them. Colonel Pongsawai appeared, and I recognized the faces of a number of other inspectors who had accompanied me on various private visits at the prison. Laughing, they asked about Paul — "the other policeman."

The colonel and Patrick disappeared into an office and came out some minutes later with large boxes which they placed in front of me on a desk. There were four in total, filled with our personal computer, iPads, USB keys, hard drives and some books. "Here's all your stuff; they don't need it anymore so you can take it home," Patrick said, smiling, as if he was doing me a favor.

I couldn't help but laugh inside. The situation felt like a scene from a movie about South American cartels. It was surreal. Patrick, the colonel and two of his colleagues loaded the boxes into the hotel limousine and I called Denis to arrange to drop them at his place for the time being.

After the drop-off, and a quick farewell to Denis, it was time to pack up and head to the airport once more. It was evening by the time I landed in Koh Samui and I barely had time to kiss Xander goodnight before he went to sleep. Thank God for my mum being there. (Again, I don't know how I could have survived any of this without her, or without the support of my dad and brother.)

Back on the island, November quickly turned into December and I had my hands full just making sure everything was in order with the resort, looking after our animals and preparing various papers for Xavier's application for a royal pardon. Xander had started walking, so I had to put fences all over the house to make sure he didn't hurt himself. It was a delight to watch him grow each day, but everything I was dealing with sapped my energy and I was starting to really look like crap.

The stress of the last few months had made me lose about 8 kilos. I never slept more than five hours a night, and I had an ulcer in my stomach and constant eczema. I felt completely at the end of my tether mentally and physically. I was living day to day like a robot.

One afternoon, when Xander was taking his nap, I decided to try and do something to get my act together. I headed to the gym and started off by running a mile on the machine. I felt like I was in a frenzy. Next thing

I knew I was pulling on my boxing gloves and punching the bag with all my might.

I couldn't stop. Tears came and a rage rose in me stronger than I'd ever felt before. I just kept punching and kicking until I gradually realized my foot hurt badly and I broke off. Afterwards, I spent a couple of days limping around before deciding I should pay a visit to the local hospital. The doctor there referred me for an MRI scan in Bangkok.

On 8 December, I told Patrick I would be returning to Bangkok and asked that he arrange another visit for me with Xavier. He messaged back that he would make sure it was a private one and that he would also send Paul to talk to us. He wouldn't be joining us himself, because his wife was close to giving birth. He also added that — as had been mentioned in the press — Malaysian officials would be coming to visit Xavier.

I immediately had a bad taste in my mouth. Surely this could only be bad news. What if the Malaysian authorities were out to harm Xavier?

I didn't know what to think but I had to keep things amicable, because I needed his help with something else — namely obtaining eight certified copies of Xavier's passport, which were required for his application for a royal pardon. The CSD still had possession of the passport but as they were in the pay of PetroSaudi, I had to have Patrick's co-operation.

He said he would get what I needed, so I asked some more about the Malaysian visit. Who were these Malaysian officials? What were their names?

"Do you already know the questions they are going to ask him?" I wrote. "And after this interview, is it guaranteed that he will be left alone? Will it help to get him out faster?" I also asked when we would find out about any improvements to Xavier's ranking as a prisoner.

He replied: "I'll be with Paul in a moment; I'll call you with him on the line."

OK, I thought: if you're hoping to discuss this by phone so there's no transcript of it, that's fine... The conversation will be recorded.

My phone rang an hour later. Paul said he would arrive in two days' time, and that he would sort out visits for me while I was in Bangkok.

Patrick revealed that he would receive questions from the Malaysians "in a little while." He continued: "I'll give them to Paul and then Xavier can see the questions and he can prepare himself with Paul. There will also be Thai officials there… Colonel Pongsawai will be there, and I'll try to get Paul to be there as well. I don't know how I'm going to do it exactly but we'll try to do it like that. It's going to be very controlled and [Xavier] will have several days to prepare."

Me: "Will his lawyer be there?"

Patrick: "I don't know yet; I think it's going to be 'Police to Police' but honestly I haven't discussed it too much with Paul yet. But once he gets there he's going to talk to the police and everyone to get [Xavier] ready for this interview and make sure everything goes well."

Me: "Who exactly are they?"

Patrick: "These are not people who are totally our friends, that's true, but that's why it's important for Xavier to be well prepared and then it's over."

He went on: "And I'm really going to ask that Paul be present during the interview... that he be given a false name, something like that, and then I don't know exactly, I have to think about it a little bit, that's all…"

Me, still skeptical: "OK."

He continued: "Paul will also see to the ranking. That's why we're sending him; he'll look at it and negotiate everything… In fact, Paul, I've just had a good talk with him, he understands exactly what needs to be done and then he's going to go and see all the people and talk to them about the ranking. Don't worry."

And there was more: "I was in the US, too. Now we've got the FBI looking at all this crap, so it's a pain in the ass. But hey… It is what it is… Life goes on."

This was a bombshell, and I wasn't sure what to make of it at the time, but as I would later discover the FBI were indeed very interested in PetroSaudi, in particular their relationships with the Malaysians and the Venezuelans.

Wrapping up, they said Paul would be in touch.

ON 10 DECEMBER, I flew up to Bangkok, and headed straight to the prison. Contrary to what I had been told, nothing had been arranged, and after a seven-hour wait I was informed no visit was possible. Yet again, I was left to wonder at the reasons. Had PetroSaudi blocked me because I refused to release the video like they wanted me to?

To make matters worse, a visit to the hospital that evening ended with me being discharged with a cast on my foot. The scan showed I had a cracked heel. I returned to my hotel, crutches in hand, on the back of a scooter taxi.

The next day, Paul came with me to the prison. He had with him a file containing a list of questions that the Malaysians would be asking, along with prepared answers for Xavier. When he wasn't looking, I took some pictures of this file with my phone. No-one seemed to have any new information, however, about the Malaysian delegation — which was already supposed to have arrived the day before.

My visit with Xavier was another short one, again in the visiting room. I warned him that he should demand his lawyer be present, and that I feared for his safety. Whether or not he shared those fears, he managed to soothe mine and to reassure me. Once more, I felt — and was thankful for — my husband's incredible strength. I showed him a few small pictures of Xander that I had hidden in my bra, and again we parted with heavy hearts.

In a taxi afterwards, Paul tried to cheer me up, but I felt increasingly wary of him and afraid of what he might be capable of. I asked him when the Malaysians were coming and said I intended to stay in Bangkok at least until Monday. There was no way I was leaving Xavier alone when they were in town.

In a moment of frustration, I added: "If anything happens to [Xavier], I'll blow it all up."

At these words, his face changed; I could tell from the way he looked at me that he knew I would do what I had just said. All he could say in response was not to worry, a phrase that I was sick of hearing from these men.

He went on to tell me that he had spoken with Patrick about helping us to sell our property on Koh Samui, so that we were ready to vacate Thailand quickly if we needed to. He said they had already found a prospective buyer. "You can sell the resort," he said. "Xavier is going to get out very soon and you can get on with your life and put this behind you." The way he smiled at me as he said this stirred in me an almost demonic vision of opening the door of the taxi, pushing him onto the highway and watching him being run over by the car behind us. Yes, I would be happy if we were able to sell up in readiness for leaving the country, but I saw no reason to trust Paul and Patrick to help us to do so.

I wrote Patrick a lengthy message explaining that despite his promises I hadn't been able to see Xavier the day before and that the visit I had just had was in the visiting room. I said that two friends who had tried to visit him recently had also been denied because the director responsible for authorizing their visits was said to have been absent. "Xavier is the only prisoner out of more than 6,000 who has to do this," I wrote. "You manage this… but sometimes I can't even see him."

I added that I hadn't even been able to give him books and magazines. Any reading materials had to be first approved by the Swiss Embassy, which happened to be open only three hours each morning — hours which, when I was in Bangkok, I usually spent trying to actually see Xavier. He also needed shoes but I had been told the only time these could be brought in was on the first Tuesday of every month. And worst of all, I had been told I wasn't allowed to give him any photos of his son "until next year."

Patrick's reply to all of this was simply: "I'll look into it right away." I felt so angry.

Meanwhile, Paul insisted I should go back to Koh Samui as planned, as it was now more likely that the Malaysians would come early in the new year. I therefore took the evening flight home to be with my son.

Imagine my consternation, then, when on the following Tuesday — 15 December — Worasit called to say the Malaysian delegation would be interrogating Xavier that morning. Crying, I begged him to go to the prison right away. I said I would pay him myself, whatever he asked for, but that he had to be there.

I was beside myself. It seemed completely obvious that Paul and Patrick had known exactly when the delegation would be coming and wanted me out of the way. I called both Paul and Patrick but of course neither of them answered.

At about 3pm, Worasit called back. He'd been to see Xavier, who he said was fine. The Malaysians had come and gone; Xavier was satisfied with the interview and had asked when I would be back to see him. At those words, I burst into tears. I had never been so scared as in the hours since Worasit's call that morning.

In the following days, Paul said he had several contacts interested in buying our resort. But fine words make fools happy. Three of his contacts never called me back and the one who said he wanted to come for a viewing never showed up — this after I had spent three days hosing down all the decks and getting the place spruced up.

Everything was a struggle. My foot was still in plaster, which didn't make it easy navigating the four storeys of the resort building or chasing after Xander.

The start of the festive season just made me feel depressed. Fortunately, my parents and my brother had all come out for Christmas to cheer me up. Again, I felt such gratitude: morally and physically they were (and are) the pillars of my life.

With everything I was juggling and the pain in my foot I decided to give up on any ideas of going back to Bangkok before Christmas. I asked Denis to go and visit Xavier and explain the situation. I had also become close to Yanna — the wife of a Bulgarian friend of Xavier's in jail — and she agreed to pass on a letter I would write.

Yanna was alone in Bangkok with her son, two years older than Xander, and she visited her husband every day. Her devotion and kindness were incredible. She gladly took letters from me on numerous occasions, meaning we were able to bypass both PetroSaudi and the prison authorities, who were not in the habit of scrutinizing other prisoners' personal letters in the same way. Yanna also helped me by making sure Xavier had supplies of necessities when I wasn't around.

Writing the letter was the hard part, though. I couldn't find the words to say; nothing seemed appropriate and I kept starting over. I wanted to give Xavier courage at the same time as warning him we were being let down by PetroSaudi — but I felt sure that would discourage him. How could I hide my own fear about what they would do to him now that they seemed to have got everything they wanted?

Even wishing him a Merry Christmas and a Happy New Year, I could hardly believe what I was writing. What had my life, our life, become?

Attaching some recent photos of Xander, I emailed my message to Yanna and told her I would reimburse her if any of the guards found the letter and demanded payment.

Altogether, it was a horrible holiday season. I wanted to stop thinking about Xavier even for just five minutes, but I couldn't. I couldn't concentrate on anything else, I couldn't sleep and my stomach constantly hurt. Time and again, I would wake up in the middle of the night with a migraine and cry alone on my terrace so as to avoid worrying anyone.

William had brought a couple of friends along and they all insisted we went out for a change of scenery. So on 24 December I joined them at a beach bar. I was as depressed as ever, but there was music on the beach, the night was warm and I had my brother beside me. He hugged me and told me to take my mind off my worries. I felt incredibly lucky to have him — my sunshine, my best friend. Xander was with my grandparents and I thought "for once, relax and let go." I ordered a cocktail and got my head out of the game just for a while.

On 25 December, we all celebrated Christmas with Xander. On New Year's Eve, I went to bed with him at 10pm. I really wasn't in the mood for fun. I just wanted to believe that this would be the first and last holiday season we would have to endure as a family riven apart.

Chapter 15

Xavier

PRISON: A PARALLEL UNIVERSE

AFTER SOME WEEKS without much communication from Paul or Patrick, Laura and I decided, in early November, that we wanted to drop our appeal against the sentence.

It was a gamble. At the time there was much talk among the VIPs about the King of Thailand granting amnesties to lots of prisoners for his 88th birthday in December. For those with longer sentences, there would be reductions. For someone like me whose sentence was relatively short, it could mean walking free at a stroke.

If there was no amnesty from the King, not appealing meant my three-year sentence would now be final. But there had been no new "evidence" to help us with our appeal, and our only other hope was that Patrick was telling the truth and would do everything in his power to get me out of jail by some mysterious "other means" by December.

Accordingly, two days before I was due to appear in court for my final bail application, I instructed Worasit to cancel my application to appeal the sentence (and by extension the bail application).

An earlier bail application (my third, following two failed applications after my initial arrest) had been made with the help of Paul and Patrick on 26 October. Paul had assured us at the time that everything was in order, and that I was sure to be released. They had brought three or four bodyguards to escort me out of the courthouse ("for your protection") if we won. And as local convention dictated (or so we were told), Laura had come with 1 million baht (roughly US$30,000) in an envelope to give the judge discreetly if I was released. I arrived at the court with chains on my feet, like a slave.

I will never forget Laura's face when I arrived at the court. She was in tears but wore a look of optimism. Deep down I didn't share her confidence, and unfortunately I was right. The application was refused because I was considered a "flight risk." How could I flee without a passport, without money and without speaking the language…?

But let's get back to the waiver of my appeal. Worasit confirmed to me on 5 November that my decision had been lodged. On 6 November, however, my name was called at 6.30am and I was informed I had to appear in court that morning to appeal my sentence. I told the guards the appeal was canceled — but no, they forced me to get on my way.

I didn't put up any resistance because, after all, a few hours away from the prison was never something to be refused. So I was led to the exit, put in chains and again ushered into a mini-van. An escort of four guards took me to court.

The situation at the courthouse was surreal. The corridors seemed strangely empty and as I walked through the building it felt like no-one was working. I soon realized that some of the staff, lurking in doorways, were discreetly taking pictures of me (to sell to the local press, as it turns out). Were they all crazy?

In the courtroom, Worasit was waiting. There was also one journalist, who had presumably been tipped off. Laura wasn't there: obviously she hadn't been notified.

I explained this to the three judges, spelling out that I did not want bail. The whole atmosphere was palpably strange, though; something just wasn't right. Worasit, who had also been summoned at short notice, told me he couldn't understand why we were there. Then I heard from the judges that my submission to cancel my appeal had not been received.

Next, they opened an envelope… and told me that my application for bail had been granted.

My response was to refuse to accept it. In large part, this was due to a sense of unease at the whole situation. By the time I was taken back to prison and then released, it would have been around 8 o'clock in the evening. Why did they want me out so suddenly, against my wishes, with no-one around to collect me and take me to safety?

It seemed they didn't want to listen to me, but Worasit insisted on presenting evidence of the withdrawal of my appeal and I repeated into the microphone — so that I could be heard by the journalist — that I *did not want to appeal* and that I wished to be taken back to prison.

Finally they assented — and Worasit whispered in my ear that he had never seen such behavior from judges in his 30 years in the profession. I couldn't put my finger on what exactly, but there was something fishy going on in that courtroom.

Eventually, I was escorted back into the van and taken back to prison — the end of my little day out.

BACK IN JAIL, the daily routine continued. Each morning I woke at 6am, after a few hours of sleep in installments of 1-2 hours. Coffee, cigarettes, reading, prayers. (Yes, we were obliged to pray two to three times a day, so I had plenty of opportunity to think about the whole situation and ask God to end this nightmare.) Day after day, nothing happened.

I lived simply in anticipation of visits. You get hardened by living in this hell day after day — or rather, you think you are getting hardened; but with each visit from a loved one your heart takes over and the longing for freedom makes you fall back into depression.

Another regular occurrence was that every month a group of monks would come to visit and the inmates — no matter how poor or wretched — would have to give them gifts. It seemed very strange to me, but the Thais told me it was just a tradition. Every month, the monks left carrying boxes full of milk, rice, water and toothpaste. They needed a truck to collect everything.

We also had a number of visits — five or six during my incarceration — from national and international bodies who went around monitoring prison conditions. These visits always had the same pattern. The guards were told in advance, so two weeks before each inspection we were all put to work. The main building was repainted; the holes in the cement were filled in; edible food suddenly became available in the canteen. And perhaps most shockingly of all, more than half of the prisoners were parked in a shed for the entire day of the inspection so that the prison looked emptier.

These same organizations would donate bowls, toothbrushes, razors and other necessities. In reality, the guards took most of this loot for themselves, or sold it outside. What a shame; and what misery.

After being released, I met in Switzerland some time ago with a Red Cross employee whose work involved visiting Asian prisons. I explained everything about my experience to him in detail. He replied that the conditions are known about but that nobody can do anything to help. If the Red Cross were to create a stink, he said, they would simply be denied access altogether. His view was that the little they are able to do is still better than nothing. Reluctantly I had to admit that he was right.

At some point, I learned from a friendly guard who had some notion of my predicament that my conversations during visits were being recorded. This shocked me but it dawned on me that I had been in Thailand long enough for nothing to be surprising anymore. I made Laura aware of what I'd learned. Of course, she already suspected it, but in any case we decided to start communicating on paper: she would write things down in notebooks and I on scraps of paper, and we would hold these up to the window separating us in the visiting room.

For my part, I would write her notes in the toilet and hide them in my underwear so as not to have them taken off me when I was searched on entering the visiting room. We had to learn to carry on verbal conversations about the weather, for example, whilst truly communicating to one another using these notes. Sometimes, we even found cause to laugh at the bizarre juxtapositions of our spoken and written conversations.

But such moments of sweetness were rare, and all I could really think of was how long I would have to wait to hold my wife and my son in my arms again.

AS NOVEMBER PROGRESSED, I waited for Paul's visits with increasing impatience. We were getting closer to the release date I had been promised: there were only a few weeks left before Christmas.

Laura brought Xander with her to visit me in prison... And it shattered me. It was the first time I had seen him in five months; I fell to my knees and cried my eyes out.

He was so handsome; he had also grown a lot and he could walk. He recognized me because Laura had shown him pictures of me and talked about me every day.

As we watched him walk around the office and played with him, I could tell that Laura was preoccupied by something. When I asked her what it was, she said she was beginning to doubt whether the PetroSaudi deal was going to happen, whether they would stay true to their word and arrange for my release in December.

Patrick and Paul came to visit me some time after. They told me, for the hundredth time, that I didn't have to worry and that they would help me get out by the "back door," but that I still had to wait a few more weeks. It was hard to believe them, but still I had to hold to that hope — otherwise it was a case of having two and half years left to go here, and I really couldn't bear to think about that. I wouldn't survive all that time.

Their news was that a Malaysian delegation would be coming in December to interview me in the presence of the Thai police. They said they would provide me with questions in advance and tell me how to answer them. This exercise would help the Malaysian Prime Minister, calm the ongoing scandal — and bring my liberation a step closer.

As I had no access to the press, I wasn't entirely aware of the extent of the 1MDB scandal. I knew it had reached international proportions, but I couldn't gauge precisely how important it was. Patrick kept repeating that it was only important in Malaysia.

In December, we learned that the King's amnesties would not be taking place this year — instead they would be saved for the following year, the 70th anniversary of his reign. It was a disappointment;, but as I hadn't allowed myself to get my hopes up I didn't feel too deflated. In fact, I had discovered that rumors about amnesties were a permanent feature of prison life in Thailand. There would be talk of amnesties to mark the birthdays of various members of the royal family, or for the cremation of a well-known Buddhist monk, or for just about any event you could imagine.

It was a beacon of hope for many prisoners, and the word for "amnesty" was one I soon added to my Thai vocabulary: *apayatot.*

Laura and I also made the decision to apply for something else altogether — a royal pardon. In this, we were able to gain the support of the Swiss Embassy, which was key to our chances. Laura and Worasit prepared all the paperwork and sent it to the Thai Ministry of Justice.

Two weeks later, I received a written reply from the minister confirming that my request had been received and forwarded to his personal secretary. The guards and the prisoners were astonished — they said these things never happened that quickly. The guards said that when inmates received letters like this, they tended to be released in about two months.

This really buoyed my hopes. I yearned to be back home, perhaps by Christmas or a little after. The director of the prison informed me that this had happened because of the friendship between Thailand and Switzerland, where the King had been educated. I really wanted to believe there wouldn't be any further complications.

In mid-December, Paul visited me with Colonel Pongsawai. He had with him 50 or so questions that the Malaysian delegation would come and ask me the next day, and we spent the day in one of the prison's offices preparing for this interrogation: I had to learn the answers off by heart. Paul said my co-operation would help to resolve the whole affair, and that the Malaysian authorities would soon issue a report exonerating Najib Razak.

The interview lasted one hour, and it went fine. The Malaysians were polite to me and thanked me for my testimony.

I felt that the investigators had some integrity and seemed to want to know the truth — but of course I had to repeat the lies that Patrick and Paul were forcing me to tell. My testimony was nothing other than what PetroSaudi had fed me beforehand: that they were a good company, and that everything had been legal. I had stolen the data and blackmailed PetroSaudi for money, in collaboration with Edge Media and some members of the opposition. I was also under strict orders not to mention Jho Low under any circumstances. And vitally, the Malaysian Prime Minister had done nothing wrong; he was a good leader.

As I waited for my pardon, the days dragged along, but there were at least some incidents to lighten the mood. On one occasion, we were treated to a concert, where the ladyboys, dressed in makeup and skirts, danced to techno music. Many of the inmates found this quite arousing (and in fact some indulged in sexual relations with these prisoners quite frequently in the showers).

For Christmas, one of the guards brought me to his office with another colleague and they asked me whether I wanted a drink. I accepted, thinking they would give me a beer, but the guard took a red plastic bottle out of his drawer. It turned out to be fertilizer for watering plants that they kept in a small pond in the building. The guard put a few drops of it in a bottle of water and shook it. The water turned red. They then took turns drinking it, and I took a sip. It had a repulsive chemical taste, and that one sip was enough for me, but the thought of enjoying a nice drink in the comfort of my own home some time soon tantalized me.

We also had regular drug tests, which involved urinating in a cup. The tests were badly controlled, and some people got other inmates to do their urinating for them. Some prisoners were found to have methamphetamine in their samples, which meant they had their sentences extended. New prisoners sometimes brought drugs in with them — concealed in the most intimate cavities of their bodies — to exchange for cigarettes or food. Prisoners who used drugs always got caught, though: they would spend their nights restless and awake, and would be easily spotted on the prison cameras.

I became very close to three VIP prisoners in my cell, and another in the cell next to mine. These men became my companions in misfortune and I will forever think of them as my brothers in arms. Their protection, advice and humanity helped me face my predicament with resilience.

Tommy had a warmth to his character and was always smiling. With his cheerfulness, he brought me comfort day after day. He came from a prominent local family and was involved in the medical industry: he specialized in stem cell treatments and owned a clinic in Germany, where I visited him much later after we were both released. In prison, he received food from his wife each day and would share it with me. He had been sentenced to a couple of years in prison over discrepancies in the signing of cheques. Despite his good humor, though, I often observed him in the middle of the night staring blankly into space. As was the case with many of us, his smile was only a façade. No one could be happy in that place.

Another close companion was a "Tsai" — a member of one of Thailand's royal houses. Everyone treated him with the utmost respect. He had a rare kindness and was highly educated. He also knew Switzerland well, having traveled there regularly. He gave me chocolate almost every day, and in return I gave him French lessons. He had been convicted in an old financial affair dating back more than 10 years. He was hoping for a royal pardon, but it was slow in coming.

There was also Tonk, a young man who also came from a good family. He had been convicted of lèse-majesté over an online post in which he merely happened to mention the name of a Thai princess. He had the same birthday as my son, which created a bond between us. He taught me to play Thai chess and it was a hobby that I came to enjoy. Between reading and playing chess, the days went by a little faster.

My biggest ally, however, was a man nicknamed Gig. We talked about football and finance — it turns out he was part of a consortium that owned a British football team. He had been convicted of embezzlement. Gig provided me with cigarettes on a daily basis and took me under his protection. He was very well known to the guards as he was also the owner of a prominent Thai football team.

Luckily, my closest friends are now almost all out of prison: at the time of writing, only Gig was still incarcerated, and I pray that he will be released soon. Only people who have spent a long time in prison can understand the bond that forms between prisoners. They are still my brothers, and even the distance between us does not change the affection I have and will always have for them. Our shared sufferings and moments of friendship remain forever marked in my heart.

Another inmate, who only stayed for two days, also marked me — and five years later we met and spoke again. He was a young Scottish man named Scott, who had come over from Malaysia and been arrested in Thailand. He knew my case well and knew who I was. He even expressed his admiration for what I had done for Malaysia. His wife was also incarcerated — in the nearby women's prison — and he told me he had information about certain Malaysian political figures in relation to another case of significant international interest, namely the disappearance of Malaysia Airlines flight MH370 in 2014. That, he said, was the reason for both of them being arrested. The parallels with my own circumstances, where I had been locked up in Thailand for offenses relating to affairs elsewhere, were striking. He told me that he had some secrets relating to the MH370 case that I wanted to hear more about some day, if he was willing to share the details. It turned out that ultimately he wasn't, which I respect.

At the time, Scott was in very poor health, and one afternoon he had a heart attack in the yard. The prisoners and guards performed CPR on him for several minutes before his heart started again. I thought he had died — but, thank God, he recovered.

Another prisoner who had a soothing presence for me was named Prawit. He was one of a number of bankers convicted in the high-profile embezzlement case mentioned previously. His only crime had been to sign documents that his superiors had asked him to sign. I implicitly understood that he had had no choice — I had learned that authority rules in Thai institutions, and that workers must blindly obey their superiors.

AT SOME POINT each week, there was an unannounced inspection of the building, with searches for drugs and pornographic magazines. (The magazines were of course lent to inmates by guards in exchange for packets of cigarettes.) When the prison warden passed among us during inspections, we were supposed to sit in the place assigned to us in our cells and look down at the floor.

My friend Gig and I would often spend our days sitting under a kind of shelter — a small area of the prison courtyard that was shaded from the sun by a sort of gazebo. One day when the warden came round, I made the decision to stay right where I was under my shelter and refuse to look down. Those who rebelled like this in the past had been disciplined by other prisoners — the ones supposedly in charge of security. But they didn't do anything to me. Seemingly I had some degree of power in the prison. This might seem like a small thing, but it gave me courage and strengthened me in facing my ordeal.

In the cell, we had two fans and a TV that transmitted only one channel — a station authorized by the military that constantly showed speeches from generals and old Thai shows from the 1960s and 70s. When the TV and one of the fans broke down, myself and two other prisoners were ordered to pay for a replacement. Laura gave the money to a guard outside the prison — about $500. I had no choice but to pay, but the principle of it bothered me.

Small-time corruption was just part of everyday life in the prison, and if you could afford to pay the guard in charge of visits, all sorts of privileges could be bought. VIPs often received personal belongings such as clothes, sneakers, food and newspapers. In my own case, being allowed to read the *Bangkok Post*, an English-language newspaper with some world news, was one of the few times I felt connected to the world outside.

The prisoner with the most privileges, though, was a former marine police commander, Major General Boonsueb Fraithuan, who ironically had been convicted of taking bribes. This guy was allowed the use of a private office with air conditioning, had fresh fruit brought to him every day and even had a team of people working for him. An anonymous letter sent to the Department of Prisons led him to having his air conditioning taken away from him, however. It was said he had been paying $2,000 every month for it.

December 31 was now upon us, meaning I had lived for six months in conditions that hardly felt human. Life in a Thai prison takes away your humanity; you feel like you are nothing. I for one felt lonely and wretched. I lived only for the next visit, and then the next. I thought about my wife and son all the time.

The only good news was that I was classified as a "good" prisoner at the end of the year. This classification was important in case the King decided to award an amnesty. You went from being a "moderate" prisoner to a "good" prisoner after six months if you didn't create any problems, and after another six months you could become a "very good" prisoner. After the same amount of time again, you could even become an "excellent" prisoner.

My progression to "good" would not have happened if I hadn't given up my appeal, because my sentence had to be considered "final" for the ranking to be revised. (This decision would prove to have vital significance later on.)

On New Year's Eve, the prisoners said they had prepared fireworks. I knew to expect almost anything: perhaps they had made pyrotechnics from some salvaged materials. But no. Around midnight they took out pieces of plastic wrapping and blew into them; the screaming sound that was produced echoed that of a rocket taking off. They then smacked the walls to make the sound of fireworks going "bang!" This went on for hours; it was so pathetic that I laughed out loud.

It didn't seem to me that there was much for anyone to celebrate, and the idea of being around this place for the next New Year filled me with dread. Truly, I had no idea what was coming for me in 2016.

Chapter 16

Xavier

THROUGH GRITTED TEETH

ON 2 JANUARY, to celebrate the New Year, the prison organized a football match between the guards and some of the prisoners, mainly the VIPs. I was asked to take part… and I agreed, thinking that it would be good for me to do some sport.

I hadn't been able to do any since arriving in jail. There was a place where you could lift weights but the entrance was strictly controlled by the prison gang. In addition, the dumbbells were homemade — just like in the American movies, they were simply blocks of cement attached to an iron bar. They looked like an accident waiting to happen, and sure enough one user suffered a broken foot when a chunk of concrete came loose and fell on him.

In advance of this football match, we were warned not to test the opposing goalkeeper, and to let the other team score as many goals as they liked. The director of the building also had to be top scorer. I participated in this charade for three minutes before making my excuses and leaving the pitch.

At the end of January, Yatavi, the guard who oversaw the foreign inmates, told me to expect a visit from the FBI "soon." My VIP cell-mates said that if the Americans wanted to speak to me, it was a good sign that I was likely to be released, as the US authorities had good relations with Thailand. This gave my morale a huge boost.

Nothing happened in the days following, which made me anxious. Then, after a week or so, Denis came to see me. He told me he had heard from Laura that the FBI had tried to visit me but that the prison officials had refused them entry. Apparently they would try to come again soon. I was alarmed that they had been denied access but happy they had tried. If the Americans really wanted to see me, maybe there was a way of getting out, and I would be more than willing to talk to them. In any case, Denis informed me that Laura would be coming to visit me soon with more news on the matter.

Another week, however, and still nothing. When I asked Yatavi why they hadn't been yet, he smiled and said they hadn't filled in the right paperwork to be allowed in. At the time, I could only guess at what was really going on, but what I discovered later shocked me. The FBI in fact made no fewer than three attempts to come and visit me, but for the first time in the history of Thai-US relations — or so I'm told — they were denied access to a prisoner in a Thai jail.

In the meantime, my "emotional lift" — a term used by many of my fellow in-mates to describe their highs and lows — sank back to basement level. In prison, any prospect of an amnesty or remission can create a moment of elation; when such hopes are dashed, the depression is absolute. I found that the only way to survive and reduce my suffering was to learn to have almost no emotions at all.

Paul came to see me in late January, in what subsequently transpired to be his last visit. He said the chief of police and Patrick's contacts in the Thai government had told them I would be given a royal pardon in May. After he had gone, however, a guard close to the VIPs whispered to me that the real reason for Paul's visit had been to erase all trace of his own and Patrick's visits. Obviously, this information was alarming. Now that they had used me for their purposes, were they preparing to abandon me?

I was fed up with his and Patrick's lies and deceptions. Thinking back to that time, I don't know how Paul, or Colonel Pongsawai for that matter, can look themselves in the mirror after everything they did to me and my family. As police officers, or ex-police officers — as turned out to be the case with Paul — they were supposed to have integrity and a commitment to justice. Instead, they were both paid criminal accomplices. Maybe they'd had noble aspirations in the beginning, but money has a way of corrupting and perverting everything.

Not long after Paul's visit, I also learned some things from Laura that shook me to the core. I knew that Paul and PetroSaudi were becoming increasingly unwilling to help us, but during one of her visits she informed me that Paul had actually made threats about what would happen if she revealed their shady actions. As she will relate in the next chapter, he told her to think about what would happen to Xander if she herself was detained — and said that he could end up in an orphanage.

When Laura told me about this conversation, she was crying, panicked. It was clear to me there and then that we needed to plan for her to get out of Thailand. I also promised myself to make them pay for the harm they had caused to my wife and family, no matter how long it took.

JANUARY ALSO BROUGHT the first of a series of regular visits from a member of the Swiss Embassy, Mr Viktor Vavricka — a man who was to become a real lifeline over several months. The first time I met him, in the visiting room, I made him understand that I could not speak freely, because my conversations were being recorded and relayed to PetroSaudi. I told him he would have to ask to be given a private visit such as had been regularly granted to Patrick and Paul. (It would take him some time for him to be granted this privilege but he got there in the end.)

As we knew the FBI was now involved, Laura and I would have to be even more cautious about evading PetroSaudi's surveillance. I started writing my letters to Laura when I was on the toilet in our cell — the only place where the surveillance cameras weren't trained on me. But even there I was still monitored and controlled. One day, coming out of the toilet — if you could call the dump we used a toilet — I saw Mike, the officer I mentioned in chapter 13 whose job seemed to consist almost entirely of watching me. He was writing on a piece of paper, but stopped when he saw me. I asked him what he was doing and he said he had to make a daily report on my activities.

He said he wrote down everything he could about me — who I spoke to, what I ate, when I used the toilet, and anything else he could think of. Mike was actually kind of a nice guy, but like all the others the system had corrupted him.

That system was like a pyramid — the higher-ups all got a bigger share of the loot, but the ordinary guards, like Mike, all took their slice. And as inmates we paid for everything. You wanted a haircut with a clean pair of scissors? That cost you a pack of cigarettes. You wanted to send mail? That meant one of your relatives slipping money to one of the guards outside. You wanted photos or books brought in? Again, that cost money. The guards earned their promotions by paying those above them, so the system forced them to be corrupt. It was a bit like the mafia.

Fortunately some of the individual guards were human and tried to help you. In fact, some of them helped Laura and I even when we didn't have the money at hand to pay them.

Another person who helped us was Yanna, the wife of Ivo, a Bulgarian inmate I had grown to be friends with. Thanks to her kindness, I was able to get letters out to Laura and communicate freely.

For Ivo, I still have unwavering affection. We shared our moments of loneliness and sadness and somehow managed to cheer one another up. As Yanna came to see him every day, he was always well supplied with food and never hesitated to share what he had with me. Without his and others' generosity, there were times when I would probably have died of hunger, because I couldn't feed myself with what was served in the canteen.

Ivo had been sentenced to 50 years for stealing $1,000 from an ATM and being in possession of 34 fake credit cards. He loudly and often proclaimed his innocence, and had hired an English guy who ran an IT forensics company in Bangkok to try and prove it, but the Thai justice system would not listen. The court had actually sentenced him to 102 years in prison (three years per card) but 50 years was the maximum sentence so that was what he was serving. It had even been confirmed by Thailand's Supreme Court. Fortunately, however, Ivo was released at the end of 2021 thanks to a royal amnesty.

What a country; what justice. By the end of his time in jail, Ivo had served more than five years — more punishment than a lot of pedophiles get — for a small-time financial scam.

In February, a new prisoner arrived and was put in an isolation cell next to ours. I was told he was a Spaniard who stood accused of murder and of having cut up the body of his victim. His name was Artur Segarra Princep. And so began my first quasi-friendship with an apparent murderer.

The morning after his arrival I went to speak to him through the bars. He looked quite normal and friendly and I spoke to him in Spanish and asked if he needed anything. All he wanted were cigarettes; for the rest, he told me, God would provide. He looked strange but I couldn't imagine him cutting up a body. As he was confined to his cell for a fortnight, I went to see him every day and gave him cigarettes, toothpaste and other basics.

After two weeks, he was let out of solitary confinement and allowed to mix with the other inmates. As with the one other prisoner in the building who was said to have dismembered someone, he had a certain instant celebrity around the place. Certain prisoners seemed to have a fascination with these sorts of crimes.

Artur had a huge tattoo of Beethoven on his back, but when I asked him if he liked classical music he told me no: the tattoo was a tribute to the superiority of the white race. He asked me if anyone had ever known of a black man to write an opera. I thought he was crazy, but I reasoned that it would be better to create some semblance of friendly relations with him than to fall out with him.

He told me he had several children, all to different mothers here and there; however, he seemed to care more for his sister's children and made me promise to take gifts to them in Barcelona when I got free. It was a promise I would fulfill.

I didn't know and still don't want to know if he is guilty. He was eventually sentenced to death, although his sentence was later commuted to life imprisonment by the King of Thailand.

One of the things I learned in prison is that solidarity cuts in all different directions. You get support from others and must show support in return to whoever will accept it; otherwise, your life will be lonely as hell. During my stay, the only pleasant moments were those moments of solidarity and sharing with others.

As I have alluded to, the prison system in Thailand grants you almost nothing. Apart from rotten food and some rationed water to wash in, you have to pay for everything. Never mind luxuries like coffee, sugar or cigarettes: even the barest of necessities — toothpaste, a toothbrush, soap, toilet paper, underwear — are precious possessions, especially if you don't have the money to pay for them.

In my case, being allowed only a trickle of visitors meant I often simply didn't have the funds. Visitors could deposit small amounts of money into your prisoner account to allow you to make small purchases from the prison shop. But as my visits were so spaced out — in large part thanks to the endless obstacles put in the way of people trying to come and see me — I was effectively a pauper.

I will never forget the generosity of those who shared what they had with me — often free of charge. Their solidarity brought me immense comfort and I made sure to give back in return by sharing to the max any meager belongings that I had. I quickly found that a shared cigarette gives infinitely more pleasure than one smoked alone in a corner. In prison, happiness comes from sharing, not possessing. And so it should be in life generally.

At times I had to endure spells when I had no idea when my next visit might be, and there was a spell in February 2016 when I saw no-one from the outside for more than two weeks. Lacking any expectation of a visit made me depressed, but so did suspecting that people were being denied permission to see me.

Besides Laura, I had visits during my incarceration from her brother William, and from our friends Wilfried, Denis, Laurent and Alex. But I know there were many occasions when they waited for hours only to be either turned away or granted as little as 15 minutes to talk to me over a tinny phone in a sweaty visiting room.

To all of you who came, I say only that those 15 minutes were worth the world to me. Your visits helped me endure months and months of loneliness and suffering and you will have a place in my heart forever.

Chapter 17

Laura

THE TURNING POINT

HAVING BEEN GROUNDED because of my foot, I needed to get back to see Xavier as soon as I could. I booked a flight for 5 January and wrote to Paul and Patrick. Paul replied saying that Patrick's wife was going into labor so he wasn't around. He also said that one of Colonel Pongsawai's bosses was "looking into everything that needs to be done to get Xavier out as soon as possible."

He added: "[Patrick] can't make it but this guy will take care of absolutely everything... He's going to make some calls so you can go and visit Xavier whenever you want with Xander. He will also be looking into getting Xavier's royal pardon and his ranking up so that he can get out as soon as possible. Patrick had him on the phone and I'm also working on all fronts!"

Reading a message like that, how would you have felt? Happy? Hopeful? I would have been too, once upon a time. But I had learned the hard way never to get my hopes up. PetroSaudi had fooled us too many times. Hope makes you blind.

I went up to Bangkok as planned and my private visit with Xavier went ahead this time without any delays or complications. When he came into the room, we burst into tears and threw ourselves into each other's arms. It was yet another bittersweet moment.

I didn't want to say anything to him but he didn't look well. He looked ravaged by events and I could tell he was at the end of his tether from loneliness and a lack of any kind of positive news.

We talked about the royal pardon and he said he had heard nothing since his application had been confirmed by the Thai Ministry of Justice. I told him I thought PetroSaudi were toying with us and would keep him in jail for as long as they could. Deep down, I think he already knew this. We agreed that we were in this fight alone, and would have to turn our ammunition on PetroSaudi if necessary.

He also told me that they were putting more and more prisoners in the cell and that he had almost no room on the floor to sleep on. What's more, new rules had been introduced: inmates weren't allowed to eat after 3pm and the water was even more tightly rationed. I felt shocked. It was unbearable to hear about this. I wanted to vomit.

I pulled out a few small photos of Xander and started to tell Xavier about his latest exploits, but when I did he just broke down in tears. I had to stop talking. My throat tightened with emotion.

I looked Xavier straight in the eye and told him: "You have to fight harder! I will never stop fighting for you, for us. So you get up and fight, OK?! It's gonna be OK, Xavier. I'll get you out of this, I promise, I swear! I need you, OK? I love you! We love you so much! Are you fighting for us?"

I knew that was the only way to pull him back. "Yes! You're right," he said, and we hugged and held each other closer than ever.

Back outside, I had to sit down on a bench. My head was spinning. Every time I thought things couldn't get any worse, they did. To see the person you love in such a state, crushed by criminals, and to be helpless to do anything about it… This was pure hell.

I went back to my hotel and sat in my room, thinking. I couldn't allow myself to slip any further out of my mind. Enough was enough. I had already gathered a lot of material about what had been done. If they weren't going to get Xavier out of jail as they had promised, I was ready to blow their schemes up. I would take them all down.

I was thankful that William was with me. He had come to Bangkok and wanted to visit Xavier the following day with me before returning to Geneva in the evening. I was less happy to learn, however, that Aziz was also in Thailand. I knew his only purpose would be to check up on me and report back to PetroSaudi.

Aziz contacted me and said he would be visiting some friends on an island close to Koh Samui and wanted to pop over and see me there for a couple of days. In the meantime, he had arrived in Bangkok… and wanted to stay at whatever hotel William and I were at. Subsequently, he did just that. With Aziz, you didn't have to be a genius to work out that his every move was carefully orchestrated by Patrick and Tarek.

When we met he was cordial enough to begin with but after a couple of drinks he started goading me. "I don't know why Xavier did this to you," he said. "Plus, he has a son. Do you really think it's fair for you to live like this?"

I couldn't quite believe what I was hearing but I decided to play along and see what he was driving at. I said: "What do you think I should do, Aziz?"

His answer spoke volumes: "I don't know, but you don't have to stay; you know, you could find someone new tomorrow."

Wow… Unbelievable. Were they actually trying to persuade me to leave Xavier? Or was he just trying to provoke me? What came next was even more revealing. "What are you going to do now?" he asked. "I mean, you didn't want to help PetroSaudi and get the tape out, so are you going to do something else on your own to help Xavier?"

I knew I was going to have to be extremely careful in how I responded, even if Aziz was more easily fooled than Patrick. Putting on my little mouse voice, I said: "What should I do, Aziz? I don't know anyone. I'm alone with my son on Koh Samui. I can't take care of our resort or sell it. Patrick and Tarek control everything: the lawyers, the justice system, the prison. I can't do anything."

After our conversation, I was furious. Did they think I was a complete idiot? I took out my phone and wrote the same message to Patrick and Paul, listing out all the ways they had failed to deliver on their promises. I said that Xavier's prisoner ranking hadn't budged, and that despite their assurances about his application being "top of the pile," he hadn't heard anything of the royal pardon. I also called out that he no longer had a dedicated guard looking out for his safety, that conditions in his cell were getting worse, that he still wasn't receiving any books, that the sale of our resort hadn't moved forward a single inch, and that I'd had to pay Worasit — a lawyer *they* had hired — myself.

Demanding answers soon, I told them: "Until now all your promises and all your words have been absolute rubbish.

Paul's response: "Wow Laura, this is not good at all, let me look at it with Patrick."

Patrick's response: "I'll look into it, I don't know what happened. And why are you paying the lawyers? It's already done."

You shits! Actions speak louder than words and it was time for some concrete progress, or else they would be the ones bearing the consequences.

ON 6 JANUARY, I contacted the Swiss Embassy to put in a request for William to be able to join me in visiting Xavier. I was reluctant at first for him to see how Xavier now lived, but they were as close as actual siblings and I was sure it would do Xavier some good to see him.

On arriving at the jail, I showed the official on duty a confirmation email from the Swiss Embassy, but he asked whether William's name was on the list of visitors approved by PetroSaudi. If it wasn't, he couldn't be admitted.

Putting on my best smile, I asked to see this list, insisting that Patrick and Paul must surely have put William's name down. A quick scan told me that my brother's name was indeed absent; however, I spotted another "Will," meaning Wilfried, on the list. Hiding the last name with my finger, I pointed to where it was written, and said: "Will, yes." The officer smiled and signed our admission paper. William and I glanced at each other and tried not to laugh.

After a two-hour wait, we were led through to the visiting room. Xavier seemed overjoyed to see William, and vice versa. We all cracked jokes and managed to cheer one another up. William told Xavier to be strong, and Xavier urged him to look after me. As William was about to return to Geneva, I said that if I also had to go back at any point, I would communicate with Xavier through his other regular visitors — Denis, Wilfried and Laurent. Discreetly, I also let him know that anything not meant for PetroSaudi's consumption would be put in one of the letters that Yanna would pass to Ivo.

As ever, the goodbyes were tearful and came too soon.

Back at the hotel, William suggested we go for a meal and a drink before he left for the airport, but unfortunately we couldn't get rid of Aziz buzzing around us. Aziz disgusted me with his aggressive questions, which had obviously been scripted by Patrick. His advice was to be nice to Patrick if I wanted his ongoing help in fighting for Xavier. I did my best to just seem sad, vulnerable and unthreatening.

When I returned the next day to Koh Samui, where thankfully my parents were waiting for me, Paul messaged me back about my checklist from the previous day: "OK Laura, I understand. I have given all the information to my police contact and he is looking into it. He will look into all the problems. I'll write to you as soon as I hear anything."

My reply: "I won't be as patient as I was in 2015."

He said he understood and that all he wanted was for everything to work out; he would look into things with Patrick and come and see me when I got back to Switzerland.

I had to go back to Geneva to tend to some administrative matters, including renewing my Thai visa. Fortunately, I was able to leave Xander with my parents on Koh Samui — but being thousands of miles away from both my son and his father tore me apart.

Whilst in Geneva, I met with Paul on 14 January at the Auberge de Chambesy in Grand-Saconnex, not far from my parents' home. Prior to our meeting I considered how I might surreptitiously record it, but in the end I felt too scared to do so in case I was discovered.

The atmosphere was tense. Paul asked me how I was doing and I told him not well, but better than Xavier. I was determined that he should know things wouldn't be the same as before — that I was now ready to fight if they didn't deliver on their promises, and fast.

He started telling me how sorry he was for the whole situation, and stressed that Patrick and Tarek were unable to control everything because they had so much to do. I replied that this was to be expected when you stole money and then tried to scapegoat someone who knew the truth.

He had nothing to say to that, so I changed tack: "When is Xavier going to get out? It's been six months now and things are worse than before for him. His royal pardon has apparently been blocked. His ranking, which you promised to have raised to 'excellent,' hasn't moved from 'good.' He can no longer exercise, because PetroSaudi blocked his access to the gym room. And he also doesn't have the close security that was originally so important to Tarek and Patrick. Any news on all of this?"

I had never been so wound up in all my life and it showed. Paul was quite speechless. I asked, sarcastically, how the two little princes, Patrick and Tarek, were doing. He said they were fine, but he knew that my tone wasn't one of concern.

When the waiter came to take our orders, I again channeled my fury. "I'd like some meat, rare; any recommendations?" Paul noticed the barb and looked uncomfortable.

The waiter left us and I asked him again, more calmly, for some answers. He took a deep breath and sighed. He seemed almost embarrassed, and stalled for a while before telling me: "As you know, I went to see Patrick and Tarek and we talked. The thing is that at the moment they can't do anything for you."

My anger burned. "Sorry? What?"

He continued: "What they told me was that you didn't want to release that recording. That could have helped a lot."

Me: "That's it? Their talk of getting Xavier out was never serious, was it? Everything Xavier went through and was forced to do for them… and now they won't release him? Are you sure?"

He became more confident: "Yes, that's how it is. That's what they told me. I'm sorry."

I burst out laughing, but my reply was serious. "'Sorry'? Really? Cut the shit! I know you're not sorry but happy to have Xavier locked up and I know you want him to stay in there as long as possible. But guess what? I'm outside, in case you forgot. If you think I'm going to drop it, you don't know me at all!"

He smiled at me coldly and spoke in a harsh and threatening tone. "If I were you, I'd be careful what you do. I would think carefully before I do anything."

By now I was shaking like a leaf, and my palms were sweating. With undisguised hatred, I asked him if he thought I was afraid of him. "Enlighten me," I said. "What exactly does 'I'd be careful what you do' mean? These are threats aren't they? What exactly do you plan to do if I expose you all?"

His calm was gone as he told me: "You know very well how it works. You know that accidents can happen. There are prisoners who get into fights and others who commit suicide, and that happens every day. And you: you're his wife; you know that you could easily be accused of complicity. And where would Xander end up if you were put in prison? In a Thai orphanage? Can you imagine?"

I had envisioned these things in my worst nightmares but hearing them verbalized shocked me to the core. MY BABY!!! NO!!! ANYTHING BUT THAT!!! What if the police came and took me away from Xander on some trumped-up charge? And Xavier: had I just put him in danger? I always knew these people had no limits, but finally here was confirmation of it. I couldn't get words to come out of my mouth.

Our food had been served but I hadn't touched any of it. The only thing on my mind was to run — to get as far away from this man as possible. I wanted to hold my baby. I wanted to know that Xavier was OK. I panicked, grabbed the waiter and asked him for the bill right away.

Paul was trying to talk to me but I signaled him to stop. I couldn't bear to hear anything more that he had to say. In a hurry, I paid for the meal. The waiter — who knew me — could tell something was wrong, but I had to just get away. I stood up, put my head down, walked out of the restaurant and hailed a taxi.

Paul was right behind me and placed himself in front of the cab. "Let's talk please? I'll talk to Patrick." Half-inside the vehicle, I stopped and turned.

"FUCK ALL OF YOU!" were the last words he would hear from me. I closed the door and the driver pulled out and away.

Some time later, I remember sitting on my parents' terrace. It was bitterly cold but I couldn't feel anything. Tears flowed on my cheeks, I could hardly draw breath and my body hurt all over like I was about to die. They had already taken my husband from me, but my baby? Xander? THAT CANNOT HAPPEN, EVER!!

After a while, I noticed that I was talking to myself. I had to come to my senses. Laura, think! What use was crying? I had to be stronger than ever, for Xavier and for Xander. I had to be ready to go to war. I had to be ready for even worse times ahead than I'd already experienced.

I put on my headphones, played some music and started to clear my head. Looking out over the Swiss winter landscape, it came over me that I now had the fight of my life ahead of me. There was no going back. For what they had done to Xavier, to my family, and to millions of Malaysians, they would pay. WE WOULD HAVE OUR REVENGE.

It is well understood that our life experience — our work, having children, even just growing older — changes us. Sometimes we don't notice it happening, or we can't think of when exactly we changed, or how long it took to happen. Even now, I still think of myself as the same person I have always been, but I also know that my husband being in prison changed me utterly. And the afternoon of 14 January changed me even more.

What Paul had said to me; what Patrick had said and done to me in Bangkok; what they had done to the man of my life, depriving my baby of his father; what they had tried to make me believe; the manipulations I had been prey to; the threats, the pressure: all of this transformed me. But in a sense it was all just preparation for what was now still to come.

I felt afraid, but not really in the way I did before. I now had nothing left to lose. This was it! By threatening me, they had played their last card and I wasn't going to cave in anymore. Now I was wholly determined to get my husband out of jail and expose what they had done to us, so that finally the whole world would realize who they really were.

Paul sent me a message later that day: "I am sorry I had to leave you on such unpleasant terms. I hope you understand that I had to tell you things, even if it wasn't what you wanted to hear!" I didn't bother to reply.

I spent the next few days sorting out my affairs in Geneva, worrying about Xavier in Bangkok and about Xander and my parents on Koh Samui. I didn't tell my mum and dad about what had happened because it would just have made them panic.

I FLEW OUT of Switzerland on January 18. During a stopover in Zurich, I called Alan, one of my best friends, and decided to tell him everything. I said I was terrified of being arrested back in Thailand, just like Xavier had been. I also told him my expected arrival time in Bangkok the next day. "If you don't hear from me by noon tomorrow" I said, "they've had me arrested at immigration for conspiracy. If you don't hear from me, please call my parents and tell them to leave Thailand with Xander immediately, OK?"

Alan promised to do what I had asked. He fumbled for some words that might reassure me but he didn't sound convinced of them. He realized only too well the dangers I faced and what Patrick and Tarek might be capable of.

At the departure gate, I suddenly felt gripped by a feeling that I was making a huge mistake. There I was, still with my leg in plaster, and being pushed in a wheelchair by an airport assistant. If the police were waiting to handcuff me in Bangkok, they wouldn't even have to chase me.

The assistant told me it was time to board and I wrestled with a desire to tell him I just couldn't do it, but the thought of Xander waiting for me in Koh Samui somehow kept me from opening my mouth. The assistant told me I looked pale. My head was spinning and I would probably have fainted if he hadn't brought me some water.

When I stopped seeing stars, the airline staff flocking around me seemed concerned. They were reluctant to let me on the plane, but I told them I would be fine and that it was just the pain from my foot that was bothering me. Finally, they agreed I could board.

Twenty minutes later, we were airborne — and I was rushing towards the unknown.

Chapter 18

Laura

MEETING THE FBI

LANDING IN BANGKOK the next day — a pale, nervous, unslept wreck — I felt almost numb with fear as I was escorted to immigration. I knew the airport corridors so well that I could count down the minutes until we reached passport control.

As the assistant pushing my wheelchair took my passport and handed it to the immigration officer, my hands were sweating and my heart beat so fast I felt like it was going to explode. The seconds seemed endless; I was sure there must be a problem.

Eventually, the officer looked up and handed my passport back to the assistant. As he pushed me through to the luggage carousel, I couldn't stop myself from bursting into tears. The relief was intense, but I realized I couldn't expose myself to this kind of danger again. Xander and I had to get ourselves out of Thailand. PetroSaudi may not have tipped the authorities off yet but Paul had been clear enough as to what they might do and I had seen with my own eyes how they had controlled things from the beginning. I would expose them in the press — but I needed to be in Geneva, where I could be safe.

I planned on visiting Xavier, staying one night in Bangkok, then heading to Koh Samui. I dropped my bags at my usual hotel — the one near the prison — and headed straight there, all the while wondering how I could break everything to Xavier. Would he be disappointed? Afraid? Angry?

I wasn't even sure I would be allowed to see him now given how things had gone with PetroSaudi. On arriving, I was able to get two signatures straight away but was told I needed a third and that there was no-one senior enough on duty to provide it. After a five-hour wait I submitted myself to the humiliation of begging the officers in charge to be allowed in regardless before visiting ended for the day. For once, they relented.

Of course, we were long accustomed to the idea of our conversations in the visiting room being recorded, but now we had to be extra vigilant. How could I communicate everything that I needed to say? As I sat waiting for Xavier to appear, I took a pen and paper from my bag and started to write down the whole scenario — all the stuff that it would be too dangerous to say out loud.

Our meeting was heart-rending. I was so happy to see him and the feeling between us as we placed our hands together through the glass and wire mesh was as intense as ever. But I had come to tell him the worst news and confirm his worst fears.

I held up a note to remind him that we had to be discreet. His anger flared but he nodded that he knew. I signaled to him to carry on our usual chit chat, then produced my next note: "Xavier, Paul threatened me, I have to leave. Tarek and Patrick sent him to tell us that there is no more deal, no more help, and that if I tried anything to help you, I would end up like you, and Xander in an orphanage. I am so sorry my love!"

Xavier stopped talking immediately. In his eyes I could see shock, rage, fear and a wild despair, a kind of nothingness. We both started to cry but I fixed him in the eye and told him he had to carry on fighting for us — and that I would do the same and never give up. I scribbled a note to say that we would be able to continue communicating through Ivo and Yanna.

I added that I would be back to see him in a week's time, and that before then I would do what I could to sell the resort and to transfer funds held in Xavier's Thai bank account out of the country. Before I left, he promised me he would do his best to stay strong. Outside, I felt equal parts fear and fatigue, and I made my way back to my hotel in a broken state. The emotions, the heat, the jetlag and the lack of sleep were all too much. In my room I called my mum and told Xander mummy would be back to see him the next day, then collapsed from exhaustion.

Seeing my baby the next morning revived me in so many ways. I spent the day glued to his side, showering him constantly with kisses and cuddles. I needed him. And again, I felt such gratitude to my parents for having looked after him.

I tried to tell them as much as I could, without saying that Paul had threatened me. I said it was now clear that Paul and Patrick couldn't help us and that it would be better if I sold the resort, went back to Geneva with Xander and worked to secure Xavier's release from there. My mum said she supported my decision as she could tell that my own safety and Xander's were not guaranteed in Thailand.

Over the next few days, I worked to load everything I could into boxes and suitcases. I asked Pon to help me hire some labor, and said that she and the others could keep or sell anything we couldn't ship. She was distraught to see me packing up, and cried with me at the thought of all our dreams being over.

At the same time, we had to keep it quiet that we were leaving. Apart from Pon, and Denis in Bangkok, I didn't want anyone in Thailand to know that we wouldn't be coming back, and I was frightened about the news spreading. Even with Pon and her family, I insisted I would come back to see them, but in my heart I knew there would be no way back.

I visited and called around several estate agents to try and get the resort sold quickly, but they all said the same thing: that the market hadn't been in a great state since the military's takeover in May 2014.

Every night as I put Xander to bed, I showed him Xavier's picture and promised him that his daddy would be with us again soon. Seeing my son bereft of his father day after day, I felt my rage rising — a rage for justice, for truth and for being able to speak out and expose the inhuman scandal we had been subjected to.

But my rage was now accompanied by a sense that I could do something about it. Following Denis' advice, I started to slowly piece together all the evidence I had gathered — the documents, the photos, the emails and WhatsApp messages, the recordings and the diary that I had been keeping over the past few months. And I began to summarize and map it all out in chronological order: all my movements; everything I'd been forced to do and everything they had forced Xavier to do; the role of Paul, supposedly a police officer from Scotland Yard, and his demands that I turn in the PetroSaudi hard drive; and much more. I took to spending all my nights working on this project.

I was also becoming increasingly jittery about our security. I slept with two of our dogs in my bedroom, and posted Veggie, our Rhodesian, outside Xander's room. I had our passports on me at all times, and kept a large iron bar next to my bed. This was how far PetroSaudi had managed to terrorize me — how far they had pushed me. I wondered if they were smart enough to realize what I was capable of after the trauma they had put me through.

On 5 February, I received a call from one of the prison staff I had become friendly with (this guy thought it was amazing that I could speak Thai). He discreetly told me that Paul had been at the prison and (after speaking to Xavier) had taken a lot of files away with him: the paper trail of official documents relating to his comings and goings. It seemed obvious to me that he would be trying to erase all traces of his own and PetroSaudi's part in Xavier's incarceration.

I had nothing to lose by demanding to know more about this visit, so I wrote Paul a message: "I am really surprised to hear that you came to Thailand to visit Xavier and didn't write to me. Could you please tell me why?"

I didn't receive a response until four days later. "Hi Laura, I tried to contact you before I traveled last week but with no response from you I thought you didn't want to talk to me anymore. If you ever want to talk to me about anything my door is always open and I hope everything works out for you and Xavier. Best regards, Paul."

In reply I wrote: "Tell me, what did Patrick really want by sending you there? You know very well that you never contacted me! So why is he sending you to the prison if they don't want to help anymore and don't care?

I added: "I have just sent you an email to your address, paulzh155@hotmail.com; I would like you to reply to this email please. This email concerns a request for the official receipt you promised to send me when you came to Geneva in July 2015, when you officially took Xavier's PC and hard drives from me for your investigation as a Scotland Yard agent."

Of course, as expected I never got an answer, far less an official receipt. I had figured out long before this point that Paul was a fake police officer; he was simply PetroSaudi's henchman, sent to Bangkok on the orders of Tarek and Patrick to do their dirty work and then clean up afterwards.

I realized that I was now in a race against time — it was essential that I contact the right people with the evidence that I had and that I do it soon.

I called Denis to tell him about Paul's visit and our exchange and he warned me I would have to be careful about my every move, and in my communications, from now on. We decided to set up an encrypted email account to communicate with one another, as well as for any official correspondence relating to the case and for keeping evidence safe in case anything happened to me.

My days were non-stop. Between taking care of Xander, packing everything up and traipsing back and forth to the post office, I wrote to Xavier to keep him updated about what I was doing and about my plans. I told him I was going to reach out to the Swiss ambassador in Bangkok and tell him everything, and that I would contact Clare again once I returned to Europe.

I also had a very interesting call from Worasit, who quietly told me that the FBI had tried to visit Xavier in prison but had been denied entry. Apparently they would be trying again soon. In the meantime, he gave me the name and number of an agent who had been in touch and wanted to talk to me. I couldn't believe it! The FBI! The plot was becoming more fantastical by the week, but one thing was clear: if American government agents had wanted to speak to Xavier, it was because they were interested in finding out the truth about 1MDB and PetroSaudi.

Worasit's call gave me hope. It also made me think that some day — when the trauma was behind us — I should write a book about it. Truly, this story had all the elements of an outlandish thriller novel: billions stolen from a country that badly needed the money by its own prime minister and a small band of crooks; drugs, decadence and gangster-like behavior; twisted lawyers; the scapegoating of an innocent man; and at the center of it all, me, a young mother who had led such a normal life, now alone with her child and living in fear.

Before returning to Bangkok, I bought a new phone and a new Thai SIM card, which I registered in my mother's name. Any conversations with the FBI, the Swiss Embassy, Clare or any other journalists would henceforth be carried out using this phone.

I also sent the Swiss ambassador an email asking for an appointment and stressing that it was about a matter of the utmost importance. He responded right away, scheduling a meeting for us on 10 February.

I flew to Bangkok on the evening of 8 February and went straight to the prison the next morning. As ever, seeing Xavier filled me with joy. As we only had 20 minutes, however, I had to make sure I covered everything I needed to communicate to him. Using our by now well-honed "system," I wrote down everything I could think of: about my efforts to sell the resort, and how it was proving difficult; everything to do with the move; the files I had been putting together; my appointment with the ambassador the next day; and the FBI contact Worasit had given me.

THAT AFTERNOON, DENIS and I ate lunch and talked about the way ahead. Even though I had a new phone, I felt that PetroSaudi might somehow be able to track my calls, so we decided I should call the FBI agent from a phone box.

The first hurdle was finding a phone box in working condition in 2016! After 40 minutes' spent riding around the city on Denis's Ducati Monster motorbike (luckily I had my cast off by this time), we found what we were looking for in a gloomy car park at an old shopping center.

As I dialed the number I'd been given, I suddenly felt nervous. Like most people, I had never spoken to anyone from the FBI before. Someone answered and said the agent in question was unfortunately unavailable. I was asked to leave a name and a number but I had resolved to be ultra-cautious so I said I would phone back.

Denis and I drove around some more, went for a coffee, then found another phone box. (I didn't want to use the same one as before as I was paranoid that someone might have already traced us there.) I called the number again. Agent still unavailable. Eventually, on the third attempt, I got to speak to him.

Right from the start, he was interested. He sounded calm and asked if we could meet. I explained that I was with a trusted friend who I would like to accompany me, and he said that would be fine. We arranged to meet the following afternoon at a Starbucks in the center of Bangkok, near the American Embassy.

Before that, I had my morning appointment with the Swiss ambassador. I had no idea how I might be received, and my nerves were shredded as I made my way to the embassy. The story I was there to tell was a difficult one — "please, you have to help me, because my husband is completely innocent and has been set up by a bunch of crooks working hand in hand with the Malaysian Prime Minister." I knew it sounded implausible, and I knew that Xavier had "confessed" and incriminated himself, exonerating PetroSaudi. Everything was stacked against him — unless I could start making people believe us.

On arriving I was taken to a large office at the back of the building. Two tall men stood up to greet me. One of them introduced himself as Mr Sieber, Ambassador, and told me his colleague was Mr Vavricka, Foreign Affairs Officer.

As we sat down, I could feel sweat on my hands and a knot in my stomach. I took a breath, told myself "OK, Laura, go!" and began recounting my crazy story. As I proceeded to spill the beans, I could see their eyes growing wider: I had succeeded, at the very least, in astonishing them.

Drawing my summary to a close, I told them: "I know how it sounds. You may think I'm crazy, but I promise you I'm telling the truth. If my husband was really guilty I would have left him by now and gone away, believe me. My husband is unjustly incarcerated here. You have to help us, please; I am telling the truth and I can prove it."

After a moment's silence, they told me they wanted to know more — that they would look into my claims and make a report. Something about their reaction suggested that perhaps my story was not entirely new to them. I told them I could give them all the evidence I had on file but that I also wanted it to be sent to the Attorney General of Switzerland.

This was the first time I had felt any kind of support or understanding from officialdom since Xavier's arrest, and I hadn't expected it. They confided that the official story around Xavier's prosecution seemed fraught with inconsistencies. They also told me they would start making inquiries after Xavier's well-being and safety — and agreed that as I felt unsafe in Thailand myself, it would be a good idea to leave the country.

I hadn't dreamt of being received in this way, so you can imagine how it lifted me. I suddenly felt an incredible sense of relief, and real hope.

I jumped in a taxi to the prison, eager to tell Xavier the good news. On arriving, however, I was told straight away that there was no-one there to sign my papers and that I wouldn't be able to see him. I begged them but they wouldn't give an inch. Lucky for me, my knowledge of Thai didn't extend to insults, otherwise I could have been spending the night in a cell myself.

I ordered food and essentials for Xavier for the next 10 days, put some money in his account, and left feeling frustrated. On the way out, however, I met Yanna, and to my delight she had letters from Xavier for me. I don't know what I would have done without this brave, wonderful woman. I told her to be careful as I knew that I was always being watched, and said I would send her a letter for Xavier soon, as I hadn't been able to see him.

Next, I hailed another taxi to go and meet Denis and we made our way to the Starbucks to wait nervously for Agent Walt from the FBI to arrive. When he appeared, he seemed very nice and understood that I wanted to be sure he was who he said he was. He showed me his official badge and said I could call the US Embassy to verify his name and number. I smiled — clearly this was no fake cop like Paul Finnigan.

He told me he had been denied access to Xavier in jail and that this was very unusual for an FBI officer anywhere in the world. In return, over the next hour, I told him about Paul, his fake identity as a Scotland Yard policeman, and how he'd convinced me to return the PetroSaudi hard drives because they wanted to erase all traces of the scam. I described how Tarek and Patrick at PetroSaudi had hired lawyers for Xavier and told them what to do and say, how they seemed to control prison officials, senior police officials and even judges in Thailand, and how they had orchestrated an international media campaign to discredit Xavier and cast doubt on the whole 1MDB scam. I also talked about how that scam had been set up.

He knew the case quite intimately and even though he couldn't tell me exactly what he knew, none of what I said surprised him. He confirmed that the FBI was conducting its own investigations and asked if I would be willing to help. I told him I had a large file of evidence that I could share with him. It was clear that he knew Xavier would be key to assembling some of the missing pieces in the case. Before he left, I gave him my new phone number and my new encrypted email address.

When he was gone, I looked at Denis in amazement. Neither of us could believe how the meeting had played out. Maybe there was a way out of this hell after all, and maybe it was the Americans who would help us.

I RETURNED TO Koh Samui the next morning, desperate to see Xander. I felt I had made progress in Bangkok but I couldn't stand the back and forth any more, and the strain of being separated from my baby.

Back on the island, however, it was just as hectic as before as I tried to finish everything to do with our move, deal with the bureaucracy of it all and finish collating all the evidence I had promised to send to the Swiss ambassador and Agent Walt. I wrote to Xavier in good spirits, telling him about how the meetings had gone. I explained that I had been refused admission to see him on 10 February but that I would come again as soon as possible.

I was still trying to keep it hush-hush that we planned to leave Koh Samui altogether, and the amazing support I had during this time from our circle of friends on the island made it doubly hard. Wilfried and Brenda, who had hosted our wedding, were always looking out for me, and Wilfried — as previously mentioned — tried to visit Xavier whenever he was in Bangkok. There were also Laurent and Billy, who called me regularly to check that I was alright, and my Thai friends, including Pon and Rot. They would often hug me and tell me that they had been to the temple to pray for me, and for Xavier.

I was also lucky enough to meet Peter, an English gentleman of about 70. He was a real estate agent and would do his utmost to help me sell the resort. I had told him a little about our predicament and he was touched and really wanted to help. He was a sweetheart.

Following my meeting with Agent Walt, we had regular contact. He wanted to know about Tarek's and Patrick's movements, and about certain transactions, investments and expenses. We also arranged for him and a colleague to pay me a visit on Koh Samui, on 22 February.

When they visited, we spent several hours talking and I answered their questions to the best of my knowledge. They also said they needed to get testimony from Xavier but that this didn't seem possible given that they couldn't visit him in prison. I told them I had a way of sending letters to Xavier directly, and that if they wanted I could ask him to put certain things in writing and collect his testimony via Yanna.

"If we can get a letter from Xavier, in his handwriting, detailing the whole financial scam, that would be extremely useful," said Agent Walt. I smiled. "It's as good as done. It will take me about a week." They were over the moon.

I had my dossier of evidence at the ready and talked them through it. They were amazed at the level of detail and the sheer amount of evidence I had gathered. In fact, they were so amazed they even asked me if I would be interested in working for them. I assumed they were joking and said maybe once I had gotten through this hell, but I beamed from ear to ear at their praise.

When they left in the middle of the afternoon, armed with my dossier, I felt happy, relieved, even proud of what I had set in motion. But I cautioned myself not to get my hopes up that everything would fall into place overnight — and in the meantime I had a mountain of other business to take care of.

There was no way I could go back to Switzerland yet, because there was just too much paperwork: paperwork relating to the sale of our property, paperwork for the bank, paperwork for the company we had set up to run the resort, paperwork for Xavier's case, for his royal pardon, for our insurance policies, and on and on. I would spend whole days fighting various corners of Thailand's bureaucracy over the smallest things. It was an administrative hell!

In addition, my runs back and forth to the post office and my constant efforts to make the place presentable continued. Each time a potential buyer was due to visit, we cleaned the whole resort; on several occasions, the interested parties didn't show up.

With everything I was juggling, I had lost more weight and really wasn't taking care of myself properly. Both physically and mentally, I felt I was in danger of burning out. I wanted to get back to Geneva as soon as I could, and from there contact Clare. The longer I stayed in Thailand, the more afraid I became for myself and Xander, and also for my mum who was still staying with us.

I kept Xavier informed as best I could in my letters for Yanna. I asked him to write a summary for the FBI — but to be extremely careful in doing so, as his every move would be under observation.

I tried to go up to Bangkok every 10 days, but with everything I had to do it was difficult to get away. I barely had time to look after Xander when I was at home, but leaving him was always a horrible wrench. My heart felt constantly torn between my two loves.

On 18 March, I went up and stayed with Denis, who — as ever — cheered me up and told me I had to carry on fighting. When I saw Xavier,

I tried to focus on the positives and told him either the FBI or the Swiss, or both, would surely help us.

He told me he had finished his summary, having written it on the toilet. When he scribbled this information on a piece of paper and held it against the window in the visiting room, I couldn't help but laugh. I loved the absurd comedy of it — and the fact that despite all our suffering, we could still see the funny side of things. That was worth its weight in gold.

I also gave him an update about the royal pardon — I had put the Swiss Embassy on the case, and they said they would chase it up with the Ministry of Justice. I was convinced that PetroSaudi had somehow blocked it.

When I received Xavier's account via Yanna, I notified the FBI and we arranged to meet at Bangkok airport on 1 April so that I could hand it over in person.

I flew up first thing in the morning of the day before and went straight to the prison. Waiting for my authorization papers to be signed by one of the prison chiefs, I noticed at the counter a register of people authorized to visit Xavier — and my eye fell on the name "PATRICK MAHONY." I secretly took my phone out and captured a photo of it. After all, what business had Patrick — or indeed anyone from PetroSaudi, the company responsible for laying charges against Xavier — in visiting him unless their case was a total sham?

By now my visiting-room routine was slick and organized. I wrote out my notes in advance, which saved us a lot of time. We had also intuitively developed a sort of code for talking about various things, and had nicknames for several people. It was pretty efficient, but also brought us somehow closer even though we were separated by a screen.

I showed Xavier pictures of Xander and told him about our son's progress, but it was often hard for him to listen. Things were looking up for us, and yet there was still so much pain. I told him again that I was fighting for us every day and that he needed to stay strong.

The FBI agent I met at the airport the next morning was a guy I hadn't met before. I gave him Xavier's letters, along with some new information I had received concerning PetroSaudi — namely that Patrick and Tarek were said to have been buying art and jewelry to try to hide their assets.

Having shared my evidence with the FBI, I was also now ready to hand it to the Swiss ambassador and I contacted him again to make an appointment. I flew up to Bangkok on the morning of 12 April and at the embassy was again led through to meet Mr Sieber and Mr Vavricka. I took out my encyclopedia-sized dossier, which I had titled "For justice to be done" and began explaining the evidence it contained of PetroSaudi's whole Machiavellian operation.

As I spoke, they again looked shocked — but they seemed ready to believe me. Why, I asked, had Tarek and Patrick done all of this to Xavier if not because they thought it would clear their own names? Why hire Paul to act as a fake detective? Why the media campaign? Why all the money spent on lawyers? What they had done to discredit Xavier and remove him from the equation was surely proof of their guilt in serious financial crimes that should be of paramount interest to the Swiss authorities.

After more than an hour, I had still only managed to skim the surface, so I left them with two printed copies and a USB stick containing everything in digital format. I also told them about my contact with the FBI, who wanted Xavier as a witness, and reiterated my request for them to send a copy of my evidence to the Swiss prosecutor. They said it would be sent right away by diplomatic air bag.

I was able to see Xavier afterwards and tell him about the meeting, which cheered him up. He was afraid for me, though, and urged me to go back to Geneva as soon as possible. I told him I would but that I had to try and sell the house first, because if he was going to be stuck in jail for more than two years we would need money by the time he got out. As my parents were both in Koh Samui, I stayed in Bangkok a few more days. That allowed me to see Worasit and ask him to try and find out why the royal pardon had been blocked. I was also able to see Xavier several days in a row.

Going back to Koh Samui felt like going home to a place where you don't feel at home anymore. There were no more photos, no more paintings, no more personal belongings. I had got rid of almost everything we had — everything apart from the hardest "belongings" of all to part with, our animals... our dogs, our cats and our parrots, including my darling macaw Blue that rolled around like a dog and danced whenever I put on music.

I begged Pon and Rot to take them all, and they accepted gladly. I knew she loved them. I said I would come and get them back some day, but I knew how unlikely that was. Separating from our animals was just one of many sad moments in my departure from this amazing island.

MY DAD LEFT for Geneva the following week — having been a huge help as I sold my 4x4, gave away some furniture to our Thai friends, and finalized my 38 boxes for shipping back to Switzerland — but my mum stayed on with me for another two weeks.

A couple of days before she was due to leave, I told her there was something I had to do that couldn't wait until I was back in Switzerland. I had to contact Clare again sooner than that — my heart told me it was the right thing to do, and my mum said I should follow my instincts. I just hoped Clare wouldn't be angry with me.

Sitting on my terrace, I nervously typed out a message from my new number: "Clare, I know it's been a while; I'm sorry but will I be able to call you? Laura." Please, I thought, just give me the chance to explain everything.

It didn't take long for her to reply: "Laura, what a surprise to hear from you. Yes of course, call me in an hour!"

A wave of relief washed over me, and I knew that if she heard what I had to say, she would understand. For the next hour, I sat alone on the terrace, looking at the sea and wondering how I had got to this point in my life as I counted the minutes.

When I called, she picked up right away.

"Clare..." I said. "I'm so sorry you haven't heard from me but I had no choice. These last few months have been like living in a movie."

She asked me to tell her everything, and over the next hour and more I explained to her what PetroSaudi had done to us and how I had been forced to cut her off. She said she had suspected Paul was a fake policeman from the beginning but that things had obviously been taken to a whole new level of deception. She'd known they were Machiavellian, but not to this extent!

She was truly shocked and said the truth ought to be exposed in the press. I said I agreed, but that first I needed to be back home safe in Geneva, with Xander. Then I would blow it all up. I said I would share all my evidence with her when I got back. To do anything rash from Thailand just felt too risky; I felt sure I was being spied on digitally and even followed when I was in Bangkok.

She said it was clear that I'd had no choice but to collaborate with PetroSaudi but that now I had stopped I was in just as much danger as Xavier. She advised me to get back to Geneva as soon as I could.

After our conversation, I felt so uplifted — and happy that I had decided to reach out. I still felt scared for my life, but for the first time in a long while I could feel a real positive energy. I felt a bit like a boxer minutes before getting in the ring — nervous, anxious, but ready to face any opponent.

I decided to go back to Bangkok quickly to tell Xavier about my talk with Clare. It couldn't wait until my mum was gone, because then I wouldn't be able to leave Xander with anyone. Taking him to Bangkok with me — and risking having to wait for hours at the prison with him just for a 20-minute visit — wouldn't have been fair on him.

Seeing Xavier kept my positive feelings ticking up. It was a thrill to be able to bring him good news in person, and as I held my little notes up for him to read, I could see his eyes light up. I told him I was building a little army to fight for him, and that when I got to Geneva everything would gather pace. I also said I would try to find him a new lawyer in Switzerland — a real one who would work to defend him and get him released. What a coincidence that I hadn't heard from the Swiss lawyers PetroSaudi were paying ever since Paul threatened me.

It felt good just to be able cheer Xavier up, even as we were gripped by the knowledge that we would very soon be apart.

As we talked, one of the other European detainees passed behind Xavier and they greeted one another. Xavier told me it was Artur and made a sawing motion in my direction. He'd mentioned this name before: this was the Spanish guy who was accused of murder and having cut up his victim's body. I felt shocked that Xavier spoke to this guy. I could easily understand that there must have been some connection between the prison's European population — after all, there were only a few of them out of 7,000 inmates. But still, it was another reminder of why I really had to get Xavier out of there as soon as possible.

Back on the island, I had the sorrowful experience of dropping my mum off at the airport the next day. She volunteered to stay, but I couldn't keep imposing on her. Back at the house — so empty now — I couldn't help but feel afraid and alone. I held my little angel in my arms that night and we fell asleep together.

The good news was that Peter had apparently found a buyer for the house. To expedite matters, I had to go to the bank and open a special account that would allow me to access the money legally overseas once the transaction was complete. Nothing was ever simple.

Just as our ducks seemed to be lining up, however, Worasit called to say that Xavier's prisoner ranking hadn't changed in the latest list of who was up and who was down. As things stood, that meant he wouldn't really stand to benefit if the King announced an amnesty for his birthday. And to top it all off, his royal pardon was still blocked.

I suddenly felt depressed again. I wondered if Xavier even knew about the rankings. After all, he didn't know much. He wasn't allowed to read the news or to know what was going on in the world, especially in relation to his case. He basically had no rights.

Worasit's news also made me doubly keen to get out of the country. I felt there was nothing more I could achieve by staying. I booked a flight to Switzerland for 12 May, 2016. All that remained was to finalize the sale of the resort and tell Xavier I wasn't leaving him in the lurch: instead, I was going home so that I could save him.

Chapter 19

Xavier

TORN APART

FROM APRIL 2016 onwards, a new rule was implemented in the prison: when we were locked in our cells each day at 3pm, we could no longer take food in with us; we were only allowed a bottle of water. The guards said this was for reasons of cleanliness, but it meant we had to go 15 hours at a time without food.

At times the temperature reached over 40°C in our overcrowded cell, and my water bottle was empty by 6pm at the latest. We were all starving with hunger and incredibly thirsty. This would be classified as torture in some countries — but in Thailand, it was explained on the grounds of hygiene.

I found this justification hard to believe; after all, the prison administration didn't provide inmates with soap, toothpaste or toothbrushes and I doubted if they really cared at all about how clean we were. I was certain that it was just another way of trying to grind us down and make us feel even more like animals. It really was inhumane, not least when you consider that there were old and sick people among us. How could it be reasonable that an 80-year-old man wasn't allowed to eat or drink for 15 hours? Some resorted to drinking water from the barrels used to empty the toilet waste.

For my part, I clung to the belief that the more these people hurt me, the stronger I got. During an argument with a guard one day, I told him they could starve me if they wanted, but that nothing they did to me could hurt me. Knowing that Laura was fighting for me, that my friends were there for her and that my son was OK made me feel indestructible. I also knew I would be out one day, while they would stay on in this miserable place. At the end of the day, a prison guard in Thailand is practically a prisoner for life — and a life filled with corruption and filth at that.

I spent my days reading and smoking, always in the little corner that my friend Gig paid someone just for us to be allowed to have some peace and quiet in. Four of us would sit there on the concrete floor in a space of about 20 square meters, but it had a wooden roof to shelter us from the sun and I felt at peace. At least we were away from the crowd. It was incredible how a little bit of silence and an uncrowded space could calm my spirit and reduce the stress of the situation.

I soon exhausted all the English books in the small library, as well as the handful of Italian and German books they had. These were my little moments of freedom, my way to escape from the hell I was living in. I felt so lucky to speak several languages, and promised myself I would teach my son to be multilingual too. Mastering languages is such a valuable tool in life.

I read about 180 books during my time in prison, including those Laura paid one of the guards to pass on to me, and the ones from Paul Finnigan. The guard who brought me books from Paul always told me they were from Scotland Yard. To the very end, in fact, the prison staff believed the fiction that Paul was an important British detective. No doubt seeing him ensconced in the warden's office helped to give an appearance of truth to his lie.

In terms of what I read, I devoured everything from spy novels, religious stories and historical biographies to books about quantum theory and even the way English girls dressed in the 17th Century. I also re-read *The Prophet* by Khalil Gibran, a book I had loved years before. Perhaps even more than before, I found so many beautiful truths in it. One passage that stayed with me was about resilience and personal acceptance. It ends: "To judge [yourself] by your failures is to cast blame upon the seasons for their inconstancy."

IN APRIL, a heatwave swept through Bangkok, the worst in decades. It was over 40°C in the shade — but shade was hard to find.

Most of the prisoners were sick and had skin infections from the heat and the grimy prison clothes. Luckily, I didn't develop any illnesses — perhaps my Ironman training had prepared me for it — but many prisoners were covered in pimples, sparking a rumor that there was an epidemic of chickenpox. It took a few days for that rumor to die down, but it caused a lot of consternation. The prison was a place where all kinds of rumors quickly swept around, many of them highly improbable.

It was a terrible time. We all sweated from morning to night, but were limited to one shower at the end of the day. Having been living in Thailand for a few years, I was used to hot weather, but this was something entirely different. You didn't sleep: it was simply impossible due to the heat and the mass of bodies. And as soon as you left the cell in the morning, your prison clothes became drenched in sweat — and stayed that way all day. The prison already stank permanently, but the added stench of sweat from hundreds of prisoners made it unbearable.

You have to stay strong, though. I couldn't give in.

To transport myself out of the place, I often imagined Laura's and Xander's days. I hoped they were still able to enjoy themselves and thought about what their daily life must be like, what their routines were. But I was always worried: I was afraid of them getting into trouble on my account, or having accidents. I felt so useless and powerless. I could no longer play the role of father and husband; in truth, I couldn't do anything for them. I constantly had feelings of guilt and shame. Because of my actions, the people I loved most in the world were suffering.

Visits from Laura and my friends (but especially Laura) were my only source of short bursts of happiness. I was happy in the days before these visits and on the day after, before often falling back into a deep depression. The utter loneliness I felt made it so difficult to stay positive. And as time passed, I could sense that Laura was becoming increasingly worried, and not just about my well-being.

As mentioned previously, Paul had threatened her with consequences if she tried to expose the truth and had said that Xander could be put in an orphanage if she was detained in Thailand. We had discussed her leaving the country several times, but it now felt like she had stayed too long.

We spoke about it again and she repeated that she didn't want to abandon me, to leave me alone in such an awful place. I was adamant, however, that I could survive in prison if I knew she was OK and that they were both safe. If they stayed in Thailand, I would never be able to overcome the stress of the situation and the fear that something might happen to them. I needed them to go back to Switzerland.

Of course, that meant I might not see them again for another two years — and the thought of it tore my heart out — but the only thing that was important to me was their safety. Nothing else mattered, nothing else.

The day we decided she had to leave, my heart was broken but I knew they needed to be safe. Patrick, Tarek and their corrupt associates in Malaysia would do anything to protect their money and their freedom. Criminals like that know only one value — that of money — and there were no limits to what they would do to ensure that they kept the spoils of their crimes. I knew it and Laura knew it too. I felt guilty enough already for her suffering; I just couldn't risk them hurting her more, or putting my son in harm's way.

Laura visited me for the last time on May 12, 2016, a day that will remain in my memory for life. I know, and have always known, that she is the love of my life. Throughout everything we have endured, she has been incredibly strong and determined, and has in turn given me the strength to carry on. I would not have survived the hell I was in without that strength. I was and am so lucky to have her in my life, and everything I have written in this book is a tribute to her strength, determination, and love.

I was nevertheless relieved and — almost — happy to see her go; she would be safe in Switzerland with her family, my family, and our friends. In the worst-case scenario, I would see her again in two years.

Two years. I could scarcely imagine two more long years of living in this misery. But I knew I could survive it; I had the strength to do so, because Laura and Xander were there for me, and they would wait for me.

From that moment on, I felt almost entirely alone. Denis came when his work allowed it, and Laurent and Wilfried from Koh Samui also came from time to time. The Thai VIPs had daily visits, whereas I had one every fortnight on average.

The main hope I clung to was that I would be included in the amnesty that was supposedly due in August that year. There were of course constant rumors about different amnesties, but nothing was ever certain. I just had to keep believing that something was possible, as the thought of finishing my sentence was too horrific. I observed some of my fellow inmates who had been given prison sentences of over ten years. Some retained hope of having a future on the outside, but others had no expectations left for their lives.

I had to meditate every morning to stay positive. One day gone was one day less to go, a week was one week less, and so on. But the more time passed, the more I began to forget what freedom felt like.

Chapter 20

Laura

PAINFUL PARTING

AFTER MY CALL with Clare at the end of April, I kept her informed about what was going on. She was worried about my safety and regularly checked in with me. She urged me to leave Thailand without delay, as did Alan and Denis. I told them things were in motion.

In the meantime, I continued to learn via contacts in Geneva about some of PetroSaudi's fraudulent investments and reported on these to the FBI. I frequently asked "the Feds" whether there was anything they could do for Xavier and informed them that I would be returning permanently to Geneva, from where I would be working as best I could to get my husband out of prison.

On 1 May , I received this reply from Agent Walt:

"I am sorry to hear your situation has gotten worse. Our efforts to speak with your husband are moving along and I suspect we will be able to do so soon. I will see if there is anything we can find out regarding his status in prison and his pending royal pardon. The NY agents intended to meet with you when they traveled here. Since it is most likely they will be here after your departure date, they may try to make alternate arrangements with you.

"Please call or text if you need anything and stay in touch. Thank you for all your assistance. I wish you and your son safe travels and truly hope your family is reunited very soon."

I prayed for them to be able to do something for Xavier, but I also wondered where our own country stood in all of this. I had confirmation that my dossier had been given to the Swiss prosecutor, but I really had no idea how long it would take for them to finally decide to help their fellow citizen and put the real criminals behind bars.

I now only had 12 days left in Thailand, and 11 in Koh Samui. I prayed for Xavier, for nothing to happen to us, for the completion of the sale of the house, for a miracle, for anything remotely positive to happen!

As I sat on my terrace after putting my son to bed, I watched the sunset and thought about the wonderful memories we had made here with our family and friends. I thought about the projects we had completed and the plans we'd had for the future; about the resort, the wedding, and the birth of our amazing son. It was so difficult to think about those times. We had been so happy, and yet suddenly our lives had been transformed into a perpetual nightmare.

I cried; I had never felt so alone. No one could feel what I felt: the frustration, the loneliness, the constant distress and anxiety, the hatred for the injustice of the situation, the anger that burned in me. In all honesty, I was really struggling to cope.

I called my mum; it was the middle of the night for her, but she picked up the phone. She asked if I was OK but I couldn't utter a word. I just burst into tears. She panicked, and pleaded with me to know what was wrong. "Mum, I can't take it anymore," I sobbed. "I'm so sorry to wake you up like this but I can't take it anymore, I can't take it anymore." I cried my eyes out. I was finally collapsing under the pressure of it all; I could no longer bear the emotional turmoil of my situation.

My mum calmed me down, reassuring me that I would be OK. She cried too, and I felt so guilty for putting my parents through all this stress.

After talking for a while, I told her that I would be alright, and that I was sorry for having woken them up.

"Laura," she replied, "call me tomorrow morning. I'll get a ticket and come and join you." I protested. I didn't want her to come back; it was dangerous enough just me being there alone. At the same time, however, I was afraid that I might have problems with immigration when I tried to leave the country. After Paul's threats, PetroSaudi could well have put Thailand's Immigration Office and the police on alert. Maybe I would need someone there to support me.

My mum insisted, and I finally accepted — in fact, I was so relieved to know she was coming. If I had a problem at the Immigration Office and they arrested me, my mum would at least be able to take Xander and return to Geneva with him. I could never let anything happen to my son. Forty-eight hours later, my mum was in Koh Samui, and I was so happy that she was back.

The final week was unbearable. I spent it packing the last few things in the house. My heart was torn between the desire to flee and the wish to never leave this place of our dreams. I didn't want to leave, but in truth I had absolutely nothing left in Koh Samui by this point except memories.

On 10 May, Pon and her family came to say goodbye, and to take our three dogs and our parrot. I knew I was leaving the animals in good hands and I tried to be strong, but we all cried. Pon held me in her arms and said they were all praying for us. She is an incredible woman. I had a huge lump in my throat as we said our final goodbyes and they drove off — my animals that I had loved and my friends that I might never see again — into the distance.

That evening, I put Xander to bed early. Once he was asleep, my mother and I admired the view one last time, gazing out from the magnificent terrace overlooking the sea. Neither of us spoke, but she knew I was in pain. She took me in her arms and comforted me.

In bed later that evening, I couldn't get to sleep. I went back out onto the terrace and stayed there half the night, thinking again about all our memories. Staring out to the sea, I tried to etch the view into my mind so that I would remember it forever. I went through all the decisions I had made in my life, asking myself where I would be if I had done things differently. I pondered every possible question imaginable, and it was approaching morning when I finally slept. When I reawakened, a page would be turned forever. A one-way ticket to an unknown future, with no way of returning to my previous life.

At 6am, our taxi to the airport arrived. On the terrace, I took one last look at our home, breathed in deeply, and felt an immense sorrow. I pictured Xavier proposing to me, coming back from the hospital with Xander, the happy times we'd spent with our friends and family. My heart was in pieces, but it was time to close the door and go on our way. As we drove off, we saw the sun rise over the sea, and the island come to life. My mother held my hand as we cried silently in the back of the taxi.

We boarded the 7:45am flight for Bangkok, and as we took off I knew it would be the last time I would leave this enchanted place. The next part of my exit from Thailand would be even harder, though. I still didn't know if I could actually bring myself to leave Xavier behind.

WHEN WE ARRIVED in Bangkok and were settled in our hotel, I left my mother and Xander to go and see my husband. It had been three weeks since my last visit, and when we met in the visiting room, we tried not to think about what was to come the next day — our farewell. The thought of not knowing when I would see Xavier again after that was agonizing.

I had written at least ten pages in my notebook explaining everything that I had done and would do. This included extensive reports about my communication with the FBI, with the Swiss Embassy, with Worasit, with

Clare, and about our plans for press coverage. I wrote about the potential buyers I had for the house (the buyer we thought we'd secured had already pulled out), and what I was doing to pursue the application for a royal pardon. I told him everything at once so that we could make the most of our last visit when it came.

In the evening, Denis came for dinner at the hotel and to say a last goodbye. In 24 hours, we would be on a plane back to Geneva. Denis promised to go and see Xavier at least once or twice a week, saying he would co-ordinate with Laurent and Wilfried from Koh Samui and make sure there was someone to visit him every few days.

I was so anxious the night before our departure that once more I hardly slept at all. After breakfast, I went to buy some books for Xavier and then headed straight for the prison. In the waiting area, I met Yanna — and true to form she had a letter from Xavier for me. He had given strict instructions that I should only open it on the plane. "I'm always here if you need anything," she told me.

Yanna said she would continue to pass on my letters and take Xavier's out with her. I left her some money, because the guards sometimes still had to be bribed for the letters to get through. She knew I was leaving that night and wished me good luck for the future. I would never forget what she had done for us; she had been a vital lifeline for Xavier and I to maintain communication, and now she was about to be our only lifeline.

Finally, it was time for our last visit. As we sat down behind the miserable screens that separated our worlds and picked up our phone receivers, we both started crying uncontrollably. More so than ever, we had to speak in code — which was frustrating, but at least it gave us something to laugh about. Xavier assured me I was doing the right thing by leaving, and said he would only be able to relax once he knew I was safely back in Geneva.

He told me he was proud of me and I replied that I admired him more than anyone in the world. I kept repeating that he had to stay strong and fight for us, and that I would never give up. The time passed so quickly, and before I knew it the final bell rang and we were told we had to go.

I knew that at the very worst I would see him in two years, but right then it felt like I would never see him again. The pain was physical and overwhelming and we were both so distraught that we couldn't be separated: we hung up our phones but our hands were glued to the window and the guards had to come and pull us both away. I left the visiting room shouting, between sobs: "I love you! It's going to be OK! Stay strong for us my love!" I held him in my sights until he was escorted from the room.

Outside, I sat and cried my eyes out. This was the most difficult moment of my life, and I felt like I was going to explode. I wanted to scream, to die, anything to stop this suffering.

It took me a while to come to my senses. The good thing about hitting rock bottom, of course, is that you can only go up, and that's exactly where I needed to go. Our enemies had made me and my family suffer horrendously and now I was going to be separated completely from my husband — but it made me all the more determined to make them pay for everything they had done.

I jumped on a scooter taxi and headed back to the hotel, where my mum and my little man were waiting for me.

We just had time to eat and finish packing before leaving for the airport. If I had any problems at the Immigration Office and got arrested, my mum was to take Xander back to Geneva. I had given her power of attorney to travel with Xander and wrote down phone numbers for Clare, Denis and Alan so that she could let them know in the event that I was stopped.

AFTER CHECKING IN my seven suitcases, we got in the queue for immigration. My hands were sweaty and I was shaking. It felt like I was carrying something illegal. I thought about Paul's and Patrick's threats, praying that they hadn't yet paid the police or immigration to have me intercepted.

I was so scared. I held Xander tightly in my arms. I knew I couldn't cry or it would draw attention. Finally, I was at the front of the queue; it was my turn.

I handed over our passports with a smile on my face, but there was a pause and I was sure there must be a problem. I felt like just running away with Xander. My mum had already passed through, and everyone else seemed to be just walking through without fuss — but not Xander and I. The officer looked at us and asked me to wait a moment, then disappeared into a back room. I thought I was going to just die. What was he doing? Had he gone to find a set of handcuffs? I could see my mum looking at me from beyond the barriers. She had tears in her eyes; she was terrified.

After what seemed like forever, the officer returned and with a big smile handed me back our passports — along with some candy for Xander! I was so relieved and so grateful that I thanked him profusely, almost shouting, in Thai. As I walked through, my mum and I both burst into tears of laughter. I was so elated, I felt like I was growing wings. But still, I told myself I couldn't completely relax until I was on the plane and it had taken off.

As soon as we boarded, Xander fell asleep in my arms. We were ready to go. As the plane began to move, I thought of Xavier and swore to myself that I would get him out of that hell. The plane taxied, the wheels were in the air, and then we were flying. I burst into tears. My mum, next to me, took my hand. She smiled at me, crying too, and told me everything was going to be OK. "You did it!" she exclaimed. I looked at her and smiled. "Yes, we did it!" I felt an incredible surge of relief. I knew my baby was safe, and I could finally get the truth out and help Xavier, even though my heart ached from having to leave him.

With Xander snuggled up next to me, I opened Xavier's letter. His words were so beautiful that I couldn't stop crying — tears of joy, relief, pain and sorrow all at once. I re-read it multiple times and prayed I would be up to the task of saving him.

Chapter 21

Xavier

SWISS SUPPORT

JUNE 2016 came around. I had been surviving in this smelly and dangerous nether world for almost a year — a year of living like an animal in a cage, without purpose, without hygiene, without anything or anyone to turn to.

As the weeks went by I could do nothing but hope for news of an amnesty, or some other miracle. But I knew by now not to expect anything. I'd had so many cruel disappointments that I was afraid to hope.

June was also when I injured my leg by tripping over an iron fence. It didn't hurt at first, but after a couple of days my wound became infected. I told the warden and he took me to get treated. It didn't look too pretty.

At the "infirmary" — which seemed more like an abandoned veterinary practice than a place for treating humans — the guard told us the duty doctor wasn't around but that he would be back the next day. He said I would have to spend the night as an in-patient and showed me to a room filled with tuberculosis patients.

I protested, saying I would rather get some antibiotics and go back to my cell. He said he wouldn't give me any unless I had money to pay him. I insulted him with words he wouldn't understand and went back to the prison.

Two days later, my leg was so swollen that I could hardly walk. Luckily another VIP prisoner, Somyot, managed to find me some antibiotics from somewhere. (Somyot was a middle-aged gentleman who had served five years of a 12-year sentence for lèse-majesté — he had been an editor and had merely published an article in his newspaper that criticized a king whose reign had ended more than a century ago. This is no joke: in Thailand anything critical of the monarchy is utterly forbidden.)

My leg healed in a few days, leaving me with a scar from the incident. I often look at it now and it brings me back to thinking about my whole prison experience.

Around this time I also had a surprise visit from my sister, Rocio, who flew out from Switzerland. She was generously escorted by Wilfried Schnider, the Swiss consul, who helped her with the necessary paperwork.

Another welcome development occurred at the end of June, when the new prisoner rankings were published: I was now considered "very good." If I kept my head down, maybe I'd make it to "excellent" in a few months.

July brought the start of the rainy season, which is usually keenly anticipated in Thailand because it tends to cool things down. But the prison wasn't a great place to be for it — in fact, in 2016, the monsoons were so torrential that the whole place effectively flooded. We walked around up to our ankles in water and the toilets backed up, spewing sewage everywhere. I had thought the smell of prisoners' sweat was bad enough; this was even more unbearable. Everything was sodden, even the floors where we slept. Apparently there was an evacuation plan but the water had to reach a certain height before it would be considered necessary to enact it. It took days for the water to drain.

Laura told me in her letters that she had been in contact with the Swiss Embassy to apply to have me transferred to Switzerland under an agreement that allows prisoners to finish their incarceration in their home country after having served some of their sentence in Thailand. According to what Laura told me, wherever I was sent to in Switzerland wouldn't be a real prison. I didn't really care — I was sure that anything would be better than what I'd experienced in Thailand. What could possibly be worse?

Mr Vavricka from the embassy visited me to sort out the paperwork. He told me that the Thai Department of Prisons had already given its agreement and that he expected the move to be confirmed quickly — maybe in a few weeks! He even showed me an article from the *Bangkok Post* in which a Thai government minister talked about my case and said I could be released as soon as September thanks to "political will from all sides." I felt almost delirious with joy — I could suddenly imagine myself saying goodbye to my fellow inmates and getting on a plane!

Some time in August, the director of the prison — during an inspection of the building where I once again refused to sit where they wanted me to — surprised me by giving me some advice concerning the transfer application. He told me to make sure all my documents were in order, and to ask the Swiss Embassy to double-check everything so that there would be no hold-ups. He seemed to be sincere; I think he knew that I didn't belong in this place, and even if he was being paid by PetroSaudi, perhaps he still had a functioning conscience.

The same month, the King also finally announced an amnesty. To mark the 70th year of his reign, he decided to show mercy to the nation's prisoners, according to their crimes and their rankings.

In my case, my sentence was reduced by one year. This meant that in a worst case scenario, I would escape this rat-trap in 10 more months. It was still a lot but at least I could see light at the end of the tunnel, albeit I was quite convinced I would be leaving Bangkok in a mere matter of weeks once my transfer was approved.

In fact, leaving for Switzerland was all I could think about. Mr Vavricka visited regularly, bringing news about my family and updates on the transfer. His confidence that it would happen — and just knowing that I had the support of my country — had a huge influence on my morale.

They knew what was going on and that I was a victim, and they weren't prepared to give up on me. That brought me much-needed comfort.

These feelings were compounded by the fact that I knew my countrymen often had to wait hours to see me; in fact, sometimes they would wait all day, only to be refused access. As with all my other visits, theirs had to be approved by the prison director himself. As mentioned previously, out of a prison population of some 7,000 inmates, to my knowledge only I got this treatment. But this didn't faze or discourage Vavricka or his colleagues.

My lawyer, Worasit — whom Laura was still paying to take care of Thai paperwork for us — also made an occasional visit. Echoing my Swiss visitors' confidence, he told me I would get to leave in September, probably on September 12. He said he had heard from the Department of Prisons that the whole procedure had been rubber-stamped.

Following that "confirmation," I was in a daze. I was completely convinced my departure was imminent and I even started saying goodbyes to some of my fellow inmates.

WHEN 12 SEPTEMBER came around, I'd had no visits, no letters, no news for more than a week. Yanna was on a trip somewhere, while Denis was also away and Worasit was busy with other clients. All I'd had to cling to was the hope that I was about to escape this hell. But then, nothing. I was stressed and anxious; I asked the officers in my building for news, but of course nobody knew anything.

The day ended, and still there had been no news. I spent the night wide awake — I couldn't work out what but I knew something must have gone wrong.

Worasit came to see me the next morning and broke it to me that the application had been refused. He didn't know the reason. I told him he must be wrong but he said he had called the Department of Prisons and confirmed that it was a definite "no."

I felt like I had been shot. When I returned to my cell, I went into a rage and insulted all of the guards. It was some time before I cooled off.

The next day, Vavricka came to see me. He explained that Najib Razak had been on an official visit to Bangkok the week before and said his hope was that the Thais had simply postponed my transfer so as not to embarrass the Malaysian Prime Minister. He reassured me that Switzerland would not give up on the application and told me to hang on.

I returned to my cell torn between rage and despair. All I could think about was Laura and Xander. Would I really have to wait another nine months to see them? Once again I'd been a passenger on the train of dashed hopes. I wasn't sure that I could ever get back on it.

A few days later, Vavricka came to see me again and confirmed what I had thought must be true — that my transfer had been canceled, despite initially being approved. Meetings had apparently taken place in New York, however, between Didier Burkhalter, the Swiss Foreign Minister, and his Thai counterpart, Thanasak Patimaprakorn, in which guarantees had been obtained that I would not be extradited to Malaysia, where my life would truly be in danger.

Vavricka at least managed to cheer me up, as he reiterated that Switzerland would not abandon me. Speaking to him made me well up with emotion, but it also bolstered my resolve. I felt that whatever the Thais or the Malaysians tried to do to me, nothing could touch me, and I would eventually leave this place and be reunited with my wife and son.

My friends in the prison tried to comfort me by proposing that we celebrate my birthday. They ordered a birthday cake from the prison kitchen; however, when the day arrived it was discovered that some of the cooks had contracted tuberculosis, and we thought better of eating anything from that source. Instead, we ate fruit in our cell and they sang Happy Birthday to me.

Not for the first time, despite my pain I was touched by their kindness. But still — I prayed that this would be my last birthday behind bars.

I continued to do sums in my head, hoping to come up with some magic formula that would make the time I had left seem shorter. Dividing it into weeks, I came up with a figure of 36.

Thirty-six weeks until my slated release. Another 36 weeks in hell. Or perhaps 36 weeks until paradise. Perhaps.

Chapter 22

Laura

RELEASED FROM SILENCE

MY RETURN TO Geneva on 13 May was the beginning of a marathon, but first I needed to buy a little car for myself — a second-hand Audi TTRS.

Cars and driving had always been my passion, and while a sports car was at the upper limits of what I could afford, I felt I couldn't afford not to have that small pleasure in my life.

Apart from that, I was entirely discreet about what I did and said. Geneva is a village, so until I was able to get everything out in the press, I wanted people to think I was just on holiday — especially Aziz, who of course was tasked by Tarek and Patrick with monitoring me.

Clare came to Geneva on 20 May to look at my cache of evidence. We met at a hotel by the airport and seemed to pick up where we'd left off a year earlier. I told her about all the files I had and she was hugely impressed with what I had accumulated — but I held back my best exhibit until last. I kept her in suspense, then pressed play on my phone. It was a clip from one of my conversations with Patrick: the first one I had recorded, back in November of 2015.

She was gobsmacked, but I had to press pause and make sure she paid attention to exactly what I wanted her to hear, which was Patrick saying: "We're all in the shit! You've got the Prime Minister of a country that is in big shit because of this too!"

Clare looked almost jubilant. "Incredible, isn't it?" I said. "Enormous!" she replied. "This is huge." Overall, she was stunned both by the volume of material I had and its significance.

I gave her copies of most of it. Meanwhile, she showed me Xavier's "confession" in full. I had read what had been published in the press but seeing the whole thing — everything they had forced him to say — filled me with disgust and made me cry with rage. Seeing my reaction, I think Clare fully understood the hell I had been living through, as a woman and as a mother.

She offered to arrange for a camera set-up and help me record some of my testimony. Once we were ready, we would also organize a press conference and put everything on public record.

At the end of May, I got in touch with Gilles Crettol, the lawyer Xavier had asked me to meet some months earlier about closing down his old company. I'd had a good feeling when I spoke to him then — I sensed he was a good person who could probably help us. Now I scheduled another meeting at his offices near the Rue du Rhône. I was ready to show him everything and find out if he could represent us.

I arrived for the appointment armed with my dossier of evidence, along with a USB stick containing digital files (including audio files from my phone), and began by saying that even though I probably sounded insane everything I was about to tell him was 100 percent truthful. By this time, I had given my presentation several times — to the Swiss ambassador, to the FBI, to Clare — and I had it *down*, as they say. At any rate, he understood right away what the evidence showed about the whole PetroSaudi-1MDB fraud and about the conspiracy to make Xavier look like a criminal so that the real crooks could clear their names.

Like the others I had told, he was shocked at what I had uncovered. "Xavier's Swiss lawyers are actually paid and chosen by the plaintiff?" he asked. He was appalled. "Unbelievable! This is contrary to the entire ethics of the law."

"If only that were all," I replied. I showed him email messages from Henzelin: they were always copied to Patrick Mahony, and very often to PetroSaudi's lawyer, Tim Buckland, too. What was clear from the chain of correspondence was that Patrick had orchestrated everything. He had not only paid but briefed lawyers supposedly working on Xavier's behalf in Switzerland, Thailand and Singapore.

Gilles quickly understood that we were dealing with a gang of diabolical shysters, and advised me to go to a public notary and have all the evidence I had collected authenticated and certified. Doing so would make it admissible when it came to making formal complaints.

He also said that while he would like to help me, he thought I should engage the services of a friend and colleague of his who had better political connections. He said he would meet this friend for coffee and discuss my case with him. I thanked him effusively for his humanity and empathy. I felt that he understood my plight and what needed to be done.

I wasted no time in following Gilles' advice by visiting a notary located near the public library, in Geneva's Old Town, who was able to authenticate the hundreds of pages of evidence I gave him. (For the audio files, he certified that they had come from my phone and had not been tampered with, and then transcribed each of the conversations.)

Meanwhile, Clare confirmed that she had found a film crew to interview me. A few days later I picked her up at the airport and we drove to Lausanne to do the filming at her brother's house.

I hate being filmed or even having my photo taken, so I was nervous about the interview, but Clare reassured me and before I knew it the cameras were rolling. Little by little, I forgot they were there and began to answer the questions with confidence and ease — all except for the ones that brought to mind painful thoughts and memories. More than once, I was moved to tears. We spent the whole afternoon and well into the evening filming.

Around this time, I was also contacted by FEDPOL, Switzerland's federal police, and at their request I sent them my evidence.

I spent my days on the phone, writing letters to Xavier, and dealing with our ongoing efforts to sell the house on Koh Samui. Most mornings, I woke at 4am so that I could reach people at the start of the business day in Thailand, but I was always late to bed in the evenings too, as I still had things to do.

On June 3, I flew to London for a meeting with the FBI and another agent who had contacted me from the UK's National Crime Agency. Clare was waiting for me at London City Airport and wanted to come with me, but I had been asked to go alone. She and I went to Berkeley Square, where Xavier and I had lived before this whole nightmare began, and where PetroSaudi still had its office around the corner on Curzon Street. So many memories came flooding back from our time in London.

Clare said it would be a good chance to take some photographs of me to accompany the content she planned to publish, so we went for coffee at the Connaught Hotel, where Xavier had met Patrick for the last time before we left the UK. I felt that would be a fitting two-fingered salute to him if and when he saw the published article.

My meeting with the FBI was a stone's throw away inside the American Embassy, on Grosvenor Square. Special Agent Joe from New York, with whom I had lately been in contact, met me at the entrance with a colleague, then took me up several floors in the lift. The door opened on a large corridor, along which I was led to a big empty office with a huge conference table. I felt very much like I was in an American action thriller movie.

The NCA agent entered and we were introduced. Everyone seemed very friendly. We spoke about the PetroSaudi-1MDB partnership and I told them what I knew, much of it from what Xavier had told me, about the absurd inconsistencies of how the deal was set up. PetroSaudi had been valued at more than $3 billion. What a joke! It never had any assets.

I also told them about Paul and his fake identity as a Scotland Yard agent. I warned them that Paul and Patrick were trying to remove any trace of what they had done to Xavier in Thailand, and explained that they had already destroyed PetroSaudi's servers, as well as trying to recover all the data Xavier had copied. With the help of Xavier's "confession," I said, they had been able to isolate Clare and undermine her credibility — as Patrick had boasted in one of the conversations I had recorded. Their only motivation had been to clear their own names in the press. (Patrick: "The courts, prosecutors, etcetera… they all base their decisions on what they read in the press.")

I asked them the same questions as I had asked the ambassador: Why would PetroSaudi go to all this trouble to get Xavier's records back? Why did they hire and pay all those lawyers? Why did they go to so much trouble running a press campaign and getting Xavier to say what they wanted him to? Why would they do all this if they weren't guilty of running the scam of the century and stealing large amounts of money? It was as obvious as two plus two and they knew it perfectly well.

For my final flourish, I explained to them about the USB stick I had "forgotten" to give back to Paul. They were very interested and I agreed to send them copies of it.

I asked if they would be able to do anything for Xavier. They said that Southeast Asia was not their jurisdiction nor Xavier an American or British citizen, but that they would do what they could to help us.

I said that I felt the only way for me to benefit Xavier would be to get everything out in the press — to which they responded that they would rather I waited. They said they were conducting their own investigations and that not all of the evidence should come out in public yet. I told them I understood their position but that if there was no guarantee of them being able to help, I had to do what I thought was right to fight for my husband's life. I said I would be willing to wait another month or so, by which point I hoped to be ready to hold a press conference — but no more.

I left after several hours of discussion with the three agents. Clare was waiting for me, along with Randeep Ramesh — a lovely journalist from *The Guardian* newspaper who was very interested in writing a long article on PetroSaudi-1MDB and my story.

He was familiar with aspects of the case but when I sketched out the full extent of what had been done and how they had tried to silence Xavier, like most people who listened he was astounded. When I played him a clip of Patrick yelling about "the Prime Minister of a country" being in "deep shit," he understood there was so much to this outrageous story that had not been exposed. He agreed to write about it after I made my splash with the press conference.

After a final cup of coffee with Clare, she kindly drove me to the airport. I landed back in Geneva at 10pm. Xander was already asleep when I got home and I collapsed from exhaustion next to him, thinking about how much I had to tell Xavier from such an eventful day.

The next day brought more welcome developments. Gilles called to say that the lawyer he had recommended, Christian Luscher, wanted to meet me and would help me. He told me to request Xavier's file from Henzelin at Lalive in writing, and sent me the exact wording to use.

It was a simple request, but it was only after more than a week and a storm of email exchanges that I finally managed to obtain the file, which I promptly transferred to Mr Luscher.

From our first meeting, I could see that he was a man of integrity and humanity. As I explained my situation and told our story from the beginning, he was extremely attentive and compassionate. When I had finished, he told me he would do everything he could to help me and that he wanted to go and visit Xavier in person as soon as possible.

His sense of injustice and his enthusiasm for Xavier's case filled me with hope. We agreed to plan a trip to Bangkok for him and also to keep Gilles informed of next steps and developments.

It was July 16: my birthday. Things were starting to look up but I wasn't much in the mood to celebrate, what with Xavier being all alone and still in danger. My friends had other ideas, however. They organized an outing to the lake — and yet again I felt so lucky to have them looking out for me.

My parents and brother also took Xander and I out to a restaurant and we enjoyed a wonderful evening together. They told me they were proud of me, and did everything they could to cheer me up. I felt immensely grateful for everything they did and had done for me.

INEVITABLY, PETROSAUDI had their little spy out trying to glean any information he could. I had frequent messages from Aziz pretending to be there for me as a friend, and finally I agreed to meet him for a drink at a bar near his place. Of course, I knew Patrick and Tarek were pulling his strings, but the thought of playing them for fools gave me some pleasure.

"What are you going to do now that they don't want to help you anymore?" he asked me. "You're not going to talk to Clare or the press, are you?"

I told him: "I don't know what to do. I'm on holiday to take my mind off things. I'm getting tired of it and I'm wondering if I shouldn't think about starting my life again."

Aziz: "You should go to Patrick and offer him a deal to help you. Maybe he can help Xavier if you do something for him."

I replied that I didn't see the point, because I had nothing more to say to them. I added that the conditions of Xavier's detention had worsened, all because of them. He played dumb but I knew he knew.

Me: "If Patrick wants to see me he can ask me but I don't need him or anyone else."

Immediately, he got his phone out, called Patrick's number and disappeared from the table for 15 minutes. Why was it so urgent? Did they know something? When he came back, he told me Patrick would be in Geneva in a few days' time and wanted to see me.

I already felt scared and paranoid. I constantly felt like I was being followed and when I made important calls I did so from my parents' phone. I knew better than anyone else what Patrick and Tarek were capable of, and yet I felt that he might be stupid enough to further compromise himself. As I was in constant contact with the FBI, I kept them informed of everything new that I learned about PetroSaudi. They were very interested in this proposed meeting.

Aziz arranged for me to meet Patrick at the President Wilson Hotel, his "home" in Geneva. He told me that Patrick only wanted to find a solution for everyone. What did this mean? What else did they want or need from us? I felt nervous and wound up. I knew I would have to resist the urge to punch Patrick in the face. I had to calm down. Again, fear of being discovered overcame my urge to secretly record our conversation.

As we waited on the pool terrace for the prince to appear from his castle, Aziz told me they had plans to go partying later as they all needed some release from their recent pressures. Nothing had changed there.

When Patrick showed up, I returned his friendly greeting with an unsmiling reply and looked him in the eye as if to say "hello, you piece of shit." I needed him to know that things would not be as they were before.

He asked me how Xavier was doing and I told him: "Xavier has nothing left. He's not even allowed to exercise. He's with so many people in his cell that he can't sleep. He doesn't have access to the books I bought for him. His royal pardon has also been blocked and…"

He cut me off with a smirk: "Of course. But I'm the one paying for Xavier in prison." He added: "I asked you to do something simple for us and you didn't want to do it."

I snapped back that I hadn't finished, but Aziz intervened, urging us to "talk calmly."

There was a long silence before Patrick resumed: "I'm here to discuss things and find a solution. I think you're talking to people, and I wonder why? I don't think it's a good solution to talk. There's also that interview that you didn't want to do; I don't know, I'll have to think about it some more, but maybe we've found a solution..."

Me: "Patrick, tell me exactly what you want. You know very well the only thing I want... but you can't or won't get Xavier out of jail."

He smiled and replied: "Very well; if that's what you think, then there's nothing to be done." It was as if he were trying to bait me. He was so sure and full of himself; the look on his face made me want to vomit.

Me: "Tell me, are you and Tarek happy torturing people like this? At least it's a change from last time when you had to pay Paul to come and threaten me instead of doing it yourself."

Looking deep into his eyes, I continued: "Patrick, I will never let go, do you hear me?

You see, I don't need you. Maybe I've even found a solution already, maybe I even still have a copy of the server."

He looked at me and laughed. I wanted to kill him but I could tell I had wrong-footed him. "I'm not the one who asked to be here, to see you," I told him. "It's you who must need something from me again."

He didn't know what to say or where to look. I could see that he was angry but more than that I had hurt his ego and he had realized I wouldn't allow myself to be manipulated by him anymore. Like a child throwing a fit, he got up and left. I looked at Aziz and remarked loudly: "Say, your friend is easily offended."

I added: "Patrick takes everyone for idiots, but not me. It doesn't work on me anymore."

Aziz looked surprised. He had never seen me like this, and nor had Patrick. They had thought they could treat me like a naive little girl, but those days were over. We said our goodbyes and he went up to join Patrick in his suite.

On the way out of the hotel, I wondered if I had gone too far. My anger was still boiling and I felt scared — but I felt proud of myself too.

A few days later, on 23 July — just days before I was due to give my press conference — Aziz called back and asked me to go for a drink with him again that evening. I told him I couldn't: I was taking the day to let off some steam by going wakesurfing at my favorite club at the Plage du Reposoir, so if he really wanted to see me he would have to go there.

He took a taxi and arrived 30 minutes later. Again, it was obvious that he was there at Patrick's bidding. We sat down and he started off by telling me that Patrick wasn't happy at all; that I should have negotiated with him, because he could have helped us.

I laughed and told him all Patrick and his gang of crooks had done was to make our lives hell. He said it was a shame that I was reacting like this and lowered his head nervously. An awkward silence followed before he told me Patrick had sent him to show me something. He pulled a phone out of his pocket, opened a folder on it, inserted some earphones and asked me to listen.

The file was of Denis and Xavier talking to one another in the visiting room. I could hear Xavier asking Denis to get me to send him $200 so that he could pay some of the guards off and be allowed to receive books and photos of Xander.

It was proof of what I already knew: that our conversations were routinely recorded and sent to PetroSaudi. But still, hearing the evidence was hard to stomach. It was such a flagrant violation of our privacy.

Tears welled in my eyes and I was shaking. Aziz, for his part, looked ashamed, and insisted "I'm only the messenger." Next, however, came the attempt to manipulate the situation to their advantage. Whatever I was planning, he said, I mustn't do it — I mustn't talk to anyone, because they had all these recordings of Xavier talking about paying off guards in the prison and they would release them to the press to destroy his credibility again. If I made the wrong move, he said, that's what would happen.

I felt so angry I wanted to scream. I gave Aziz his phone back and told him I had to leave. I couldn't bear to see him a moment longer. Sickened, I went and found my car and drove off. My recurring fear of Xavier being hurt plagued my thoughts.

Driving helped calm me, however — and I started to think. If their plan was just to release the tapes from the visiting room, it didn't actually seem like much of a plan. Would it really damage Xavier? For one thing, it would show the lengths to which he had to go to be allowed a modicum of dignity. For another, it would show that his accusers — PetroSaudi — had spied on him.

The more I thought about it, the more I realized how stupid they were. I was actually laughing. I hoped they had nothing more evil and twisted up their sleeves, but I couldn't see how releasing the recordings would help them.

When I told Alan, Denis and Clare about the Aziz episode, they were all incredulous, but they all told me the same thing: "Be very careful, Laura. These people will stop at nothing."

I begged Denis to go and see Xavier and tell him we had confirmation of the recordings. I also told the FBI and the Swiss Embassy. None of it did my anxiety any good.

CLARE TOLD ME the conference room at the Holiday Inn at Geneva airport was booked and that she had contacted a host of journalists she trusted — in other words, none of the reporters who had so far done PetroSaudi's bidding.

She also put me in touch ahead of our event with a contact of hers who she said I should speak to. Pascal Najadi was fighting for justice for his father. Hussein Najadi had been a famous banker in Malaysia and the founder of the country's AmBank back in the 1970s, but in 2013 he was murdered on the street in Kuala Lumpur. Pascal believed it was because his father knew too much about the 1MDB scam. I called him and we spoke at length, comparing our stories and what we each knew about the affair.

Forty-eight hours before the press conference, I got another call from Aziz. I decided not to answer, but he sent a string of messages. He was insistent: "Call me, it's really important." Had Patrick found out that I was about to go public? I called back and turned on the recording function. The more evidence I could gather, the better.

Aziz: "Look, the thing is, apparently Clare is going to do a press conference with everything you recorded."

Me: "A press conference? What do you mean?" They had tried to take me for a fool for so long that I had no qualms about playing dumb. I wanted to make him squirm, because I doubted that he would say out loud what they were worried about. Patrick would have warned him to be careful.

The conversation was very cagey. I asked him who had told him there would be a press conference. He said Patrick had told him — and had said "it won't work."

I asked him why and he repeated that they would be able to release recordings of Xavier talking about paying off guards, and "all that, I don't know what."

Me: “What is he going to say? That Xavier is obliged to pay [for things]?”

Aziz: “I’m scared, that’s all. I see that it’s going to shit. I’m saying to myself ‘I don’t know…’ That’s why I wanted to put him through on the phone so he can speak with you.”

Me: “But I don’t see what there is to say, Aziz... [Patrick] wanted a deal... Three weeks ago, I went there on purpose to see if he could do something for Xavier as he had promised from the start, and then he tells me what? Instead he insults me, he wants something else…”

He repeated the stuff about Patrick’s recordings incriminating Xavier, and I told him I had proof that the payments were necessary because Patrick controlled Xavier’s existence in prison and had chosen to cut him off. I also put it to him that if these recordings were released they would simply show how PetroSaudi had orchestrated everything to do with Xavier’s imprisonment. Were they stupid enough not to see that? He then said that I must have supplied Clare with information for the press conference. “Only you could have,” he said.

I continued to play dumb. “Absolutely not, I don’t see what I could have given her… Maybe someone hacked my email, I don’t know.”

He persisted in asking me if I would talk to Patrick. I declined: I didn’t want to be threatened anymore, or to be talked out of what I had resolved to do. The discussion was becoming absurd — and kept going round in circles. I told him: “I don’t want to talk about Patrick anymore. Now that he’s in the shit, let him deal with it himself.”

I asked him if he’d seen how Xavier was being treated in prison, and if he thought Patrick’s actions were normal. He replied: “Yeah… yeah… Well, I hope it doesn’t get too violent.”

I was fed up with their threats. I said angrily: “You know, Aziz, I’ve had people in prison from the start who told me that the conversations were recorded. I was told the prison sent copies to the CSD and the CSD sent the copies to Patrick and Tarek… So he can release the recordings;

they'll just confirm what I am saying and he's going to look even more like a buffoon. You can tell that to Patrick, OK? Let him do what he wants. I'm done."

He answered in a diminished voice: "OK… Well I'll tell him. Alright." And with that, we said our goodbyes. I knew very well that I would not hear from this hypocrite again. And that wasn't the only plus: I had another recording that would strengthen the case against them. I was still scared but I was ready to face whatever came next.

THE TWENTY-EIGHTH of July 2016, a Thursday, was the big day — the day when I would shake myself completely free of PetroSaudi's manipulations and tell the truth about them. I prayed that by doing so Xavier would gain his freedom and be able to return to a normal life.

Clare managed the whole set-up, including making sure the journalists arrived on schedule. We spent the morning preparing — and I had the chance to meet Pascal, who was accompanied by his steadfast and adorable wife Anna.

Ahead of proceedings, I had never been so nervous in my life: I was shaking, my hands were sweating and my stomach ached. This was the moment I had wanted for so long, and I couldn't mess it up. Clare and Pascal assured me I would be fine, and I was grateful to them for having confidence in me.

As the journalists started arriving, I counted about a dozen of them in total, more than I had expected. At 2.10pm, Clare switched the microphone on, introduced herself, and began a summary of the 1MDB affair and how Xavier had been caught up in it.

She then introduced me and it was my turn. My throat tightened as I started speaking, but soon the words came pouring out and there was no going back. I presented my summary, including key pieces of evidence, and stated loudly and clearly that I had been threatened by PetroSaudi as recently as 48 hours ago. As I spoke I gained confidence: it came to me that this was my story and I had nothing to hide; on the contrary, I wanted the world to know what had been done to us.

After my presentation, Pascal took the floor and talked about his father's story, which I found to be both moving and disturbing. As I watched the journalists taking notes, I hoped and prayed that they would put the truth about our cases in print and online for the world to see. Once again, it struck me that if I wanted to tell my whole story I would need to write a book.

Next, it was time for questions — and they came thick and fast. Journalists being journalists, some were skeptical and some asked for more proof. Someone said they knew Xavier's Swiss lawyers and that the claims I was making against them sounded defamatory, but I replied that I had evidence to back everything up. Most of all, though, they were interested, even shocked.

Clare had imposed a time embargo of 7pm that evening for publication of any articles. Randeep would be publishing a long read in *The Guardian*, accompanied online by a few minutes of the phone conversation I'd had with Patrick in which he referred to Najib Razak.

Clare also had her own article ready to publish, and would be posting my video interview with her on YouTube.

One thing I stressed to the assembled reporters was that PetroSaudi would try to stop them from doing their jobs and telling the truth: "They will do everything they can to prevent you from getting your stories out; they will threaten to drown you in every legal procedure imaginable. Don't let yourself be swayed or influenced by them!"

True to form, some called me later in the day to say that they'd had threatening calls from PetroSaudi's lawyers. I reminded them that these lawyers were paid with stolen Malaysian money and that everything I had said was right, verifiable and indeed verified.

Clare had work to do so I left her to it. Back in my car, I breathed a huge sigh of relief. I couldn't quite believe what I had just done. Now there would be a waiting game to find out what came out in the press. I decided to take a walk to clear my head, then go home and spend some time with Xander, my parents and my brother.

At 7.25pm, Clare sent me two links: one to her own article, the other to the long piece in *The Guardian*, which included the audio clip I had given them. *The Guardian* story was headlined: "1MDB: The inside story of the world's biggest financial scandal."

Minutes passed and more articles appeared. Finally, after all this time, the truth was out. I didn't have to lie to my family and friends anymore, I didn't have to hide anymore — and above all, if anything happened to Xavier, everyone would know who was responsible. I cried from happiness with my parents and my brother. Even though I was still afraid of how PetroSaudi might respond, I knew I had done the right thing and that it was our best chance to get Xavier home and protect ourselves from PetroSaudi.

For the first time in more than a year, I felt free and alive again. I smiled and said to myself: "Take that, you bunch of crooks! This is just the start. Nobody touches my family. Nobody threatens me."

I would have given anything to see their faces right at that moment, to feel the panic and confusion they were in. I felt so jubilant knowing that I — the naive young mother they thought I was, the gullible wife they had tried to silence — had landed this blow.

After celebrating at home, I got in my car and drove to the lakefront to have a moment to myself. I wanted to tell everyone I knew about what had happened, so I composed an emotional message, copied the links to the articles and my video interview with Clare, and started contacting everyone we knew: friends, acquaintances, old colleagues, journalists, people we hadn't seen or spoken to in years, friends of our families… the list went on. I had taken the decision some time before to delete my

Facebook and Instagram accounts, because I needed to protect my privacy when I spoke to the press. Now, however, I wanted the people who knew us to understand the truth and know why we hadn't talked about what was happening until now.

I held back from copying my message to Patrick — but I did send it to Aziz. It gave me pleasure to imagine him showing the others what had been revealed and them being compelled to look at my interview and see what was written about them.

I only wished Xavier could share in all of this, but I knew that when he learned of the revelations, he would be filled with hope.

Immediately, I started receiving calls, emails and texts of support. It was hard to keep up. In the following days and weeks, there were letters, requests for interviews, even offers of work. It was stressful dealing with it all but there was now real momentum. I continued to do interviews and share evidence with journalists, and positive articles kept appearing in the press.

I also stayed in constant touch with Clare and with the lawyers, Gilles and Christian. The Swiss justice system seemed to be finally looking into PetroSaudi; and in Malaysia, even as Najib Razak clung to power, there was mounting pressure against him from civil society, opposition politicians, the country's central bank and overseas prosecutors.

In Bangkok, Denis, Laurent and Wilfried were still visiting Xavier regularly and keeping him up to date on developments. Meanwhile, Yanna continued to help us communicate through the letters she would smuggle in and out of the prison. Like many people in our day and age, I rarely wrote anything apart from phone messages, but these letters were all we had and had become extremely precious to us. Waiting for the next letter, the next reply, was an acutely bittersweet feeling.

RUMORS CONTINUED to circulate that an amnesty would soon be announced in sight of the 70th anniversary of the King's coronation. If so, Xavier's sentence would be reduced. I had Worasit on the phone every other day to ask him about it, and Yanna told me it was all but finalized.

Then, on 9 August, Mr Vavricka from the Swiss Embassy called to confirm the news: an amnesty had been announced. Xavier's sentence had been reduced from three years to two.

I was stunned. Obviously I wanted him out sooner, but this was a step in the right direction. I felt overjoyed and had a new energy. Xavier now had only nine months left of his sentence to serve, and I was determined that he should be transferred to Switzerland. My lawyers told me that if this happened, he might well be released sooner, because the Swiss authorities would likely take the harshness of his incarceration in Bangkok into consideration and deduct time.

In communications between the Thai and Swiss authorities, a transfer date of September 12 was mentioned. If there were no further administrative hold-ups, that would mean we would be reunited in less than a month!

On 31 August, however, the news came that the transfer had been postponed. Why? Well, it just so happened that Najib Razak was due to visit Bangkok on 8 and 9 September, and I was reliably informed by contacts in Malaysia that Xavier remaining in Thailand was a top priority for the prime minister.

I was beside myself. We'd been told he was coming back to Europe; now I was terrified that he might be transferred to Malaysia, which was too alarming to contemplate.

I went into a frenzy of activity: I called the Swiss Embassy in Bangkok and told them that if Xavier was taken to Malaysia his life would be in danger, and that Switzerland couldn't turn a blind eye. I also reached out to the FBI and NCA agents I had been in contact with to alert them.

Christian and Gilles were on the case, too, but Clare told me she was worried, as did others.

I couldn't sleep or eat. The wait was interminable. Finally, on 14 September, we received confirmation that there would be no transfer to Malaysia. We were also given notice, however, that Xavier's move to Switzerland had been officially denied. We later learned from the Swiss Embassy that the Malaysians had put enormous pressure on Thailand to get him extradited, but luckily Swiss diplomatic pressure was stronger and prevented this from happening. The cancellation of Xavier's return to Switzerland was explained by telling us that it was against the rules to transfer someone who had less than a year left of their sentence. That seemed like a fabrication.

I was disgusted and depressed. I didn't know what more I could do. I prayed for a miracle to release my family from this hell and to have a normal life again. I was living a life that was alien to me, that was not of my own making; and yet, I had become adapted to it and had discovered I was better at facing adversity than I could have imagined. I reflected on what I'd learned about human beings and our capacity to function like machines. The mind can win out over the body. But for how long?

I knew I had to just keep staying strong: I had no choice but to keep getting up and carrying on the fight each day, even as I was being eaten up inside. I had to just keep going — writing to journalists, pressuring the authorities, making sure Xavier was not being neglected. In truth, I was too afraid to find out what would happen if I stopped.

Chapter 23

XAVIER

CIRCLE OF LIFE

BY THE END of September, rumors about the King's failing health were rife. If he were to die, the beginning of a new reign would bring an amnesty for thousands of prisoners. The prison organized daily prayers for his recovery, but many inmates privately wished for him to die so they could gain their freedom.

The atmosphere was frenetic; everyone spoke about the King's condition. One of the prisoners in my cell, the "Tsai" I mentioned earlier, had a family member in the royal council, and confirmed that the King would not be around for much longer, that he would probably only last a few more days. It was horrible but we all willed it to happen. I had never wished for anyone to die, but the prospect of a reduced sentence was always on my mind.

On 13 October, news of the King's death rippled through the prison, stirring a sense of panic and excitement. Everyone thought they would be released, that the new King would do what his father had done 70 years ago when he succeeded his brother — that he would free all the prisoners. Even the murderers and pedophiles now anticipated being released.

I thought they had all gone mad, but in my heart I hoped that at least I would be spared. Days and weeks passed without an official announcement. The atmosphere in the prison soured as doubt planted itself in our minds, but my Tsai cellmate assured me the amnesty had been approved and that the royal council was just working out the details. Easier said than done, but we just had to carry on being patient.

At the end of November, my new Swiss lawyer, Christian Luscher, came to visit me in prison. I knew him by reputation as a politician — he was and is a member of Switzerland's National Council — and as a fine lawyer, and I learned from Laura that he cared about our story and would take charge of my case. I soon realized what a good and just man he is.

The relationship with Luscher was established through Gilles Crettol, a lawyer Laura had contacted in Geneva. I had first met Gilles in 2010 when I was setting up a consulting company; then Laura had gone to him to close the company, which was inactive, in late 2015. She had told him a little at that stage about our plight and then reached out to him later when it was clearer that we were being deluded by PetroSaudi. He immediately wanted to help and put Laura in touch with Luscher.

Luscher was accompanied by Vavricka from the Swiss Embassy when he came to see me, and the visit took place in one of the offices where I had previously met with Patrick and Paul. What a turnaround in events. At first we were suspicious and combed the office for microphones or cameras that might have been planted there by PetroSaudi, but we found nothing. It was such a relief to be able to speak freely.

Luscher told me the Swiss authorities had pushed for my transfer to Switzerland but had been unsuccessful. More importantly, however, they had taken the necessary steps to rule out the possibility of extradition to Malaysia. That this threat no longer existed was a huge relief to me and I was extremely grateful that my country had stood up for me.

I told Luscher my main concern was now around the amnesty, and that I feared that somehow the Malaysians and Petrosaudi would find a way to influence the Thai government and have me excluded from it. I'd had so many false hopes that I was wary of being optimistic about anything. I couldn't imagine another disappointment and didn't think I would be able to recover.

This time, I needn't have worried, however. At the beginning of December, the names of the first batch of prisoners to be given an amnesty were announced over the loudspeakers in the jail. And mine was one of them.

I WAS STUNNED. I couldn't believe it. I found a hiding place and just sobbed. I didn't want anyone to see me in this state.

Many of my fellow inmates came to me and hugged me. They were happy for me — even many of those who were not eligible for release under the terms of this amnesty. Despite the fact that I didn't speak Thai and they didn't speak English, a bond existed between us. Seeing me being allowed to leave gave them hope that one day they too could get out.

Under the amnesty, sentences were reduced or wiped altogether according to the severity of what you were in for and your classification as a prisoner. My eligibility stemmed from the fact that I had less than two years left to serve and was rated as "very good"; I'd had a few moments of rebellion but I had avoided fights and generally kept my head down.

I was overjoyed: I was going to see my wife and son again! I was going to live again, to be a human being again. But I was also saddened that many of my friends would be staying behind — my brothers in arms, my comrades in sorrow, the guys who had supported me when I needed it.

The exact date of release had not yet been announced — only that it would happen in a few days' time. Given the number of times my hopes had been dashed since my arrival, the wait was unbearable.

Officials from the Swiss Embassy came to visit me. They said they would be waiting for me on my release and would accompany me until I had boarded the plane. They explained that the Swiss authorities had reached an agreement with the Thai government to be allowed to protect me until I left the country.

Finally, I was given a release date of 20 December. In the days prior, I didn't sleep at all. I could only think about my return to freedom, about which I had refused to dream for so long. After so many false dawns, I finally knew it was a reality.

On 19 December, at 3pm, I entered my cell, supposedly for the last time. My mind replayed memories of everything that I had experienced over the last 546 days. So many things had happened that were inexplicable, illegal, unbelievable.

As I reflected on these, I was surprised to hear my name called for a visit. This was unusual, as the visits usually stopped at 3pm and it was now 5:30pm.

My heart raced. Was there a problem? I was sure it had to be bad news and that my amnesty had finally been refused at the last minute for some obscure reason. I struggled to stand up and was afraid I might faint.

I was escorted from the cell and taken once again to the private office where I used to meet Patrick and Paul. I was in a state of complete distress.

Two people, a man and a woman, were waiting for me, and the guard greeted them with the greatest of reverence. The man introduced himself and explained that he worked for the Thai secret service. He wanted me to tell him what I had experienced in prison, who Mr Finnigan and Mr Mahony were, and why they had come to visit me.

I was reluctant to open my mouth. I said that trusting Thai law enforcement had already cost me 18 months in prison, that I was getting out the next day and that I didn't want to take any risks. He patiently explained that he just wanted to know what had happened, that he wasn't going to take notes and that there were no recording devices in the room.

Nothing I could say would cause me problems, he said, adding that the Thai authorities wanted to return me safely to Switzerland and that protective measures for my release were in place.

I hesitated a little, but decided to talk. I told him about the false confessions, the lawyers paid by the men who put me in prison, the false trial, the visits from Patrick Mahony, Paul Finnigan and the Malaysian delegation, the questions I had received in advance, the manipulations of the prison authorities... and all the other shady elements of the story that I could think of. I was satisfied with my explanation; it was more or less complete.

The agent didn't seem surprised. He informed me that there might be a Thai investigation into my case, thanked me for my co-operation and said there would be a police escort to take me to the airport the next day. He added that there had been rumors in the press that I might be targeted by assassins who wanted to stop me from leaving Thailand, but said I shouldn't worry.

To be honest, I was hardly listening to him. Now that I knew I would definitely be leaving, my heart had already soared out of the room. Back in the cell, my companions wanted to know what had happened. I explained and they shared my relief and once again hugged me. I started to cry — the first time I had shown emotion in front of other inmates.

Of course, I didn't sleep for a second that night. I could only think about my departure, and about Laura and Xander. I visualized my arrival at the airport, the boarding gate, the seats of the plane, the meal tray.

On 20 December 20, at 6am, my cell door opened. I drank one last cup of coffee with my mates and smoked one last cigarette before the prisoners being released — a few hundred of us — were all led outside to a tent for an hour of prayers for the new King's health. I didn't pray, but I thanked him for letting me go home.

After prayers, we were taken to fill out various items of paperwork for our release. Unlike the other prisoners, I had an official looking over my shoulder as I filled out the necessary forms, and unlike the others I wasn't given any documents to take away with me. But I didn't care. I couldn't stop staring at the exit door, some 50 meters away.

Another rule that only applied to me was that I was forbidden from taking any papers or documents from my cell. I decided I wanted one memento of my time in prison, however, so I peeled off the picture on my locker — the one that had been taken of me the day I arrived, after I'd had my head shaved — and stuck it between my buttocks. It was childish but I felt I had to take something with me.

The whole release process ultimately took hours due to the sheer numbers leaving and the dearth of staff to handle us. True to form I was the last man standing — all the others had filled in their paperwork, collected their belongings and walked out the door. At that point, I wondered again if I had been duped. Would I ever be released?

Everything I wanted was behind that big iron door. Laura and my son were in Switzerland waiting for me; now I was so close to being reunited with them.

In Thailand, the death of a King gives life to ordinary mortals. Just a little more patience and I would finally be free.

Chapter 24

Laura

AN EXCRUCIATING WAIT

WHEN WE SAY that one person's misfortune is another's joy, sadly it's sometimes true. The news of 13 October 2016, that the King of Thailand was dead, was like music to my ears. In the language of a prisoner's wife, it could only mean one thing: an amnesty.

I spent all of that day on the phone trying to find out if and when it would be announced. Xavier wrote to me to say that he'd been told it was certain to happen and that by his calculations he would be out by December. But I wouldn't be fully convinced until it was official — and it wasn't official yet.

The days and weeks passed without any confirmation. On 10 November, I met with Christian Luscher and Gilles Crettol to take stock of the situation and talk about Christian's forthcoming trip to Bangkok. He planned to visit Xavier on 24 November.

I told him there could be obstacles to his visit when he arrived, but he said he would take the precaution of asking someone from the Swiss Embassy to accompany him. Even if PetroSaudi were paying off the entire prison system, it seemed unlikely that they would be able to blackball both Xavier's lawyer and his country's official representative, especially after I had just exposed the Thais' corrupt collusion in what was an international scandal.

Before he left, I gave Luscher a letter for Xavier and some pictures of Xander. I warned him to be wary of being recorded by PetroSaudi in the room, and I also suggested that he meet while in Bangkok with Denis, who would be able to testify in his own words to just about everything PetroSaudi had put us through.

On the day of their visit — morning in Bangkok, but the middle of the night in Geneva — I couldn't sleep from nerves. I got up at 4am and paced around the house trying not to wake everyone up, until finally I heard from Christian. He told me everything had gone well and that Xavier was in good spirits — that he was full of hope and fully believed he would be released in December. I prayed with all my might that he was right.

Christian made me laugh by telling me about how they'd searched the entire room for hidden microphones. He also said they had spoken at length about Xavier's safety, and about his case. It was clear that he was more determined than ever to help us.

On his return, we organized another briefing with Gilles. Things were happening fast and my marathon had become a sprint. I was still constantly on the phone — keeping family and friends updated; dealing with the property agent on Koh Samui; paying bills; and making sure Xavier had regular visitors. I also spoke to Pon to assure her we hadn't forgotten about the animals.

By writing to Henzelin and asking to see Lalive's files from Xavier's case — which they were obliged to send me by law — I uncovered a treasure trove.

For a start, the files contained details of the fees levied by Lalive for supposedly representing Xavier. These had been charged to KBSD, a small PR firm run by one David Scholberg.

This is when I learned, with a little digging, that Scholberg had traveled to Thailand with Patrick and the Lalive lawyers in August 2015, and had even stayed at the same hotel as all of us. How did I find this out? Well, he wasn't very discreet or smart about it. His Facebook account was open and right there for all to see was a post on his wall that put him at the Bangkok St. Regis at exactly the time when the media campaign was being put in motion. The post included a beautiful picture of a huge suite with a jacuzzi overlooking the park in the center of Bangkok, all of it paid for by PetroSaudi of course. How vain.

The most curious part of it all, though, was that — as mentioned previously — I never got to meet Scholberg. Neither Patrick, Paul, nor the Swiss lawyers ever mentioned his existence. He had been with them at the St. Regis at the same time as me, but they'd conspired to keep him out of my sight. In chapter 9, I mentioned that during that trip I was told by Paul one morning that I should stay out of the lawyers' way. With hindsight, it's obvious that they simply didn't want me to know about Scholberg.

I believe there were two reasons for this. Firstly, PetroSaudi used Scholberg to pay the Swiss lawyers' fees to disguise the fact that they were in control of Xavier's legal team. And secondly, it was Scholberg who provided the contacts and the strategy for them to discredit Xavier in the press.

If Xavier was supposed to be Lalive's "client," I wondered in what sense they had worked for him. It was scandalous that one of Switzerland's biggest and most respected law firms had been paid more than 200,000 Swiss francs to purposefully work against the person they were nominally "helping." All they had done was follow PetroSaudi's orders and travel first-class to Bangkok, where they were put up in a five-star luxury hotel, all expenses paid. Their transport to and from the prison, with Patrick, Paul and Scholberg, was in a limousine.

The USB from Lalive was in fact very much like opening Pandora's box. Everything I discovered seemed yet more shocking and disgusting. For example, there was an email from Scholberg to Lalive's Sandrine Giroud, which read:

"Attached and below are some materials that you can give to the PR firms when they are evaluating the situation and the appetite to take this on and work with Swiss-based (or international if they think they have the contacts) journalists. What we are looking for is basically a journalist willing to write the true story. The story out now is a simple one of whistleblowing where the means justify the ends — so basically they committed crimes but they were uncovering crimes, so it is ok. However the true story is one of people with no intention of whistleblowing but rather a greedy former ex-employee only motivated by money and opposition politicians who used him for their political goals. There is no whistleblowing, just crimes of dealing in stolen goods, money-laundering and using a poor Swiss guy for political gain. Somebody has to be interested in that story and getting the truth out there. Preferably a journalist who doesn't like Le Temps *and their editorial freedom and lack of fact checking (they are completely in bed with Clare Rewcastle Brown (who has the most to lose if the truth gets out) and they have confirmed to Laura Justo that they are working with her). We can offer a lot of case evidence to back these claims up to someone willing to take this on as well as interviews with Xavier and Laura Justo...*

"(Whatever you give them, please make sure my name is not on it. Best to just let them read this stuff only for now and then take it back. Whoever we decide to work with can then keep copies and also get all of the supporting evidence.)"

De: David Scholberg <d.scholberg@kbsd.ch>
Envoyé: mercredi, 5 août 2015 00:59
À: Giroud Sandrine
Objet: Fwd: PR Firm Materials
Pièces jointes: Events and Timeline Summary.pdf; ATT00001.htm; Project X V3 5 13 July 15.pdf; ATT00002.htm

Subject: PR Firm Materials
Date: 2 Aug 2015 22:14:44 GMT+2
To: David Scholberg <d.scholberg@kbsd.ch>

Attached and below are some materials that you can give to the PR firms when they are evaluating the situation and the appetite to take this on and work with Swiss-based (or international if they think they have the contacts) journalists. '

That this email chain actually started on 13 July — BEFORE PetroSaudi even told me that they were hiring Swiss lawyers to work for Xavier — indicates that they had the whole thing worked out in advance, and that Lalive knew from the outset they weren't being employed to represent Xavier in good faith.

THE TIME FOR accountability would surely come, however. My immediate priority was having Xavier safely back in Switzerland, and my mind flitted between a sense of elation that our nightmare would soon be over and absolute fear and dread of some new disaster.

On 12 December, Worasit called and confirmed that the amnesty was happening. Xavier's sentence had been reduced by half, which meant he would be released, and home, before Christmas.

I couldn't believe it — the impossible was coming true! I cried, trembling with joy. My parents and brother saw me and understood right away. We all stood in floods of tears. I took Xander in my arms and held him tightly, telling him: "Daddy's coming home, my love."

He smiled at me, the tears welled again, and we all hugged. It was a magical moment. I finally felt that everything was going to be OK.

I spoke to Denis, who confirmed the news. He had visited Xavier and said he'd never been better. By this point I was smiling from ear to ear, my head was in the clouds and my heart felt lighter than it had ever been. All I could think about was the moment when we were together again.

Clare wrote to me to say that one of her sources in Kuala Lumpur had heard that Xavier was not expected to get out of Bangkok alive. It was alarming but I thought steps could be taken to protect him. I notified Christian and Gilles and they said they would request help from the embassy to ensure all the paperwork for Xavier's departure was in order and that he be given a security detail to get him from the prison to the airport.

Meanwhile, the FBI were in touch to say they wanted to speak to Xavier when he was released as he would be a key witness in the case they were building on 1MDB.

On 15 December, the Swiss Embassy confirmed to Christian that Xavier would be released on 20 December and that his flight had been booked. I was breathless with excitement but still terrified of anything that might happen to stop him boarding that plane.

On Monday, 19 December, at 9:07am Swiss time, Christian emailed me: "Things are moving, let's talk in the afternoon ok?" I scrolled down: Xavier would be released the next day at 10am.

I cried once more. The next several hours were going to be excruciating. I couldn't eat and I knew I wouldn't be able to sleep. In fact, I would have stopped breathing if it was possible. Was the miracle I had longed for about to actually happen?

Chapter 25

LAURA

DREAMS BECOME REALITY

ON 20 DECEMBER, at 6:03am, I received the most beautiful message of my life, from Christian Luscher: Xavier was free. The message was accompanied by a picture of him outside the prison, standing alongside prison officials and Swiss security men.

I broke down. I had waited so long; now I just wanted to hear my husband's voice. It had been 222 days since we had last spoken, since I'd last seen him.

Denis called and said he'd just been with Xavier, and that they had hugged. He hadn't been able to stay with him but he said Xavier was well and would call me as soon as he could. I felt so excited I didn't know what to say but asked him to hang up in case Xavier called.

Ten minutes later, my phone rang again. It was an unknown number, but I knew it had to be him. I answered the call and heard: "Loulou!"

In tears, I trembled: "My love!" Neither of us could speak. For several seconds, hearing each other breathe was enough to make us happy. It was such an intense feeling, knowing how much we'd suffered to get to this moment. Being able to finally hear one another was so comforting.

For the next 15 minutes, we chatted, laughed and cried with joy. I told him we were waiting for him and that very soon he would be able to hug his son. Just hearing Xander's name made Xavier cry, and I felt overjoyed at the thought of them being reunited. He rang off and said he would call back later as he had to be escorted to the airport.

At 16:28, Christian, who was in touch with the ambassador, Ivo Seiber, sent me a photo of Xavier's boarding pass and a message saying he was at the airport.

At 17:35, Gilles texted our group to ask if Xavier had boarded yet. Christian replied with a photo of Xavier taken at departures, smiling broadly in a yellow t-shirt. I was over the moon to see him looking so happy.

A short while later, he called again, this time on video. Again, we laughed and cried with happiness. We said we loved each other and that we couldn't wait to be together in just a few hours more.

18:15: Christian texted to say "TG970 takes off in 40 minutes."

18:29: Another text. This time, they were about to board, and there was a photo of Xavier standing by the gate with the Swiss security agent and Sieber. My beloved was edging ever closer to me.

18:37: Another text… They were on the plane!

19:07: The plane was still at the gate!

Of course, it's not unusual for planes to wait awhile on the runway after boarding but my imagination ran wild. I wouldn't be at peace until I knew they had taken off.

19:16: Another message: "The plane has left the gate."

19:24: The status of the flight on the Suvarnabhumi Airport website showed: "Departed."

What a feeling! I finally knew that Xavier was safe and sound — and that we were going to be reunited. For the first time, I let my relief overcome my stress. As I put Xander to bed, I was able to promise him, truthfully, that our family would be whole again.

Still, the night was endless. I couldn't have slept if I had tried. I spent it on an adrenaline overload, checking the progress of flight TG970 every other minute online.

The flight landed in Zurich on 21 December, at 6.55am, and Xavier called shortly afterwards. Just knowing that he was back in Switzerland was an amazing feeling. In about two more hours, we would be together.

A private meeting-place for us had been organized at Geneva airport, near arrivals, where we would be away from any media or other on-lookers. The plan was to meet there at 9:30am.

Christian was there when I arrived with Xander. We had a view onto the runway and Xavier's plane had just landed, although no-one seemed to be coming out. I felt so nervous, just waiting. Then, suddenly, he was walking towards me.

I thought my legs would give way as the tears streamed down my face and we hugged, holding one another like only a husband and wife can after being kept apart for so long. The world seemed to stop spinning; it felt like we were the only people on earth and that this moment was all that mattered. Xavier took Xander in his arms and we hugged all together. Christian, looking on, immortalized the moment with a family photo that will live with us forever.

Finally we were a family again, together, safe and happier than words can ever express.

Chapter 26

XAVIER

THE SWEET SMELL OF FREEDOM

AT AROUND NOON on 20 December, I was still waiting alone by the prison's great iron door. Beyond it lay freedom.

Officer Yatavi appeared and told me some officials would take me to immigration. He then uttered the last sentence I would hear in prison… a sentence that makes me laugh to this day. He said that his family sold rice and that he would be grateful if I could help him find buyers for it when I returned to Switzerland.

Finally, the prison door sprang open to the world. The first thing that I noticed — and which I hadn't encountered for 18 months — was trees and greenery. I had been in prison, away from everyone and everything, for 547 days. It had been 547 days of simply surviving.

A Caucasian man approached me and shook my hand. He introduced himself as Jan, a security officer from the Swiss Embassy in Bangkok.

Jan quickly briefed me on what was going to happen. Thai special forces police would escort me to immigration, where I would have to wait for a few hours before being taken to the airport. He himself would follow the Thai police vehicle to immigration. The Swiss consul would meet us there, then the ambassador would arrive and stay with me until my plane departed. Before I got in the police van, however, I had to have my photo taken — seemingly for administrative purposes — with various police personnel and prison officials.

Inside the vehicle were four armed officers. They looked exactly like the ones who had led me to prison at the start of this nightmare. How things had changed: now they were making sure I escaped it safely.

My first glimpses of normal life, as we drove through Bangkok, were of streets, passers-by, shops, parks. Freedom washed over me.

Outside the immigration department, in the city center, some journalists were waiting for me. I gave a brief statement to the effect that I hoped to be home very soon. I didn't really know what to say as my mind was completely elsewhere.

The consul, Wilfried Schnider, was there and had brought me some clothes for my trip. I asked him if I could borrow his phone to phone my wife. I dialed her number and it rang. Suddenly I was speaking to Laura for the first time in more than seven months — although at first I was too emotional to say anything.

We managed to talk, and cry, for 10-15 minutes. Such bliss. Finally, I allowed myself to believe I was going home.

After a couple of hours the ambassador, Ivo Sieber, arrived — a tall, elegant and charming man. We spoke at length and I found him to be pleasant and funny. He told me he had spoken to Laura several times and that he had promised her he would stay around until the plane was airborne. He was in contact with Christian Luscher and would notify him when the plane took off.

I asked if it would be possible to have a shower as I had been in the sun most of the morning and wanted to be reasonably clean to meet my wife and son. I was taken to a cell that had a shower room (and where I met a French prisoner who told me he had been waiting for three months to be extradited). After showering I wanted to get on my way and rejoin the ambassador but — were the Gods laughing at me? — I discovered I was locked in. I had to yell for some time before anyone came to free me.

As the time for departure neared, my Thai immigration officer and the ambassador told me they had worked out a plan for me to leave by the back door to avoid any risks.

In the meantime, however, I was approached by another Thai officer who said that while we waited he needed to put me in handcuffs. I immediately told him that was out of the question and after a slightly heated exchange he backed down, muttering that he had made an administrative error. I wasn't about to give up on my new-found freedom just because someone in a uniform fancied bossing me around.

When I asked the director of immigration for my personal documents — my passport and papers proving that I had completed my sentence — he replied that there were no documents for me, and that my passport was in the embassy's possession and would be returned to me when I was back in Switzerland.

I later learned from Worasit that Thailand had actually banned me from returning to the country for 100 years. When I subsequently asked two other Thai lawyers to verify this, they did — adding that they were astonished because it was unheard of. That the Thai authorities were so bent on punishing me in this way seemed to me to offer further proof of their complicity with PetroSaudi and Malaysia.

I've never felt particularly sad about being unable to go back to Thailand as that stage of my life has passed, but I would have enjoyed showing my son where he was born and spent the first year of life, and of course meeting some of our old friends.

Eventually, I was driven to the airport in the back of a police truck, along with a dozen other ex-prisoners I had never seen before. The journey seemed endless but it was worth the wait: arriving at this modern airport that I knew so well felt somehow luxurious. Only one Thai officer, in civilian clothes, accompanied us through the departure hall. Strange to relate, but just seeing people — clean, well-dressed people — and smelling the scent of the perfumes they wore, made me quite emotional.

The ambassador and I were taken to a basement area, where I was asked to wait for an hour or so before boarding. There were some papers to sign — all in Thai, so I had no idea what they said… but I didn't care anymore. Before I knew it, the flight was being called and it was time to go to the gate. As the ambassador and the security officer accompanied me all the way to the door of the plane, tears filled my eyes. I felt very proud to be Swiss.

I found my seat, put on my seatbelt and looked in a sort of wonder at all the buttons on the screen in front of me. I was alive again!

When it came time for the plane to taxi to the runway and begin accelerating, I had a lump in my throat. I still couldn't quite believe this was happening: I was going to see my wife and son again in a matter of hours.

I decided to order a glass of wine to celebrate the moment but my body had obviously become too unaccustomed to it and I almost threw up. I also couldn't sleep for a second during the flight, so I tried to watch films — but my mind was already in Switzerland.

When we arrived in Zurich it was dark outside and I couldn't see much, but — as the ambassador had promised — I was met on the tarmac by a policeman in civilian clothes who was to escort me onto the plane for Geneva.

This officer knew my story and was very kind to me. As we waited, he bought me a cappuccino at one of the airport bars — my first coffee as a free man. When we were ready to board, the hostess checking tickets asked him if I was a criminal; he responded that I was an important traveler who was under his protection. I'll never forget him.

Day was breaking as we took off for what is only a 30-minute flight. I could feel my heart beating at 100 kilometers per hour and thought I might be sick. I looked out of the window and recognized all the familiar landmarks — the lakes, the mountains, the towns — as we neared Lake Leman. When Geneva came into view, I couldn't stop myself from crying again and tried to hide my face from my fellow passengers.

Another policeman, again in civilian clothes, was waiting for me when I exited the plane. I followed him to the arrivals building, where he had a police car waiting for us and proceeded to drive it at what felt like 200km per hour back across the runway to a side building. Getting out of the car, I looked up and there — standing by a window — were my wife and son.

Seconds later, I was jumping into Laura's arms and holding Xander. It was an incredibly intense moment and even now as I write about it, it brings me to tears.

Christian Luscher was there too and after giving our family the moment we craved, he wanted to shake my hand. I felt his kindness and class immediately. As a politician, he could easily have publicized my arrival and used it to put himself in the spotlight, but no — his priority was to keep Laura company as she waited for me, and to welcome me back to the country.

Laura had brought her parents' car and we drove it back to their house, where we planned to stay for a while before finding our own accommodation.

It was three days until Christmas and I'd quite forgotten how cold it gets in Europe in the winter. Cold, yes, but to me so beautiful.

My in-laws were there to greet me when we arrived and there were more tears all round, but also champagne: the occasion called for a little celebration. My own family also came to visit a little later.

Laura's parents were kind enough to go and stay with some friends, giving us the place to ourselves for a couple of days. The privacy and the time to readjust mentally were welcome and much-needed. For one thing, I couldn't sleep for several nights: I wasn't used to the dark anymore, and sleeping on a mattress made me feel seasick.

Meanwhile, Laura took the time to tell me in detail everything that had happened while I was away, everything that she had experienced at the hands of corrupt criminals who had done their utmost to ruin our lives to cover up their actions. The way they had treated a 28 year-old mother with an eight month-old baby was unforgivable — and indeed I will never forgive them.

Chapter 27

XAVIER

STAYING TRUE

THE DAY AFTER my return, one of Switzerland's Italian television stations asked if they could interview us for a report they were producing about the PetroSaudi-1MDB scandal. We gladly agreed.

The report provided a truthful summary of the case, citing plentiful evidence of PetroSaudi's wrongdoing. We were confident that it would hasten the company's day of reckoning — and rather frustrated when afterwards they seemed no closer to facing justice.

As I acclimatized, I experienced many pleasures, but few were as precious as being able to see close friends again. It was as though our shared life had simply been paused. As the saying goes, friends are like stars: you can't always see them but they are always there.

There were lots of emails and letters people had written to me while I was in prison — letters Laura had been unable to convey to me. To this day, I read them from time to time: they are rich testimonies of friendship and will be forever dear to me.

People were generally surprised to find me in good spirits. I tried to explain that being released from prison had freed me of the burden I had carried. I truly didn't feel any mental after-effects — I didn't even have nightmares. Maybe it was the therapy of being surrounded by the people I love and who love me, simple as that.

I was also in good shape physically, as confirmed in a medical check-up with my doctor and by the blood samples he took. He told me that in times of great stress the body either weakens very quickly or gets stronger. Luckily in my case it was the latter. I was sure that this was thanks to my family and the unwavering support of my friends.

My only health issue was in fact a dental one — the lack of hygiene in prison had taken a heavy toll and I had to have nine teeth treated. But still, I felt I had escaped lightly.

Shortly after my return, Laura received confirmation that our house on Koh Samui had officially been sold. The sale price was a fraction of what we had paid for it, but the market had changed considerably and it was a huge achievement to actually complete the sale from 12,000 kilometers away. It was a weight off our minds and gave us enough money to survive on for a while.

Luscher was in touch and I agreed to visit the Swiss Federal Prosecutor's office later in January once I'd had a break and the chance to spend some time with my loved ones.

The FBI were in touch, too, and wanted to meet me in New York. I declined: after discussions back and forth with them and our lawyers, it became clear that Laura had given them all the information we had and that my presence was not paramount. They were friendly, thanked me — and in particular Laura — for what we had done, and wished us well.

They also confirmed that all the investigations into the Malaysian scandal stemmed from the documents I had provided. Knowing that the biggest money grab in history had been exposed by our actions was a source of satisfaction. For all that we had suffered, morally we had done the right thing, and I felt sure that good would triumph over evil.

We were advised to remain on our guard — advice which made perfect sense. That meant never taking the same route at the same time twice if it could be avoided, and staying constantly alert when we were out. Luckily there were people tasked with protecting us. I can't mention who they were, but we remain eternally grateful for their vigilance. After a while, however, we knew that we couldn't live like this forever: we had to go about our lives. Let criminals live in fear of retribution; we had done the right thing, and after the last 18 months of hell we felt we could face just about anything.

Every other day, I searched the web for new information about the PetroSaudi case and about myself. On one occasion, Xander was next to me when I clicked on an article which displayed a photo of me when the Thai courts had served me up to the press. Seeing me flanked by armed officers, he happily declared: "There's Dad with his friends!" Bitter though the memory felt, I laughed out loud.

On New Year's Eve, we went to the mountains with some close friends, did some sledging and enjoyed a good meal. Back in Geneva, we lived quietly, enjoying the novelty of a normal family life — walks with Xander, meals with friends and time to ourselves. Gone were the material luxuries that come with big salaries but we relished the greatest luxury of all — simply being together.

Christian and Gilles asked Laura and I to attend a meeting they had arranged with Henzelin to explain his side of the story and his collaboration with PetroSaudi.

The conversation, at Christian's office, started badly, with Henzelin arrogantly declaring his innocence and asserting that he had simply been doing his job. Confronted with the evidence that his "job" had been to destroy me and walk away with more than $200,000, he reluctantly admitted, however, that he "could have been" manipulated by Patrick Mahony.

At the end of the interview I watched him leave with a certain disgust. It seemed to me that he had sold his soul for cash.

A few days later, I went to Bern with Christian for a hearing with the federal authorities, who were at this stage investigating four individuals in connection with the 1MDB affair — namely Jasmine Loo and Casey Tang, both 1MDB officials from Malaysia, and two co-conspirators from the UAE, Mohamed Al Husseini and Khadem Al Qubaisi .

Present in the room besides myself, Christian and the prosecutor were three lawyers acting for the accused. We had traveled up by train and I felt very relaxed — I couldn't have been more ready to tell my story and I knew it by heart.

For the next seven hours, I answered questions and gave testimony of everything I knew about PetroSaudi.

I began by telling the prosecutor I had known Tarek Obaid for 20 years and PetroSaudi since its creation. I told him how the company never had more than two employees before the Malaysian deal was signed, and that its only activity prior to this was a failed venture in Latin America.

Next, I covered how PetroSaudi, an empty shell of a company, used a farm-in agreement to bring oil field assets into play which did not belong to it, thereby obtaining the false $3billion valuation of itself that allowed it to go into partnership with 1MDB.

I then described how money started to be laundered out of 1MDB through financial chicanery — in particular through the payment of $700 million to an account at Coutts Zurich that had nothing to do with the PetroSaudi-1MDB joint venture and in fact belonged to Jho Low, and also through the creation of what was essentially a fake loan from PetroSaudi to the joint venture, the reimbursement of which was presented as accounting for this missing $700m, which in reality had been siphoned off.

Under questioning I explained that of the $1.8 billion received by PetroSaudi from 1MDB, only $300m was ever invested in legal activities. I also outlined that in addition to the $160 million paid into Tarek's personal account prior to my departure from PetroSaudi in April 2011, a further $260 million was transferred to it for him to help Jho Low and his associates acquire Malaysia's Utama Banking Group, a move that bailed out various people close to Najib Razak.

Most crucial of all to me was my explanation of how I had acquired the data to prove all of this. I recounted in detail how it was given to me by "S.T.," the IT services provider to PetroSaudi. I told the prosecutor PetroSaudi had insisted I declare in my forced confession that I had stolen the data — because they knew this would make it inadmissible as evidence in court.

At the end of my deposition, I was asked if I had anything to add. I said I had two things on my mind: firstly, I was shocked that PetroSaudi still had the power to threaten to bring charges against the media and individual journalists for reporting facts; and secondly, I was disgusted that they were still able to enjoy billionaire lifestyles with what was stolen money.

On my way out, I spoke to the prosecutor about the snail's pace of justice and he commented that in a sprawling case like this, involving dozens of people and hundreds or even thousands of bank accounts, things could take time. It seemed to me that for any "ordinary" criminal who got caught, prison was a foregone conclusion, whereas for those who stole hundreds of millions of dollars there was nothing inevitable about it.

The US Department of Justice had by this time seized more than $1 billion in Malaysian assets originating from 1MDB which had been illegally invested in the US, and had clearly mentioned PetroSaudi — and the names of Tarek Obaid and Patrick Mahony — in proceedings. This was a victory for us and a flag to other countries, including Switzerland, that they should be taking the matter seriously. Surely, arrests would soon follow…

It ought to be stressed that the data I had passed on not only incriminated PetroSaudi — it also had a domino effect in exposing others who had been in league with 1MDB, not least Goldman Sachs.

The American banking giant collected hundreds of millions of dollars in commission on bond issuance activity that normally only would have earned them tens of millions. In their case, greed won over financial probity, but at least they were brought to heel: in 2020, the bank negotiated a settlement with Malaysia in which it agreed to pay over $2 billion in fines. Not enough for my taste — but again, a victory.

Laura and I decided there would be time enough to launch our own complaint against PetroSaudi — naming Tarek, Patrick and Paul — once it became clearer how things were progressing with the overall 1MDB case in Switzerland. In the meantime, we felt it would do us good to go abroad for a while as a family. We chose Spain, where the winter weather is nice and where we could be away from everything and just recharge our batteries.

Having that spell of tranquility and rest did us a world of good, and we returned to Geneva in May 2017.

Unfortunately there were other problems waiting for us. We needed to find somewhere to live, but found our attempts to obtain a lease thwarted. It transpired that my family and I were known around town — however, people tended to know only scant details about our case and assumed we were guilty. One potential landlord even told us he feared there might be a bomb in the car park if he let his apartment to us.

And my daily problems as an ex-prisoner didn't end there: I was also unable to open a bank account... in my own country. You can bet that neither Tarek Obaid, Patrick Mahony nor any others of their circle had such problems. The PRs they had paid to discredit me and paint themselves as the victims had been highly effective, to the point that in the city where I had lived for most of my life, I constantly had to justify myself and try to explain the truth to people. It was exhausting: I just wanted to be able to live quietly with my family.

Finally, through a friend, we found a flat in the Pâquis district where I had grown up 50 years earlier. It was a return to my roots. We moved in during July, and for the first time had a taste of traditional Swiss family life.

The same month I also had to return to Bern, this time for a confrontation — as part of the same investigation — with S.T., who now denied having given me the hard disk with the data from the PetroSaudi server. (Incidentally, and somewhat incredibly, he still worked as a consultant for PetroSaudi. Moreover, in May 2018 he became a Director at the company. What better way to keep him on their leash?)

I brought technical proof showing that the data couldn't have been taken from any of PetroSaudi's computers in London, and that therefore I couldn't have been the one who extracted it. S.T., on the other hand, had had access to the server in Geneva, and possibly remotely. He was clearly uncomfortable with what I presented, but continued to insist he had played no part in the leak.

I could understand his predicament, because if he confessed to having given me the disk he would surely be accused by PetroSaudi of theft, but I begged him to tell the truth and stop covering for people he knew to be criminals. I also asked him to forgive me for breaking my promise not to pass on the data — and asked him to consider that the theft of billions of dollars from Malaysia weighed more heavily than the betrayal of such a promise.

I could see that the police believed me, but S.T. wouldn't budge and the conversation ended in a stalemate. In fact, we traveled back to Geneva together on the train, and managed to avoid any further discussion of the case.

IN SEPTEMBER, CHRISTIAN and Gilles proposed that we start gathering everything we needed to file our complaint.

This was no small undertaking: we had to get hundreds of pages of evidence translated into French. Mainly thanks to Laura's extraordinary intelligence and determination, however, a lot of the painstaking work of cataloging the evidence and putting it in order had already been done, and once again she set herself to the task with amazing industry. The support we had from Gilles and Christian was also indispensable.

We lacked no motivation for pursuing the case, but it was clear that revealing the truth and making the real criminals pay was going to be an arduous battle. Not only did we want justice for the wrongs committed, but our family name had been sullied by PetroSaudi, often with the help of lapdog journalists, and we needed to restore it. We knew there would be obstacles put in our way, and that expensive lawyers and PR firms would be enlisted to try and manipulate the judicial process and the media narrative.

It strikes me that the world would be a different place if lawyers didn't make exorbitant sums of money from abetting criminals. The 1MDB-Petrosaudi scam was set up by law firms and tax experts. They created the structures to launder money and received millions for doing so, but it's unlikely that they will ever have to pay anything back. Sophisticated criminals can afford to buy the services of people whose talent is devoted to manipulating the law. For the normal citizen forced to defend himself, justice is slow and expensive.

But you need to focus on the positives — and in late 2017 we had some good news. We had left three dogs, as well as numerous cats and parrots in Thailand. The parrots were untransferable as they had no papers and the cats were free spirits who came to us when they wanted and then disappeared for months on end. But one of the dogs — Veggie — had always occupied a special place in our hearts.

Trying to get her back from Thailand was no small challenge. Suffice to say that dealing with Thai bureaucracy again brought back some painful memories. Happily, though, we managed to get the paperwork over the line. The day we picked her up from the airport we promised ourselves we wouldn't cry — but as anyone who keeps animals will know, such promises are worthless. When Veggie was brought through customs, we shed tears of pure joy.

With her addition, our family was complete and ready for the challenge ahead. After all that we had survived since I had last seen her, nothing could cower us.

Chapter 28

Laura

DAVID VERSUS GOLIATH

TOWARDS THE END of 2016, and ahead of Xavier's release, I had been contacted by journalists who were working on a TV documentary for one of the Italian networks in Switzerland about the fate of the Italian Swiss bank BSI. At the time it was in the process of being swallowed up by another Swiss bank, EFG, having had its banking license revoked in Singapore and having come under investigation by the Swiss regulator over its involvement in transactions related to 1MDB and PetroSaudi.

I spent two days being filmed and interviewed at my parents' house by two very talented reporters, to whom I gave substantial amounts of evidence and source material. It was a case of re-telling, again, my incredible story, with all its unlikely facets and twists. Their response chimed with that of many others who listened — they said the course of events Xavier and I had weathered was worthy of a movie.

By coincidence, the documentary's broadcast date was a couple of days after Xavier's release, and so they asked to interview us both live afterwards. As we watched the show being aired, we had to fight back tears — re-living the nightmare didn't get any easier. But the show felt like a triumph; despite the efforts of PetroSaudi's lawyers to stall it, the film didn't pull its punches. It was another battle won and made me believe there was no way of stopping the truth from winning out.

Curiously, a handful of journalists, mainly writing in obscure blogs, continued to try to discredit us, but if Patrick and Tarek were trying to wage a PR war via the media, we were confident that they would lose it. At the same time, we knew we had to keep the momentum going if we were to restore Xavier's good reputation and achieve justice. Along with Clare's excellent interview with me, this TV documentary helped to keep the pressure on the authorities to act.

In January 2017, our lawyers arranged for a sit-down with Henzelin and Giroud to discuss their so-called defense of Xavier during his incarceration and the absurd fees they had charged for it.

The atmosphere was tense from the beginning and in his opening remarks Henzelin was scathing about our reasons for calling the meeting. Christian Luscher pushed him to explain the extravagant fees paid to Lalive not by PetroSaudi but by David Scholberg's company, KBSD, a third party whose involvement had been kept secret from us. Henzelin became agitated and told us he did not understand how I could have failed to know about KBSD, given that Scholberg had been at the Bangkok St. Regis at the same time as me, as part of the team acting on Xavier's behalf.

His answers were evasive, like those of a politician, so I put it to him directly that it had in fact been his duty to mention Scholberg, at least to Xavier. "When you sign a mandate to defend a client," I said, "you know that you must keep him informed of everything that concerns his case. Mr Scholberg's name was never once mentioned to us; however, it's in your files that he discussed matters of strategy with you by email even before Xavier signed a mandate for you to represent him."

I further commented that such conduct was ethically indecent and a disgrace to the legal profession. That kind of brought the discussion to an end. Henzelin and Giroud left offended and angry, but I hoped their anger was also mingled with guilt and anxiety at knowing they could be in trouble over what they had done.

As the weeks and months rolled by, the press coverage continued. Xavier even featured in a *Vanity Fair* article, his image appearing alongside that of Leonardo DiCaprio, whose name became connected to the 1MDB affair after it emerged that "The Wolf of Wall Street," a movie in which he starred, had been financed with 1MDB money by Najib Razak's stepson, Rita Aziz.

SEVERAL MONTHS OF media glare can be intense, so we decided to get away from it for a while and decamp to the south of Spain. It was a smart move. Finally we were able to decompress from our ordeal, get back to appreciating the simple things of life and spend quality time as a family. We enjoyed every second of it — laughing together, talking, being happy. My parents and my brother joined us for a couple of weeks, and we also managed to go on a trip to Fuerteventura, in the Canary Islands, where I got to indulge my passion for surfing. Finally, we finished up our Spanish adventure with ten days in Barcelona.

All in all, it was an incredible break, but we knew that hard work lay ahead of us on our return to Switzerland and that our complaint against PetroSaudi depended entirely on my evidence being completely bulletproof. We also had other challenges to confront as we attempted to re-assimilate to life in Geneva — for example, our "fame" made it difficult for us to find an apartment. It seemed landlords thought we could be a risk to their property on account of Xavier being targeted by unscrupulous enemies. It was enormously frustrating but made us all the more determined to reverse the damage to his name by making sure the Swiss justice system did its job.

In May, I received a shocking phone call from a journalist, let's call him "Henry," from an important Swiss newspaper. It transpired that Patrick Mahony had filed a complaint against him following an article he had written in October 2016 that included a link to an excerpt of a recording I had made of a conversation between Patrick Mahony and myself. Patrick's charge was that Henry had published a recording that had been made without his knowledge.

Henry asked if I could testify and bring evidence to help him during his hearing. I was, of course, more than happy to do so, and a few months later I was called to appear at the Public Ministry of the Confederation (MPC) in Geneva.

The case didn't directly implicate me but I was nevertheless wracked with nerves, because it was my evidence and its validity that were under scrutiny. If Patrick were to lose against this journalist, it would be a strike for us. Gilles Crettol accompanied me and fortunately the hearing went smoothly: I merely had to answer the questions put to me simply and truthfully.

Key to my evidence was that I was able to demonstrate how Patrick had ordered Aziz to install an application on my phone in order to record my conversation with Clare Rewcastle Brown — and that he should therefore have been well aware of its existence on my phone. I also showed that I had written to Paul to express concern that using the application without Clare's consent would be illegal — and that this supposed English police officer had replied that it was absolutely legal and that Patrick wouldn't have asked me to use it otherwise.

Eventually, Henry called me with the news that Patrick's complaint against him had been thrown out. What a vindication! Patrick had tried to discredit my recordings as evidence on the grounds that he hadn't given his consent — but in fact he was ultimately responsible for the app being used. He had been fooled at his own game.

In July, we finally moved into a new rented apartment in Château Banquet, a building in Pâquis, right in the heart of Geneva and near the lake. The simple act of finding a place for ourselves after so long felt incredible. I decorated the whole apartment, including a beautiful room just for Xander, and we were soon making the most of our new home by inviting friends over regularly.

On 16 July, I celebrated my birthday and it seemed to me that for the first time I had everything I had ever dreamed of, all in one place. Surrounded by the people who meant everything to me — my friends, my family, my husband and my son — I felt truly fulfilled.

We spent an idyllic summer walking in the mountains, barbecuing with friends, and enjoying watersports on the lake. We also took Xander swimming almost every day. Time passed and we savored all the things we had missed when we had been separated and forced to fight for survival; but neither did we forget about what needed to be done.

Slowly but surely I started to put everything in order that we would need for our complaint against PetroSaudi and their partners in crime. It was a titanic job and took many days and nights of sifting through hundreds of documents — everything from photos and other evidence proving the involvement of Paul Finnigan, to emails by David Scholberg about the plot to destroy Xavier's reputation, letters, testimonies, transcripts of phone and text conversations, and much more, all proving the web of deceit and corruption these people had spun around the world. It was a daunting task but ably supported by Gilles and Christian. They — and Xavier — assured me I had done an extraordinary job.

We eventually filed our complaint with the Swiss Prosecutor General on 23 October (which by a twist of fate that gave us a good laugh also happens to be Tarek Obaid's birthday). It contained no fewer than 13 charges: threatening behavior; blackmail; extorsion; coercion; sequestration; endangering the lives of others; slander; slanderous denunciation; misleading the courts; bribery of foreign public officials;

forgery of documents; criminal organization; and money laundering. I remember feeling an indescribable sensation of joy and freedom when we received confirmation that it had been received and I hoped with all my heart that I would be called quickly to give testimony. I desperately wanted to put my story on public record and for the authorities to dole out justice. Our lawyers cautioned that the wheels would probably turn slowly, however, and much to my frustration they were right.

After the passage of several months with no news, we decided to call a press conference in Zurich to make our complaint public and to let our targets know we still had them firmly in our sights. It was a stressful thing to pull off but it went well and managed to generate a significant amount of favorable press coverage.

As ever, PetroSaudi's lawyers were quick to deny everything and assert that their clients had done nothing wrong. Of course, white collar criminals always find a way of passing the blame around like a hot potato, and a pattern was beginning to emerge in 1MDB-related inquiries and litigation around the world. PetroSaudi's position was that they had been manipulated by the Malaysians and by Jho Low. Jho Low in turn said he was manipulated by Prime Minister Najib Razak — and Najib's defense was that he was manipulated by Jho Low and by PetroSaudi. The truth was that they had all ended up with hundreds of millions of dollars in their own bank accounts, and in an attempt to wipe the slate clean they had silenced Xavier by having him thrown into a Thai snake-pit. So much for being manipulated by other parties.

Our questions to journalists were designed to put the spotlight firmly on PetroSaudi's guilt: Why was their response to the original revelations a kangaroo court campaign to make Xavier go away? If what we were exposing to the world was false, why didn't PetroSaudi file a counter-claim against us? And why hadn't Tarek, Patrick or Paul ever had the courage to face questioning by the press?

In April 2018, we heard rumors that the Swiss authorities were negotiating an out-of-court settlement with PetroSaudi. We were deeply alarmed. Apparently it would involve fines and suspended sentences for Tarek and Patrick, but no prison time. This couldn't be right. Switzerland had turned a blind eye in the past to shady financial practices but the country was supposed to have turned over a new leaf. How could the justice system be contemplating such a pact with the devil? We were determined to oppose any such deal, and fortunately to date it has not come to pass.

Meanwhile, Xavier was asked to attend a few conferences to talk about his experience of corruption and to explain how organizations were still able to commit such crimes despite new banking regulations and scrutiny. His message was simple: you can put in place all the safeguards you like to prevent financial crime, but if the people responsible for enforcing them don't do so, or do so badly, then the crimes will continue to happen.

Often he was asked if he considered himself to be a "whistleblower." We discovered that people often think of whistleblowers as being like a cross between Nelson Mandela and Mahatma Gandhi. In reality, it is rarely as simple as that: whistleblowers are citizens like any others and have to choose between morality and their own safety and security.

Xavier began his banking career in 1987; I started mine in 2006, not long before the PetroSaudi-1MDB scam got going in 2009. In the two decades in between, the financial world actually changed a lot — and had gotten used to new regulations monitoring suspicious transactions, new rules aimed at making financial crimes harder to pull off, and the rise of compliance officers.

Had anything really changed, though? Had things got better? In fact, no: there have been more, and bigger, financial crimes than ever before. For all the regulatory oversight, and for all the digitalisation in the sector, transactions are still conducted by human beings, and by nature human beings are corruptible and manipulable.

How many people feel compelled to report nefarious activities they see at work if such reporting involves compromising the company that pays their salary and ultimately feeds their family? How many people will put their careers at risk by going against management? Every action has consequences, and denouncing a crime can be very costly — as our family has learned the hard way.

AS WE SETTLED into life in Geneva we found some consulting work that allowed us to keep our necks above water. I also took on some translation work. We continued to keep an eye, however, on any and all developments relating to 1MDB's undoing. As Xavier will relate in the next chapter, something big was brewing in Malaysia — events that coincidentally or not also resulted in the resignation of Patrick Mahony as a director of PetroSaudi on 11 May, 2018, according to the business and enterprise register of Switzerland.

On June 1, I traveled to London to attempt to file a complaint with the Metropolitan Police against Patrick Mahony, Tarek Obaid and Paul Finnigan. Xavier had gone to Malaysia but planned to join me at the end of my London visit.

The policewoman assigned to talk to me seemed more interested in the box of donuts brought to her by a colleague than she was in what I was trying to tell her. I knew my narrative sounded somewhat fantastical, but I couldn't help but wonder if she thought I was crazy. She looked simply overwhelmed by it all, so I offered to send her web links summarizing the 1MDB case, which I assured her had gained significant international exposure. I also told her I would follow up by sending her all the evidence I had in English translation.

Afterwards, I found I had to chase the matter up by email just to get a case number, and on several subsequent occasions I emailed to ask for news and received no reply. It troubled me that a former British police officer who passed himself off as being a current Scotland Yard detective had been hired by criminals to go after an innocent man, but that the police in the city where these criminals had conducted much of their business had almost no interest in finding out more. To this day, I have never had any follow-up communication or feedback regarding this complaint.

Chapter 29

Xavier

A HERO'S WELCOME

IN THE RUN-UP to Malaysia's general election of 9 May, 2018, the ruling Barisan Nasional coalition, led by the incumbent Prime Minister Najib Razak, had been in power for more than 50 years and was favored to return to power again — even despite the 1MDB embezzlement scandal and the public exposure of Najib's direct involvement.

There were credible voices in Malaysia hinting that a change was coming, however, and that gave us some hope of Najib being ousted.

As the results came in, Laura and I followed the changing electoral map live online. The day started badly, with Barisan Nasional parties — chief among these the United Malays National Organisation (UMNO) — leading the race. But gradually the opposition parties, led by Mahathir Mohamad, began to gain ground.

Dr Mahathir had been Prime Minister from 1980-2003 and was very much an establishment figure, but in 2016 he had quit the UMNO in protest at Najib's corruption, and in 2018 he led the Pakatan Harapan ("Alliance of Hope") grouping, a faction that also included the reformist People's Justice Party led by Anwar Ibrahim (more about whom in due course). As the count continued, Mathathir suddenly emerged as the favorite to form a new government, until eventually it became clear that history had been made and the Barisan Nasional had been ousted — thanks to backing for Mahathir and Anwar.

Dr Mahathir's victory was a cause for celebration as far as we were concerned. We even shed a few tears as we popped a bottle of champagne that we had been saving. It felt like a victory that we could share in and one that went some way to extenuating our suffering since 2015. We were in contact with various friends and contacts in Malaysia and were touched by their sense of joy and relief, and their appreciation for the part we had played in uncovering the 1MDB fiasco.

Two days after the election I received a call from a man named Kamal Siddiqi. I didn't know him, but it seemed I had mentioned him in my false depositions to the press in Thailand, where I had been forced to describe him as a player in a purported plot to overthrow Najib.

He asked me to come and visit him in the UK to talk, and I agreed to fly over later that week. A little research told me that he was an engineer and a successful entrepreneur in his mid-50s who was known for introducing the first electric cabs to London.

He sent a driver to pick me up on arrival at the airport and I was taken to a location in Surrey, in the countryside outside London, where Kamal ran a factory making prototype electric trucks and vans.

He showed me to his office, which was adorned with pictures of Dr Mahathir, and congratulated me on what Laura and I had done to help his country. He then proposed that I go to Malaysia… to meet the new Prime Minister! I told him I was sure that I was likely to be on a list of people banned from entering the country, but he promised me everything would be taken care of, that I needn't worry, and that an official would meet me the moment I stepped off the plane.

True to his word, that's what happened when — a few days later — I touched down at Kuala Lumpur: a government official met me at the arrival gate.

Unfortunately things didn't go entirely smoothly after that. No sooner had my passport been scanned at immigration than an alarm went off. The document was whisked from hand to hand and an immigration officer told me to follow him. As I had predicted, I was still on the banned list.

Left to wait in an office, I could see people outside peering in at me, talking about me and trying to discreetly film me. Here was my introduction to the fame I had lately acquired in Malaysia.

I didn't feel worried but I had been rather looking forward to going to my hotel and having a shower before I was due to meet Dr Mahathir. Eventually, after about two hours, a driver brought documentation from the Prime Minister's office and I was allowed to officially enter Malaysia. A car from the Shangri-La was waiting to pick me up, but there was no time to stop at the hotel: we had to go straight to the Prime Minister's residence. I sensed the driver was more stressed at the situation and by the thought of seeing the PM than I was.

It was about 5pm when we arrived at our destination — a modest-looking house in an upscale neighborhood that seemed to be part of a golf course development. On entering the building, I took off my shoes and was shown to a room where Kamal Siddiqi and Mahathir Mohamad were waiting for me.

I suddenly felt a little anxious and emotional but the Prime Minister quickly put me at ease. I felt immediately that he had an aura about him, and he spoke to me in a soft and agreeable voice.

Over the course of an hour and a half, we talked about 1MDB, PetroSaudi and my experience of prison. It was late when we wrapped up but before I left I asked if I could have a photograph with him. He assented and Kamal did the honors on my phone camera.

Back at the Shangri-La I called Laura to tell her about the meeting and share something of the moment with her. And finally, before falling asleep at around 2am, I decided to post the picture with Dr Mahathir on Facebook.

When I woke up I discovered to my amazement that I had thousands of Facebook friend requests, as well as dozens of requests from journalists for interviews. My phone didn't stop pinging all morning.

The messages happily included one from Kay Tat, the editor from *The Edge* newspaper to whom I had given a copy of the PetroSaudi server in February 2015, and who I had neither seen nor spoken to since. He told me that all of KL was aware of my presence. We agreed to have lunch the following day and talk about the incredible events of the past three years.

By then, I was on the front page of every newspaper in Malaysia — and in fact this was just the beginning of my media exposure in the country. I would be a "face" in the newspapers, and on television, on many more occasions to come. In truth it gave me a weird feeling to see myself in print or on screen, and still does.

Even the employees and staff of the hotel now knew I was "famous" and would ask me for photos and autographs. I wasn't at all keen on being a celebrity, but I did enjoy these moments of recognition and friendship.

I accepted some but not all of the requests for interviews — I had been advised that many of the country's newspapers remained close to Najib and would have an agenda against me. I did not have experience of dealing with the press, but I quickly realized it's relatively easy to communicate effectively when you are telling the truth. Only liars have to go to the effort of concocting a story.

Over the course of a couple of weeks in Malaysia I met the Prime Minister several times, always in the presence of Kamal Siddiqi. Besides the topic of 1MDB, they often spoke about potential electric vehicle projects in the country, which I found interesting. I also met several other key people involved in digging into the 1MDB affair, and spent many hours at the premises of the Malaysian Anti-Corruption Commission (MACC).

Everyone at the MACC seemed kind, respectful and patient as I told them everything I knew about the 1MDB-PetroSaudi scam. Again, I found myself being held up as a poster boy as they asked me for autographs and selfies and told me they were touched by the sacrifices I had made for their country. Only when I asked who they had been investigating before Najib's electoral defeat did they turn bashful. It seems the corruption watchdog's hands had been tied by the ruling elite.

I returned to Europe at the end of May and went to meet Laura in London. She had just lodged an official complaint with the Metropolitan Police against Tarek Obaid, Patrick Mahony and Paul Finnigan and we followed it up by submitting hundreds of pages of evidence by email. It made perfect sense to us that we should do so; after all, PetroSaudi had been allowed to operate in the British capital. To this day, however, we have heard nothing back from them. Similarly, there was never any follow-up from the UK's National Crime Agency, whose agent Laura had met in 2016.

Having lived in London, I can attest to the fact that much of the real estate in the city's finest neighborhoods is owned by people whose funds are more than suspicious. If the UK were to properly investigate these people a large part of London could be freed up for citizens with normal jobs and normal wages.

I traveled again to Malaysia in June to provide the MACC with additional information and documents and met again with Kamal and the Prime Minister. Each of these meetings was unforgettable: Dr Mahathir has an incredible charm about him and a very sharp mind. He is well into his 90s but remains in incredible shape physically and has a brain like that of a 20-something.

Some months later I also found myself in London again — this time for a dinner in celebration of the victory of what had been for so long Malaysia's opposition. I was introduced and treated as a hero, which seemed a little excessive but also felt nice and helped to counteract some of the suffering our family had endured.

Ultimately, I see myself as an ordinary person who had to make an important moral choice and in doing so helped to advance democracy in a country that deserved better.

Shortly after my return to Europe from my second trip to KL, Najib Razak was arrested over his involvement in a related scandal involving the misappropriation of millions of dollars from SRC International, a company that had been formed to handle infrastructure projects. Without going into detail, the pattern of corruption was the same as in 1MDB's dealings with PetroSaudi: the Prime Minister had hoarded public funds for his own personal use.

Even though Najib remained free on bail, we thought of this as a win. It was a win, certainly, relative to what was going on in Switzerland, where the authorities had failed to move against Tarek and Patrick, both of whom were still at liberty and enjoying their stolen money.

Geneva is a small city where news gets around. We knew they were continuing to party in all the old places and with the same careless abandon. At times, the thought of it made us mad with rage, particularly as we were essentially struggling to make a living.

In July, the Swiss authorities finally announced Tarek and Patrick had been placed under investigation for, *inter alia*, bribery of a foreign official, forgery of documents and aggravated money laundering.

I was more than convinced that the Swiss — and the Malaysians, and the Americans for that matter — knew these two men were guilty and had the evidence to prove it; and yet at least for now they still remained at large.

IN THE AUTUMN, two journalists from the *Wall Street Journal*, Tom Wright and Bradley Hope, published "Billion Dollar Whale: The Man Who Fooled Wall Street, Hollywood, and the World," a book about the

1MDB affair with a particular focus on Jho Low's part in it. I had been glad to assist them by sharing documents and spending many hours on the phone explaining PetroSaudi's role in the scandal. The book highlights both the staggering corruption perpetrated by Jho Low, Najib Razak and their co-conspirators, and the need for justice.

Another book, published around the same time, was Clare Rewcastle Brown's account of the scandal — "The Sarawak Report: The Inside Story of the 1MDB Exposé." I found it to be the better of the two accounts published, and full of searing insights and anecdotes. It is also a testament to Clare's love for the country in which she was born, to British parents, and where she has spent much of her life.

In October, I participated in two conferences in Kuala Lumpur, again focused on corruption and economic crimes. At the second event, there were over 1,000 participants, and once again I was on the receiving end of some effusive Malaysian appreciation.

On the same visit, I also gave a radio interview and a live interview on television. The latter was a little nerve-wracking, especially as the journalist told me before we went on air that he was known for being somewhat aggressive. I rose to the challenge, however, and told him to enjoy himself as I had nothing to fear from him by telling the truth.

At some point around this time, I was also interviewed by an Al-Jazeera reporter who asked me perhaps the most pertinent question of all relating to my entanglement in this whole sordid affair. This journalist wanted to know what would have happened if PetroSaudi had simply paid me the money I was due. Would I still have exposed their crimes?

My answer was, and still is, that I don't know. All I can say is that it's an honest answer. I hope I would have still done what I did — and what's more I *think* I would have done it, because I'd like to think that's who I am and who my parents taught me to be. But in the end, I'll never know.

Besides some other press interviews, further visits to the MACC and another audience with the Prime Minister, I also got the chance to meet in KL with another veteran politician. Anwar Ibrahim had been Finance Minister and then Deputy Prime Minister during Dr Mahathir's first long tenure in office but later spent many years in prison on charges — which he has always denied, maintaining they were politically motivated — of sodomy, a crime under Malaysia's penal code. His relationship with his former boss might best be described as complicated, but by 2018 the two had put aside their differences and following Dr Mahathir's electoral triumph, Anwar was immediately given a royal pardon. He would later succeed Dr Mahathir as head of the Pakatan Harapan coalition.

I discovered Anwar to be another extremely fascinating and inspiring individual, and a man who overflowed with energy. Despite having spent a decade or so in prison all in, his commitment to political change had been unwavering. I found his extraordinary resilience greatly to be admired.

Back in Europe, Laura and I considered that it was time for another change of scenery. We had become too well-known in Geneva and, as alluded to, Switzerland is not exactly a whistleblower's paradise. We made plans to move to London after spending Christmas and New Year as a family in Malaysia. These plans came to nought, however, after several friends and acquaintances cautioned us against the move. London was simply not an option as England's libel laws are such that PetroSaudi could have drowned us in litigation proceedings.

AT THE END of January 2019, as our holiday in Malaysia was drawing to a close, Kay Tat called me to say that Kooi Ong wanted to meet us. Apparently he was keen to make a donation to us for the help we'd given his country. I was surprised and frankly amazed but at the same time inwardly delighted as things had been difficult for us. At the time I had a couple of projects on the go in real estate and consulting but these were likely to take several months to come to fruition and we were strapped financially. In fact, at the time we were living on money a friend had lent us. Now it seemed we were to be offered a new lifeline.

We went to see Kooi Ong at his office and — on the spot — he produced a cheque for 8 million ringgit, which is equivalent to about $2 million.

Laura and I were utterly astonished. I had never seen nor contacted Kooi Ong after meeting him in February 2015, but it was Chinese New Year, which he said always made him feel generous. He explained that he liked stories where the good guys win in the end and that he wanted to thank us for the sacrifices we had made to help Malaysia. He also showed us the Monet painting that he had wanted to give me as a guarantee when we had met in Singapore.

Our response to his gesture was one of pure relief and gratitude. Most of our savings and the money I had been paid by PetroSaudi had been sunk into our Thai venture. Some of that had been recouped when we sold the resort, but taxes, legal fees and other costs had eaten up a lot of what we were left with. Kooi Ong had obviously been sensitive to the precarity of our situation; but now, thanks to him, we could see a new beginning in front of us and have confidence for the future.

After abandoning our London plan, Laura and I had made tentative arrangements about going to live in Spain; however, on the insistence of Kamal and others, we decided to settle in Malaysia instead, at least for a while. We had found it to be a beautiful country with incredibly friendly people and we now had contacts who could surely help us find jobs and earn a living.

I had opened a new company in Geneva after coming out of prison and decided to now close it down and clear out of Switzerland entirely. Inevitably, however, this was easier said than done, as the notaries I contacted to take care of basic administrative procedures didn't seem to want to help and wouldn't return my calls. Not for the first time, I felt that being all over the internet for having been in prison had made me persona non grata.

Finally, I was able to find a notary's office that agreed to take care of things entirely online without putting obstacles in our way. It was a weight off our shoulders — life could go on and we could set our course for a new chapter in Malaysia.

Further obstacles lay in wait, though, as banking the cheque from Kooi Ong proved a little more difficult than we had imagined. The first bank we tried asked for resident visas. We had started the process of getting these but it was going to take time. Another bank said I was too well-known in the country; in fact, the person we dealt with even said that if Najib Razak ever returned to power, he didn't want to be found out as having allowed me to open an account.

This sentiment was one I was to become familiar with in conversations with various people — including some of the most prominent figures in Malaysian society. They might have been glad to see Najib ousted, but deep down they were afraid that one day he and his cronies would return to power and they wanted to protect their positions. Their caution unfortunately turned out to be partly justified.

In the end, I asked someone close to the Prime Minister if his office could give us a letter of introduction to be able to open an account. This was granted and we were finally able to bank the money on 15 February, 2019.

Shortly afterwards, I received a call from Kamal asking me if I would be able to lend him some cash. He sent me papers showing that his company would soon be floated on the London Stock Exchange at a valuation of several hundred million dollars. These were genuine documents stamped by Swiss banks, and I had no reason to doubt Kamal, having listened to him talk at length with high-profile businessmen and public figures about his plans to set up a factory making electric vehicles in Malaysia. He said there would also be an opportunity to join the company when the factory was built; otherwise, he would be able to help me establish my own business, for example in helping foreign firms set up in Malaysia.

Kamal said the IPO would likely take place in the next few months. After speaking with Laura, we agreed to lend him half of the money we had received from Kooi Ong. Morally, we felt that investing Kooi Ong's cash back into Malaysia was a good thing to do.

After paying various expenses, taxes and legal fees, as well as reimbursing some friends who had helped us, that didn't leave us with a whole lot in the bank — but we trusted Kamal as a friend 100 percent.

ON 14 FEBRUARY, I received messages from three journalists — one at Reuters, one at Bloomberg and another who wrote for *Le Temps* in Switzerland. They all wanted to speak to me urgently as apparently they had learned that in November 2018 Swiss federal prosecutors had opened an investigation against me following a complaint by PetroSaudi of industrial espionage.

I was stunned — I had never been given any information about such an investigation. The journalists didn't reveal their initial sources, but it was obvious to me that they must have been tipped off by PetroSaudi's retainers. What they did confirm was that the office of the Attorney General had told them this information was correct and that it had indeed opened an investigation following authorization by the then justice minister, Simonetta Sommaruga, two months previously.

Again, there was no doubt in my mind that this would have been the result of pressure exerted by PetroSaudi's lawyers. The whole business made me wonder how Switzerland could be said to be any different from a banana republic.

I contacted Christian Luscher right away and he said he had likewise been completely unaware of any such investigation. We decided to wait in case we heard anything from the Swiss authorities. Almost four years later, there has been nothing.

After communicating with Christian, I wrote back to the Reuters and Bloomberg reporters — both of whom I had spoken to about 1MDB matters before — and told them the same thing, which was that I had received no information from the Swiss authorities about any investigation against me and that publishing reports of one could only sully my name.

They both responded within minutes to say that they would therefore refrain from publishing anything. Thank God they were both journalists of integrity. The same could not be said, unfortunately, for the reporter from *Le Temps.*

This journalist had in fact been one of the first to cover the PetroSaudi case in Switzerland. I had met him several times in Geneva and given him numerous documents to help him with his articles, but they always seemed to skew towards siding with PetroSaudi. Laura and I had talked about suing him for defamation but never had the resolve to go through with it.

On a telephone call, I told him the same thing I had told the other reporters, and added that I knew he knew the details of the case, including who the culprits were. He responded by asking for an on-the-record statement and I told him it was clear to me that PetroSaudi were trying to smear me and divert attention away from the real questions they had to face about their criminal activities.

He said he was aware that I was due to speak at a conference in Switzerland and asked if I wasn't concerned I might be arrested. Of course, I replied that I wasn't concerned in the slightest.

In the event, the article he published contained none of what I said and raised this notion of my possible arrest. It read like it had been written on behalf of PetroSaudi.

The day of its publication, my 80-year-old mother called me in tears. She had read in her newspaper that I could be arrested if I came back to

Switzerland and she was worried and scared. I don't wish ill on people in principle but perhaps someone close to this journalist will some day suffer in such a way that he will reflect on his own conduct.

WE RETURNED TO Switzerland for a few months to prepare everything for our move back to Asia. There was still no news of our complaint against PetroSaudi — but by now we had learned that justice moves at its own speed.

In May, I met in Geneva with a journalist from Tamedia, a Swiss media company, who told me she was about to land a scoop linking Tarek Obaid and Switzerland's Attorney General, Michael Lauber. True to her word, on 12 May the story appeared. It claimed that a man named René Brulhart, one of Mr Lauber's best friends, had received more than two million dollars from Tarek in exchange for unspecified services. The story wasn't hugely surprising to me, but I rather hoped it wasn't true and that it didn't account for the aforementioned snail's pace of the government's investigations.

Chapter 30

Laura

A FALSE DAWN

IN JULY 2019, we left Switzerland with the intention of building a new life in Malaysia. This time, we traveled together as a family — the three of us plus our beloved dog, Veggie.

We stayed initially at a hotel before deciding where we wanted to live. After looking around, we settled on a beautiful place in Bukit Damansara, a quiet neighborhood that is only a short drive from the city center. It's also close to the French School, where we enrolled Xander.

From early on in our new adventure, we had friends and family come to visit us, and when the school holidays came we took the opportunity to travel around and take in more of the country's astonishing beauty.

Life was good, but of course like anywhere else Malaysia has its share of problems. We soon discovered that every year there is a serious environmental issue arising from fires caused by deforestation for palm oil development. The fires are mainly in Indonesia, but fine particle pollution often reaches Kuala Lumpur, causing smog and prompting the government to close schools. The destruction of biodiverse forests and their replacement with unsustainable plantations seemed to us yet another example of humanity's priorities being all upside down.

We were guests in this part of the world, though, and for that reason we made sure not to venture too many opinions. Malaysians in fact often wanted to know what we thought about local politics, but we mostly avoided weighing in.

Thinking back, however, one thing I could never quite fathom was how a country's politics could be so overshadowed by ethnicity. Malaysia's three largest population groups — Malays, Indians and Chinese — exist as distinct power blocs and there are unmistakable tensions between them. Perhaps being Swiss gave Xavier and I a unique perspective on this: Switzerland is a small country with four languages and distinct communities which have lived peacefully together for hundreds of years. It could be an example for other places to follow. Admittedly, Malaysia is a much younger country than Switzerland, which was established more than 700 years ago. Maybe it just needs time.

One question Malaysians often asked us was why their government had not rewarded us for our sacrifices. Our response was that it was never something we expected or desired. We never asked to be compensated — but more than that the gratitude we had encountered from everyday people, and the satisfaction of having participated in the expulsion of a government that was stealing their money, felt like reward enough.

The wall of official silence and public suspicion we had experienced in Switzerland contrasted markedly with the recognition we received in KL, where hardly a day went past without someone expressing thanks on behalf of their country. Xander, who had just turned five, was beginning to understand that we were quite a famous family, although thankfully he was still too young for us to have to explain it all to him.

At times, we actually felt that our "fame" prevented us from integrating better with Malaysian society. People were sometimes awkward or embarrassed around us, and perhaps others were afraid to associate with us. Whatever the reasons, we found it hard to build much of a social life.

In spite of this, I did make some good Malaysian friends. Unfortunately, the current political situation in the country does not allow me to mention them by name, but they know who they are and that they have a place in my heart.

My personal goal in Malaysia was to study for a cookery diploma at KL's Cordon Bleu Academy. To be accepted as a student, however — and for Xavier to be allowed to start a company — we needed to have residency permits, and these were slow in coming.

After a while, we tried to expedite matters by asking the Prime Minister's office directly. We were instructed to contact Muhyiddin Yassin, who was at that time Dr Mahathir's Minister of Home Affairs. Unfortunately, despite repeated follow-up inquiries, nothing came of this connection and our permits were never granted. So much for my ambition to attend the Academy.

Was Muhyiddin's refusal to help deliberate — a snub to his then boss? Again, I can't offer any answers but I do know that our Malaysian friends were mystified that we didn't get our permits.

While we waited for officialdom to give us a helping hand, I found I had rediscovered my appetite for sport and fitness and started running regularly in the hills near our house. It helped me to clear my mind and I loved getting back into shape.

Another joy was rediscovering the beauty of the temples of Angkor, in Cambodia. Almost a decade after my first visit, with Xavier, we went again with Xander on the school holidays and fell in love once more with the beauty and serenity of the place. Xander was enchanted; I'm sure it felt to him like discovering a new world. As for me, I hadn't experienced such an intense feeling of peace for a long time.

IN OCTOBER 2019 — fully two years after we had filed our complaint — we heard from the Swiss police that they wished us to attend hearings. Mine was scheduled for 19 November.

Their summons letter stated that they had been instructed by the judicial authorities to move forward with the case on May 15 — in other words, three days after the story broke (as described in the last chapter by Xavier) about the federal prosecutor's friend having received $2 million from PetroSaudi. It's not for me to speculate as to whether this was a mere coincidence.

Back in Kuala Lumpur, meanwhile, Najib Razak's trial was underway. Many journalists contacted us for comment but we stayed silent as we didn't want to be seen to be trying to influence the judicial process in any way. I was just delighted that finally one of the perpetrators in the whole outrage was being made to answer to what had happened.

Late in 2019, Xavier was invited to attend a conference in Wellington, New Zealand on the subject of financial crime. The invitation came from the New Zealand police, who had organized for him to fly business class and to be put up in a nice hotel for four nights — but that didn't stop New Zealand's immigration authorities from denying him permission to fly. Xavier called me from his stop-over in China to say that he'd been told he couldn't enter New Zealand because he had a criminal record. It was just another example of the problems we'd faced ever since Xavier's release, but this one seemed particularly farcical. It was as if the right hand didn't know what the left hand was doing.

It was also an illustration of how the internet skews reality. Xavier was an innocent man, but if you looked online you might not think it. Against such a weight of "evidence" it's very hard to fight back, because for a lot of people whatever they read on the internet must be true. In Xavier's case, the fact that he was an ex-prisoner was like an indelible mark that made him automatically unwelcome in certain countries. It was something we had to learn to live with, but we weren't about to stop fighting it either.

Another conference Xavier was invited to attend was in Dubai, but this time we stayed away of our own volition due to the UAE's ties with Saudi Arabia. There was no point in putting Xavier in the way of people connected to Tarek who might hope to harm him. Instead we passed the invitation to Clare, having established an arrangement with her whereby we often exchanged invitations depending on our availability and hers.

In mid-November, I returned to Geneva alone to be interviewed — finally — by the federal police in connection with our complaint. Xavier also flew back to give his testimony, but only once I had returned to Malaysia as this way we didn't have to disrupt Xander's schooling.

One of the police officers involved in handling the case told me that if it was up to them they would have moved much quicker. He said the case had proceeded slowly because of "discussions" between the prosecutor's office and our adversaries.

Yet again, I was shocked. What did a country like Switzerland have to "discuss" over such a prolonged period with people against whom there was such a weight of evidence?

Whilst in Europe, I also made a trip to London to see Kamal Siddiqi. I told him we were going to need the loan we had given him in February repaid, as our costs were starting to pile up. He had said the loan would only be for a few months. Now he wanted us to wait a few months more, and assured us he was about to secure financing from Softbank; apparently this would allow his company's IPO, which had been delayed, to go ahead. We decided to let it drop for the time being.

Back in Malaysia, we spent the holidays in Penang, a beautiful island in the north of the country. Again, everywhere we went we were lauded as local heroes — much to Xander's delight.

In February 2020, Malaysia finally asked Interpol to put Tarek and Patrick on its "Red Notice List," the closest thing you can get to having an international arrest warrant against you, although it doesn't actually compel countries to make arrests. To us, this was not a moment too soon.

The move was reported in various media, including Singapore's *Straits Times*, whose story was headlined "Tarek Obaid, Patrick Mahony join Jho Low on Interpol list."

At the end of the month, meanwhile, we had a visit from two Thai opposition parliamentarians. They came secretly and said they were building a picture of the Thai government's involvement in the 1MDB case. A big part of this obviously related to who knew what about Xavier's imprisonment.

Over several days of meetings, I gave them a complete dossier of everything I knew that might help them. They were flabbergasted and said they intended to raise the matter through parliamentary committees and expose the Thai authorities in the press.

True to their word, soon afterwards the details began appearing in Thai newspapers, and serious questions began to be asked. Of course, the Thai government denied any knowledge of or involvement in either Xavier's case or the 1MDB fiasco more generally, and unfortunately the campaign to expose the truth became sidelined as Covid-19 swept the country and everything stopped.

Shortly before the whole world came grinding to a halt, however, a new political bombshell hit Malaysia.

We were once again on holiday in Siem Reap, in Cambodia, when we heard the news that Mahathir Mohamad had resigned. Factionalism in government, and Dr Mahathir's refusal to work with figures from Najib's regime, had led him to walk away.

Our friends and contacts in Malaysia assured us the situation was only temporary and that even as a new government was formed under Muhyiddin Yassin, Dr Mahathir would soon be returned to office and command a government of national unity.

We were gravely worried, however, and returned to Malaysia immediately. The situation seemed all of a sudden unstable and with Yassin in charge, we couldn't be sure what might happen next. Therefore, we decided to pack up and leave Malaysia without further delay. Without telling anyone, we booked plane tickets for a couple of days later.

Our departure was both frantic and tearful, but we couldn't take the risk of political elements sympathetic to Najib and his allies regaining influence and attacking us. Already, Xavier was receiving threats of violence on Facebook and we were genuinely worried about our security.

A close friend helped us to pack what we could into a dozen suitcases, but we left everything else behind. It was essential that we be as discreet as possible under the circumstances. Painful memories of my departure from Thailand came flooding back, but whereas I had left Bangkok with my mum, this time Xavier and I took the extra precaution of booking ourselves on separate flights: I would fly with Xander and Xavier would fly alone. At least Covid gave us a reason to wear masks, but this being Malaysia people still recognized us at the airport.

Besides our belongings, we had to leave Veggie behind — again, she would stay on with a good local friend. I hoped and prayed we might have her shipped in a few days or weeks, but my prayers were to go unanswered: we would wait the better part of a year before being reunited.

Not for the first time, we were returning to Geneva with no home, no work and with our resources stretched to the limit. It was both an emotional and a financial hammer-blow. And on top of all that, we had to isolate because of the pandemic.

In Malaysia, Covid allowed the new government to silence the opposition and establish its grip on power. Similarly in Thailand, it gave the authorities cover to shut down discussion of the 1MDB affair and to dodge scrutiny of their part in it.

During lockdown in Switzerland, we stayed with my parents. It was an arrangement we were familiar with and as before they were remarkably supportive.

We were down on our luck, but life carried on and nothing had dented our resolve to bring PetroSaudi to justice. In early autumn, the US

Department of Justice moved to seize $330m in assets held by PetroSaudi in London and we were determined to keep up the pressure via the press to make sure that any frozen assets were never returned to them through legal manipulations or judicial failures. The money was from Venezuela, where Tarek and Patrick had enriched themselves at the expense of the Venezuelan people by basically bribing executives at the state-owned oil company PDVSA. The set-up was not so very different from how things had worked in Malaysia.

The United States of America (the "government") brings this complaint against the above-captioned asset and alleges as follows:

PERSONS AND ENTITIES

1. The plaintiff is the United States of America.

2. The defendants in this action are all funds held in escrow by Clyde & Co. in the United Kingdom as damages or restitution in the 2017 UNCITRAL arbitration between PetroSaudi Oil Services (Venezuela) Ltd. and PDVSA Servicios S.A. *et al.*, as more particularly described in Attachment A ("DEFENDANT ASSETS").

3. The persons and entities whose interests may be affected by this action are PetroSaudi International; PetroSaudi Oil Services (Venezuela) Ltd.; 1MDB PetroSaudi, Ltd.; Tarek Obaid; and Patrick Mahony.

NOW THAT WE were back in Europe, we resurrected our previous idea of going to live in Spain. We made trips to find accommodation and a school for Xander and in August we packed everything we had into a van and set the satnav on another new beginning. It was time to start living again.

Not long after settling in our new place, just outside Valencia, we were contacted by a journalist who said he had received documents that contradicted everything we claimed about PetroSaudi but insisted he wanted to be able to give our side of the story.

He seemed friendly and spoke about having a child the same age as Xander and about wanting to fight corruption — so Xavier took him into his confidence and shared details of our case and the evidence we had.

It was a mistake. This fake journalist simply published, in a blog he had just started from scratch, the usual lies peddled by PetroSaudi. The next day, his drivel appeared on about 50 other sites published in places like Russia and India, but none of it was picked up by any credible media. What this told us was that Tarek and Patrick were still up to their old tricks of trying to manipulate public opinion and the justice system. They were again trying to discredit Xavier ahead of him giving testimony against them in the Swiss investigation. Xavier may have fallen for the trick this time, but really it showed how just desperate they actually were.

Xavier traveled to Bern in mid-October to give his statement to the prosecutor in charge of the Swiss Confederation's investigation into Tarek and Patrick in relation to aggravated money laundering, bribery of foreign officials, forgery of documents and other offenses.

He came out of the hearing mentally exhausted but confident that justice would be served, however glacial the pace of it. Our family needed that to happen — and we knew that Malaysia needed it too.

We continued to have almost daily contact with certain Malaysian officials, who kept us informed about the political situation. They assured us that a new alliance between Dr Mahathir and Anwar Ibrahim remained possible provided they rallied the support of some smaller political parties. For the time being, Muhyiddin Yassin clung to power.

The latest from Kamal was that our loan would be settled by the end of the year. He reiterated that we shouldn't worry about it — his, and our, situation would soon improve. I badly wanted to believe him. Worry had been my companion for too long and I was ready to be done with it.

Epilogue

Xavier and Laura

AN UNFINISHED VICTORY

EARLY NOVEMBER OF 2020 brought news of a fresh catastrophe. Kamal, to whom we had entrusted half of the money given to us by Tong Kooi Ong, had suddenly died of a heart attack.

We were devastated. We had considered Kamal a friend, but frankly we had to think about our financial survival. The loan we had given him in February 2019 was only supposed to have been for a few months. Where did we stand now in terms of its repayment?

We started to panic when we were unable to contact Kamal's family. After several attempts, we reached his son, Noamaan, to offer our condolences and to express our concern for the outstanding loan.

After that conversation, we never heard from them again. We sent them proof that we had helped their father and that he had promised to return the money, but they stonewalled us with silence — and even today we haven't heard a word from them. At one stage, we made inquiries with Dr Mahathir's assistant; he was able to reach the family, but he replied to us a few days later saying we couldn't expect anything from them. We later learned from Kamal's lawyer that he had gone bankrupt and that there was no money to settle his accounts. It was a depressing situation but we were well aware that Malaysia had bigger problems to solve than Kamal's debts.

The loan's default had immediate consequences for us. We had been counting on its reimbursement to continue living in our new place in Spain and for being able to set up some new business ventures, but for now we had to abandon those plans and move from our house in the countryside to a smaller and cheaper apartment in the city.

Fortunately, we were able to count once again on the generosity of our family and friends, who helped us to muddle through. We also began selling some material possessions, mainly watches and jewelry, to bring in some extra money. We were fully in survival mode.

As we settled down in our new life, one piece of good news came in the form of Veggie being returned to us from Malaysia. Having her back didn't change our predicament but it brought us happiness and optimism and made us feel whole again as a family.

IN DECEMBER 2020, Xavier got into a Facebook exchange with Najib Razak, who had tagged him in a post erroneously connecting him to his SRC trial (which had nothing to do with PetroSaudi and therefore nothing to do with Xavier). It was a fresh reminder that neither Najib nor any of the others involved in this whole saga seemed capable of remorse, shame or regret.

More edifying was that Xavier was nominated for "Whistleblower of the Year" by Constantine Cannon, an English law firm. He didn't win the award but it was a sign that our struggle was still in the spotlight. More importantly, it introduced us to Mary Inman, a remarkable woman who worked for the firm and whose support and encouragement have been a real help to us.

Life was still an uphill battle, though. Until we were able to find permanent jobs and plan properly for the future, we would remain indebted to those close to us.

Exposing wrong-doing had ripped our lives apart and we were still suffering the consequences, but our experiences at least gave impetus to an idea that we could be useful to other whistleblowers. Accordingly, we set up a small not-for-profit company dedicated to helping those who want to speak out against crimes. Through it, we have been able to put several people in touch with reliable journalists whose aim is to tell the truth about corruption and malpractice.

In our own battle for the truth, there was welcome news in March 2021 as we learnt that PetroSaudi's attempts to have the data from PetroSaudi's servers made inadmissible in the Swiss judicial process had been rejected.

But for every step forward there has been at least one step back. For example, we were shocked to discover that PetroSaudi's legal team had made several attempts to have the prosecutor in charge of the case against them dismissed on a technicality relating to some documents from Malaysia that he had failed to share with them. These efforts did not succeed, but of course their only purpose was to try to slow the investigation down and push the case beyond its statute of limitations so that their clients can walk free — something that will transpire in October 2024 if justice is not served before then.

These are the underhand tactics such lawyers specialize in. On many occasions, we have asked ourselves how we could possibly hope to win against people who have access to millions to defend themselves. A friend once told us that to fight against billionaires you have to be a billionaire. But how could we ever accept that? We know we have right on our side and that justice should not be rendered according to the wealth of the people under investigation, whether honestly begotten or otherwise.

To this day, we have no money to fight the case, almost no work and have had to sacrifice many of the things that give family life its full flavor.

But we refuse to give in and will continue to fight for what we know to be a just cause, namely the rule of law and equal justice for all.

As a couple, we remain as strong as ever — but we've endured a lot these past few years and the struggle continues. We have often grappled with feelings of guilt and doubt about the validity of our decisions. We've also been robbed of precious time in the life of our family that we can never get back. Most painfully, our entanglement in the 1MDB affair deprived Xander of many important moments with his parents.

Ultimately, we made these sacrifices because we convinced ourselves we could help a country that had been cheated, a country that's not our own but which we later came to love. At times it has been frustrating to watch Malaysia squander the mandate its citizens delivered in 2018, and to fail to put the iniquities of the old regime properly on trial, but we live in hope that justice will prevail in the end.

Apart from those we have directly asked for help, few among our friends and family know how much we have had to go without or the reduced circumstances in which we have been living. We wake up each day wondering if we'll have enough to pay the rent at the end of the month, or for our son's schooling. We live a much more basic life, but perhaps that has its advantages too — perhaps we have learned to appreciate the things we do have more, not least each other and the values and integrity we have fought to defend.

Another positive is that in Spain we are anonymous. Like true Swiss, we never wanted to be in the spotlight. Here, we can go about our daily lives in tranquility. Taking Xander to school in the morning or driving to have lunch at the beach as a family in our little car are simple pleasures that may have passed us by when our lives were more hectic and harassed.

We are often asked why it has been so difficult for us to find work. The answer is simple: we have been told consistently that we are too well-known and too much of a reputational risk. Given that we have often been applying for jobs in the financial sector — where a fresh scandal is exposed every other month — this is almost laughable.

We have sought employment in other fields, too: for example, Xavier has applied to organizations involved in fighting economic crimes or pushing for transparency, but without success. You would have thought he would be an asset to such organizations. Apparently not. The rejections have been discouraging, but still we refuse to give up. Apart from anything else, we have to prove that there is a way back after you've been dragged through the mud by criminals.

A particularly bizarre episode began in September 2021 when Xavier was contacted via Clare by a fund manager in London named Maarten Petermann, who amongst other things owns one of France's top football clubs, Lille. He said he had been a friend of Kamal's, knew Xavier by reputation as a man of integrity and incorruptibility, and was interested in his knowledge of Venezuela as he was involved in some deals in connection with the refinancing of Venezuelan debt.

Xavier went up to Paris and spent the day talking to him and one of his employees. They subsequently stayed in touch over several months and said they would hire Xavier on a consulting contract, to instigate which he sent them various documents they asked for. Abruptly, however, Maarten simply stopped responding to messages or emails and the contract vanished with him. After checking with one of our contacts in London, we came to the conclusion that he was just someone who liked hanging around with people in the news. The world is really crazy.

At the end of 2021, we were also contacted by Khadija Sharife from the Organized Crime and Corruption Reporting Project (OCCRP), a consortium of journalists. She wanted to know what parts of the 1MDB story had not been covered in depth. We pointed her towards looking into the roles played by lawyers and tax experts to enable the scam and to conceal it. People in these professions were involved at all stages of the creation of the PetroSaudi-1MDB deal but have escaped scrutiny.

In return, Khadija was able to help us — by pleading our cause to Delphine Halgand, Executive Director at the Signals Network, a foundation that supports whistleblowers, for financial assistance. It turned out to be a good tip, as the foundation awarded us an exceptional grant of 6,000 euros. In former days, this would have seemed a modest sum to us, but in 2022 it helped us keep the proverbial wolf from the door for several months.

As if to illustrate our point about the "rule of lawyers" in the whole fiasco, in December 2021 we also discovered to our horror that a British judge had allowed PetroSaudi to withdraw $1 million per month, from an amount of $330 millions dollars frozen in London pending the result of a dispute involving PDVSA, Malaysia and the US Department of Justice, to cover "business and legal expenses." How disgusting that these criminals were allowed to use stolen money not only to defend themselves but for "business" purposes too.

Once more this illustrated the value to Tarek and Patrick of paying top dollar for the most expensive lawyers in Switzerland. At the same time, as mentioned previously, it was becoming increasingly clear that their main strategy was no longer to actually defend themselves but simply to play for time using tactics such as challenging the Swiss prosecutor.

Around this time, we were also in touch with another consortium of journalists — Venezuela's Armando Info — and were glad to assist their research into what really happened in relation to PetroSaudi's contracts with the state company PDVSA. In Venezuela, as in Malaysia, the PetroSaudi crooks enriched themselves on the backs of poor citizens.

In the good news column, 2022 also brought the return of conferences and seminars as the pandemic receded, and Xavier found himself in demand. These engagements aren't sufficient to feed a family in the long run but they have certainly helped us. Some more finance and real estate consulting projects, as well as ongoing translation work, have also kept us going.

In addition, we signed a contract with a producer who has followed our story since the beginning and with whom we have built a relationship of trust. The hope is that he will develop a film or TV series, based on this book, that tells the story of the injustice we have suffered as a result of daring to blow the whistle on white collar criminals whose sense of entitlement led them to operate beyond the bounds of morality and decency. We're confident that it will highlight the story we want to tell: a story that focuses not simply on the crimes of men in suits but that shows the human consequences of their crimes too.

At the beginning of 2022, Xavier was once more nominated for an award, this time the Allard Award for International Integrity, a prestigious prize given by Canada's Allard Foundation that recognizes exceptional contributions to the fight against corruption and for human rights. Xavier wasn't chosen for the prize but he was named on a shortlist of nine selected from hundreds of nominees. It was another moral victory and a huge psychological boost.

BY HANDING THE copy of PetroSaudi's hard drive to the press in 2015, we triggered — by domino effect — exposure of what emerged as one of the biggest financial scandals in history, enveloping not only 1MDB and its subsidiary SRC International but its Abu Dhabi partner Aabar Investments and the investment banking giant Goldman Sachs.

In fact, across the whole set-up, the role of banks in accepting and moving the stolen cash was fundamental. For years, banking controls have been multiplying and compliance departments have mushroomed, but financial scandals have not been eradicated. On the contrary, they have increased. It's clear that the systems of supervision are not working. It has been exasperating that some of the same banks that have refused to open an account for Xavier have been among those continuing to accept deposits in countries where official corruption is endemic.

Equally exasperating has been learning how far the justice system can be manipulated by unscrupulous lawyers paid exorbitant fees by rich thieves trying to evade the law. We are not angry with the Swiss prosecutor in charge of the 1MDB case. On the contrary, we recognize that like us she is fighting with unequal weapons in a system that favors and even protects criminals. But what message does this send to young people who want to study hard and earn an honest living? If Tarek Obaid and Patrick Mahony get away with their actions because the statute of limitation expires, the lesson would seem to be that with the right lawyers you can get away with anything. Only by punishing them for their illegal and immoral acts can the system answer to the verdicts that will be passed by our children and future generations.

In terms of where Switzerland is at in confronting the 1MDB scandal, the fund's money that ended up in the country has been frozen, but the two main culprits are still free and enjoying lifestyles that are denied to ordinary, honest people.

And what of Malaysia? In August 2022, Najib Razak's conviction for having received illegal transfers of $9.8 million via SRC International was upheld. He has yet to be definitively judged for his part in the wider 1MDB case, but the ruling was a remarkable victory for truth and justice. Most crucially, he is now in jail, having become only the second person — after Xavier — to suffer such a fate in this whole twisted story.

November's general election also brought some more welcome news. The vote ended in a hung parliament but in the aftermath Anwar Ibrahim was finally given the chance to form a government. For us personally, this felt like another vindication of our suffering. Anwar has campaigned against corruption for decades and with a reformist like him at the helm, there is again hope that the era of kleptocracy that flourished under Najib's rule is truly over — and that changes can be made that will consign such corruption to the past.

As for Tarek, Patrick, Paul and Jho Low, we still hold out hope that our struggle will win out in the end and that they will be put where they belong — behind bars.

For us, ultimately, being able to look at ourselves in the mirror and feel proud of our choices despite their costs is reward in itself. We often think of the men whose crimes we interrupted and about their relationships with their loved ones. How do they justify themselves to their family and friends? How do they reconcile themselves to lying all the time? We may have suffered but we've never had to face these agonies.

Writing this book has been a painstaking job that we've accomplished little by little each day. It's not something we ever imagined doing and many of the episodes it contains have been difficult, even painful, to relive. The main motivating factor has remained constant, however: this book is for Xander, so that he will always have a record of the real story of what we endured as a family. He is, after all, one of its unwitting protagonists.

Having survived the toughest time of our lives, we've been able to make a home for ourselves as a settled, happy family in a country whose beauty, and the kindness of whose people, comforts us every day. No matter what victories or disappointments lie ahead, in many ways we feel richer than anyone who profited financially from this whole sorry tale.

"Never be afraid to raise your voice for honesty and truth and compassion against injustice and lying and greed. If people all over the world...would do this, it would change the earth."

–William Faulkner

Acknowledgments

THIS BOOK WAS WRITTEN for and is dedicated to our incredible and beloved son Xander.

We hope that, regardless of how painful it has been, our experience can show him the right path to follow in life.

Love, family and friendship have given us the strength and courage to endure our ongoing tribulations. The people closest to us have our eternal love and gratitude.

Laura: I thank my lovely and extraordinary mother Kate, my wonderful father Walther and my incredible brother William, who have supported us with unconditional love and without whose constant presence, I could have never survived the ordeals described in this book. And to you Xavier, my dearest husband, my everything: I have always admired your integrity and determination. Your love for us gave me the strength to carry on through the darkest time of our life.

Xavier: I thank my loving mother Maria, who has always been there for us, and my late father Andres — my example, my friend and above all, my hero. To all my former companions in prison and the people who visited me, your kindness and affection brought light in my life during this sinister period. And to you Laura, my huge-hearted lioness: without your love and dedication I would not have made it. You are the true definition of a passionate warrior, my inspiration, the source of my courage and my true love.

To all our dear friends who supported us with absolute devotion and affection, there are too many of you to mention here and not enough words for us to thank you as you deserve. Your friendship is the best gift we could ever have dreamt of.

To Gilles Crettol and Christian Lüscher, our white knights: you are both shining examples of integrity, justice and kindness.

A huge thanks to our favorite editors, Kenny Hodgart and Johan Nylander, who believed in us and in our story and who helped us to put into words this "rendezvous with injustice."

You will ALL be forever in our hearts.

Laura and Xavier

Support Us

THANK YOU FOR TAKING the time to read our book. We hope our story can strengthen resistance to corruption in all its forms and advance the cause of equal justice for all. If you would like to support that cause — and our desire to live in a world where criminals are made to answer for their actions instead of being allowed to persecute innocent people with impunity — you can make a donation to help us meet our costs by visiting gogetfunding.com/justo-family.

We hugely appreciate all of the amazing support we've had over the last few years.

BIBLIOGRAPHY

THE FOLLOWING ARTICLES ARE directly referred to in this book. You can also find more sources, documents and links at rendezvouswithinjustice.com.

- 'US probes Barclays over ties to Saudi prince': CNN, May 12, 2013.
- 'Tony Blair: the former PM for hire': The Guardian, 28 April, 2016.
- 'Swiss freeze millions amid investigations of Malaysian fund': CNBC, Sept 2 2015.
- 'The Khashoggi killing had roots in a cutthroat Saudi family feud': The Washington Post, November 27, 2018.
- 'Raking In The Profits From Malaysia': Sarawak Report, 12 Oct, 2015.
- '1MDB: The inside story of the world's biggest financial scandal': The Guardian, 28 July, 2016.
- 'Held Hostage By Najib And PetroSaudi: The Justos Speak Out': Sarawak Report, 28 July, 2016.
- 'MACC issues alert to Interpol for Jho Low, PetroSaudi duo': The Edge Markets, February 12, 2020.
- 'US moves to seize $330m of alleged 1MDB assets held by UK law firm': The Guardian, 18 Sept, 2020.

Laura and her assistant, 2007

Xavier with his Ferrari, 2006

Our resort on Kho Samui

On our first trip to Thailand, 2009

Our wedding day on Kho Samui, 2013

Taking Xander to school in Kuala Lumpur

With all our wedding guests

Almost ready to pop

Laura with the employees of our resort

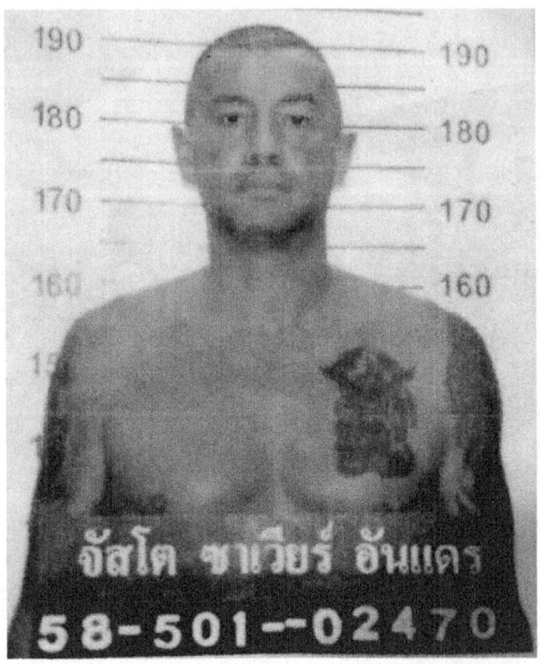

Xavier's prison photo

Xavier on his release, with prison officials and (second from right) a Swiss officer

Xavier at Suvarnabhumi Airport, about to fly home

Xavier's first meeting with Dr. Mahathir Mohamad in Kuala Lumpur, 2018

Xavier meets in 2018 with Anwar Ibrahim, now the Prime Minister of Malaysia

Reunited in Geneva

Our family in Valencia, December 2022

Made in the USA
Monee, IL
11 January 2025

76429843R00225

"In a time when most people return to houses—shells really, in non-descript towns, Connie reminds us of the deep meaning and understandings by returning *home* to a community—our herd. (Horses *do* always know the way home!) And in this place, where we can truly explore finding and giving *love,* with clarity and consistency, we can discover ourselves, our spirituality, and who the Creator intended us to become.

The book challenges us to be more observant, and trust the rhythms and miracles in this incredible place which we are blessed to live, and the creatures that share it with us. In a pleasant format, Connie weaves metaphors and lyrical stories into a tapestry that inspires me to listen to and observe more closely the lessons of the horse.

To an ol' ranch girl, much of this discovery may seem like new-age (or age old?) mumbo-jumbo. But quite frankly, it is the roots in the earth with the animals, particularly the horses, which make her book resonate with this cowgirl! The old timers, and true horsemen and women of today, take time to *observe, reflect, think and feel.* These people were great storytellers, often times in very *simple* terms—just not *easy* to fully grasp the meaning of their tale. One day it becomes clear to you what they—what the horse—was trying to portray. How wonderful that we could be life long learners! Connie's book helps to remind us of the power and introspection and growth that we have easily within our reach if we simply observe, listen, and act out of love."

~ Alice Trindle
T & T Horsemanship, author of *Horsemanship Principles: The Art of Developing a Willing Partnership*

"Constance Funk has given us a feel/see picture of her transformational journey with the help of her lovely horses. Her personal stories of learning facilitated by the horses at Woodylane Farm, the games she co-designs

Praise Qu

Beauty From Brokenness

Bits and Pieces of My Journey into Wholeness

"Connie's journey is a heart-warming, eye-opening story, It is sure to resonate with all horse lovers. Put this book on your 'must read' list!"

~ Jane Savoie
Olympic Reserve Rider and 3 Time Olympic Coach,
Author of *That Winning Feeling!*

"Constance Funk's ability to create *Beauty From Brokenness* is an inspiring story. Gathering the shards of a set of antique bowls accidentally shattered during a family dinner, she creates an intricate mosaic on a French flower pot and plants sunflowers, transforming a moment of seemingly irreversible destruction into a work of art. This becomes the central theme of a book that explores her search for ways to deal constructively and artfully with life's injustices, in her family, in her horse and herself. A soulful, thoughtful, heart expanding journey, *Beauty From Brokenness* contains much wisdom conveyed with humor, grace and honesty."

~ Linda Kohanov
Author of *The Tao of Equus, Riding Between the Worlds* and *The Way of the Horse*, New World Library Publications

"Connie gives us all an example of the highest form of courage, the courage to look within and transform daily trials into the raw materials from which dreams are made."

~ Stormy May, Producer,
The Path of the Horse documentary

with equine input amazed and delighted me. I learned a great deal. Thank you, Connie."

~ Barbara K. Rector,
Author/Founder of *Adventures in Awareness: Learning with the Help of Horses*

"This is a wise and insightful book. In *Beauty From Brokenness*, author-equestrian-artist-mother Connie Funk shares her healing journey with horses as the catalyst for well-being. Her stories are rich with the magic of symbolism. If you are a horse lover or interested in exploring the depths of your being to better not only yourself, but the entire world, you will enjoy and benefit from these stories. I anticipate great things as a result of this book!"

~ Elisabeth Bart, M. Ed.
Author of *Go for the Joy: Your Gateway to Creating and Maintaining Optimal Health*

"Connie Funk's unique style keeps readers engaged and comfortable as she shares her personal experiences and journey through the unconditional love of horses. Reading this book enables anyone to apply Connie's acquired wisdom with the their own lives regardless of experience with horses or lack thereof. *Beauty From Brokenness* is definitely a useful tool for those who seek answers to a multitude of life's crazy questions."

~ Leah Juarez
Founder/CEO
Equesse, Inc.

"Most of the time when we are looking in on someone's 'charmed life,' thinking ours is so much less so, we need to remember that we are all on our own 'hero's journey,' as Joseph Campbell said. All of us are dealing with something, and it is not outside of us, but our own inner journey. I think everyone who is on their own spiritual path will connect on a heart level with Connie's story. While she experiences the path to self-discovery through her work with her beloved horses, it is the story of everyone who truly seeks to be their authentic self. We all have different paths, but our true hero's journey will lead us 'Home'—to the God connection where we are all one."

~ Susan Rios
Suan Rios, Inc. --artist, author

"What a blessing Connie has created. She so beautifully captured the wisdom offered in horse medicine and combined a powerful message with insight, her personal journey and the gift of the written word. Her masterpiece touched me emotionally and spiritually. Truly a healing message. Thank you for taking me to such a tender place!"

~ Joanell Tylor
C.N.M., C.N.T., Essential Wellness

"This is a beautiful story of a woman's journey to find 'what makes your heart sing.' Through truth and love, Connie and her beloved horse, Chasta, found the courage to reclaim what was lost. Now they dance together to the music of their hearts."

~ Rita Dulaney

"Memories of my own childhood rose from the depths. Connie eloquently describes the magic of life and synchronicity when we are in the presence of horses."

~ Bonnie Treece
Founder, Horse's Way Equestrian Arts

"I appreciated the weaving into her story citations of many of the noted leaders in the field of inquiry into human and animal energy and natural therapy. I was pleased to note how once again their insights and techniques were helpful to someone with the courage and determination to make personal, positive changes. That in my experience is the toughest challenge of all: the self-discipline to take 'the road less traveled' and transform it into your life path. Partnering with equus on this path opens a vast new world to us on all levels, as Connie has discovered. The heart-wounding is part of the bargain, alas!

Her book is very readable, very honest. She has taken the brave journey. I hope her book will encourage others to do so as well."

~ Mary-Charlotte Shealy
Brindabella Farms, Success-Centered™ Riding/Training

"*Beauty From Brokenness* is a lovely story covering all aspects of human emotions—faith, healing, love and compassion. At 91 years of age, I was delighted to read it! Truly a beauty!"

~ Betty Chowka

"A beautiful memoir of discovery demonstrating once again the healing power of animals."

~ Dolly Joern, ARNP

Beauty from Brokenness

Bits and Pieces of My Journey into Wholeness

Constance D. Funk
Woodylane Farm

Foreword and Illustrations by
Kim McElroy

PublishingWorks, Inc.
60 Winter Street
Exeter, NH 03833
603-778-9883
For Sales and Ordering information:
1-800-738-6603
www.publishingworks.com

Printed in Canada.

LCCN: 2008925796
ISBN-10: 1-933002-80-8
ISBN-13: 978-1-933002-80-4

Beauty from Brokenness

Bits and Pieces of My Journey into Wholeness

Cover Photo Art: Diane Williams, equine photographer.
www.dianewilliamsart.com

Vintage china mosaic frame by Constance D. Funk,
Woodylane Farm, www.constancefunk.com.
Cover design graphics and text design by Davina Andrée,
www.arrowheadgraphics.com

When Diane sent this photograph to me, I was amazed, and my first reaction was that it may have been computer enhanced. No, her ability to see my shadow cast on my horse, Chasta, while standing with her, inspired her to shoot at an angle that would reveal only mare and shadow.

Horses do reveal our shadow selves, and by shining light onto them, we are able to heal and integrate, becoming whole in mind, body, emotions and spirit. What remains are the shades of gray and my stories are about finding the beauty in the shades of gray.

Please notice that my shadow is superimposed over Chasta's heart – where all healing takes place. My experiences realizing wholeness with horses for myself and my desire to share them with others is my castle in the air....

"If you have built castles in the air,
your work need not be lost.
That is where they should be.
Now put foundations under them."
~ Henry David Thoreau

Contents

Dedication

Thank you, God
for blessing Me
with your creation
and the heart and desire
to share these stories
they are dedicated to all of the souls
within these pages
especially Gary, Evan, and Chasta
and to those I have yet to meet

Foreword

Some people are born artists. From an early age they seem to have their own unique capacity for self-awareness and the ability to witness their own experiences not only for themselves, but for their potential to be meaningful for others. Their memories must be recorded in a special place within; a place of dreams and metaphors, synchronicities and spontaneity where wounds become opportunities for healing, and joy bubbles over in the knowing that it must be shared.

Connie Funk is an artist of life. Her heart has stored her experiences like fine wine until they reached the perfect maturity. Along the way, as if she knew she would be writing this book, she collected meaningful quotes from gifted authors that have profound meaning for her. Words that have spoken her own truths. It is fitting that someday she too, will be quoted.

Like the beautiful mosaics that she creates from broken china, the bits and pieces of Connie's life make beautiful patterns that are meaningful and wholly new.

I have been blessed to be a part of Connie's journey over the past few years. She has profoundly affected my life in ways too numerous to count, and I have come to realize it is not only because I have spent time with her, but because every encounter with Connie, whether in person or at a distance, leaves one buoyed up by her presence, her amazing capacity for the wonder of life, and her dedication to embracing its challenges.

I know that each person who reads her book will be similarly caught up in the stories which unfold as beautifully in the telling as they would if they were sitting across from her. Her contagious positive energy resonates just as powerfully from every word and punctuation mark she has so lovingly placed within these pages.

Just as horses have carried her on her journey of transformation, may *Beauty from Brokenness* carry her humble but powerful wisdom to the hearts of those who, once touched by her inspirations, may remember to celebrate and cultivate their own.

~ ***Kim McElroy***
Spirit of Horse Gallery

Introduction

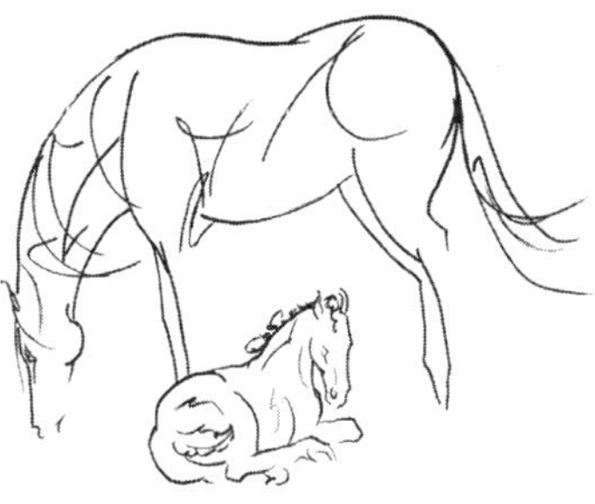

Whenever we write a story, it is a reflection of who we are at that point in time and the sum total of our experiences and how we perceive them.

While these stories seem to start at midlife when I was gifted with an extraordinary and troubled horse, it was because it was high time for me to have my world turned upside down. To shake up a lifetime of memories, emotions, beliefs and all I *thought* I knew. My new horse was the creature that could—and did—accomplish the mission. Because of her, my world expanded, and the trajectory of my life felt like it went from black and white to technicolor. Not because it has been glamorous, that's for certain! The process has been downright messy. Or that it has been simple or easy (which I have found are two *very* different things)—far from it—but because I feel as if I woke up to a new beginning. An awakening. At the very least, we are seekers on a journey together. A journey of healing that has changed, and in fact, enriched my life to the point of rescuing it from an inner soul death that was keeping me from being fully alive.

My experiences have been so meaningful for me that I felt compelled to share them. I refer to many authors, clinicians, and modalities that have influenced our healing. At the end, there is an extensive resource list with titles, websites and other contact information. My hope is that it will provide you with a roadmap of sorts that you may use to choose what calls to your heart and mind and spirit to pursue further your path to wholeness.

James Herriott, the beloved author and veterinarian from the Yorkshire Dales who wrote the *All Creatures Great and Small* series, has truly touched my family over the years. We have read and reread all of his books and later blubbered and howled our way through the BBS Film Collection that we purchased through Public Television in America. And isn't that how God touches and expands our hearts—through tears and laughter? Whenever interviewed with rave reviews, James always modestly said that he simply recorded the life he had so gratefully been given.

I have been similarly blessed to share my life with rich characters—two and four legged and winged, who have given me an amazing tapestry of experiences—*great and small*. They have been my guides, mentors and companions. And in the case of the mare named Chasta, who prompted me to put pen to paper, my soul mate. Now if that sounds romantic, don't let me mislead you! I loved hearing Wayne Dyer, the bestselling author who I have been greatly inspired by share his definition of a soul mate on one of his CDs. He describes it as another being who challenges us regularly. Keeps things stirred up. Real. Authentic. Kind of like a burr under your saddle at least to the extent that it gets our attention and in this case, from the horses point of view, appropriately. Yep, that's Chasta. *She got my attention!*

I grew up hearing my father say that God looks out for fools and children. Having been the recipient of grace, I believe it to be true. While Chasta is fascinated by and generous with the innocence of children, she has a very low tolerance for fools. In calling me on my darker and yet very human and important emotions, she has helped me to regain my innocence and to see it in all life. As poet Maya Angelou so eloquently reminds us, "We do what we know, and when we know better, we do better." Chasta created opportunities for me to live this experience. Again and again!

It was also clear to me from the beginning that I could offer her the same relationship in return. Whatever the sum total of her experiences were before coming to us, there was no question that she brought her own accumulation of traumatic baggage. Even though horses respond to and live in the moment, what came before for them influences how they behave. Between the two of us, we were definitely not traveling light! Interestingly, my most disquieting and frequent recurrent dream/nightmare had been *frantically* trying to jam copious amounts of *stuff* into numerous suitcases, while being *lost* and *late* to some *unknown* destination/flight/departure. *Whew!* It was a broken record that ached for resolution. It has faded in frequency and intensity, but still occasionally visits.

Enough to remind me that the ongoing goal of my life is to continue to learn to let go of excess baggage in my life, both literally and metaphorically and *travel light*—mentally, emotionally, physically and spiritually. To rise up in the company of horses—and all life—and soar, any place in time, in waking and night dreams.

Thank you for taking your time to share my journey—
may it inspire you to travel light.
Constance D. Funk
Woodylane Farm

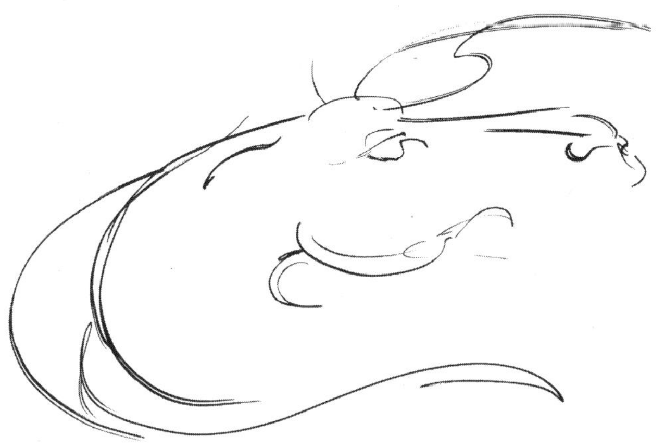

PART ONE:

The Awakening

Chapter One

Enter Chasta, My Gifthorse

I have always loved exclamation points. As a child, they seemed like pogo sticks jumping for joy at the end of a sentence. Even after DANGER! KEEP OUT! they felt important in a hopeful sort of way. It was as if the exclamation point was saying "I *mean* it!" And if it came in multiples, "I *really* mean it!!!" I am not sure if many published authors use multiples to express themselves, but children often do as they learn to put their feelings onto paper. I did. Today I realize that little symbol of punctuation helped me to feel as if I was heard, if only to myself. How important it is to be heard – to have our feelings considered. How many generations of children have been affected by the expression that *children should be seen and not heard*? It's a package deal. To not be heard is a form of being silenced. Silence can be golden, to be sure, but for a child to find his or her own place in the world, being heard is essential. Feeling heard allows each of us to develop our own unique voice. Each of us has something to say that contributes to the equilibrium of the Universal Story, the Grand Symphony.

Including horses. For me, especially horses. When I was given a Palomino colored horse for my 47th birthday from my husband and son, I did not realize the spiritual awakening her presence would ignite in me. It turns out this horse, a mare named Chasta, would provide a mirror for me to see myself. But this mirror reflected much more deeply than what could be seen on the surface. This mirror could hear me and feel me to the depths of my soul as well. Chasta came to me, clearly wanting to be heard. She wanted to be seen for who she was, and to have her feelings considered. Horses demonstrate this for us mostly through body language. Early in our relationship she used her enormous hooves to express herself. She stomped the ground for exclamation and emphasis. Often she used one hoof and then the other. Sometimes she reared up and came crashing down in front of me. She was clearly saying, "I *mean* it!" and "I *really* mean it!!!" using her own unique form of equine punctuation. She awakened in me *my* own deep need to be heard. And she helped me to develop my own unique *voice* also.

I am not an expert horsewoman or rider nor mother, wife, writer, daughter, sister or friend—for those are only roles and do not define me. Instead I am gently working in the present moment at living fully in the awareness of becoming better about recognizing who *I am* without the scrutiny of an unruly ego. And for that opportunity, I am truly thankful.

These stories are bits and pieces of my life that have led me to a place where I am *remembering* the person God created me to be. Take what you need and leave the rest. Each piece is a prayer on my journey to wholeness.

Chapter Two

The Mare with the Mirror and the Microphone

When I said that Chasta's presence ignited my spiritual awakening, it was more like spontaneous combustion. Her resistance and reactions were huge. Sparks flew. They connected me to a fear and an angry fire deep within me. Where were these emotions coming from?!

I believe that God reveals Himself to each of us in ways that we can understand and relate to. For me, the face, voice and peace of God has always been associated with His creation: People, animals, all of nature. Clearly, this mare seemed like an exception. I wanted the peace and connection that animals had always so willingly given me. It was as if she held up a mirror and a microphone, interview style, and asked, "Actually, how do you *feel* about your anger?"

This wasn't exactly riding off into the sunset on my golden horse as in my childhood dreams. Did I even sign up for this course? Actually, no. She was a gift. Quite literally, a *Gifthorse*. Ironically, I *did* dream of a golden horse while lying in my bunk bed as a little girl. Didn't everyone? After all, I grew up in America in the 1950s when Roy Rogers had his beloved Trigger and Mister Ed, the talking horse, entertained us from the black and white TV set, which was still in its early days.

With Chasta, things were different. In the first week of our time together, it became clear that she would change my life forever. It has been said that when the student is ready, the teacher will appear. I like to think that it was readiness on my part, but it felt more like Divine Intervention.

Immediately, I wondered why she responded to me with such extreme resistance. Our first horse, Chad, had been gentle and willing. Although chestnut colored, he acted more like Trigger and Mister Ed. After his death, he was buried under a giant fir tree on our land, and still feels like a strong anchor for my heart, giving me a safe harbor to retreat to.

While I was wondering what was wrong with Chasta, I am quite certain she was thinking the same thing about me! My inner anger was affecting her and my fears were red flags that aroused her instincts as a prey animal. And what *was* triggering this response in me, anyway? I thought I had dealt with all of that "forgiving and letting go" process. *Apparently not. "Moi?"*

I have always loved words. Anyone who loves to read and write does. Thanks to my mother, Kay, encouraging me, I developed the habit of looking up definitions and being mindful of spelling. She inspired me to become a wordsmith, and I became fascinated with word and phrase derivations. My mother shared my passionate interest and gifted me with a wonderful little book many years ago called *A Hog On Ice & Other Curious Expressions,* written by Charles E. Funk, ironically the very same name as my late father-in-law for whom our son Evan Charles was named for.

The complete expression is *"independent as a hog on ice"* and is meant to connote supreme confidence. It was an expression used by my maternal grandmother, Helen, during my childhood along with many other colorful phrases that she learned growing up on a ranch that painted a vivid picture in your mind's eye.

When I realized that Chasta truly *was* my gifthorse, I felt intrigued to know the meaning of the expression *"looking a gifthorse in the mouth"* from Mr. Funk's charming and informative book. Reading his text, I knew I was guilty of doing just that which he describes.

To paraphrase his research: This is a very old expression that has been attributed to the writings of Saint Jerome, one of the Latin Fathers of the fourth century church. This phrase has been translated into many languages, and it refers to the poor manners shown by someone who receives a gift and then examines it for defects. The age, and presumably the usefulness, of a horse can be determined by looking at the teeth.

Was I looking for the gift horse's weaknesses rather than what I needed to do to improve my own? Was I searching for what others could do for me before I thought about how I could serve them? Why should this be any different with a horse? Clearly, my gift of an accountability partner for my own growth had arrived. A truth teller. *Ready or not.*

Here is a pearl of wisdom that I have heard but do not know the source of: *Change is inevitable. Growth is optional.* With a deep breath (actually it was quite shallow at the time, but more on that later) and a trembling heart, I chose the growth option. Like poet Robert Frost's less traveled path in the woods, it has made all the difference.

Chapter Three

Ask: "I Need Help!"

I needed help with a capital H. This beautiful animal appeared to be in as much pain as I was. Pain is pain and often cannot be differentiated as to what the source is, but this shared resonance was in our minds, bodies, emotions and spirits. Chasta and I were embarking on our journey to learn to feel and move through pain over time and shared experience.

Chasta had been attempting to communicate with me in significant ways since day one. Because my only true experience with horses had been with our first horse, Chad, and he had been so well trained and docile, I had not been challenged to think like a horse. To use a phrase well known in the horse world, he was *filling in* for me. In other words, he was compensating for my ignorance. The level of my ignorance? *Beyond belief*! That is because once we acquire some knowledge, we realize how much we do not know.

Here goes: My new golden horse was out in the pasture on the first day of the rest of our lives.... Arrrrgh! *That's* how naïve I was! Did I take the time to get to know her? No. I went into the tack room to get the saddle that my husband paid extra for and put it on the rail of the fence. Groundwork? At the time, I did not know the meaning of the word. Weren't horses meant to be ridden?

I went back into the stable and got the groom box. When I came out, I was stunned to see that Chasta had pulled the saddle off the fence with her teeth onto the ground and over twenty feet and was stomping on it with gusto! Now hindsight is always 20/20, but it seems pretty clear that there was something about that saddle that stirred some pretty powerful emotions in her! Turned out it was far too small and pinched her terribly, and that was before a rider ever got aboard!

It did give me pause at the time, but *not enough* to keep me from proceeding with *my goal*: to ride my beautiful new horse. Chasta had other ideas. Thanks to her, I am learning to be *far more aware* of the feelings of others and *my own agenda*.

Chasta warily allowed me to put on the offensive tack, but clearly was not happy engaging with me. She gave me the sense that I was violating her, though my intentions were not overtly to dominate my new horse. How often had I had that sense but chose to ignore it, whether I was imposing it on others or experiencing it myself? Her stiffness and brace touched off a rigidity on me—or was *I* her trigger? She held her breath and I responded in kind, or was I her mirror? We were the proverbial chicken and the egg.

The sensation of a question forming, either from me or from her, was fleeting, so I set my jaw and got the job done, however insensitive to feeling deeply what was going on for either of us. I mounted and tentatively asked her to move forward the only way that I knew how at the time—by putting pressure on her sides in the form of a kick. She pushed against my legs with her barrel as if she had become some huge blonde equine balloon. Nothing happened to move us forward. So I kicked again. Still no movement, so I kicked harder and started clucking in an agitated way. We were a total vision of disharmony.

Finally, because she (or both of us) needed to take a breath, Chasta moved forward, taking me straight to the fence and parked herself. With everything she could demonstrate nonverbally, she said loud and clear: *"Ride's over!"*

Baffled, I persisted. In an attempt to turn her around and try again, she set her parking brakes—she planted a hoof on each corner of her body and increased the silent volume. *"I said, Off!"*

I got down, powerfully humiliated and ashamed that this lovely animal had rejected me and though I could see that she was struggling with her own emotions, selfishly had a pity party all for myself, pretending I had more compassion for her than I truly felt deep inside at the time.

It didn't help that she ran to Evan whenever she saw him and looked gratefully at Gary when he came up the driveway in the evening and plucked an apple off the tree for her.

Some fencing needed repair so I hired a handy cowboy to do the job and she flirted with him shamelessly, pulling his coat off the fence and taking a pack of cigarettes out of the pocket with her teeth like they were old pals. I was really starting to get an inferiority complex, but was not asking good questions. Reduced to an insecure adolescent by her rejection, I asked in a whining way why she didn't respond to me. *"Aw,* she's just *spoiled,"* this longtime horse handler told me as he retrieved his cigarettes. "Just show her who's *boss!"*

That mentality had never jived with me so the next time I took her over to the pasture where he had done the repairs, I saddled her up there, ready for a new start, *still* without a plan for success. She continued to resist me, with threats to bite and kick, but I *did* try to put on a tough act, thinking it may have actually improved things a bit. Remember Dom DeLuise in the Mel Brooks movie satire *Blazing Saddles,* with his megaphone shouting, *"Wrong!"*? You get the picture.

She started out moving off at a walk and I felt myself thinking, "Well, *that* is more like it!" until she picked up the pace and got halfway across the pasture and then came to an abrupt halt. I completely ignored her urgent stop as a sign that she had something to say. Coaxing her on with my legs, within a split second I was standing up in the stirrups with my full weight as she reared up and wildly pawed the air! We came down with an enormous crash and she crouched into the position to release a mighty buck followed by another—and another. I could feel my spine as if it were a xylophone being played in fast motion. It stunned me at that moment that people actually did this for a living!

I was still not off, so she blew out at a gallop as if she had been shot out of a cannon, and my mind and body finally reconnected long enough to think about bailing as it seemed like the huge fir trees ahead were moving toward us rather than the reverse—kind of one of those "your life flashing before your eyes in fast motion moments." But just when I thought I would jump off to the right, she would zig to the left, then zag back to the right, like a halfback trying to score a touchdown through the defensive line. She took another sharp left, a few inches from a huge tree, then took a colossal leap down in to the open door of her stall! At the last possible second, I hunkered down over her back or I would have been knocked off or decapitated.

She was standing perpendicular to the wall, in the same position as our first ride, but with her sides heaving and her entire body shaking. I was so stunned and scrambled that I just *sat* there, my head near the ceiling, feeling grateful we had built such roomy stalls!

Finally it occurred to me to get down—sort of like your hand on the hot stove without the appropriate withdrawal. Also, somewhere in my mind was the ridiculous myth that you could "never let the horse win." When had I become so disconnected from myself and how could I change that? And what was she showing me? These were not the questions that I was able to ask at the time, because I just felt so badly. I later learned from the accomplished Olympic reserve rider, author and inspirational speaker, Jane Savoie, that in order to have better answers, *we need to ask better questions*. In her powerful book, *That Winning Feeling*, she teaches fantastic visualization techniques that create powerful connections between horse and rider, and apply to improving *any* aspect of our lives. But at that moment in time, I only felt hurt, rejected, and afraid.

I led her out of the stall and into the sunshine, pulling off her saddle and other tack, and fell to my knees, sobbing. She turned and went back into her stall, out of view. As I cried, I felt as if I was tapping into a reservoir of tears as deep as the ocean, feeling the extreme emotions of every time I had felt like a failure.

Within a few minutes, she emerged from the stable and came to stand next to me, her head close to mine, and proceeded to moan in some otherworldly primal way. It was low and guttural and eerily soothing, like the sound of the giant whales, her face near my ear. It was transporting us into some other place in time when I felt something ancient rise in me until we were abruptly interrupted when a friend of mine who is admittedly afraid of horses pulled up our driveway. She saw me on the ground and yelled with urgent concern, *"Oh my God, are you all right?"* as Chasta beat a hasty exit.

Maybe if we had been able to finish what was happening for us, I could have tuned in sooner to what she had to teach me, but deep in my heart, I held the memory as reason to go on trying, beginning to truly understand that we needed to heal *together*.

We found a lovely, older, well-trained Arabian horse named Ritzy to keep Chasta company, hoping that it would help her to relax, and they bonded instantly and completely. Time went by and I summoned up the courage to try again. My limited experience riding horses on trails seemed to give them a purpose that they readily understood and enjoyed so my next idea was to take her off our property on a *real ride* and show her that I meant no harm. With the anxious memories of my previous scenarios planted firmly in my mind (a recipe for disaster, of course), I saddled her up at the trail head behind our home.

Without going into further detail, suffice it to say that in my anxiety, we were both exhausted on every level by the time I threw a leg over her back. It amazes me *still* that I had such a complete lack of awareness that we were *not ready* for a riding relationship! If we could not truly connect on the ground with a mutual language, how could I expect her to balance me while on her back without communication and confidence?

In three strides, she was in a bolting gallop, *OFF* the trail leaping over everything in our path. By the grace of God, I stayed on, in direct response to my prayer that reverberated throughout the forest—*"Dear God, help me!"* I yelled the words as spontaneously as she had gone into wild flight. We came to a clearing and attempting to turn her, I was able to use a single rein to bend her head and come to a wild, circling and eventual stop. I dismounted, and we stood trembling together, terrified of our roller coaster of emotions that had left the track. My son, Evan, who had anticipated a quiet trail ride had cantered up on his Arabian horse to rescue me, shaken by the sight. Initially, he had been quite impressed that his silver-haired mother had blown by them on the trail until he realized that we had created our own path in thunderous crashing and he heard my cry for help. I thanked him and his beautiful boy, Ritzy, and sent them home. Chasta and I both needed to learn to stand on our own two and four feet. Victims no more. I trusted that we could walk home, on the *ground*.

Horses and women have been victims of domination since the beginning of time. Chasta helped me to experience the duality deep within my being between feeling like a prey animal/victim and the emotionally charged predatorial aspects of myself.

I also knew that I could not change this situation in my own strength. My pounding heart, breaking through years of numbness, allowed the tears to flow. I say *the tears,* because they felt like much more than just all my own. I realized at that moment that God never asks us to do anything in merely our own strength. I looked up into the deep blue sky and asked for help. In response, Chasta dropped her head and blew, a horse's sigh of relief.

Chasta's wild ride was not like a doozy at the carnival or amusement park that titillates you at the moment with an adrenaline rush that you walk off on the way to the next one. It was a potential near death experience. These moments can create life shifts that do not allow for going back because they are turning points in a new direction.

The out of control experience left me with so much adrenaline that I still felt shaky when my husband, Gary, got home that evening. Lying in bed in the dark, he apologized for getting me the "wrong horse." I was so confused and emotional that my words were not really coherent. Then he shared his heart.

He said, "Her *eye* asked me to *please* take her home. She said, *"Help me!"* in a way that I *knew* I had to respond to."

Wow! Those are the kind of intuitive flashes and messages that I receive regularly. I started to cry.

"What do you want to do?" he asked. "Do you want another horse?"

Did he feel like he was the wrong husband? Had I given him cause to feel that way? For many years? Never quite my shining knight in armor on a great steed?

"No," I answered softly. "Something *very* powerful happened out there today. She came here for a reason."

Gary reached over and put his hand on my arm in the darkness, and then began stroking my hair, something that has always touched me deeply. "You have got to learn how to trust sometime, Connie. I am one who has broken you and maybe she is one who can help heal you."

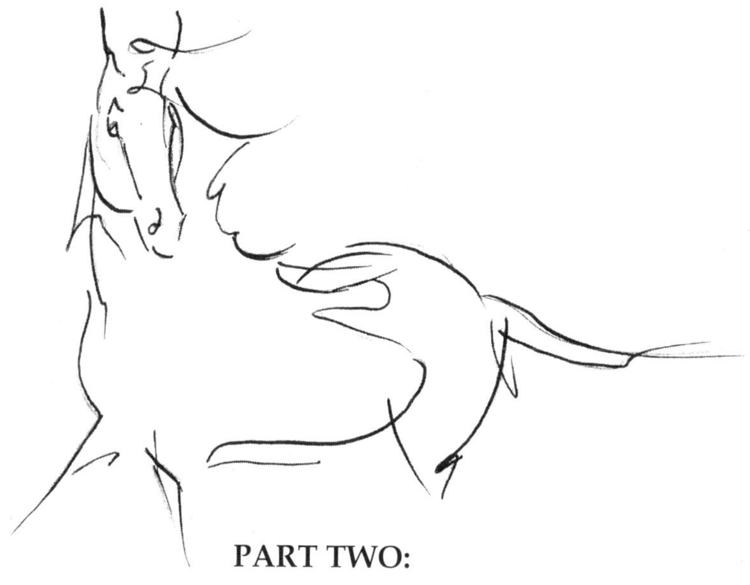

PART TWO:

The Gifts

Chapter Four

Receive: Answered Prayers

My early experiences with Chasta nearly scared me to death. As terrifying as a few of the episodes were, after the intense adrenaline subsided, I noticed something profound. I *felt. Deeply.* In every fiber of my being, I ached, but it felt like I was waking up, like signals were being felt and heard, one cell at a time. Too big to ignore, deny, or suppress. I realized that she had scared me to *LIFE!* She had jump started my heart, equine electroshock therapy style. *I wanted to live, really LIVE!* To become fully alive in a new and lasting way. It became my mission to feel and learn the messages behind the dark emotions that my helplessness had revealed and were causing me pain and anxiety on every level. A teacher, this sentient being would take me on a soul journey like no other. Chasta and my body were collaborating to get my attention!

Very soon my prayer was answered in the form of a beautiful woman named Kathy Yeager. Recommended by a friend, she agreed to come and meet with Chasta and me. A natural with animals, Kathy had developed her abilities growing up on a huge cattle ranch in South Africa. Her confidence immediately put me at ease and my journey to become a student of natural horsemanship had begun.

Kathy had a fascinating life story of her days as a child growing up with domestic and wild animals. A combination of her vast experiences and her own highly honed instincts gave her an ability to relate to Chasta with a calm and confident presence that I did not possess. She connected me to the Parelli Natural Horse-Man-Ship™ teachings, led by master horsemen, Pat and Linda Parelli. This term was created to describe a shift in traditional thinking about horse-human interactions that is more relationship-oriented and considers the horse's point of view. The Parelli model is about developing leadership skills in the human that creates a partnership with the horse where the dignity of the human and the dignity of the horse are of equal value.

As Kathy shared her knowledge and skills with me, it became clear that the onus was on me to learn to communicate effectively and do my part to create the intimate connection that I was looking for. I also realized that Chad, our first horse, had come to us with an unusually calm and willing nature, and he was able to offer us easy going responses. He was well trained, and had a vast repertoire of experiences before coming to us as a senior horse. This had been my *previous* experience, but it was not what Chasta presented at that time. Chad had been the one who carried us, and not just on his back.

My husband, Gary, and I bought tickets to attend the Parelli Tour. Pat and Linda Parelli and their magnificent horses travel the globe to make the world a better place for *all life* by teaching humans about their incredible communication system. When Gary came down the stairs, I was pleased to see that he was wearing cowboy boots, feeling like he might be as excited as I was to learn more about bridging the gap between Chasta and me. My pleasure was short lived when we pulled out of our long driveway and he made the first of a long string of business phone calls. I stuck my nose in the Parelli book that I had ordered, thinking it would have been a better idea to attend this event with one of my horse women friends.

When we arrived, we met up with Kathy and her wonderful husband, John, and a large group of Parelli devotees from our area. I looked over to see Gary on his phone, as if he had never left the office. As we made our way to the bleacher seats, I had the feeling that it might be a *long* weekend, being with someone whose mind was somewhere else.

Then Pat Parelli rode in on his breathtakingly beautiful black horse named Magic, and the excitement in the air was palpable. *"Raise your hand if you love horses!"* he hollered, as if speaking to each one of us individually. My heart beat wildly in response as my hand shot up. I looked at Gary and he was suddenly perched forward, like a horse with his ears pricked in full attention. Within the next few hours, my Type A husband had requested my notepad and was wildly scribbling such "Parellisms" as "Take the time it takes and it takes less time," and "you have to be willing to be *inconvenienced* for success."

I never saw his phone come out again until a break toward the end of the last day when he was talking to one of his managers back at the office. "Yes, we are still at this horse deal," I overhead him say. "This guy is *fantastic.* Anyone who can get me to sit for two days on cold metal bleachers has something to say."

Gary discovered that weekend what I had realized—this was about *life.* The horses were the experience that allowed us to learn the lessons. I remember a moment when Pat Parelli was demonstrating with a troubled horse that had been brought to the tour session by a horse owner in need of help, like me. The horse went from having extreme reactions with his owner as they came into the arena to a calm and accepting demeanor when he was with Pat for just a few minutes, following him like a happy puppy. I looked down the row at Kathy, and we beamed smiles of recognition about our mutual desire to reach Chasta. I knew I was in the right place.

Pat believes and teaches that humans are the ultimate predator and horses are a prey animal. It is amazing that there can be such profoundly beautiful relationships between the species. The teachings are about learning to work on *yourself* by becoming balanced in mind, body, emotions, and spirit, and offer that integration to your horse as you develop a partnership together. It is a transformational experience for humans because horses teach us to understand our own nature.

Humans *are* the ultimate predator, as the natural horsemanship teachings inform us, and as far as the food chain goes, it is true. Unless we are outwitted and eaten by another carnivore. But we also need to remember that humans, other than purist vegetarians, are omnivores and also have a prey nature. Especially women.

Linda Kohanov, the founder of the Epona Approach™, teaches us about the yin/yang duality of human nature. The yin, or more feminine nature, is part of the balance that we all need to strive for, but is most natural for women. Women have historically been seen as prey, and dominated by the male of the species, and in extreme cases, possessed. So not only can women easily relate to horses from their prey nature resonance, we can often respond to them in a sensitive yin manner, treating them as they would like to be treated, and yet if we are not aware, can become too passive. On the flip side of this coin, when motivated by fear, a woman's yang or more masculine nature may be triggered *in the extreme* and we can attempt to dominate and control, with horses or any of our relationships. This sets the stage for women (or men) to have the tendency to develop passive/aggressive personalities—and I was one of them with these traits, *however much I did not want to admit it.* Chasta taught me to recognize and own it , so I could change it.

Striking a balance for both genders is the key, neither dominant aggression nor passive submissive behavior is effective for either horses or humans. Assertive confidence with a willingness to be aware of the other person or horse's point of view is the secret to building mutually beneficial and satisfying relationships. Learning to be "matter of fact" and at the same time nurturing has been a tremendous challenge for me as a person, but the more I observe horses, the more I see the leaders among them model this. They *care deeply* about the survival of the herd, but are not wishy washy or overly sentimental—they lead from their hearts that are intimately connected to their instincts and knowledge.

And when it is all said and done, relationships are all that truly matters in this life. The rest are merely creature comforts since we can't take them with us. Many years ago I was having tea with my dear elderly neighbor lady, Faye. She was an incredible gardener and lived in a charming cottage style home on a large corner lot surrounded by her amazing plantings, fragrant pink peonies as big as dinner plates being my personal favorite. Her adult daughter had developed a debilitating disease and Faye had a wing built onto her home for her daughter and her husband to live, and they were to move in soon from out of state. During our visit, the phone rang and she picked it up, delighted to hear her grown grandson's voice. "Oh, *Honey!"* she exclaimed, "How *are* you?"

I was sitting so close that I could hear the entire conversation through the phone lines. He was calling to warn his grandmother that his mother had packed too much furniture and other belongings to fit into the space that Faye had created for them, and the movers were on their way.

"No problem! I'll just get rid of some of mine!" was Faye's *immediate* response. Her grandson was very aware of the charm and attention to detail of the décor of her place and returned with, "Oh, Grandma, you can't do *that!"*

"And *why not?!*" she exclaimed. "I can't take it with me where I am going—it would probably just get hung up on a tree!" So don't you worry about a *thing!*"

The last time I corresponded with her, she had just celebrated her hundredth birthday, not surprising with a perspective like that, is it? For Faye, her relationships were what she treasured above all else. And since Chasta has taught me so much about what it means for me to be in relationship—with myself, with God and all life—I think of Faye often and am inspired by her values and the choices she made to uphold them.

So we learn to use our emotions as information to become our authentic selves, in touch with our feelings. That is precisely what horses do—everything that happens in their environment registers with them quickly as information to help them make their next move. To engage playfully with a herdmate or run for their lives. They do not label the information as good or bad—just what it is—input to help them make the best decision. They model emotional agility: pay attention to the environment/information and how it makes them feel, respond and then return to a neutral, yet fully engaged enjoyment of life. They do what they do best, being a horse—*in the moment*—which usually translates to a contented snort and attention to what sustains and nourishes them: the garden that is their natural habitat. In other words, *return to the pleasure of the moment ... to life.* Wouldn't life be more wonderful if that was our consistent response as humans? And that we, too, could return to the garden from which we came?

Pat Parelli makes statements about the horse/human relationship regularly that I hear, understand, and respond to experientially. Then a few months later, I feel that I understand it on a deeper level, and can respond more effectively. Over time, I have come to understand the profound depth of what he knows on a *feeling* level because of a lifetime of interacting with these amazing creatures. I also must acknowledge Linda Parelli, for her *phenomenal* ability to interpret Pat's depth as a horseman for the rest of us. She is an *incredible* and inspiring teacher who makes learning fun and fascinating. I also personally feel the reason that the Parellis lead the natural horsemanship movement (and, in fact, coined the term) is because they balance each other's male and female energies *perfectly*— I think she has enhanced his feminine yin energy in the same wonderful way that he has enhanced her masculine yang energy—not one more than the other. *And the horses know it and show it!*

We can no longer live in a patriarchal society in the world today that is so intimately connected through technology via the media. Nor strictly matriarchal—it must be unity between the two as it is in the wild horse world. The stallions lead by protection and procreation and the lead mares and mothers teach and guide. It is *cooperative* and *dynamic*. And in my opinion, breathtakingly beautiful.

One of the things that I heard Pat say early on is: "Your horse does not care how much you know until he knows how much you care, and the very best way to help him know that you care is to take the time it takes to help him build his confidence." Well, that seems simple and straightforward enough, but it could change the world in an instant if that were the way that we approached every relationship! *All* of us need encouragement and help with our confidence in life. Think about it!

And to "take the time it takes" in this world of instant gratification and "quick fixes" is a new challenge to truly learn to be in harmony with horses. A friend helping me to expand my computer skills sat in a chair next to mine and complained that my program was *"So slow!"* Compared to hers, it apparently is, but when did mere seconds cause us such agitation?! Although there is more to life than increasing it's speed, our frenetic pace often dictates our emotional responses and behavior. *And it is contagious.*

The other statement that has really affected my thinking that Pat says is, "Your horse is often frozen between the desire to please you in the moment and to preserve his own survival." That is a very provocative statement and seems to relate mostly to the horse, who is hardwired as a prey animal for self-preservation in a big way. And yet, the more I experienced that sensation in awareness when working/playing with my horses, the more I realize that humans operate in the same way much of the time. So many of our subconscious and habitual behaviors are really tied in with our deep patterns of survival, even if there is no longer a tiger at our tail. It may have been at one time (eons ago), and we are wary that it may jump out from behind a rock again. Of course, for humans in the urban jungle today, the situations are different, but the emotional juices are the same when we go into the "fight and flight" response. I realized that my horses' body language when they were at that point of "frozen concern" is often what I see and feel in other humans, and can relate to it very strongly in my own behavior. We want to be in relationship with others, but may feel deep down that intimacy will compromise our very lives!

So if we think about the other person or horse's point of view from that standpoint in our interactions, what amazing connections we could make by *helping each other!*

Horses are huge and powerful athletes, and in order to be effective with them, we need to possess *true* confidence to be their partners. They need us to be physically, mentally, emotionally and spiritually fit. I realized at midlife that my comfort zone where I felt this confidence was getting smaller and smaller. I was comfortable only doing what I was good at—where I felt *safe*. In reality, this need for safety was creating a need for control. The subconscious mind is not comfortable with change—it prefers the familiar. But remember the "change is inevitable" quote? That *is* a constant. The only constant *is* change.

Author Anais Nin states: "Life shrinks or expands according to one's courage." Like the dear old Cowardly Lion character from our collective childhood, I needed to find my true courage.

In the outstanding body of work by cellular biologist, Dr. Bruce Lipton, called *The Biology of Belief*, he explains that cells can either be in a fear/protection or growth/health mode. Either/or, but not both at the same time. The *protracted* state of fight and flight from being in a fear-based mode affects us at a cellular level and sets the stage for chronic illness. That comes from thinking/feeling the tiger is at your tail *constantly!*

I had been struggling for years with my physical health. The kind of autoimmune challenges that left me feeling sick and tired all the time, drained of strength and energy. Feeling sick and tired of feeling sick and tired is not what life is meant to be for any of us. And these symptoms have become epidemic within our culture to the point where conventional medicine is unable to even completely recognize the complicated origins—just painting illness with a very large brush as various "stress syndromes." Instinctively, I knew my journey with Chasta was providing the path to true wellness on every level. *My life depended on it.*

Chapter Five

Believe: In the Infinite Possibilities

Dr. Lipton emphasizes that it is our *beliefs* that create our biology. Our beliefs are based on our *perceptions – how we see the world.* On a conscious level, I had a positive outlook on life, but what was this darker underworld that Chasta was so unnerved by? It was time to know and heal all of me from the inside out. All of our experiences shape who we are, and again, it is our *perception* of those experiences that makes the difference. Buried in our subconscious minds are the core beliefs that affect our behavior. These patterns become stored in cellular memory and impact everything we do. After reading Dr. Lipton's book in the midst of my challenges with Chasta, I began to ask myself, did I play a part in my destiny or was I just reacting to the circumstances in my life? I believe that God has a beautiful plan for all of our lives, and my faith is strong. Why then all of the fear and anger and unresolved conflict within me? Obviously, I was disconnected from the power of God within. And confused. A God who promises freedom from constant fear and a peace that the world cannot give. I believed that, but was not living it too much of the time.

What Chasta helped me to realize was that God created strong emotions for a purpose: to help me to feel when my boundaries were being violated. He created anger and fear as signals to stand up for myself and proclaim my truth as I understand it.

My story is not much different from anyone else's, regardless of age or background. I want to belong—to be loved. To realize my dreams—to share my unique gifts. To serve and love.

Yet I learned early in life that the best way for me to get along in every situation was to be good. Nice. A high achiever. People pleaser. Don't rock the boat. It felt like the only way to get the love that I needed and wanted. It worked at a level of approval, but did not allow for a full range of emotions. Besides, no one can maintain this behavior constantly, especially a child, so being real and expressing *all of my emotions* did not feel safe. I developed my own inner critic early in life to keep myself in line and on my toes. It was hard work for me *and* my head chatterer. Exhausting, actually.

Especially since I was a highly sensitive child, and the one most likely to respond to the proverbial elephant in the living room or the Emperor when he had no clothes on in the parade. To feel safe, I had to conceal the way I was *really* feeling and perceiving life for the sake of "getting along." So when I lost my voice, because it was suppressed deeply at times, it bobbed close to the surface, wanting to emerge.

Now my level of understanding about *emotional agility,* a term developed by Karla McLaren, helped me to understand that God designed *all* emotions into our consciousness and they only become extreme when we ignore or deny them. The emotion is the messenger and often societal constraints advise (or force) us to "shoot the messenger," by conforming to what is "expected" of us. After all, what would the neighbors think?! And did you ever get the feeling that the neighbors, or even strangers, or "they" were more important than how *you* felt? Or told that you were too sensitive and therefore somehow flawed and making life more difficult for others?

My father had such an unstable and chaotic childhood that to his credit, he vowed to himself not to repeat the darkness of violent upheaval with his own family one day. He has a brilliantly creative mind, so he envisioned a perfect world for us with calmness and serenity, filled with beauty and free from strife. And he felt it was his job not only to create this but to enforce it. The only challenge is that when your family of origin was four babies and a dog in suburbia, life got a little messy, noisy and unkempt. It created habits that caused me to develop a sense of editing out the dark stuff of life when in reality, it was good, bad and sometimes ugly. What I finally realize today is that these are just labels—it is all really about opportunities to learn. And grow. But at the time it can be really painful and when you are a little girl, you do not understand why. You just soak up what is being modeled for you.

Outward appearances showed many successes in my young life, but increasingly, I felt afraid to reveal any emotions that seemed negative. At that time, I couldn't fully imagine and accept that even God could love me unconditionally. No one *but* God really knew how lost I felt.

I had married someone much like myself. We shared the same strengths as well as what I still consider our "works in progress." We were already engaged when I realized, however fleetingly, that Gary had a closer relationship with alcohol than he did with me. It took many years before he was ready to embrace true sobriety. There was great affection between us, but also tremendous confusion and betrayal. Both of us contributed to what was healthy in our relationship and what was not.

Alcoholism is a part of every family system but was not the pattern of my nuclear family of origin, so I did not fully understand the deep woundedness Gary had developed because his paternal family line had all been consumed, literally, by the most powerful and common addictive drug on the planet—and the gateway drug to all others. Gary's father, a kind and extremely tender and sensitive man, died of his disease without ever telling his son in so many words that he loved and approved of him (which, of course, he did *deeply,* but was unable to show), and it took Gary's father's death and his *own* son's birth before he began to heal.

During an equine facilitated guided discovery session at the Epona Center, founder Linda Kohanov made a very astute and insightful observation when the group was working on being very tuned into our sensory awareness in present moment time.

Once focused in that awareness, smells are richer, the landscape colors more brilliant, sounds are intensified and bodily sensations are more readily felt. At the end of the session, the participants and Linda as facilitator all read their observations aloud to the group and Linda described how she could hear distinctly from a distance one of her horses cribbing against a fence.

Cribbing is a chronic habit and coping mechanism common to horses who are kept in stalls for long periods and are claustrophobic and/or bored and that leads to the anxiety of feeling trapped. In the wild, horses travel from twenty-five to fifty miles per day on the average, so imagine how unnatural it is for them to be confined to a small space.

They discover that cupping their lips over something and pulling down while sucking in breath rhythmically produces the calming effects of endorphins released into their bloodstream. It becomes a powerfully addictive pattern and it is a very reasonable response to an animal who is designed to be in a herd dynamic, and who may be hungry and thirsty for more than companionship.

Yet this horse that Linda could hear cribbing was turned out with his buddies on a lush, green pasture with a huge trough of fresh water from a deep well on the historic ranch on a weather day that could be described as idyllic. He had acquired this habit before his days at Epona, but in spite of the fact that his conditions were now as ideal as they can be in domesticity, his addiction continued.

Why then, the cribbing—the addictive behavior?

That is a question that has confounded therapists, scientists, writers, poets, wives, husbands, employers, children and friends since the beginning of time.

We learn in recovery that alcoholism—or *any* addictive process—is cunning, powerful and baffling on every level of our being and those effects are not limited to the addict, but all those who are connected in intimate ways, and in the bigger picture, to everyone.

Humans and horses are pattern animals, with built in instincts for self-preservation. Both species are emotional creatures who seek comfort. Comfort is often what feels *familiar,* even if it is less than ideal or what a reasonable person would chose on a conscious level. There can be subconscious triggers to repetitive behaviors that are associated with entrenched patterns. So freedom from pain becomes a very high priority, and the pattern to self-medicate common to both, even if the environment changes in a positive way. I found this insight to be profoundly fascinating and extremely perplexing.

The key to change is identifying the addictive, *"remembered"* unhealthy pattern, and interrupting it and replacing it with a new positive pattern. Easy to state, and challenging to accomplish. We must learn to remember in a way that *feels* better than the old pattern. This is the dance of life, and sometimes it requires not only healthy partners, but a very talented and inspiring instructor!

With God's grace, Gary and I made a decision to be willing to go to any length to heal our marriage. We decided to take our individual *hero's journey*, as described by author Joseph Campbell, together. Somewhere along the way we were shown a diagram of a triangle with God written at the top and our names on either side at the bottom corners with arrows pointing upward. It was a graphic way of saying that the closer each of us got to God, the closer we would get to each other. It has been true for us.

We were blessed with a beautiful son, Evan. My friend Judi called him "Evan from Heaven." Truer words were never spoken. Being a mother brought me the greatest joy that I had ever known. I had glimpsed the miracle that I am through his birth and finally knew what it meant to be reborn. Much of the grief and deep pain inside me lifted and I knew true forgiveness and gratitude in ways that I had never experienced. His childhood had reacquainted me with my little girl self, and I thought I was doing pretty well ... *until I met Chasta.*

What I was learning from being with horses is that feeling *all* emotions, and being able to understand the messages behind them is the way to whole health. As Dr. Candace Pert describes in the paradigm shattering and reconstructing research in her book, *The Molecules of Emotion*, we must feel and move through the emotions that are often thought of as negative, such as fear and anger. She states: "To repress these emotions and not let them flow freely is to set up a dis-integrity in the system, causing it to act at cross-purposes rather than as a unified whole. The stress this creates, which takes the form of blockages and insufficient flow of peptide signals to maintain function at the cellular level, is what sets up the weakened conditions that can lead to disease. *All honest emotions are positive emotions.*" Italics mine.

I had conformed by becoming a "nice girl" (or at least what I wanted the world to see) all of my life. And, as family systems go, I had watched my mother and grandmother model that behavior to the point that I often did not even know how I *did* feel—I became numb. No wonder I was angry and did not know it or own it on a conscious level! I also believe that Chasta had been handled by some humans who gave her the same message: *You must conform! And be good! And your feelings will not be considered!*

Chasta had given me the opportunities to learn to feel and work through these emotions. Fear is a normal response in humans and horses, and is designed to be able to save our lives. *We must neither ignore it nor stay stuck in it, but learn from and move through it.*

Little by little, we were starting to get the hang of it. I was introduced to an amazing teacher and author at the annual Parelli Savvy Conference, Dr. Stephanie Burns. She wrote a book called, *Move Closer, Stay Longer*, that describes how we can grow by moving out of our comfort zones a little bit at a time, and staying there a little longer before we and/or our horses go too far over a threshold that creates fear and panic. She has a remarkable gift of teaching her concepts and a terrific sense of humor that also kept Gary in rapt attention. What impressed us both the most is that when the Parellis sought her help to support their concepts, she decided the only way to be truly effective was to become a student of the horse herself, so she bought a house in the country with acreage and her first horse, so she could be practicing what she preached and learning along with the rest of us! *Bravo!*

One of the biggest challenges I faced was accepting that I would need to learn to drive a horse trailer and load and travel with my horses. Horses are justified to not want to walk in a box that in their minds might be a meat locker. They are hardwired *not* to walk into confined spaces, especially with someone waiting to shut the door! Plus driving with the extra length behind me, turning wide in traffic, and the responsibility of traveling with such precious cargo seemed overwhelming to me.

The Parelli program has helped me, *experientially,* to learn *not* to focus on what might seem like the enormity of the overall goal, but to become proficient by focusing on each small step along the way while being aware of the bigger picture. The *move closer* (toward the goal, one step at a time) *stay longer* (working toward achievement) philosophy and practice of Dr. Stephanie Burns applies in every situation we face and every dream we want to pursue. Dr. Burns is an expert on how adults learn (or don't!) and she and the Parellis gave us great tools.

So, *onward and upward!* Two steps forward and three steps back? Sometimes it feels that way, but what I was learning is that *both advancing and retreating are equally important steps in the dance of life. Especially* dances with horses.

Chapter Six

First, Heal Thyself

It was time to take a good look at my shadows, the strong emotions that being with Chasta evoked. I read avidly about communication with horses and everything I could about understanding them. I was completely spellbound reading books about the nature of horses and their history in civilization and all I could find about exploring the horse-human bond. I attended fantastic workshops with Jonathan Field in British Columbia, Canada. Jonathan is an *extraordinary* horseman and a wonderful human being who truly opened my eyes and heart to the possibilities. He taught me and continues to teach me skills to go with my heart and desire. His phenomenal abilities as a horseman have been profoundly affected by the teachings of Pat and Linda Parelli, and other outstanding mentors. It has helped me to bridge the gap of understanding between Chasta and Me.

I made good progress with my knowledge and abilities. When Chasta had shined her light on my deepest fears, it allowed me to *feel* them. At the same time, it created an opening for me to *discover the information behind them* in true and lasting ways. The vicious circle of experiencing anger and fear had created tremendous guilt in me. Why were these feelings so hard to shake when I was truly aware of my blessings and deep faith?

I believe that if we continue to ask for help, we will be guided to our next step. And the next. It truly is a matter of trusting in the process of living our Divine Plan—aligning ourselves with God. I began to learn that *horses do reveal what we most need to heal. I have come to understand it as God's gift for us.*

Chasta had multiple owners in her young life before she came to us. She was struggling with *her* confidence and trust as well. In the horse world, we were a mismatch. Her resistance and fear required a confident leader in whom she could place her trust. Too often in our interactions she read the telltale signs that my emotions were all over the map. Was I worthy of her trust? Could I be consistent in my requests and responses? We had a dance that could be described as, "I'll trust you when you trust me—*You go first!"*

Many knowledgeable horse people suggested that I sell her. It reminded me of the many well meaning people who had advised me to get a divorce from Gary. Cut your losses. Move on. Like the time I was outside in the garden of the first home we had purchased together in the early days of our marriage feeling tired, weak, confused and afraid after Gary had stayed out all night. Again. Digging in the earth seemed like the place to be where I could feel connected to something bigger—to renew myself.

Instinctively, I knew by observation that my mother and grandmother had soothed their spirits in gardens. I saw a peace and contentment revealed on their faces amidst their flowers that stood out uniquely without words. Neither of them spent much time with me showing me *how* to garden, but their look of connection showed me *why* to garden.

I knew choosing alcohol and everything that came with it was what had kept Gary out all night and ironically, I had used it, too, as an anesthetic for my own pain over being a young bride left alone with my fears and tears. It was quickly becoming an unhealthy pattern in my own life. Now I had a morning-after headache and queasy stomach to deal with when a friend and colleague of mine pulled up in his truck as I bent over my shovel in an attempt to turn our new home into the ivy covered cottage of my romantic dreams. We talked for a few minutes when he asked me where Gary was. I have never been a good liar (heaven knows how hard I have tried), so I responded with "I don't know." After another brief interchange, he advised me to *"shitcan him!"* I wasn't familiar with this expression, but I was pretty sure it meant to dump or dispose of him. This man, older and wiser, was offering a simple solution to a complex problem. Isn't that what we are doing when we give children drugs because they cannot sit still and pay attention in class? David Suzuki, the brilliant author and environmental leader, says children actually have a *nature deficit* rather than an attention deficit because they are disconnected from their own natural rhythms, and that is why they cannot function in conformity well. The more sensitive the child —and often the most deeply wounded—the more there is a challenge. And all children are sensitive. It is the human condition. And wounds are part of everyone.

My own mother was sitting in her elementary class the day after her father's funeral when her emotions of grief and fear rose to the surface and she began to weep. Her beloved Daddy had been hospitalized for an aggressive form of lung cancer that had developed quickly and took his life suddenly. She never got to say goodbye to him or he to her. At the funeral, she was lined up with everyone else to view his skeletally thin body with cheeks that were rouged in the style of the day, in an attempt to cover the pallor. She reached out to touch the face of the father who had loved her so tenderly and recoiled as she felt her fingers on what seemed like cold stone. Her mother, who had faced the deaths of both of her parents and a beloved brother to military training maneuvers in the previous few years was now forced to find a job to support her two daughters during our country's great depression. Now *there* is an oxymoron.

What happened next has had an impact on my mother that I am strongly convicted has contributed to the chronic and debilitating illness she suffers from today because it created a tremendous psychic wound, and unless healed, these wounds continue to undermine our health. In response to her tears, her teacher, a *woman*, pulled her out of her chair and into the hall where she admonished her harshly, "Stop crying this minute! *You need to be strong for your mother!"*

Can you imagine?! A small child who is facing the loss of her father to death and her mother to a new job and her own grief? *Overnight?* Being told it was not OK to *feel? Dear God.*

My mother, with her kind and generous spirit, has spent her life trying to live up to the impossible task of being strong for everyone else on the planet but herself. How could she possibly take care of herself while she was taking care of the rest of us? The heartbreaking part is that I never heard this story until recently while we sat together in my car outside of her neurologist's office, tying to make sense of the diagnosis that was causing her to lose her physical functions in a rapid decline. And now I could better understand why she was unable on a deep level to know how she truly felt about the world around her and that conforming and being strong for others was imperative behavior for her. She had been *commanded* to *conform* and *not feel* at the most vulnerable time in her life!

So back to my friend's response and Gary's all nighter. I am sure his advice was meant to be protective of me—he could see that I was hurting and knew this was a pattern. But the situation begged for more questions, rather than a knee-jerk reaction. However inappropriate the behavior was, was it not fair to consider how Gary's behavior was influenced by how much *he* was hurting to make those choices? And how was *my* behavior contributing to the situation?

I am not suggesting that a woman *deserves* to be abandoned, betrayed or otherwise violated. Blindly "standing by your man" is *not* my recommendation. Today, after years of self discovery, *I know* I would not choose to stay in a relationship where there was active alcoholism. With *anyone*. However, had I not been willing to take a look at my own unhealthy and codependent behavior, best described by Melody Beattie in her book, *Codependent No More,* I would have been destined to repeat it in future relationships.

Codependents are people who have lost sight of their own lives (or never developed that sight in the first place) to tend to the drama of someone else's, becoming psychologically dependent on that person in an unhealthy way. Another definition that I read on a recovery website is: waking up and asking the person that you are enmeshed with — *"so how do I feel today?"* It would be funny if it were not so tragic.

When talking of her bestselling book, Melody stated: "I wanted to call it *Codependent, Not So Much,* but the publisher said that it would never sell." She realized that we are works in progress. The good news is that because of my time spent with Chasta, I am more aware of my codependent behaviors, and working to make positive changes. "Progress, not perfection" is a slogan we humans can be helped by to support us toward growth.

My own wounds were revealed in behavior patterns that lacked integrity while I was attempting to preserve the façade of the stalwart wife. Imagine my horror a few years later when a counselor at the alcohol treatment center where Gary was admitted told me that the codependent is as sick or sicker than the alcoholic! *Huh?*

It would take years of denial, confusion and stuffed emotions for me to start to understand and appreciate and find peace in the lessons that I was learning. Chasta came along to help me erupt my internal volcano. My own personal version of Mount Vesuvius.

Airing our dirty laundry is not intended to be hurtful to *anyone* or to place blame. Everyone is aching for and deserving of forgiveness, whether they are aware of it or not. It is that I have come to realize that what we have struggled with can be seen as a gift to help us to feel gratitude for our growth and to share that with others. Besides, the best thing to do with dirty laundry is to give it a good scrub and leave it out in the fresh air. One of the slogans in the alcoholic recovery process is *"You are only as sick as the secrets you keep."* At least the dirty ones.

So sell Chasta? Our animals have always been members of our family and hadn't I been willing to go to any length to heal my marriage and family? This was about healing *me*, and I knew it.

I grew up hearing "love God" and "love your neighbor as yourself." I think the second commandment is the hardest one to follow and the basis for many of the world's conflicts. We don't love our neighbors because we don't love ourselves first. I have come to believe that we *must* realize self-love. It is the most important work in the journey of life. How can we give from an empty cup? How can we trust anyone if we do not trust ourselves? If we can truly embrace that *God does love us unconditionally*, we can experience self-love and be able to live in praise and gratitude. Then in a deep and abiding way, we can offer that love to the world and truly understand our connection to all life.

For years, I had struggled to overcome my autoimmune illnesses. Physiologically, it means self-attack. When did my inner critic gain so much momentum that it took on a life of its own and had power over me on a cellular level? And since I was imposing this on myself, what was I projecting onto others? My need and desire to be a confident partner for Chasta gave me the courage to reclaim what I believe is our universal birthright: to know and love ourselves for the Divine Children that we are so that we can offer our unique gifts to the world.

I researched the name Chasta, pronounced *Shasta,* and discovered that it means purity. *We could find our pureness of heart and Divinity together.*

Chapter Seven

From Touch to Trust

In the first days and weeks with Chasta, she moved away from my attempts at the gentle grooming efforts that most horses enjoy and pushed *into* the pressure intended to move her. Her reaction mode was one of opposition and self protection.

I was used to the responses of our first horse, Chad, who when seeing the groom box, walked over to it and lifted a hoof on his own without having been asked, readying it to be cleaned. He moved freely at the slightest suggestion. Our Arabian horse, Ritzy, has a history of nearly falling over in a state of ecstasy during grooming sessions whenever one of us found a "pleasure center." He has always loved to be vacuumed with the rubber massage tip when his winter coat sheds out, in spite of the roaring noise.

In horse vernacular, Chasta was *headshy*, meaning that she did not welcome people in her head space, much less allow or enjoy touch there. Now you can imagine this being a challenge when it comes to the basics of putting on a halter or bridle.

I began to learn about the energy fields that surround a horse with Sandra Wallin, founder of *Chiron's Way Centre for Equine Guided Development.* Sandra is a talented and insightful counselor and teacher of the equine facilitated therapeutic process. She taught me more about her Epona Approach™ training that explains how horses as well as people become aroused by being approached from levels significantly further out than their head and heart space and to notice their body language with all of your senses when they seem to be reaching a threshold or change within them. At that moment, pause, roll your weight back, or even take a step in that direction, and sigh, releasing your breath. This demonstrates your respect and awareness before you come closer. She taught me that every sentient being has a physical space and their energetic boundaries exist beyond what we can see with our eyes. We are not taught this as small children and it can challenge us our entire lives until we can understand it and set healthy boundaries—literally—for ourselves and be aware of and respect them in others. We can be unaware of being violated and violating others if it is all we have ever known.

I believe that was true for Chasta and for me—we had allowed people to trod all over our personal boundaries, both physical and emotional, for too long, and she recognized the resentment I had bubbling up in me, sometimes white hot. We also share the trait of being highly sensitive, although I believe this to be true for all loving creatures to varying degrees.

Linda Kohanov, founder of this approach taught at the Epona Center in Sonoita, Arizona, says that: "This basic lack of respect for space is a major source of fear and anger in humans and horses and I believe, some 'learning disabilities' and ADHD in children."

Much of this socialized conditioning is on a subconscious level. Imagine crowded city streets around the world where this lack of regard for personal space is a constant where many people make an effort to avoid eye contact and awareness of others altogether. This undercurrent of created separation divides us all.

Sandra exposed me to exercises that helped how I approached Chasta, in awareness of her hypersensitivity.

It became a dance of "approach and retreat" and asking permission to come into her personal space at close range. It was startling for me the first time I felt that I could actually palpate in the air the "energy bubble" around Chasta's head and heart space. I asked her permission to touch and groom her there, several feet away from her physical body. I will always remember the gentle look of what appeared to be appreciation when I carefully stroked the air around her with my softest brush.

Then I purchased my first book written by Linda Tellington-Jones, called *Getting in TTouch: Understand and Influence Your Horses Personality*. Linda is a gifted and accomplished lifetime equestrienne who has developed her own unique series of bodywork touches influenced by the mind-body integration for the nervous system from one of her mentors, Dr. Moshe Feldenkrais. After Chasta allowed me to practice these touches *near* her body, slowly she began to accept them more readily *on* her physical body parts. Specific touches are designed to alleviate fear and pain, increase confidence and create a healthy overall flow of energy and promote well being.

One morning I came out and presented the horses with their morning grain. Ritzy zoomed in and ate lustily, as usual, when I noticed Chasta outside, next to a tree, turned away. I called to her, and she turned, slowly and stiffly, and looked in my direction. Normally, she would have raced Ritzy to the feed buckets. I approached her slowly and asked her permission with my mind and voice to come close enough to touch her body. Her head hung listlessly, and her eyes revealed pain—she flinched at my touch. If a horse could look nauseated, she did. I looked quickly for wounds and felt her hooves for heat. Everything seemed normal until I touched under her belly and found it was turgid, distended, and again, she flinched. Having no previous experience with this, I had an intuitive hunch that it was gas colic, somewhat of a generic term for abdominal pain. In this case, the distention appeared to be related to gas. Sandra was teaching me to trust and act on my instincts, my inner knowing, that I possessed even as a novice horsewoman. I assured Chasta that help was on the way and ran in to call my son, Evan, and our veterinarian. Asking Evan to go and stay with her, I attempted to make an appointment for an emergency vet call.

When I came back outside, Chasta had gone to the sand inside the round corral and laid down, in obvious misery, with Evan at her side. I asked him to run into the stable and get my Linda Tellington-Jones TTouch™ charts. I had laminated the collection and put them in a three ring binder so that I could refer to them outside in all weather conditions. He ran out and handed them to me and I looked quickly for a touch designed to relieve gas colic.

The chart said to do *Ear Touches*, starting with small circular strokes at the base of the ear and then placing the hand over the ear and moving towards the tip where acupressure points are stimulated. Chasta laid there, now looking to me for help. I was talking out loud, mostly for my own benefit, in an attempt to stay calm and focused, and I told her that I needed to gently touch her ear, something she had always resisted. I was kneeling at her left side, and began the circular stroking process. Within mere seconds, I heard the loudest, longest expulsion of gas that I had ever heard from any creature in my life! It sounded like the *Queen Mary*, ready to leave the dock! Because I was touching her, I could feel the reverberations throughout my body as well. We both sighed in unison in relief and not a little amazement, when she looked *right* at me, and twisted her head *completely* around to offer me her other ear! It seemed so obvious that I responded by more ear touches on that side. You guessed it—another *long* boom of flatulence within moments. The *Queen Mary* had returned to port! When the sound finally subsided, we both looked at each other—our relationship new. *A bond of intimacy created by entering a crisis together and moving through it.*

I stroked her back and belly for a few minutes and then moved away as she pushed herself up to her feet. She walked away, in the direction of the feed bucket, then stopped and turned, looking back at me with a long gaze that appeared to be approval. I was elated!

Touch that hurts and wounds, and touch that helps and heals are both stored in the cellular memory. Chasta obviously knew of the former. It is true that I did as well. She and I were discovering together the touches that lead to trust. With horses, a simple gassy bellyache can lead to a life threatening form of colic when the bowels become twisted. Chasta knew she was in trouble, and that my intentions were to act on her behalf. Beginning to string together these small triumphs of understanding between us was thrilling me daily, not unlike the moment when your child smiles and reaches for you and for the first time says, *"Mama!"*

I have often been accused of anthropomorphizing my animals. That is, attaching human characteristics to them. It *is* true that I am in the process of learning to think less like a human and more like a horse (or dog, cat, duck ...) in our interactions these days, but this much I *do* believe: Animals are emotional beings and each has it's own unique form of intelligence, it's connection to God. I have often heard, "It's *just* a horse," or "all animals *have* are instincts." If I were to adhere to these limiting beliefs, I would miss the greater richness that God is offering me. *The Mystery*. The more I open myself to the possibilities, the more they are revealed to me.

Did I mention that Chasta has *loved* to have her ears stroked ever since then?!

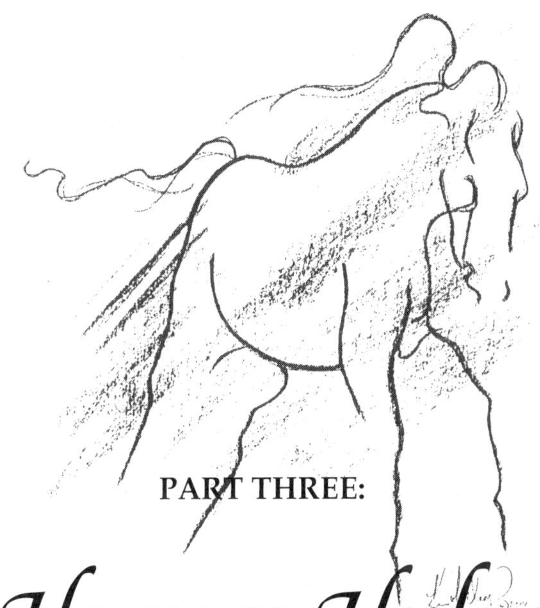

PART THREE:

Horses as Healers

Chapter Eight

Signs of Synchronicity Along the Trail of Truth

My mare and I had taken leaps forward together. Literally, *Quantum leaps*. It was an epiphany for me when I realized that was what Chasta and I were doing crashing over fallen logs in the woods, careening dangerously out of control. Control. What does that mean, anyway? *Nice* girls like me do not want to be thought of as control freaks. I just wanted to be safe. There we go again with safety. Wanting to feel safe is a universal desire but mine was *far* too restrictive and small. It was based in fear. Daily I could sense that my time spent with the horses was expanding my connection to the world. I heard the universal horse herd calling to me in my day and night dreams. Then I found Linda Kohanov's *incredible, transformational* books: *The Tao of Equus* and *Riding Between the Worlds*. They gave voice to my feelings and more and more I knew this passion to heal with horses was my true spiritual path.

My good friend Joanne Mitchelle, a licensed massage therapist, was giving chair massages at a street fair on a sunny weekend. On a break, she wandered through the vendors' displays and saw a woman who had wonderful merchandise from around the world—works of art and antiques. She saw an amazing antique beaded cape that had been worn by a horse in a marriage ceremony in India. Excitedly, she told the woman that she had a friend who she knew would love this remarkable piece and wrote down her contact information to share with me. The next time I came in for a relaxing and heavenly massage, she gave me the website address. Following a massage is never a good time to have to retain my wits completely and who knows which compartment of my purse or wallet or pocket it vanished to? I thought of the beaded cape many times, and even looked for the piece of paper from Joanne, but it would leave my consciousness as quickly as it had entered.

One day, the thought returned to my mind and refused to budge. I called Joanne and sheepishly told her that I needed the information again. *"Wow!"* she exclaimed, "I was just cleaning my desk and recycling things when I came across the name of the woman who has the cape. I actually thought how strange it was that I had not heard from you, since I was sure you would check it out and love it. I was just sitting here contemplating whether to toss this in the recycle bin or call you!"

I looked it up online and ordered it—a rare and beautiful treasure! Beaded into the design were two horses the colors of Chasta and Ritzy and a golden dog just like ours—incredible! While talking horses with the shop owner, Jeri Hansen, she asked if I knew her neighbor, internationally known equine artist and writer, Kim McElroy. Her name sounded familiar, but I wasn't sure. Looking up Kim's website, I realized that I had been sending her horse art greeting cards for years and had always been powerfully drawn to them. I called Kim to order her book of art and stories, *From Heart to Art,* and shared my admiration for her talents.

As we connected, we began to discuss spirituality and horses. Kim mentioned that a story about her mare, Darma, had been featured in *The Tao of Equus*. I told Kim that I was scheduled to take a workshop with the author, Linda Kohanov, and her Epona Approved Instructor, Sandra Wallin, at Sandra's *Chiron's Way Centre* in Canada. Amazingly, a last minute cancellation on a waiting list allowed Kim a spot and she was asked to bring some of her incredible equine art to display. We decided to share a ride and lodgings. Since, remarkably, it was Kim's birthday the day we left, I suggested we enjoy a celebration lunch in LaConner, the historic channel town near where I live.

Meeting her for the first time in my driveway, I felt as if we had been friends forever. I showed Kim my most favorite of her paintings in her book and asked if I could order a print. She smiled and said that she would contact me with the details when we returned from our week in Canada and also share a special story about the painting. It is magnificent: A very powerful image of a light-colored horse that strikingly resembles Chasta and an owl ascending together in the starry sky called *Silent Night*.

We enjoyed a lovely lunch and had so much to share that time got away from us—I realized that we needed to head north and Kim asked that I drive through the old town along the waterfront on the way. Before they were married, she and her husband, Rod, had been to LaConner once before, in a foggy mist, and she said that there was a very special building that she wanted to point out to me. Both she and Rod had been mesmerized by this old landmark that housed treasures from around the world, eerily like the shop her friend Jeri owned. They had been inspired to buy rings for each other there that day as a symbol of their new love. She told me that the energy there felt sacred and palpable, but she could not be certain why.

"There it is!" she pointed. I smiled as goose bumps prickled my neck.

"That building belonged to my parents," I said. "It used to be my father's architectural design studio. We had our wedding reception there. I threw my bouquet off that balcony."

"Omigosh!" was her stunned reply.

"But that is not all of it. What you were responding to most of all is that it was built as a livery stable around 1880. *It is the horses that you sensed.*" Kim's business is called *Spirit of Horse Gallery.*

We sat for a moment in reverent silence. "My parents dug up a horseshoe for me when they were restoring the foundations," I told her.

Kim had an incredulous look on her face as she shook her head slightly, as if in disbelief, eyes wide. "Now I can tell you the story of my painting." She proceeded, "That night as we drove slowly out of town in the fog, we turned onto the country road that I *now* know is toward your home. Suddenly, a huge white owl flew up on the passenger side just outside the car window and it looked *right at me!* When we got to our home that evening, I began painting *Silent Night.*"

A large framed print of the beautiful and inspiring image hangs in a place of honor in our dining room, ascending the high wall above the antique sign that named our home: Woodylane Farm. *Being aware of our kinship with all of life, in awe and gratitude, creates the space to live in this flow of synchronicity and wonder.* I remember hearing that synchronicities are God's exclamation points. Maybe *that* is why I am blessed with so many of them!

All of these synchronous events helped me to feel the hand of God guiding me, blessing me with kindred spirits, both two and four legged, to help me on my journey. My path to wholeness. To the light.

For it was in the light of the harvest moon that I first saw Chasta and was given this gift of awakening and now a spiritual kinship with a new friend that made my heart leap for joy with a gratitude as immense and bright as a full moon, complete with the owl as a symbol for the wisdom I was gaining in my new awareness.

“Silent Night” by Kim McElroy

Chapter Nine

Horses as Teachers: Frank

Kim and I arrived in British Columbia, Canada at Sandra Wallin's *Chiron's Way* equine facilitated therapy workshop led by author Linda Kohanov and Sandra, who is trained as an Epona Approved Instructor as well as having her own practice. Linda is the founder of the Epona Center, an equestrian based conference and retreat destination in Sonoita, Arizona. I began to understand that Linda and Sandra live and love the path they teach. They have become lead mares extraordinaire by living and working/playing with horses. A wild horse herd is a matriarchal society where the lead mare guides and makes decisions for the greater good, assisted by the patriarchal protection of the stallions.

We introduced ourselves the morning of the first day, as we gathered in a circle, and some of us looked like deer in headlights as we tried to clarify what prompted us to be there. I heard the words of Pat Parelli in my mind about the need to be willing to be inconvenienced in order to succeed. It felt as if I was embarking on a wonderful adventure and yet I felt vulnerable at the same time. Many of the other participants had traveled from great distances to be there and had little to no experience with horses. I had planned and sacrificed for over a year to find myself registered for this important workshop, but I still felt a little wobbly. Personal growth, it turns out, is truly hard work sometimes! As open as I felt I was to the possibilities, the process was still beyond my imaginings.

Some of the interactions between horse and human take

place in a small corral called a round pen, where we were instructed to focus on the presence of the horse and how it may affect us. In my "reflective round pen" session, I was standing about ten feet from a huge gray horse named Frank. He had seemed quite indifferent to my outpouring of tears and the accompanying snuffling after we had done an exercise to let go of the inner critic (our false self/Ego) and accept our divine and authentic selves. Linda had helped me to reflect on what messages came up for me *in my body* that were life affirming and those that limited me in an unhealthy way, guiding me through the process.

I have told you that I often see the face of God revealed in animals, but imagine my surprise when *I very clearly saw* an image of George Burns standing at the head of this enormous horse! Remember the movie *Oh, God!*? *It was him! George as God. Standing there smiling and seeming to tell me not to take myself so seriously*. I blinked and he was gone, but it had been so *real*! My knees were knocking and I was sure that I had been out in the sun too long when Frank walked across the corral toward a bucket and kicked it—*hard*. Now that in and of itself is not such an improbable thing for a horse to do. *But it just looked so deliberate.*

He looked right at me, walked over, and kicked it again. Then he stopped and looked at me as if to say, *"Get it?!"* My mind reeled. I felt as if I was on *Candid Camera*.

Kick the bucket? That's my message?! Oh geez—my inner critic/false-self/Ego kicked back in (even though we had just completed the exercise to lose it—see how much practice I needed?) and chided, *"Guess you're gonna die!"* Then just as suddenly as I had felt myself tighten up, I relaxed and started to smile. It was just my false self/Ego (my inner critic) dying—and good riddance! Did Jesus not tell his followers that we must die to be reborn? And the final line in the "simple prayer" made famous by

Saint Francis of Assisi says "that it is in dying that we are born into eternal life." Other faith traditions teach dying to self as well.

Once I relaxed, I stood quietly expressing gratitude to Frank (and George!) when I heard in my mind distinctly: *Be still and know that I am God. Clear as a bell.* My eyes felt fuzzy and my vision softened and Frank's horse body seemed to dissolve into the rugged gray mountains behind him until they were one. It was surreal. My entire being felt bathed in the Holy Spirit. I felt truly connected to all life in that moment.

Linda Kohanov also exposed me to the concept of'intersubjectivity. We have grown up with the models of the objectivity of the scientific method that gives credibility to our rational minds and the one of subjectivity and how we individually perceive life, but the concept of *intersubjectivity* allows for an interplay of the more balanced ideal. Rather than looking at life from the outside of things with objectivity or from our own viewpoint with subjectivity, we can learn to live in the state of intersubjectivity where we are in the 'flow'—the stream of consciousness where we are accessing information from every cell in balance from within and from the outside and our interconnectedness to all life. This experience with Frank was a profound example of this understanding for me—an opportunity for me to embody what I believed.

When I experienced my authentic self in that guided experience with Frank, it was the divine spark that helped me to feel connected to the whole of creation and the feeling of truth within my every cell.

When it came time for me to share with my support group (my homies for the week), I was speechless. They had been outside the corral, supporting me by *"holding the sacred space of possibility"* reverently, and recording what came up for them as they observed with all of their senses.

This expression was created by Kathleen Barry Ingram, a colleague of Linda's, to describe a new way of turning the notion of an audience into something different than what we think of traditionally. In the typical definition, the audience is the group that is expecting to be entertained and to judge the performers in terms of their own desires and needs. In the "holding the sacred space" model, the person in the arena does not have the responsibility to entertain. The audience is there to support the person for the experience in feeling safe to experiment, make mistakes, express authentic emotion and to be witnessed and supported without judgement. It is a powerful experience for all participants, and one we do not often receive or give in ordinary life, from ourselves or to others, yet it is a model that could make life so much richer for all of us in so many positive ways!

In a squeaky voice that came from my awe and wonder, I recounted my experience. As I shared my tears about my inner critic insisting that I was not good enough, smart enough, pretty enough, etc. enough, a beautiful man named Ed from New York held up a note that he had written during my original sobfest. It read "You are *more* than enough." He had been responding to what I had earlier been experiencing in my mind with no words exchanged aloud!

The energy of the group felt completely united when I went on to describe Frank *becoming* the far off jagged peaks. Marion, a fantastic artist from Ontario, simply held up the drawing that she had made while I was in the experience. *It was a mountain.*

In the final hour, the entire group of fifteen human participants, five human facilitators and five horse therapists gathered for the closing ceremony. In a very moving way, we talked of our sacred responsibility to take what we had learned out in to the world and the importance of maintaining a community of support. We all walked in a serpentine, led by an aging sorrel chestnut gelding named Sundance. Blind in one eye and ravaged by time and illness, thinking of his great dignity still moves me deeply. At the end, Sandra's beautiful black mare, Grace, her long plaited mane shining, regally wore my antique beaded horse cape that was the gateway to this adventure for me. Linda then turned the entire procession in the opposite direction, with Grace now in the front of the line. It was then that I heard the words to the time honored hymn in my mind, *"Twas Grace that led me safe thus far and Grace will lead me home."*

When I did return home and described my adventure to my husband, a graduate of the recovery process, he said that it sounded like I had gone to "treatment."

"I did," I smiled.

Chapter Ten

Frank's Apprentice: Eclipse

The morning of the final day of the workshop, my group was gathered for an active round pen session. The idea of this activity was to engage the horse of your choice in an interactive dance of movement using body language to invite the horse to move willingly with you.

My fellow participants had become dear friends in this special and authentic setting. I sat watching them in celebratory awe as they stepped into the center of the enclosure to learn more about themselves and how they relate to the intimacy of the horse dance, especially with an audience, though we understood that our role was very different than in the conventional sense. My job in that moment was to hold the space for them in a supportive and sacred way as they would do for me when it was my turn. We were to choose a horse from the herd that had been assembled for the workshop. Two people in my group, back-to-back, had chosen a beautiful young leopard spotted Appaloosa named Eclipse. Each of them had a lovely experience and toward the end of the second session, I noticed that Eclipse was very relaxed and looked quite sleepy. He even rolled a few times in the sand and I wondered if he would stay down for a nap. He didn't, but stood quietly, eyes at half mast. I smiled and thought of my own horses at home, likely resting in the morning sun. It was a gentle closure for the session.

In that moment, Leslie Ross, trained in the *Adventures in*

Awareness™ guided development process, our wonderful facilitator and owner of Eclipse, told me I was next and asked me to choose a horse. Just the simple decision-making process sent me into a habitual pattern of trying to make it work for everyone involved, even if that meant I never even considered how *I* felt about the situation. Eclipse seemed tired, I thought, and would probably welcome a break, but I did not want to hurt his feelings by not choosing him, especially in front of the group! Or inconveniencing anyone else to have to get another horse. And what if the horse I wanted was someone else's choice who might be disappointed? There went the mind chatter again! At least I had become more aware of it! While I was trying to recover by remembering my new techniques to let go of the noise (sooner than later) and just *feel* in my body what my true self wanted, Eclipse turned and looked at me and deliberately walked over from the other side and stuck his nose through the rails and touched my belly where I was experiencing the sensation. *The precise moment that I shifted my awareness to embody what was going on for me, he had responded.* There was an audible inhalation from the group and Leslie smiled and said, "I think you have been chosen."

My entire body relaxed in relief that a decision had been made, thanks to Eclipse. As I made my way toward the gate to go inside the corral, he looked lazily off into the distance, leg cocked and totally relaxed. Within a split second, his entire mood shifted and he bellowed a frantic whinny and took off running. He had nowhere to go but in circles, which only escalated his wild energy. Again, the group's emotions, in unison, appeared to mirror Eclipse and suddenly everyone was wide-eyed. He blasted another shrill whinny and in frustration, started crow-hopping and kicking out.

Leslie looked at me and asked how I felt *now*. *"About Eclipse?"* I responded. "Yes," she replied." Are you afraid to be close to him?"

The instant that Eclipse had shifted from a relaxed to a panic mode, I had noticed his horse friend, Frank, being led from the round pen within Eclipse's vision to another around the corner and out of sight. *Horses notice everything, and I realized in that moment that they were teaching me to be more aware of the bigger picture, too.* I knew his reaction was entirely due to separation anxiety of his pasture mate and leader. Instantly, he felt vulnerable, alone and frightened, which had prompted his reaction.

"No," I said. "I am not afraid of Eclipse—he is only upset because his buddy just walked out of sight—Frank is his security." And then, in the flash of an instant, my emotions boiled to the surface in the form of heaving sobs. My group reverently supported me in silent concern as my tears flowed. Finally, in a quiet voice, Leslie asked, "What *are* you afraid of?" Without hesitation, I blurted out how afraid I was for my son, Evan, to go out into the world and *my* separation anxiety around it. I felt terrified of the culture changing the close bond we shared. Leslie suggested that when I felt ready, to go into the round corral and interact with Eclipse. She knew that I had my own horses, unlike many of the participants, who were engaged with them for the first time.

As I entered, our mutual need for connection was palpable, and Eclipse ran to me and we both melted into the moment, sighing with relief. As we stood together, I placed my hands on his heart and withers, the prominence at the base of his neck, and I could feel him blowing softly against my face. He smelled sweet and sweaty, and I felt a deep connection to the powerful scent that a baby evokes for his mother. Leslie and another excellent facilitator, Jennifer Jackson, an Epona Approved Instructor, made quiet suggestions that helped me through the process. Jennifer offered for me to think of Evan in a little boat, with me on the shore with a line between us. She told me that it was important for me to visualize letting the line out and allowing Evan to drift out to sea, knowing that if it became stormy, I could reel him into the safe harbor of his mother's love. As that feeling began to resonate within me, on cue, Eclipse moved gently away from me to the edge of the pen and called, but this time less urgently.

All of us were very moved by what was unfolding. I watched him for awhile, then asked him with my mind and body to return to me. He did. We walked together, quietly, and I cried anew. This time, they were tears of joy (which Evan had coined "happy tears" when he was only three years old), trusting that the bond I have with my son would survive the stormiest seas. I also realized in that moment that Eclipse, in horse years, was a teenager like Evan. I felt a weight that had been developing over time, shift and release, seeming to fly away toward the nearby mountains. Even the name Eclipse seemed very significant, since its meaning is the partial or complete covering of one celestial body with another. Celestial bodies refer to the sky and heavens, and my relationship with Evan has always been Heaven on Earth for me. And didn't I want Evan to reach for the sky with *his* life? Eclipse's leopard spots even had meaning for me since I have always associated power and strength with the big cats. As a mother, my greatest desire for Evan is for him to develop his faith and come into his own power with God.

Now to share the amazing addendum to this experience. About a year later, I attended another equine facilitated growth workshop at Sandra's *Chiron's Way Centre*, co-facilitated by the brilliant Barbara Rector, one of the great visionaries in this field, creator of Adventures in Awareness™, also a program for Equine Facilitated Personal Development. Before I left for the workshop, I needed to wrap a gift that I intended to take for Sandra. Inside my large box of gift wrap, I shuffled through the papers to find a suitable piece. Right near the top was something that startled me into stunned reflection. It was a piece of artwork that Evan had created in school, maybe in the first or second grade. It was a painted paper collage. It has a small figure of himself in a little boat, cut and pasted onto the choppy seas of his green and blue paint. His name was written in his sweet little handwriting, and there was a line out from the boat to the shore. I wept in gratitude to God and His mysterious horse and human angels.

I brought it to share with the group and was especially happy that Jennifer was there to see her healing metaphor in another form, created years before my experience with Eclipse! I shared that it had fascinated me to realize that I had only a vague memory of ever having seen it before and absolutely *no idea* how it ended up in that box and not amongst the artwork collection that we have saved and displayed over the years.

As I shared my story, Barbara smiled and said, "It was in with your gift wrap. The horses always have gifts for us, we just need to unwrap and receive them."

And cherish them forever.

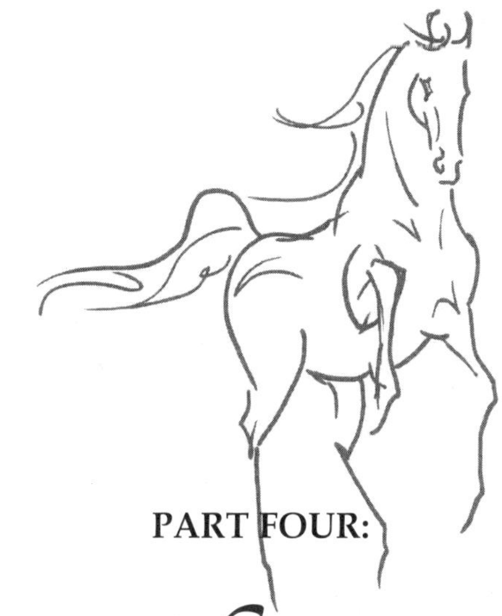

PART FOUR:

Life: A License to Learn

Chapter Eleven

Beauty from Brokenness

I believe that God sent Evan as a special angel to heal much more than our marriage. When I say that, I do not mean that is his *job. It is just who he is, a gift.* He gives us the opportunity, like all children do, to experience love and be changed for the better. It is *not* his responsibility to heal us, just to be himself, which is love. It is our job to allow the Holy Spirit to heal us, so we can feel the love. Evan spreads seeds of compassion and joy wherever he goes, and like his father, has a very tender heart.

When he was just a little fellow, he and Gary planned a surprise dinner for my birthday. When I got the call to come home, after being sequestered at my parents' house, there was a sign over our front door that read: "Funk and Son, Italian Bistro." I was greeted by a smiling Evan with a linen napkin over his arm and a mascara moustache, apparently not able to speak any English as he motioned me to my table set with a single rose and our best dishes. Chef Dad entered with my piping hot seafood lasagna, dripping with cheesy marinara sauce and a gorgeous salad of baby Italian greens, which I enjoyed immensely.

After the meal, I was sent upstairs to read while they prepared to make me a carrot cake, my personal favorite. A cake from scratch on a school night when it was nearly bedtime? A very sweet idea, but my mother/bedtime police instincts kicked in, so I went to the kitchen to help move things along. Gary was leaning down to look for a grater when his elbow connected with a stacked set of antique bowls on the table. They landed on the floor with a sickening crash and there were shards everywhere. I looked in dismay at my formerly lovely bowls, collected over many years, and then into the eyes of my husband and son. Evan started to cry and wailed, "Now we have ruined your birthday!" "Hardly," I said, "You have both made it very special. I *am* disappointed, but I will have them made into a mosaic of some kind. Thank you for my special party." We enjoyed moist, spicy cake with a sunken center from being covered with sweet cream cheese frosting while still steaming hot from the oven. No birthday treat ever tasted better.

The next day, I called my dear friend Joanne, who amongst many other talents, is a mosaic artist. When I asked her to make something from my shards, she said she was too busy and that I should create something myself, especially since the pieces had special meaning. "I'll talk you through it," she said. And she did. I used the shards to cover a French flower bucket, and have used it every summer since for bouquets of sunflowers.

I was hooked on this new way to express my creativity. I began creating "bits and pieces" mosaics from vintage china and realized that creating beauty from damaged goods had been a significant theme in my life. I love to restore antiques, create handcrafts from old found materials and find new ways to use worn and abandoned things.

What began as gifts for family and friends became a passion that I began to share by teaching my techniques. I read an interview with the one of the greatest singers in history, Tony Bennett. His two great passions in life are his music and his art in the form of painting. The magnitude of his stature as musician and artist is due to his dedication as an ongoing student, and his desire to constantly improve his crafts. He states that "I do not sing or paint because I want to, but because I *have* to." *That* is passion. I will always remember the Tony Bennett records (huge black vinyl discs on a turntable) playing in the background of my childhood, and hearing my father love to tell the story again and again of how Tony auditioned forty-five times before he was hired, and that was in a small (and probably seedy) lounge. Tony had the belief that God had given him the gift to *sing*, and his voice as an instrument has brought joy around the world for over sixty years.

Mosaics are an art form as old as time and belong to every culture. It became apparent that broken vintage china was a very evocative medium. Every ethnic group uses clay from their area of the earth to create decorated china and most of our sacred celebrations include meals together that record these patterns in our memories. Holiday meals, weddings, and even funeral celebrations of life. These are the settings where we are most inclined to have powerful emotional responses—our juices really get flowing and are stored most significantly. People are fascinated to see shards incorporated in my creations that were their grandmother's china pattern or from a ceramic bowl they remember that came in a box of oatmeal during the depression years of their childhood.

As I taught classes, I shared the meditative process this medium had offered me. Every piece felt like a prayer to create beauty from the brokenness that I felt inside.

Damaged goods made new. It was as if I was reconstructing and birthing integration and wholeness from within. Scientist and author Dr. Candace Pert explains in her landmark book, *Molecules of Emotion*, how being in a meditative state during a focused process actually creates the body's own natural chemicals called endorphins, which are associated with pleasure and deep connection to life.

Dr. David R. Hawkins has written one of the most provocative books I have ever enjoyed, titled *Power VS. Force*. To quote a passage, he writes: "We know clinically that alignment with beauty is associated with longevity and vigor—because beauty is a function of creativity, such longevity is common in all creative occupations." For me, the part about vigor is most appealing—my idea of fully living is to be *vigorously* healthy. And I believe it is not *which* process of creativity that we choose to incorporate into our lives, but simply that we *do something* on a conscious and consistent basis.

What is it for you? Playing the piano for your own pleasure and/or for your community? Growing an abundance of organic vegetables that grace your family table and are enjoyed by your neighbors? Teaching an illiterate adult to read? There are so many ways to develop and express creativity and are as individual as we all are. Go for it—for your health and the health of the planet!

This healing process had a direct affect on my ability to connect with Chasta, and with all of my relationships. Each day I perceived the two of us less as damaged goods and felt us heading towards magnificence. In fact, I began to proclaim it!

Many of the people taking my classes have thanked me for encouraging them to do the same in their own lives. Each of us must create our own healing process, but an encouraging word may be the permission we need to give ourselves. The connections I have made with my mosaics have been so powerful, because the creative process unites us all. I had taken on the role of the wounded healer as teacher. We often teach what we need to learn. By realizing the gifts that my mosaic process was offering me, I could share those insights with my students.

Sandra Wallin's business name for her Equine Guided development practice is *Chiron's Way*, named for the centaur (a creature both man and horse) in ancient Greek mythology who was a kind and gentle healer, and became accidentally wounded by one of his students. The subtitle of the book by Henri Nouwen called *The Wounded Healer* says it all. "In our own woundedness, we can become a source of life for others." This passage in Henri Nouwen's book defines it for me: "Making one's own wounds a source of healing, does not call for a sharing of superficial personal pains but for a constant willingness to see one's own pain as rising from the depth of the human condition which all men share."

So it is important that we not become so attached to our pain as to perpetuate it and remain in the role of victim, preventing our healing by creating a vicious tapeloop of all of our suffering. Rather, to identify that which has injured or limited us and take responsibility for making positive, life-enhancing choices in the present and share our suffering *only to the extent* that it gives us a heart of compassion for our fellow man and that we understand experientially the interconnectedness of all of life.

It has been a special joy for me to help people create meaningful mosaics from their broken family heirlooms that can live on in a new form. Change! Make new! I recently saw a wooden sign in a catalog that read: *Life is short – use the good china!* Advice taken, since you can always create a beautiful mosaic if it breaks!

And finally, a sweet story that comes to mind when remembering creating special mosaics. An antique kneeling bench called a prie-Dieu, French for "pray to God," was found in the basement of the historic church that we attend. A family had taken it home so that I could pick it up since I had agreed to restore it and apply some mosaic decoration. When I went to their home, the oldest children, Sarah and Katie, had a story to share with me. The night before, as they were practicing their piano lessons, they heard the voice of their five-year-old brother, Charlie. They looked to see him in the corner of the room, kneeling on the bench, with his little hands folded in prayer and his eyes closed. "God," he prayed aloud, "Please make me into a better boy. But if you don't, it's OK, 'cause I like myself the way I am." We enjoyed a laugh together thinking of the many delightful things Charlie had said in his young life. But the more that I thought of it, the more it felt like Charlie had really struck a balance in his innocence. He was in touch with God, asking to be better, but happy where he was *in the moment*.

"Out of the mouths of babes," and "straight from the horse's mouth" are both classic phrases that we can ponder here. *I believe that children and horses will continue to lead us into the kingdom of Heaven.*

Chapter Twelve

Pay It Forward

On a beautiful autumn day I met a very special friend of mine along the street of the small town where we live. We walked and talked until we came to the studio office where she has her counseling practice. Her name is Elke Macartney, and she has remarkable healing gifts and has a heart filled with love for all life. I admired a beautiful metal sculpture of feathers in her office. It was stunning. She said it had been a gift from a friend, and wrote his name, James Montgomery, on a slip of paper for me. Some days later, I called his number, but his answering machine was full, so I could not leave a message to express my interest. I intended to try again, but never did and the paper vanished into the same place a sock in a dryer must go.

The following spring I took our Arabian horse, Ritzy, to a horse camp in Canada with my dear friend, Amelia, and *her* Arabian boy, Mariner. We had the time of our lives. Our hosts at the Quilchena Ranch were delightful, and our equine leaders, master horseman Jonathan Field and his beautiful wife, Angie, made it a mountaintop experience -literally.

Our first family horse, Chad, had been Amelia's childhood companion. She needed to find a family who could give him an easy, caring retirement so she could pursue her athletic goals riding with a younger horse. We got Chad and she got Mariner. Perfect. Amelia is young enough to be, and often mistaken for, my daughter, and the perfect age to be Evan's big sister to look up to. We felt blessed to say that in acquiring Chad, we added *two* members to our family.

There were many highlights to our trip, but a very special one was captured for us by Amelia with her camera. It is a photo of Ritzy and me in the rushing creek up to his belly, mane flying in the wind, enjoying the cool water on his legs on a hot day after a long ride. The sun is setting in the background to complete the picture.

On the last day of camp, we drove the long haul home together and said our final goodbyes. I came in late and my family was asleep. I checked a stack of mail and my phone messages. One was from a man named James Montgomery who said that he had tried to gift his friend, Elke, with a sculpture of a horse, but that she had told him to give it to her friend, Connie Funk. She gave him my number so he could call me. He asked that I call him with my address, so that he could ship it to me.

Here I was, late at night, still smelling strongly of horse, and euphoric from my trip. It felt like déjà vu, but we will get to that in a moment. It was too late to call, so all I could do was go to sleep and dream of horses.

In the morning, I called James and introduced myself. He was so kind and said that he was pleased to send me this gift. "Would you like to hear about it?" he asked. "Yes, please," I replied. "I created two horses," he started. "One is a silver one that I kept for myself and the one for you is a golden one with a white blaze in the shape of lightening." His voice continued, but I could not hear the words over my tears, which stunned me with their intensity. After a few moments, he paused and said, "Are you all right?" I struggled to regain my composure and quietly told him that I had a golden horse with a white blaze with a lightening shaped scar over it. "Oh, my," he said, "tell me about her."

"It's a long story," I began. "I took a trip to France with my parents and brother but had never left Gary and Evan for any period of time before. It was very tender for all of us to be separated over such a long distance. I was gone over my birthday in September and they phoned the six-hundred-year-old chateau where we were staying and Evan played his cello and they sang *"Happy Birthday"* to me through the phone lines. The next day they went and bought Chasta for me from a young, dark-haired man named Damien, while I, at the same time across the ocean, was horseback riding on a bay colored Paso Fino with a guide in Provence—a *young, dark-haired man named Damien!* After our return flight home, I dropped off my parents and was too jazzed to fall asleep. Gary and Evan had left that morning for a school field trip to mountain camp and we had agreed that *they* would feed all of our animals in the morning and *I* would feed them dinner when I returned that night.

I came into our kitchen about 1:00 a.m., checked my mail and listened to my phone messages. Then I saw their note. It said: "Happy Birthday—we bought you a horse! Her name is Chasta—we hope you love her." I was so tired that I didn't fully comprehend it, but decided to investigate. *No wonder* our dogs were in my face—they weren't just happy to see me—there was a new *horse* in our pasture!

I grabbed an apple, took a juicy bite, and wandered out into the autumn darkness. I saw a light form in the moonlight, and as I got closer, I could see her dark eyes in contrast. I had a sharp, visceral response in my gut as if sparks flew off her face. I noticed that she had a jagged scar across the slender white blaze and star on her face. She was very wary, but finally took the apple and backed away. It was eerie, and I slowly turned to come in after watching her from the distance that she had created between us. I went inside and fell deeply asleep and woke up in a dreamlike state. I dreamed I went to France and rode a golden horse.... My night and day dreams had combined.

Then I told James that Chasta's scar used to make me feel sad, because I felt certain it was the result of trauma, but that going through the fire of transformation together that we are both stronger and now I feel our scars are becoming beauty marks. Partnering with a horse is like any relationship—the more you offer, the more you receive, especially when you are bonded by mutual trauma, *and the release of letting go of it.*

Now it was me who paused.... "Are you all right?" I asked. Through an emotion-cracked voice and tears, he said that his father had been a gifted horseman and that horses had been calling him. He said that he was thrilled that his sculpture was going where it had such special meaning.

I told him that I had admired his feather sculpture and had never made a follow up call about it. "What is your fee for the horse sculpture?" I asked. "It is a gift for you—all that I ask is for you to *pay it forward,*" he insisted.

I was stunned at his generosity and we exchanged information and hung up. Although the phone lines had disconnected, I felt a powerful hookup remaining with this stranger who was now my friend.

About a week later, I came home to find a large box on our veranda porch. I recognized the return address. Eagerly, I opened the box on my hands and knees, and unwrapping the packing material, gasped. It looked *just* like Chasta! I pulled it out and held it to my chest, weeping. *At that very moment,* Amelia and her dear husband, Erich, pulled up our long driveway to help me repair some fencing. She got out of the car and approached. *"It's the horse, isn't it?"* she asked. I turned it around so she could see it—she gasped too, recognizing Chasta down to the details of her markings. We hugged in mutual gratitude for these amazing animals that had brought us all together. Another shape in the box caught my eye. Carefully wrapped within was a full moon to go with Chasta and a feather sculpture like the one that I had admired! There was also an envelope with a photo of the beautiful silver horse sculpture that James had made for himself. Amelia and Erich hung the sculptures on our stone fireplace and they still fill me with awe and gratitude as they remind me of the deep connections we are gifted with in life and I know they always will.

Here is where the story gets even more interesting. I was trying to think of a gift to send James in gratitude for his generous spirit. I knew that telling our story would be a form of "paying it forward" but nothing else special was coming to mind. The next day we had breakfast with my parents at our favorite restaurant in LaConner (owned, not surprisingly, by a couple who have two horse ranches!) and I gave them a copy of the photo that Amelia had taken of Ritzy and me in the churning water. I told them that I wanted them to come to our home after our meal to see the amazing gifts that I had received.

My father, Glen, said, "That is really interesting, because I have a gift of art for you, too." When we went out to his car, Dad handed me a painting that he had just finished. I looked in awe as the hairs on the back of my neck stood up. My father said, "I have no idea where this image came from—I just knew that it was for you, and that is before I knew you had such a great experience with Ritzy!" The canvas revealed a man in a long, dark coat and hat on a silver horse that looked *exactly* like the one in James' photo! They were in *deep, churning waters in a lightening storm!* "It's called *'Knowing the Way Home"* he said.

Gary and Evan were admiring it when I said, "Dad—now I know this is for an artist named James." When we got to our home, I took him in and told him the story. "May I send it to him?" I asked. "Of course, now *I know* why it flowed through my hands." I mailed it to James with a card saying that it may represent his earthly father and his strength and love and trust of horses and how grateful I was for this amazing experience of the interconnectedness of our creative spirits. Soon after I received the most beautiful letter telling me that the painting had been the impetus for a very profound healing as well as a transformation within himself.

I have yet to meet James in person, but we signed our cards "sister" and "brother" and one day Elke promises that she will bring him and his family to meet me and mine.

Thank you to Elke, James, our fathers and the silver and golden horses. And to God's mysterious ways that connect us all. *Horses always know the way home. They help us to understand that indeed, we do, as well....*

I shared earlier that my father had a very traumatic childhood. He moved sixteen times from birth to the age of nineteen when he joined the Navy to escape his home life and had his seventeenth relocation. He attended fourteen schools, missing significant portions of every level and the sixth grade altogether. He remembers skipping school to relieve the trauma of being so far behind, creating more of the same. He dodged the truant officers by hanging out at Woodland Park Zoo in Seattle, feeling a connection to the animals and the natural beauty there. He recalled that he noticed signs that identified where the animals had come from and told various species that he would try someday to make sure they got back to the wild of where they came. He especially promised this to the horses, for he knew firsthand of their wild nature and beauty.

One of the only periods of his young life that he remembers as happy was when the family moved to Prosser, Washington, to be close to his maternal grandmother,

Emma Hobson. Emma was the cook and housekeeper for a widower and his young daughter, Mr. Knute Hunton, who had a ranch in nearby Mabton.

Dad remembers the great love that Mr. Hunton had for his horses that plowed his fields and carried him on their backs over the vast acreage. Knute Hunton was an early pioneer there, homesteading Washington State from Oklahoma. He rode west horseback on his own and got as far as the prairies of Wyoming when he became ill with a high fever from the exposure. He was so weak that he had to dismount and lay down on the ground for several days. His faithful horse never left his side, and licked his forehead and face to cool him. Finally, the fever broke and he was able to get to his feet and mount his loyal horse to continue their journey.

He cared for his horse for the rest of her life, knowing that she had saved his. This experience meant a great deal to him and he impressed the fact that horses are remarkable creatures upon my father.

At the edge of town where my father lived, the land rose up for several miles until it reached the area known as *Horse Heaven Hills.* The children from the neighboring farms and ranches all had their own horses so Dad remembers riding bareback with his pal, Billy, at great speeds, jumping over irrigation ditches and the ever present tumbleweeds all without benefit of a lesson—just the relaxed confidence from the natural state of being a kid in the country, connecting with animals and nature.

He said that at the crest of the climbing hill country, the land became a plateau and there were wheat fields as far as the eye could see. Often when the kids ventured up into the hills with a pouch of vine ripened tomatoes from the garden and carrots for the horses, they would bury potatoes covered in tinfoil under rocks in a campfire to return to later after a ride. Dad remembers carrying a salt shaker in his pocket for seasoning! On those special occasions, he and his friends would often see what few people in the world have ever had the privilege of witnessing: the wild herds of *Horse Heaven Hills*.

He described in detail the thundering sound of the pounding hooves and the huge cloud of dust their movement created in the distance. He said that the horse leader was evident and often stood on a rocky prominence to look out to the horizon with the eye of the eagle before moving on. Nothing in the Saturday movies that he loved as his escape from the life he led at home could compete with *this* real life experience!

The kindness that Mr. Hunton offered my father has remained with him to this very day. I cannot help but think that Mr. Hunton's great love for horses and James' father's great love for horses was a special part of this creative interchange. They are why we can continue to pay it forward. *For it is in giving that we receive.*

As this remarkable story illustrates, the concept of "paying it forward" is not merely linear. *Love moves in circles*. All true gifts from the heart create a circle of love, whose concentric rings just keep getting bigger, like skipping rocks on a still pond.

And what prompted Gary and Evan to find a golden horse for me on my birthday as a surprise when I was halfway around the world? A gift so personal after telling them that I was not able to face loving another horse after the death of Chad when I had built a wall around my heart to protect me from the pain? After I had begun using the stable as my art studio, trying to heal my grief?

What a mixed soup of emotions I had! How could a person who loves horses as much as I do not be thrilled at such a thoughtful gesture? But since most horses live twenty to thirty years, shouldn't I have been involved in the decision? Chasta was blasted in the crossfire of my emotional quagmire for some time while I adjusted.

I will never fully know what truly happened that day with Gary and Evan on a conscious level, but this I believe: My highly sensitive husband and son were both just acting as directed by a power greater than all of us that I know as God to bring home a horse who would help me find *who I am.*

by Glen Bartlett

by James Mongomery

Chapter Thirteen

Listen Up

With the help of horses, I felt my patience for learning level expand. Since horses communicate primarily with their *bodies,* we need to learn to *listen* in new ways. It is all about *feel* and the focus that creates it. Focusing near and far, using more of our peripheral awareness—all valuable practices to learn to be more present in whatever we are doing. And it takes practice.

While volunteering at our local elementary school, I met a lovely man named Andy who had brought his seeing-eye dog to meet the first graders. After his presentation, he and his beautiful golden retriever visited with me in the back of the classroom. I knew from reading an article in our local paper that he was an accomplished martial artist, so I asked him more about it. "Well," he replied. "I just took an advanced level midnight blue belt test." His task was to spar with two opponents half his age coming at him with knives at the same time. He told me he listens with his whole body, but that he had a terrible sinus infection at the time and wondered if he should postpone his test. He went deep within and made the decision to attempt it. His awareness was so perfectly in tune that he listened and *felt his way through the entire experience.* He passed the test and advanced.

I draw on that image to develop my own skills. More practicing. Pat Parelli reminds us that we need to "learn to feel and know what happens before what happens, happens."

Horses do. That is why being near them increases our

awareness. I sat down to dinner recently to a beautiful organic chicken salad with goat cheese and fresh local beets. My son asked if he could take a bite of the succulent roasted chicken off the top. I thanked him for asking and said, "sure," and then he took another. And another. So I gave him a *"that's enough"* look (like a horse would, without words) and he smiled, (message received) and we went on with our meal. I got up to get a glass of water and could sense him stabbing another bite of chicken off of my plate, even though my back was turned as I walked away.

"Save some for me!" I implored. When I returned, he said, *"Whoa, Mom! how did you see me do that?!"* I reminded him just *who* he was dining with, proud of myself that I was becoming more horse-like. Mothers have a tremendous capacity for this "knowing sense of what happens next," and how many of us were certain that our own mothers had eyes in the back of their heads!?

I saw a woman at an airport recently whose children were starting to have a meltdown from the stresses of the "hurry up and wait" and the long lines that are part of these days of travel. As her son wheedled and whined and finally took a mighty swing at his sister, this confident mother continued to focus ahead with a look of composure as her arm raised up in a block like a masterful martial artist to deflect the blow that she had anticipated was coming and then did the same when her daughter retaliated. Her steadiness and leadership defused the situation completely, and soon the kids were quietly moving forward in the line. This is the kind of confident leadership that helps all of us, horses and humans alike. How many times have we witnessed the reverse of that situation when a harried mother starts screeching loudly at her unruly children and it continues to spiral downward toward total chaos. Horses respond to screeching about as well as children do—*they don't!*

So careful listening and anticipating helps me to hear the beauty of birdsong with greater appreciation and intensity. I hear the call of the geese long before they fly overhead in formation, so that I can be ready to watch their amazing flight patterns and be filled with awe and gratitude for being alive. It also helps me get into the stillness better even when I hear sounds that I perceive to be unpleasant. Practice. After thirty years, I am *still* working on getting used to Gary's snoring! I think God has a sense of humor pairing heavy snorers with light sleepers! But there *is* progress, and *better is better*.

My friend, Robert Eagle Bear, a Native American storyteller, told the children from the LaConner Boys and Girls Club when they were here for a field trip that our Creator gives us two ears and one mouth so we should listen twice as much as we speak. It is good advice. Practice. *Boy, do I need practice!*

I come from a long line of excessive talkers. Most of us talk incessantly because we have to compete for airspace to be heard, but no one is really listening well, since we are all jumping in whenever possible to talk some more.

Because being around horses creates the need for careful listening and observing keenly for changes in their arousal levels and their resultant body language, I am learning slowly but steadily that my family and societal patterns have not modeled that we need to be aware of other's reactions as we speak. To watch and see how our speaking is affecting them, so that we can modify our behavior to attempt to stay in rapport in healthy ways.

What I did not realize until I started studying natural horsemanship and the Epona Approach, is that we often disassociate and relieve tension through excessive talking because of our state of over-arousal that gets stimulated for numerous and ongoing reasons, especially those of us who are hardwired to be highly sensitive. Just think of only the basic background noise of life that is constantly with most of us, much of which is our own egoic mind chatter!

So I am working on catching myself sooner than later and watching for what might trigger me, feeling that in my body, and deciding before I start rambling whether I really have something to say that will be of value. If not, best to keep my lips *zipped!* The emphasis on body language instead of verbal language in the natural horsemanship methods has been very valuable for me in this regard. My goals are to get from talking too much, to whispering more, and ultimately to silence. *To find the stillness within.*

In our bedroom, we have a small antique framed Victorian motto, hanging from a chain. It reads: *Look up.* It always makes me feel hopeful and helps me with my perspective. So I thought of a way to use a well-known saying in a new context—in a way that I would be reminded about *hearing* our connectedness to all life: *Listen up.*

The awareness that helps us develop a sense of "feel" with horses is hard to describe and even harder to learn. It is about observation and listening using all of our senses. Deep listening involves paying attention to our bodies and feelings as well as the environment and the reactions of others that we see, feel and hear.

The late Tom Dorrance, considered one of the most influential of the quiet pioneers who shared the gentler ways with horses and revered by all who knew him, talks about *feel* in his book, *True Unity*. We can have a direct feel when we are coming into contact with the horse with our body, ropes or reins, which we want to be light and fluid. And the more intangible indirect feel that comes from our focused mind and intention. Indirect feel can be every bit as powerful as direct feel or more so.

Choosing to become a lifetime student of the horse gives me an opportunity every day to use my senses and beyond to develop timing, rhythm, focus and ultimately the magic of *feel*. To attempt to become as perceptive as a horse will be of benefit to me wherever I go, whatever I do, right where *I am*.

Chapter Fourteen

Remember to Breathe

Remember to Breathe. I saw those words on a bumper sticker. Inspiration comes in unlikely places, so pay attention to tailgates! I actually laughed out loud when I read it because I was holding my breath, however unintentionally—at the time. I am still working on it on a daily basis.

The horses have been my incentive to get well and be well—that much is clear. To say that breath is basic to life is an absurd understatement, but I had a lifetime habit of shallow breathing with tightness and bracing that constricted a healthy flow of breath. Learning with Chasta has provided me the opportunity to practice to breathe deeply, with awareness. Jonathan Field, our friend and trainer, taught me to whistle or sing if I feel tense when I am interacting with her, so that I can keep my breathing pattern moving in an easy going way. What a difference it makes! You can't be tense and whistle at the same time, he told me, and it's true! One day I was in a session with her at his place, *The Field Horsemanship Centre*, and we were moving on the ground at liberty and I felt frozen—stuck, unsure what to do next. Jonathan instinctively turned on the most beautiful music, and I felt a deep sigh and release of held breath come from within both Chasta and me, and we were able to move on with fluidity.

Being fluid on a horse either on the ground or on their back requires breathing *with* the movement. Practicing Tai Chi, Qi Gong, dance or Yoga are some of the wonderful ways to learn to connect movement with breath and help us to embody our spirituality. Our Western society has trained us to stay in our minds, and is to the peril of our *entire selves*. I had done much healing work with my mental, emotional and spiritual health, but it has been my body to be the last to come aboard. The ancient wisdom of the mind, body and spirit connection is finally being recognized in our culture. Dr. Candace Pert, a brilliant research scientist, author and speaker, asserts that we must heal the body through the mind and vice versa—it must be an interaction. In fact, she uses the term *bodymind* to express that *there is no separation*.

One of the most healing forms of integrative therapy that focuses on breathing with movement that I have experienced is an amazing technique called *Watsu*. I read an article that explained it as a water therapy approach based on Shiatsu that combines the healing touch of massage, acupressure and physical therapy in a pool that is heated to body temperature. The article prompted me to make my first appointment, where I experienced the movements facilitated by a therapist, that are so fluid and relaxing because the water creates a warm and buoyant environment that allows for gentle and pain-free stretches. Not only have I received tremendous relief from pain and stiffness on a physical level, there is a distinct emotional release component as well that creates an intense spiritual connection.

As a small child, I fell into water over my head and surely would have drowned if it had not been for family close by. In a Watsu session, I was in a deep meditative state from the focused awareness of my breath and I felt as if I was in the original experience of falling into the water and being trapped under the blackness of the dock. Instead of feeling frightened, I could see the dark corner of the dock and my outstretched hand in an attempt to reach it, and, in what felt like slow motion, my body rising toward the light. It felt as though the original trauma had been revisited in a healing way. Without thinking about it intentionally on a conscious level, I had a similar experience with revisiting my wildest and most terrifying ride through the woods with Chasta. During Watsu, where I was floating on the surface of the water with my eyes closed and having my body guided in gentle movements by my wonderful therapist, Liz Bart, I felt as if I was on Chasta's back in the water and instead of feeling the terror of riding a bolting runaway, we were in slow motion, riding the waves together in perfect harmony. Now I have *that* memory to call on when I am with Chasta, rather than the traumatic one. I have had many amazing insights during and after Watsu sessions that have contributed to feeling more centered and grounded in my awareness.

The horses have taken me to the ground in new ways, helping me to become stronger in my core and in touch with my breath. We have a huge playground on our property that we call "The Horse Course" with many obstacles where horses and humans have the opportunity to think and play together. The obstacles are metaphors for the challenges we face and how to solve the puzzles of accomplishing them together. I learned these concepts studying and practicing the Parelli Program™. I had a profound experience one day there that truly helped me to *embody* my faith in the interconnectedness of all of life.

Chasta and I were playing on the ground at liberty—no ropes or tack. Your horse has the choice to be with you—or not. We were running side by side and I could feel the pounding rush of her huge energy field co-mingling with mine. We jumped up onto a platform between two giant fir trees and off the other side, turning to run toward a series of barrels to jump over. As we landed the jump simultaneously and continued running, I had a tremendous sense *of being myself at about age seven* running and whinnying at recess with my friends as we pretended to be horses. We were a herd, blowing and pawing and shaking our manes. Chasta and I finally came to a panting stop and she *offered* me her head and pressed it against mine in quiet communion. I am sure her heart felt my inner child as well, because her eyes were soft and reassuring. Then I felt it—*joy! She had awakened true joy in me.* Horses, like children, are in present moment time and are masters of joy. *Take joy!*

Because of my early challenges with Chasta, I have been motivated to learn much about equine behavior. It is important to understand how horses relate to each other in a wild, natural setting as well as their group dynamics in domesticity. We need to be aware of the prey/predator relationship and how each of us is hardwired. We must understand the importance of creating a true partnership. It is imperative to think like a horse and use horse psychology.

But deep in my belief system, I know, as many other horse and *all* of nature lovers do, *there is something more.*

I felt it that day when I was on the playground with Chasta. I have witnessed it watching others with their horses. I have vivid day and night dreams about the deep connections between all species. I think about it when the mated pair of wild Canadian Geese that enjoy our pond as their summer home call out their honking greeting when they swoop down and land in our pasture and how Frank and George, our domestic ducks, run as fast as they can with their little webbed feet to go and greet them. And I remember when we raised Frank and George from ducklings in the orchard (and yes, I *did* name them after Frank, the big gray horse and George Burns!). Evan and I built a shelter and a ramp down from it into their wading pool where they would run and cavort and splash with apparent delight while Chasta would hang her head over the fence in rapt attention as if she was watching Saturday morning cartoons. Not only did Chasta love the handful of corn I would give her when feeding the ducks, she just was plain *interested* in their comings and goings.

When the neighbor's dog killed two of the ducks, we

were so sad. They had just learned to enjoy their freedom at the big pond, no longer confined to the fencing of the orchard. While our dogs live in peaceful coexistence with our other animals, the ducklings were just too big a temptation for this young dog. What began as a romping chase had fatal consequences. Yet each day, all the small birds living here could be prey for the bald eagles that fly overhead.

The final blow was when our female duck disappeared. This time we felt crushed as we had so anticipated ducklings on the pond that would be raised naturally by their mother instead of us tending ducklings from the feed store. Each day I was outside somewhere on the property when Chasta would call to me. I would go to her, give her a scratch and a stroke, and tell her that she was a good girl. After several days, her calls became more urgent, and I noticed that she was standing in the same place, an uncharacteristic spot. The next morning, she was hanging her head down over the fence. At this point, I *at least* knew she was trying to communicate something to me, but *what*? I went out of the garden and around to where she was and asked her what she needed to tell me, but she would not budge from her spot, her head hanging still stretched down over the fence. I stood next to her and looking down from her vantage point, saw our female duck sitting on a nest she had built in an old tool box in the garden! I realized that Chasta had been standing in this spot daily for nearly a week, letting me know Mama duck was safe *and expecting* and *I had just missed it!*

We can agree that when our dog or cat goes to the door and squeaks or scratches, they are attempting to communicate: they want out! It's a no-brainer, yet why is it such a stretch for us when they have other, seemingly more complex things they want to express?

My heart tells me to continue on the path of *something*

more. I believe that every species is hardwired for love and connection. God in every cell.

Thinking of the special kinds of intelligence that God has designed into every living creature reminds me of a powerful true story. My friend and veterinarian, Dr. Greg Ingman, knows how fascinated I am about learning more about animals and the importance of interacting with them for our own health and growth. He shared a story with me from his practice.

One of his elderly clients, a widower, has a mixed breed dog, his faithful companion. The gentleman had to go in for heart surgery so the dog was being cared for. The entire time his master was in the hospital during his surgery, the dog lay uncharacteristically quiet. Then his owner was released to go to a care facility for convalescence before he could go home. When the dog had the opportunity to be let out, he took off, on a mission.

The next time the dog was seen was outside the window of where his master lay in the care center, jumping up and barking a greeting as if to say, "Here I am, your reason to get well—your reason to live! It's me!!"

The care center was twenty miles from their home and the dog had never been there.

I have read and heard of *hundreds* of similar stories, many of them involving animals who saved the lives of their humans.

Who but God can create or explain that kind of intelligence?

Chapter Fifteen

Patience

Here is another bumper sticker worthy of mention: "Patience, I want it and I want it NOW!" Patience is a virtue and we cannot charge it on our credit cards. Just like other character flaws and incongruent emotions, horses will shine a light for you to see just where you are in your responses. Impatient? *Busted!* The horse will tell you. I have had many people tell me that they just wouldn't have the patience to work at the play sessions that I *now* have with my horses. *Precisely!* Here is an opportunity to develop it. Patience certainly isn't a need exclusive to working with horses. It's across the board. How about being a parent? A marriage partner? Rush hour traffic? Waiting in line? Just being alive qualifies us for the need to cultivate true patience.

How often in our impatience and frustration do we just want to give up on ourselves and others? Discord and divorce are rampant. Battlefields are everywhere—in homes, schools, businesses, churches and sadly, on a large scale, in the trenches of countries around the world, as the death toll continues. What if we did not think of life as so disposable—that I need to get rid of this horse or this husband because they are not what I need them to be in this moment?

Again, I am not advocating allowing abuse or accepting behaviors that are dangerous. But so much of what is wrong and not working with life can be overcome by focusing on *what is right*. With this mate, this child, this home, this job, this body, this horse. Gratitude and appreciation for where we are and what we have helps us to get where we want to go and to what is possible.

I had an amazing experience at the Epona Center in Sonoita, Arizona, with author and founder Linda Kohanov. She had guided the participants of a workshop in a visualization to "*Become the Horse,*" to deepen our understanding about what it means to interact with these marvelous creatures, who as a species, Pat Parelli affectionately calls, "*Nature in its finest form.*" When we came to the end of the guided visualization and opened our eyes, each of us had been assigned to a small horse herd at the Center and we were to spend time with them cultivating our awareness in this heightened state of "being" a horse.

My imagination had taken me to a beautiful place on that warm, sunny day where I felt as if I was a sorrel chestnut horse with a white blaze. As I wandered toward the horses that I had been assigned to, I felt deeply connected to the earth and her smells and colors, the sounds of the horses snorting contentedly, aware of the birdsong of the desert and the huge birds of prey who prowled overhead. I slipped through the rails of the fence and looked quietly at the closest horse, a leopard Appaloosa who I had enjoyed a lovely private session with the day before. We picked up where we left off and had a nice scratchfest together. Then I made a wide arc behind the other two horses that I had never met at the back of the pasture, just making them quietly aware of my presence. They continued grazing, but pricked their ears in my direction.

At that point, in my peripheral vision, enhanced by the feeling that I was now in a horse body for this exercise since they have an enormous field of sight, I saw a sorrel chestnut horse with a white blaze far away in the next pasture looking intently at me. So I did the horse dance of greeting from a distance and he came to me as I approached the fence line. There was a hotwire at the top, so I got on my knees and we exchanged breath a few feet from the ground. Looking into his gentle eyes, it felt like looking in the mirror, since I imagined myself to have his coloring, and I realized in the moment that in the horse world, that the two of us were as common as to be *very ordinary,* and yet all I could see was his complete and total magnificence, as if he were the most beautiful horse ever to grace the planet. I felt like I was plugged into God with a very strong connection, with an extra heavy duty extension cord. And as I beamed the love that I felt God was coursing through my veins and every cell, that is what I felt in return from this kind horse, the sweet, warm smell of his grassy breath coming into my nostrils in gentle blasts. I asked nothing of him, and had no carrot to offer. I experienced love, only love, yet *completely and wonderfully and powerfully love.*

Wow! I felt dizzy with joy, deep into the mystery. I saw another horse way across his pasture who looked like a mare to me so I decided to try to affect her with this connection from a distance. I took a deep breath and beamed her love for all I was worth. Her head was on the ground grazing, and within about two seconds, she lifted it, *looked right at me* and made a beeline in my direction like I was a bucket of sweet grain! My magnificent horse friend stepped aside so she could greet me with an exchange of breath. Sitting on the grass, I realized that I had been perched on an ancient flattened pile of horse manure and smiled and realized that must have been part of the magic formula to ground me to be a conduit for all of this energy! All I could do in the way of direct touch was to scratch their muzzles with a finger through the fence, but it was enough. As the three of us were communing, I saw a third horse from their pasture coming to join us, and realized that the three in mine were also approaching. I continued to focus on the lovebeam, and within a few minutes, I was surrounded by six horses in a space where we could have fit into a large elevator together! The elevator is a perfect visual since elevated is how I was feeling—floaty and euphoric. I let each of them know silently that they were magnificent and how much this experience had meant to me, and I finally walked away, feeling weightless, slipping back out through the fence rails and changed from within.

The next morning at the airport, I was still basking in the way the horselove connection had made me feel, and decided to do a little experiment. There I was 1500 miles from home, missing my family and animals and not knowing any of the people I saw milling in all directions and forming lines. I decided to concentrate on one living soul and see if I could focus that amazing energy that I had experienced with the horses. My eyes took me to a young man in a Goth-looking t-shirt, skate board shoes, with an earring and a tattoo.

Again, the deep breath and a prayer for God to pour it on. I beamed away with all I had, and within a few seconds from across the crowded terminal, he looked in my direction. Now, since I was old enough to be his mother, I decided to just smile and then look away, lest he think I was a very looney, lonely old gal, but I kept my focus on sending him the beam of love and that he was as magnificent a young man as I could ever imagine. It felt wonderful to me, indeed.

My line moved and I printed my boarding pass and checked my baggage. I had a bit of a wait at my gate, so I took a walk, had a snack, and finally sat and read before the announcement came to board. I was seated on the aisle midway back in the plane, and there was a friendly woman next to the window who noticed my carry on bag covered with embroidered horses.

"Hi!" she smiled, "I just took a horseback ride in the mountains yesterday in Arizona for my friend's fiftieth birthday. It was wonderful!"she enthused. I smiled back and told her that I had just been with horses in a very special way myself, including a ride in the mountains not far from where she had been. Then we discovered that she lived about twenty minutes from my home! Next we heard an announcement that the plane was full and to please share the overhead compartments as the last of the passengers boarded. I stretched my legs and got out my eye covers, anticipating a rest on the flight home. *God had other plans.*

The final person to come down the aisle was the magnificent young man who I had beamed the love on earlier that morning, and he took the last seat, the one sandwiched between me and the women who had been hanging out with horses! How could I have known that he was even on my full flight, much less seated next to me? Because God reminds us constantly that we are *all* magnificent, if we are listening.

My new friend smiled shyly, and then spent the flight telling me the story of his life. There were many parallels between us, and I felt like a loving auntie, like I do with my own nephews. When we had landed he said quietly, "Could I tell you something?"

"Sure!" I smiled.

"Earlier today I noticed you from a distance and you stood out and I saw light around you. That has only happened to me once before in my life."

"That is because there is a light all around us that is much bigger than we are, don't you think?" I offered. He shook his head up and down and smiled. I did not share that I had chosen him for my experiment, as I felt that it was *me* who had been chosen for the honor to participate.

We walked off the plane as if we had been traveling together and headed to baggage claim where he retrieved my luggage off the conveyor belt like an attentive bellhop. When I told him that I had really enjoyed getting to know him and that he and his family would be in my prayers, he gave me the most sincere and lovely hug, which I can still feel in this moment.

So my next experiment was with Gary, beaming love and gratitude at him instead of wishing that he would pick up his socks off the floor or remember to roll the garbage can to the end of the driveway. And Evan, turning up the voltage on the lovebeam when he deserved my support and encouragement more than he needed my critique. And on Chasta, when she seemed bracey and unwillingly to connect with me.

And it's working! I am also remembering to coil myself up in the extension cord of love and shine the beam on myself. That way I remember there is always lots of juice left for everyone else.

So these days Chasta *fascinates* me. The Parellis have a motto that their program helps us to "turn our fear and frustration into fun and fascination." It's true. Once Chasta and I became less fearful and more trusting, she became incredibly curious and I became fascinated. She is a master of escape. I have seen her untie knots that would defy Houdini. She has undone gate latches with her mouth and chewed through ropes with her teeth. She is cool as a cucumber about it, too.

One time I made a tape fence around some young trees to keep the horses away so they could get a foothold on their growth. She knew the tape was not electrified, and wanting to get at the longer grass around the trees, knocked the bottom section down with her hooves, and limboed under. How do I know this? Because Evan and I watched her in amazement and head shaking delight from a distance. She does this with acres to graze on *because she can.*

For a period of time, she was finding shorts in the electrical tape fence that were no longer hot around the pasture that our neighbors had let them graze on, happy to have their field mowed. Again, she would take down the bottom section with her hooves and roll under. The temptation of the fallen pears in the nearby orchard was just too much. I would hear Ritzy whinnying in a frenzied panic and know she was out again. I made an appointment with the friend who built them to have the fences secured, and he argued, "She *can't* have gotten out again!" *But she had.*

In the meantime, I went out with some stakes and tape. She was standing behind me while I hunkered down to make a physical barrier. I decided it was high time to give her a stern lecture to let her know just how much consternation she had caused Ritzy and that this nuisance and unsafe behavior *had* to stop. I was rambling on, stringing the tape in elaborate "X" designs that looked ridiculous. "*I* know this isn't hot and *you* know this isn't hot, but until the fence is replaced, I expect you to respect this," I said menacingly. I finally straightened up and turned around and found myself looking directly into her gigantic horse face. She had a huge mouthful of wadded up tape, hanging in great loops around her chin, as if to say, "And *this* is what I think of your lecture!" In that moment, she spat it on the ground with a loud *"pthooey"* for emphasis and walked away. *I kid you not.*

I have been able to become fascinated by her because her intelligence and unusual (by horse standards) behavior has gifted me with increased patience. Now when she does something that challenges me, I am more apt to step back for a moment and wonder what the next best move is for me to make, rather than react in impatience. Linda Parelli calls it the *"hmmm ... how interesting"* pause. It applies to so many areas of my life! It really gives you a moment to reframe things in a way that truly does make life more interesting instead of frustrating or annoying. Linda and Chasta have helped me expand my emotional fitness and coping skills.

I have an observation about the horse/human relationship when it comes to developing a true partnership. As humans playing with horses, with patience and kindness, we can help them to develop the left side of their brains, the thinking and rational side. I am learning this by studying the Parelli Natural Horse-Man-Ship Program™. This expands their mental and emotional health, which supports their physical health. As prey animals, they are hardwired to respond with fight and flight in their right brains, their reactive side. Many of them too often live in this fear-based state in the unnatural world of the human in domesticity. With *both* sides of their brains developed, they live far healthier and happier in a whole-brained state.

Humans are the same, but opposite. We have two hemispheres of the brain as well, but our society favors a left-brained rational state where things can be measured and proven, so this is where we may be more developed. Interacting with horses can help us to get in touch with our right brains more and to develop our intuitive instincts—our inner knowing. Our Divine self. Author Linda Kohanov wrote a beautiful essay/chapter called "Intuition" in her third book, *The Way of the Horse,* which is beautifully illustrated with cards by equine artist Kim McElroy, and it is *fascinating*. Linda says: "Intuition not only connects us to a more soulful consciousness, it reminds us that the universe is a latticework of relationships."

So horses help offer us the whole-brained state of integration that we offer them. This is our gift to each other through interspecies communication, allowing access to both hemispheres in a flow that taps into the best information available: calm wisdom.

Super learning and unity is possible in this "humans heal horses" and "horses heal humans" healthy whole-brained integration mode. And the wonderful thing is that our relationship with each other and all of life is enhanced since the whole-brained state is how we can see the world through a perception that it is a friendly place and that peace and joy are for all.

Learning this potential helped me to see the perfect dovetail between equine facilitated growth and healing and a method for the psychology of change called Psych-K™. Partnering with Dr. Bruce Lipton, author of *The Biology of Belief,* the creator of the Psych-K system, Rob Williams, explains how much of our behavior is shaped by our subconscious beliefs in his book, *The Missing Piece/ Peace in Your Life. If our subconscious beliefs do not support our conscious goals, it will create continual conflicts.* Horses sense this incongruence and open us up to the possibility of integration. *They read us like a book!*

Dr. Bruce Lipton's endorsement on the back of Rob Williams book reads: "The 'secret of life' is BELIEF. Rather than genes, it is our beliefs that control our lives. Psych-K is a set of simple, self-empowering techniques to change your beliefs and perceptions that impact your life at a cellular level."

I have found the Psych-K methods to help create healthy alignment and remarkably significant transformations. After taking the fascinating and interactive workshops with Psych-K approved instructors Dhebi DeWitz Jensen and Larry Valmore, I felt that I had a new and profound confidence in my ability to know and love myself and others and a strength and peace that felt like I had released a huge amount of baggage around life limiting subconscious beliefs that I had stored within me for years. I came home and realized that my desire to write this book was enormous and sat down to have it pour out effortlessly. Like a visit with an old friend. *(A patient one!)*

The Psych-K techniques are an extremely self-empowering tool accessing the body's own biofeedback to access the Divinity within each of us. I believe self-acceptance and peace begins *within us,* and is the beginning of peace on the planet. It starts with the individual. It is the coming together of science and the Divine. Science is essentially the explanation of nature. There truly never has been any separation. With the increased understanding of quantum physics, we are finally beginning to be able to prove it. Regardless of the advancements in technology and science, we still cannot unravel the great mystery of the Divine. The more we understand, the more the Mystery. Rob Williams reminds us that on a jet flight we are told to get our own oxygen masks first if we are to help others. Love yourself so that you *can* love your neighbor. By doing that, we love God. And God is well pleased.

People often remark that they feel like a "completely new person" after practicing the psychological kinesiology techniques that Psych-K offers and is named for. Participants in the equine-facilitated therapy process regularly say the same thing. I am learning from my wise teachers, both human and equine, that it is actually that people are becoming more like themselves—*who they were created to be.*

And people who knew Chasta when she first came to us and know her today remark that she, too, is a "different horse." Two things have happened—first, she is mirroring a healthier person that I am becoming and she is also closer to her own true nature by what I have done to support her, *with a lot of help from my friends*. I am pleased to report that I consider all of my mentors to be friends—comrades in open and loving arms. Our wonderful neighbor across the fence from the lower pasture, Nonie, who at eighty looks and acts at least twenty years younger, used to call Chasta *"that blonde!"* and now, with great tenderness, *"My girl."* She also believes that since Chasta was the inspiration for this book and that I am merely the ghost writer, she would rather have the opening sentence be: *"I am a very smart horse!" You* decide!

These processes of natural horsemanship and Psych-K truly do dovetail – what a beautiful symbol of peace, and the Holy Spirit. The Holy Spirit represents the feminine mother nature of God for me, and the dove is the perfect soft, winged messenger.

Chapter Sixteen

Liberty

Horses really only have liberty and freedom where there are no fences, and sadly, few wild herds remain. But in domesticity we are given a chance to truly bond up close and at a distance when we play at liberty—no ropes or tack involved. The horse has a chance to participate or not. Many amazing horsemen and women have achieved astonishing relationships with their horses at liberty. The human and equine artists of *Cavalia,* the spectacular touring performance, have changed the way we see horse/human relationships. The Parellis, Klaus Ferdinand Hempling, Lorenzo of Provence, Carolyn Resnick, Liz Mitten Ryan, and many others have achieved true unity at liberty, and give me much inspiration to aspire to.

Being on the ground, literally, is a very healthy place to be for humans and horses. *Down to earth.* It is one of the biggest challenges we face in the modern world. So much of our earth is covered in concrete and asphalt and we spend so much time on artificial surfaces indoors that we literally have lost touch with the magnetic energies of the planet that were designed to keep us balanced and on our feet. Those energies have information and nourishment for us that help us to develop a strong inner compass and compassion for all of life. Why do you think that we are inherently drawn to walking on the beach or hiking in the mountains? Because it reconnects us and renews our batteries in a way that no computer or television ever can. Those are the things that keep us trapped in our heads rather than living in our bodies.

Learning to play this way with my own horses has been

so liberating for *me* as well. It has given me a chance to practice clarity in my mind and spirit, to develop the power of focus and intention. To learn to pay attention and live in awareness. To *be in my body.*

One of the most significant books that I have read on learning to feel emotions and how they affect and inform our bodies is called *Bio-Spirituality*, by Drs. Peter Campbell and Ed McMahon. They discuss the work of Dr. Eugene Gendlin, the originator of a technique called *Focusing*, where a person develops an ability to know what he calls a *felt sense* of what is happening for them at that moment. Once felt in the body, they can experience a *felt shift*, or transformational change. Again, they speak of merging the body and spirit, and not living exclusively in the mind. Their book is so informative and useful and it reads like poetry. These gentlemen are *walking their talk.* Which is truly just a way of saying they are embodying their spiritual lives which is what their book is about!

Drs. Campbell and McMahon are priests with a global perspective, and a passage from Bio-Spirituality reads: *"There is support within our bodies for unitary consciousness. Focusing, we believe, can contribute to a spirituality that nourishes cosmic congruence irrespective of a person's religious affiliation.*

Without some practical "look-out point in the universe," world religions and all people who espouse unitive teachings face an indescribably bleak alternative. Unless we can find a way to live these noble teachings, unless we take concrete steps to put our bodies where our good intentions are, unless we discover some path through the barrier of impotence that so impedes progress in religion today, we risk falling victim to the growing technology of planetary destruction. Focusing touches the feelings of fear, frustration and lack of presence that nourish the suspicions, mistrust and hatred that inevitably lead to war.

The way ahead, of course, lies within ourselves."

These men are the kind of leaders that our world so needs today, and each of us can join them in our daily lives as we become aware of connecting with our own feelings by using the *Focusing* techniques and getting to know them.

Author and equestrienne Carolyn Resnick wrote the amazing story of her life in her book, *Naked Liberty*, sharing her remarkable childhood growing up with a herd of wild horses. The following paragraph speaks of the profound connections that she came to understand: "Harmony and teamwork is how horses are able to survive the elements, and when we put our focus on building these skills with horses, we can connect into a one-mind consciousness in the unity of shared movements like the ones found in nature. We can see this connection in schools of fish, migrating birds, stampeding horses or the harmony of a foal shadowing his mother in flight. While it is beautiful to watch, it is more powerful to experience."

I had the privilege of studying with one of Carolyn's premiere liberty instructors, Bryan Smith. He taught me more about what it means to be aware of my body in ways that are horse-like, imagining that I have their heightened perceptions and even perceiving my upright body as a forehand (arms) and hindquarters (legs) as I move. By acting more like a horse, I am becoming increasingly aware of my own movement and feel more *embodied*. Horses are fully present and live in the moment. If we are to be like them, we have the opportunity to practice that awareness.

I have also learned more about the relaxation process from being near my horses than most anything I can think of. Grooming them and scratching their itchy spots and just to be in their presence always slows down and deepens my breathing. When they are free to choose to go or stay with me, each moment we have together is a gift. I feel my arms as well as the soles of my feet on the ground as I reach to brush under their bellies and over the top of their tall backs. I sense my body parts working independently and connected to the whole of me. And the smell of horse sweat is completely tranquilizing as far as I am concerned. It is a scent as old as time. Primal and real. *Much* better than anything at the mall. A beautiful way to remember this body-spirit awareness is a quote by Ronni Sweet, "It is the horse's gift to connect us with Heaven and our own footsteps."

Our founding fathers promised liberty as the freedom to choose. Giving my horses the freedom to choose to be in a relationship with me has expanded my vision of what it means to be free. Anne Frank gave testimony in her diary that it is possible, even in the most horrific situations that *we are free to choose a perception* that people are basically good and in spite of some circumstances, the world is indeed a friendly place. Choose forgiveness … Choose peace … Choose love. The words seem simple enough and resonate with truth. Why does it seem daunting sometimes in practice? That's precisely it. It takes practice … Repetition. People are pattern animals. That is how we learn—horses too.

I have a quote on my wall that I pass daily by Mother Teresa that reads: "If we have no peace, it is because we have forgotten that we belong to each other." She lived her life remembering, and inspiring others to do so.

One of the most Godly men I know has spent a lifetime choosing to practice forgiveness, peace and love. His name is Father William Treacy, an Irish-Catholic priest. Each time that I have had the privilege of being in his presence, I can see light radiating from his eyes and around his face. He is the co-founder of *Camp Brotherhood*, an ecumenical retreat center dedicated to honoring different faith traditions and promoting world peace and unity. He was a panelist on a debate format television show in Seattle with Jewish Rabbi Raphael Levine and they became lifelong friends, purchasing an old farm to dedicate to their mutual vision—to love and serve and heal hearts with God. After Rabbi Levine's death, Father Treacy continues to lead this legacy of united hearts. Rabbi Levine was a talented artist and craftsman and I will always remember how moved I was when I saw a large mosaic that he created for the center where different faith traditions share perspectives and break bread together. It reads: "All paths lead to God if they are paved with love." It should come as no surprise that horses have always lived at Camp Brotherhood, contributing to the peaceful atmosphere there.

One day I visited with Father Treacy over tea and muffins at a local Starbuck's™, and he shared with me how knowing and caring about close friends from other faith traditions over the years had enhanced his own because the love in action that he had experienced helped him to embody his faith's teachings. He spoke of his dear friend Jamal Rahman, a Muslim clergyman, who had shared

the writings of the Sufi mystic, Rumi, with him and what beautiful love poetry it is. I agree.

Every year my family attends the annual celebration at Camp Brotherhood and so enjoyed hearing the stories of an interfaith pilgrimage to the Holy Land by a group represented by the Christian, Jewish and Muslim faith traditions. They traveled together, visiting holy sites that had different significance for each faith. They supported and honored each other along the way, celebrating their friendship by holding hands and floating together in a circle in the Red Sea.

With my great love of words, the first one that comes to mind here is: *Wow!*

That seems like true liberty to me.

Photo by Kevin Morse

PART FIVE:

Gaining Momentum

Chapter Seventeen

Love: The Universal Solvent

Help comes in many forms once we ask for and are willing to receive it. Dr. Nels Rasmussen is a human and animal chiropractor who was recommended to me shortly after Chasta joined our family. When I described her extreme reactions to him, he quietly asked if I thought it might be possible that I was contributing to our challenges. *"Absolutely!"* I replied, "I am truly hopeful that you can help both of us."

Dr. Nels practices the B.E.S.T. (Bio Energetic Synchronization Technique) originated by Dr. Ted Morter, Sr. The sessions help to balance the body by facilitating emotional release. Over time, I have felt stronger, more confident and "lighter" in spirit. I believe Chasta has as well.

Dr. Nels invited us to attend a weekend seminar with the Morter Health System Team and I used the fact that it fell on my birthday as leverage to get Gary to agree to go. The recurring theme of amazing things happening on my birthday reminds me that we can be reborn every day if we allow ourselves to choose gratitude for our lives.

We arrived at the hotel and went to the large meeting room to join a few hundred others. The day began with a fantastic presentation by Dr. Ted Morter, Jr. who spoke eloquently on holistic health, peppering his remarks with a liberal dose of his disarming humor. Next, his sister,

Dr. Sue Morter, got the crowd on their feet with her amazing energy and charisma. She spoke of the power of our thoughts to impact our health and the possibilities for healing with focusing on love and forgiveness. She proclaimed, "Love is the universal solvent—pour enough of it on and it can dissolve any challenge." The dynamic duo kept us all on the edge of our seats until the lunch break.

Gary went to get in line for a table at the restaurant next door when I saw Dr. Nels heading out. I wanted to thank him for inviting us to such an outstanding and inspirational seminar when we were approached by Drs. Ted and Sue. "Hello," smiled Sue. "Do you two know each other?"

"Yes," I replied, "Dr. Nels is my practitioner and the person who recommended we attend. My husband and I are loving this!"

"Terrific!" she said, "We had just discussed that we wanted you and Nels to participate on stage tonight for a demonstration. Will you do it?"

"Sure!" boomed Dr. Nels, and I followed with "Wow, what a great opportunity—I'd be honored." "OK, great!" she continued. "Please go out to the entry and sign the release forms and we will call you up later."

Dr. Nels and I headed to find their staff members and got the form. A waiver of liability form is standard operating procedure for most any kind of participation, but suddenly I felt a knot in my stomach reading the fine print. Working at being in touch with my body signals, I looked at Nels, who was happily signing away. "Uh, I'm feeling a bit of anxiety about this," I started. "Do you want to do a balance around it?" he asked. "That would be great!" I answered. The balance I am referring to are the techniques he practices created by the Morters. He assisted me in balancing for the fear that came up for me and I felt myself relax and return to the enthusiasm I had felt earlier. I signed my name, grateful for having been chosen.

Gary and I enjoyed a lovely lunch and agreed this seminar was inspiring like the Parelli events that we had attended and felt so glad we had made the effort to come.

Later, as a prelude to the final event of the evening, Dr. Sue drew us all in with her talk about the power of our individual and collective thoughts to be in "possibility." She said that four people had agreed to come up on stage and demonstrate the principles. She told the audience how important it was for them to offer support and belief for the process. Then she and Dr. Ted called us up and told the crowd the other pair were to be our "spotters." Then Dr. Ted picked up a long piece of iron rebar to show the audience, demonstrating how stout it was by not being able to bend it with his hands or feet. As I watched, I thought maybe Nels and I would be doing the limbo! What's the worst that can happen here, I thought? I'm reasonably flexible, and I can be a good sport. It doesn't bother me to be in front of a crowd—I have had experience teaching and public speaking, so I was feeling relaxed, but excited.

Then Dr. Ted told me to take off my leather soled shoes, since I might slip on the hardwood stage. Suddenly my mood shifted when they lifted the iron rebar and placed it into the hollows of our necks! It had rubber tips on the ends, but just the weight to hold it in place was quite uncomfortable—in fact it hurt—and I went from eagerness to anxiety and soon to complete fear. At that time, I had a history of health challenges with my throat and neck, which was why I felt so vulnerable. My inner tape loop went on fast forward and my first thought was a rational one; I knew at any time that I could change my mind and remove the bar with my hand and go back to the audience. But, trying to be brave and wanting to challenge myself, I attempted to breathe deeply, and to remember the strength in my core that I had been developing through Tai Chi and my horse studies. But it was all I could do to listen to Dr. Sue describe the process. Exactly what *were* we doing up here? Was the other pair going to limbo under the bar first? *Then I heard it!* With total enthusiasm, Sue announced, "With the power of their focused intention, Nels and Connie will bend this bar in half!" *Oh, my!*

Then she approached Dr. Nels and asked, "Please state your intention!"

"To help heal the world!" he roared, the iron bar stuck in his neck as though he had nary a care. Then she looked at me. I could feel my face flush along with the rest of my body. "And Connie, your intention?"

I tried to find the confidence to shout a response that I had no time to prepare for, but all that came out was a throaty whisper, "To be a bridge to love." "Perfect!" she enthused. "Now, Dr. Nels, you start by stating your intention again and nod at Connie. Then Connie, you follow and nod at Nels. Then, *push!*"

I wished at that moment that I had removed my socks, too, because I felt like I was standing on an ice rink. Dr. Nels was *so* focused, confident and determined that it unnerved me completely. What did they possibly see in me that made them think that I could accomplish this? Here was a man who I trusted and admired and suddenly he felt like a fierce opponent, even though we were a "team." He boomed his intention statement and nodded. *It was now or never.*

I heard myself repeat my statement and I gave a tentative nod, completely absorbed in the pain at my throat. Dr. Nels came at me like a bulldog and my fear changed to terror. I forgot *everything* that I had practiced about a balanced stance and could feel myself moved backwards. *Fast.*

I knew that I could *still* use my hands to remove the bar and save myself from this fear and discomfort, but deep within I felt myself rallying. Why had I waited so long before remembering to pray in earnest? Suddenly I experienced the feeling of the power and exhilaration I get when I have run on the ground between Chasta and Ritzy and the huge forward pull of energy it creates. It gave me the courage to feel the fear. I realized the fear was completely inhibiting my strength when I heard in my mind distinctly, "*perfect love casts out all fear.*" I thought of Dr. Sue's statement that love is the universal solvent and is bigger and stronger than any fear. *I realized that I believed that at my deepest core, in my soul.* Once I *acknowledged my belief of the truth* of the words from scripture, I looked at Dr. Nels and he was suddenly surrounded by Christlight. I saw outstretched arms behind him, coming through the light.

Crash! The iron bar bent and hit the floor. It happened so fast and with so much force that the four of us were catapulted in to a group hug, then quickly joined by the Morters. Stunned, I looked down and saw the bar on the stage, bent in a perfect U shape!

When we described our experience to the cheering crowd, I realized that my strength had come from within and from all of them. *The Holy Spirit works in each of us for all of us.*

Dr. Nels said that at the moment the bar bent, he had realized he was pushing too hard and had backed off. "You cannot push love," he shared. *Both of us had been focused on perfect love at the same time, and so had our community of support – that is when we succeeded.*

A line of people came up to talk with us as the evening came to an end and their shared experiences were amazing. One woman told me she was on the edge of her seat, trying to get strong in her core for me, when she looked down and realized her entire row was doing the same thing! A gentleman told me he felt tremendous discomfort in his own neck and that it released the moment the iron bent. Another told me that she had been so frightened for me until she remembered that her worried thoughts were hurting, not helping me. Dr. Sue had told us earlier that worrying about people is like "throwing mud on their pie." Instead, we need to offer them loving prayers. So the woman continued to tell me that she had shifted her worried thoughts to *"You can do it!"* and *in that instant,* the bar bent. She was thrilled! "*You* gave me the courage!" she told me, while I was feeling the same thing about her.

A darling elderly lady came up to me slowly with the aid of her walker and told me that she had written down everything that I had said and that it was going to be her new affirmation. Her cheeks were rouged and her eyes glistened. Gary came through, hugged me tight and told me he was proud. He said he *knew* I could do it!

Then a beautiful woman approached holding a gorgeous tapestry coat with images of horses on it. She passed it to me ceremoniously with tears in her eyes and said, "I want you to have this." "Oh, goodness, no," I stammered, "I can't accept such a generous gift!" "Please, it would mean a lot to me," she smiled. I had never met her, but had admired the coat earlier in the day while we were in the ladies' room. This wonderful gift brought the experience full circle reminding me of the strength I have gained from my time shared with horses!

Dr. Nels and I now share "custody" of our bent iron bar and it is a potent reminder of God's love for us. It is in our garden now, over a statue of Saint Francis, known for his gentle spirit, quiet strength and the love that he

shared with all of life. He is also possibly the most famous animal communicator in history!

Saint Francis devoted his attention to the whole of creation and considered the sun and stars and moon and trees and animals to be his brothers and sisters. Of animals and all of nature he wrote: "Not to hurt our humble brethren is our first duty to them, but to stop there is not enough. We have a higher mission—to be of service to them whenever they require it. "

Amen.

Chapter Eighteen

Inner Guidance

Flies are a problem for horses. Besides looking gorgeous, that is why God gave them tails. Their own built-in shoo fly. I use a natural insect for fly control in the form of a small predator fly that eats the larvae of the flies that annoy horses. This is much like releasing ladybugs to control the aphid population in your garden. We live adjacent to a dairy farm and a cattle ranch and are therefore in a fly zone, whether we like it or not. Just add sunshine and horse manure and you have the need for "pest management." Not wanting to use chemicals or disturb the ecosystem, it is always a challenge.

Flies are attracted to sweaty horses and their mucous membranes. That is why you will see concentrations of them around their eyes and mouths on a hot day. Horses are *so sensitive* that they will swish off a single fly with their tails, so imagine a conglomeration of them on their faces. Annoying? It's downright miserable for them.

Daily in fly season I apply non-toxic herbal repellants and cover their faces with see-through fly masks. I used to drive by horses in pastures looking like Zorro and wonder if they appreciated such a garment. Now that I have horses of my own, I realize they would put them on themselves if they could.

After reading J. Allen Boone's *amazing* book, *Kinship With All Life*, where the author describes his remarkable personal relationship with a housefly, it gave me new affection for the under appreciated insect, but I still needed to control them in areas the horses frequent, especially near their water sources. So I bought some "fly sticks" at our rural feed store. They are a long cylinder that looks like a giant firecracker. Remove the outer wrap and there is sticky fly paper underneath, the kind that was hung up in the cabin where I stayed as a Camp Fire Girl in my youth. Only these are huge, about two-and-a-half-feet long.

I went outside to hang them up and decided a good location was down by the horse's loafing shed near the pond, a shelter where they get protection from the elements. The horses followed, always interested in me, especially if it involves treats. I *love* to be popular, so I am usually good for at least a carrot. I hauled the ladder out and hung one up where I thought it would be out of reach, unless the horses stood up on their hind legs to investigate. For an average horse, that would not be an issue. For Chasta? By now, you know that she is a horse of a different color!

Knowing Chasta, I admonished her to leave it alone. Ritzy, having had his snack, was happy to go back to being a horse and left us so he could graze. Chasta watched my every move. "You need to leave these alone, my dear," I started. "They are here to give you relief, but touching them will only cause trouble."

Gary Larson, the famous cartoonist who created outrageously funny scenarios between man and the animal kingdom, designed a strip for people like me. It has one of his absurd looking human female characters and her little rotund dog. The first frame has the woman blabbering on incessantly to her dog, something akin to "Now be a good doggie, Ginger, and come and eat your dinner and then we will ..." The title of the frame is: "What the human says." The second frame says: "What the dog hears" and the "bubble" coming from the woman's mouth that contains her words says "Blah, blah,

blah, Ginger, blah, blah, blah …" In other words, all the dog hears and knows is her name. It's hilarious.

But, it is my belief that Chasta *can* read my thoughts, at least in pictures, and feel my intentions. Science has proven that images in the form of pictures can be translated from the frontal cortex of the brain to be interpreted by others. We all form images as we think of something—if you don't believe it, right now as you read this, whatever you do, don't think of a red balloon! See what I mean? So, though I attempt to frame things in a positive light, if my intentions are for Chasta to "stay away from this fly stick," it becomes the forbidden and, therefore, has *high intrigue* for her.

If there is *anything* in her pastures that can be moved or knocked down, she will do it. Ritzy would walk by a wheelbarrow of manure every day with nary a glance, but Chasta will knock it over every time. Sometimes I haul obstacles and toys out into one of the big pastures and invite a group of friends to bring their horses for a day of fun and learning. If I leave the obstacles out, in the morning the carefully assembled playground will look like the remains of a wild party—everything upside down and strewn recklessly. Chasta at work/play.

I forgot about the fly sticks until a few days later when I was inside working on locating records for our taxes when I would rather have been outside with the horses.

It's not that I mind paying our fair share of taxes. I am proud to be an American and grateful for the tremendous freedoms we enjoy in this country that are so easily taken for granted. I just do not often agree with how our tax dollars are being spent. While I deeply appreciate every man and woman who have served our country to defend us, I do not personally know a single person who is enthusiastic about spending federal money building bombs, especially when there are nearly forty million people in the United States of America living at the poverty level and the numbers continue to grow. I read a quote by George McGovern, not a politician who I ever became familiar with, but that states beautifully what I feel about being patriotic. He said: "The highest level of patriotism is not blind acceptance of official policy but a love of one's county deep enough to hold her to a higher standard."

Our family systems, whether they are a nuclear family, a corporation, a sports team, a church, a government, or a horse/human partnership are *only as healthy as the leadership that is intended to unite them.*

But that is another story. Or book. But I digress.

Back to where I was, head mired in paperwork, when I lost my tenuous focus and heard distinctly, "Chasta needs You." Sure she does, I thought, interpreting it to mean I needed and wanted to be outside instead of trying to organize my piles. So, more urgently I heard, "Chasta *needs* You." The words came loud and clear. More aware than ever of heeding my inner signals by at least checking in, I felt the need to get up and go the nearest window.

About 300 feet away, *directly in my line of vision,* Chasta was rearing up, pawing the air in movements so violent that it appeared she was having a seizure! Then she fell to the ground, rolling and thrashing wildly. My heart lurched as I ran to the door. If she had been *anywhere* else on the property she would have been outside my area of vision from where I was standing.

By the time I raced to the fence, I was able to see what was causing her hysterical reaction and Ritzy's frenzied galloping. They were both in a literal lather down their chests in response to the neon cylinder sticky fly paper stuck to the side of her blue fly mask like some sinister sword. Attached to the back of her huge jowl, it was even *chasing* her, threatening to stab her at any moment. Comical as it may sound, to them, the unknown of this perceived danger was very real and Chasta was convinced that her life was being threatened. Ritzy felt powerless to save her from the savage beast.

I resisted the temptation to chuckle and walked through the gate and called to her in a low, calm voice. "Chasta, come here. I know *just* what to do." Her ears pricked toward me at the sound of my voice and she turned on a dime on her haunches and flew to me at a thundering gallop and then, as she drew near, tucked her hindquarters under and came to a sliding stop that would have won a competition. Finally, she thrust her head toward me, heaving for air. Confidently, I raised my hand and peeled off the offending assailant.

Even through the mask, I could see that I had become her safety. To a horse, safety is number one. I stood quietly, stroking her, again resisting saying "I told you so." *I am sure she knew I was thinking it!* Horses learn *quickly*, and chances are good she would not stand up on her hind legs any time soon to disturb a fly stick.

Ironically, other than when humans apply them, horses don't wear masks like people do. And they assist us in removing ours: Our masks of false bravado when we are really afraid, our masks of acquiescence when we are actually seething and all the others. *"Horses getcha real and they keep ya real!"*

What is the message here? For me, it is to listen to and learn to trust and act on our inner guidance, whether it is a recurring thought, a vision in a meditation, a tightening in our gut, or a message in a dream. Investigate, go deeper. Ask for help. Pray about it.

My greatest hope is that I can consistently become the port in the storm for Chasta. To maintain an inner calm that is real in whatever situation arises. *To intend to be that for myself so that I can offer it to those I love and to the world.*

I sent Gary a card many years ago that read: "God does not offer us freedom from the storms, but peace within the storm." It is faded and dog-eared, but we hung onto it, literally and metaphorically.

Trust your guidance. It is God on the inside calling. "Pick up! *It's for you!*"

You Look So Familiar

A variety of expressive arts are often offered in conjunction with equine facilitated therapy and personal growth and development workshops. The rationale for this is that interacting with horses creates an opening that allows for a healthy state of vulnerability in people. Following a session with an equine partner is a wonderfully creative moment to journal, paint, write poetry or many other possibilities that lead to transformational self-discoveries.

Sandra Wallin hosted a workshop called *Touch Drawing*™, a process created by a remarkable artist, Deborah Koff-Chapin. This time it was not in combination with any equine learning experience, and in fact, was held at a community arts facility rather than Sandra's *Chiron's Way Centre*. Sandra e-mailed me to share her enthusiasm for the process and invited me to attend. I looked at my calendar and felt the familiar feeling of overload. Then I looked at the course description of the *Touch Drawing*™ and had a change of heart. It truly resonated with me and I registered for the one-day workshop.

Up early on the designated day, I made the drive North over the border to Canada. It is interesting to me that so many of my healing experiences have been on Canadian soil since it has thrilled me to travel there since I was a small child. A foreign country! The British influence in the charming city of Victoria and the cosmopolitan and ethnically rich metropolis of Vancouver have always been enormously appealing to me. Both are in the beautiful province of British Columbia, where I was headed, ninety minutes from my home. And the Canadian people are as engaging as their homeland—friendliness is their hallmark.

Allowing extra time to navigate, I arrived early and was happy to greet Sandra and meet Deborah. Other participants came in and started to gather and exchange introductions. An attractive woman with tremendous energy approached me. With a quizzical look in her eyes and a smile on her face, she asked, "You look *so* familiar! How do I know you?" Not recognizing her from any of the workshops I had taken with Sandra or with horseman Jonathan Field who I trained with nearby, I introduced myself and tried to find our common ground. We ended up shrugging and agreeing that we were both eager for the experience.

Then Deborah gathered all of us in an opening circle so that we could share our backgrounds and our interest in the process. Most of the participants were therapists who intended to incorporate what they learned with their clients as well as for their own inner work. She asked that we partner up and share a table. The woman who had greeted me previously smiled at me from across the room and used body language to ask me if I wanted to pair up. I smiled back and nodded yes.

The *Touch Drawing*™ process uses paint squeezed onto a special board and covered with tissue like paper. Using your hands and/or other body parts, the impressions made on the paper create the art. Once removed from the board, it is a very evocative form of expression, unlike anything that I had ever experienced.

With lovely music in the background, my partner and I set to work. We had been advised to immerse ourselves in the process and to minimize interactions amongst the group. Occasionally both of us reached for the same tube of paint without really looking up and touched hands and exchanged a few words, but otherwise worked independently about four feet from each other.

Toward the end of the morning, Deborah announced that we would soon break for lunch and encouraged us to stay and share our drawings, again choosing partners. She said our job was to listen first to the person's feelings about their work and then offer insights that it may evoke for us. My table partner and I agreed to stay together.

Both of us had been remarkably prolific, amassing a large number of drawings. She started first and I was enchanted with her distinctive artistic style and her ability to express what she was feeling with detailed clarity. After sharing a quantity, she peeled off the next painting, still slightly tacky. A puzzled look came over her face. She studied it a bit longer and finally said emphatically, "I have *no idea* where this came from! And then continued, "It is obviously a female form, coming out of some kind of lidded box or trunk—it looks like she is escaping—only a toehold left. Maybe it's Pandora, but I think it's too late—she's *outta* there!"

Sitting next to her in stunned silence, my jaw gaping, I looked at the ghostly sylphlike form. She *was* on her way out! I was covered in goose bumps and the hairs on the back of my neck were at attention. At least three times that I could recall within the week, I had said aloud to female friends that my inner work and personal growth had been challenging me to the point where I questioned whether I should have opened my own personal Pandora's box and that I sometimes felt like pushing her back in and closing the lid! As I shared this with my new friend in incredulous tones, she, an art therapist herself, said "Well *now* I get it! This was *your* drawing—I just executed it!"

It was an incredible shared moment as we sat next to each other, realizing that our energies had collaborated in a mystical way. Emotional resonance—entrainment—coherence. All terms described by Dr. Candace Pert in her newest book, *Everything You Need to Feel Go(o)d*. Our experience was one for the record books!

But there was more. She progressed down her pieces of art until she got to the final image. It was a *beautiful* depiction of a horse's face. But not just any horse. Looking back at me through those eyes was Ritzy, our sweet boy, in every detail. She paused and said, "Hmmm, now I am stumped again—this one drew itself, but I don't know the significance of the horse."

Oh my! I had taken a truly magnificent ride on mountain trails with Ritzy the previous day, taking the afterglow into my night dreams and thinking about our time together all the way to Canada that very morning.

His image surfaced through *her* hands, but was vibrating through *my* heart. When I shared this information with her, she smiled and asked how to spell his name so that she could title the painting correctly.

I have experienced many amazing examples of emotional resonance and overlapping energies with humans and animals—Evan and I constantly say the same thing at the same time, down to the inflection—but this one took the cake.

So I started paying close attention to people saying *"You look and feel so familiar to me,"* realizing it was happening on a regular basis by strangers of all sizes, shapes, colors, ages, ethnic backgrounds and faith traditions. The more I noticed it, I realized the frequency had taken on comical proportions—I had come to expect it! Airports, restaurants, grocery stores—people smiling tentatively and then approaching me, asking where we knew each other from.

The word familiar shares the Latin root with family. One of the definitions for family from Webster's Dictionary is: "a group of similar or related things." With sincere humility, it is my belief that the more I am familiar with and know myself, the more others see and know themselves in me. Our emotional resonance for each other reminds us that we are related. That we are at least as *similar* as we are different. Back to the commandment to love your neighbor as yourself—if I can see the divinity in myself, I can see it in others. Then we can be mirrors for each other, reflecting back the love from within.

That is why I felt I *knew* Kim McElroy on the day we met. Why she felt so familiar to me. Like so many people who are touched by Kim's art, I had resonated with the essence of who she is through her creations, which are her gift to the world. I could relate to her through her art because we are related to each other and to the horses we share a mutual love for.

And speaking of Kim, there was another postscript to the synchronicities of the day. The workshop ran a bit late and Sandra asked that I go meet the friends we had scheduled to have dinner with that night while she finished up. I went off into the night in an unfamiliar city with a little map she had drawn and ended up at a restaurant called *Palomino* (Chasta's coloring) *that felt so familiar* to me. When everyone finally arrived, we still had to wait for a table in the large and sprawling dining space. As I felt myself slide into the booth, I realized that this was the *exact table and spot* where I had been sitting when Kim and I enjoyed a meal there when we first came to Canada to the workshop with Linda and Sandra!

As different as geographies, cultures, languages, faith traditions and species are, we truly are similar. Related. Familiar.

One Family.

Chapter Twenty

The Fire of Transformation

It was a wild winter in the Northwest. Tons of rain, record freezes and gale force winds—all this, and it was only November! We had four enormous trees blow down on our property, three Cedars and a Douglas Fir. Fortunately there was no severe damage but the largest Cedar, actually a fusion of several trees which had formed a large base, had crashed down in the severe winds and damaged limbs on a number of others. The area where it happened has been a very special place for me—a place where I have spent a lot of memorable time with the horses over the years.

On the day our first horse Chad arrived, I got up three times in the night and stood under those trees with him, pinching myself to make sure this dream was real. I was forty but felt as if I was five. It was where I first saw Chasta in the moonlight on our eerie first encounter. It has been my favorite place to take the time to groom Ritzy's long winter coat that makes him look like a cinnamon bear. I call it "The Sacred Cedar Circle" due to the arrangement of the trees, and it has been a sanctuary for all of us.

The image of a purple blue horse in one of Kim McElroy's paintings that she calls "Halcyon," has come to me there regularly in prayer and meditation. I love to perch on a large rock near the trees or even on the ground and rest up against them and spend silent time with the horses nearby. Located behind the stable, the horses get relief from the shade of the trees and from bugs and the wind. The tree that fell was a favorite rubbing spot for their itches. When it blew down, the trees it landed on prevented it from hitting the ground.

When our friends who are professional tree trimmers came to cut it up, the stump popped back down and remained. But since there were large holes and roots, it posed a safety problem for the horses, so we decided to burn it. My heart felt so sad, so Evan and I approached it tenderly, like an old friend that we were laying to rest.

We fed the fire all day and sat next to it while we ate our lunch. It felt wonderful on a cold winter day and the scent of an outdoor fire is always something special, taking me back to all of the good times spent around camp and beach fires. We shared memories of times with our animals over the years. Evan's recollections are a treasure for him because, without siblings, his animals have been his constant and devoted companions.

Chad, our first horse, is buried close by and we remembered the eerie beauty of first one, then two bald eagles circling uncharacteristically low over his grave on the day he died. We recalled the way our golden retriever, Charlie, lay like a sentinel next to the cross we made for Chad's grave from fallen limbs. Now Charlie is buried next to his old friend. Also how our little cat, Gussie, Chad's best pal on our farm, disappeared on the day Chad died. She used to be wherever he was. She had often slept on the ground with him, between his massive front legs. When his saddle was lying over our round rail fence, she would take a nap in it while we groomed him. The day Chad died, she was nowhere in sight. She returned one month later, thin and frail from her apparent mourning. Soon she was her feisty self again.

Then I recalled Chasta and I running at liberty the first time I jumped through the U-shaped tree on our property and she followed me, jumping through as well, and what a thrill it was for me to feel that powerful connection.

And on warm summer nights, "Camp Chasta", the place in the round corral where I set up my chaise lounge and bedroll in order to sleep outside in a desire to gain her trust. The gate to the round corral left open, and free to be wherever they wanted within the pasture, I noticed the first night that Ritzy stood guard while Chasta slept within about ten feet from me. The next time she was half the distance and by the third night, I opened my eyes in the morning and she was sound asleep standing up with her head directly over my heart!

Revisiting all of these special memories together gave us a feeling of profound gratitude for all that we had been through as a family over the years—the pleasures and the struggles. Chad had been a source of joy and a strong anchor for us with his sheer size and strength and gentle demeanor and willingness to be close with us. People so often do not like to talk about difficult times, but as the fire crackled, Evan and I recalled the confusion and fear we felt when Gary was suffering from a debilitating depression when Evan was six years old after his father *finally* made the choice to become *continuously* sober. Not temporary rides on the wagon before falling off, as had been the pattern. He was ready to choose to become the wagon master.

Ironically, alcohol is a depressant, so most alcoholics are chronically mildly to moderately depressed for the years they are actively addicted but when an individual attempts sobriety and there is no longer the option of the release valve that a relapse and use of alcohol *seems* to provide, true and *acute* depression is often the result. Just like a pressure cooker, the steam builds up from inside and the valve provides the release to keep from blowing the lid and contents sky high. If humans do not have safe and effective strategies for releasing the inevitable pressures as they come along in life, such as prayer and meditation, volunteering to help others, a strenuous physical workout, connection to a community of support, journaling, etc. (which are all choices to be present), then using alcohol as anesthesia to cover the pain seems like a reasonable and familiar choice/pattern.

Acute depression overtook Gary on Christmas day. Holidays and old painful memories can be subconscious emotional triggers, and just before dinner, Gary announced that *"I have to go."*

"Where?" I wondered aloud, since Christmas dinner was nearly ready to serve.

"I don't know," he announced. And he didn't. Sober for a number of months, he had been struggling with terrible business challenges and pressures that were really tied in with his identity. He was feeling overwhelmed by some of the wreckage of the past from old choices, now that he was no longer drinking and had to take a hard look at them.

We had spent a nice Christmas eve and Christmas day morning with our families and now it was just the three of us and suddenly he sat there, perched on the end of the sofa, looking like the father in the old black and white Disney™ movie from my childhood, *Hans Brinker and the Silver Skates.*

In the vintage film, Mr. Brinker was in an accident and has developed amnesia and does not recognize his family and sits in a darkened corner with his head bandaged with a look of confused terror on his face and the family does not have the means to get help from a doctor. I remembered watching it as a child and was haunted by the blank yet fearful look in his eyes and the crushing worry of his family, feeling powerless to help him.

It was truly Gary's dark night of the soul, as depression has often been described, and as a result, we went into the darkness with him. He would sit at look at Evan, the love and joy of his life, and stroke the side of his face with the back of his hand, the only real physical gesture of affection that I ever saw Gary's father offer. There was recognition, but it was from far, far away.

It was a number of months before the light returned to his eyes and he looked like Gary and Daddy again and regained his familiar scent. During acute depression, those vital things vanish and leave loved ones feeling like the Brinker family. Lost and confused. Our animals gave Evan and me a comfort that truly sustained us.

During that period, God also graced our family with some wonderful people who gave us unconditional support and were there for all of us. *We must ask for help when it is required!*

One friend referred me to a man who provided counseling from his home about an hour north of where we live. Following the directions, I arrived at a small, humble place in a quiet old neighborhood and found a dear, elderly gentleman with gold-rimmed glasses and eyebrows as white as his hair at the door who guided me to his study. He was a wonderful listener as I poured out my heart and shared my pain and fears. His responses were simple and he shared a few very comforting lines from scripture, but what profoundly affected me the most was that he told me that I just needed to *"outlove him."*

By that he did not mean a competition, but that then and at the end of it all, that I would need to be there, arms outstretched like the father for the prodigal son, regardless of what Gary decided to do in the long run. He assured me that I had the heart to do this and that everyone does, and in essence, it is what we are called to do and that it is all there is. I never saw the kind counselor again, but that hour session changed my life.

If I am to succeed with Chasta, I must *outlove* her, and be there, at the end, with my heart open, willing to smile and continue to learn and try again. Get up when I fall, literally or figuratively, and believe in a new moment in time, the *present* moment, which is the true gift.

It is my life's goal and challenge to simply receive and accept that gift.

And we *were* there, when Gary found his smile again, and renewed his commitment to be our husband and father, and picked up our healing journey of life where we left off, much stronger on every level for it. Evan had a new tricolor Jack Russell Terrier puppy named Cosmo and they both had six-year-old grins as they played on the floor with him, feeling new themselves.

Remembering this time in our lives and grateful that it was behind us, my strong and gentle son and I continued stoking the fire of the burnt-out fallen tree. It finally got dark and Evan left for the evening to be with friends. Gary came home from work and we went for a nice, long walk in the moonlight, turning off our lantern on our country road unless a car approached.

As we walked toward our long drive on the way home, I noticed the fire was still glowing in the wind, which had picked up considerably. I said a final goodnight to the horses, as I always do, and suddenly I had a sense that I needed to go check the fire. Not from a safety standpoint, but from a knowledge that it held a message for me.

Approaching with my lantern, I stopped and stood transfixed. The formerly massive trunk, which had been nearly five feet across now had only a few inches around the perimeter remaining, the entire inside burned away. To my complete amazement, I saw *very clearly* a pair of three-dimensional silhouettes of horse heads burned away by the fire and the wind. Where an eye would be, was a glowing ember—the rest was black. The dancing wind and flames created a kind of movement as if they were running. Now you may think that I have a fertile imagination, and you would be right, but I believe God gives us eyes to see Him *where we are*. Because I have had a heart for horses since my first memory of them, I see them *everywhere*, strong and free.

I turned off the lantern and stood in the glow of the fire, thanking God for the heat that was melting my heart, erasing the walls of my own fearful imaginings—the

guilt and worries that had burdened me over the years. The sadness and pain over being both betrayed and being the betrayer. Having to give up the fairy tale illusion of having "the perfect life" and feeling profoundly grateful for the one that I had. Working at letting go of the plethora of mistakes and poor choices that I had made along the way and understanding how all of it has contributed to my personal growth. I would still miss the beautiful old tree, but was grateful to God for what it had meant to us and to the horses.

Excitedly, I went inside to tell Gary about my discovery. He had gotten into the bathtub to warm up and said he was happy to take my word for it! So I took my camera out in the hope that I could capture the images that were so clear and amazing to me.

Evan returned home an hour later and was game to go take a look, putting his arms around me and giving me a long, tight squeeze. As we came around the corner, I looked up to see that the burnt horses were gone—erased, too, by the wind and fire.

Galloping off into the winds for all time, the winds of change and transformation.

Chapter Twenty-One

Letting Go

Horses are wonderful teachers for learning when to hang on (sometimes for dear life) and when to let go. They have incredible memories, but are great examples of living in the present moment. If they get into an altercation with another horse, shortly thereafter, they may be seen grazing together side by side. "Live and Let Live" and "For the Good of the Herd" may well be their mottoes.

Humans have a consciousness about living for the greater good and universal abundance with love for all, too. Often it is just buried in our society's models for competition by being stuck in the ego, creating divisiveness and fear.

It is so easy to ride a horse with one foot on the accelerator and one foot on the brake in fear, not trusting them to stop or go. Smooth acceleration and deceleration *depends on trusting the process and our part in it*. It is truly difficult to see the bigger picture when we are stuck thinking it is all about *us*. Keeping a perspective on where we fit into the grand scheme can be tricky, to be sure, but nature gives us a beautiful model for understanding my son's favorite passage in Ecclesiastes: *There is a time and purpose for everything under Heaven*. Including a time to die.

Our beloved Arabian horse, Ritzy, had been ailing on and off for some time. He always seemed to keep going, like the Energizer bunny. But during the cold days of winter, he seemed to be in his final decline. I went out one morning to find him relaxed and ready to eat breakfast but the bottom of his blanket was iced over.

Puzzled, I checked his inner wool blanket. It was bone dry. That is when Gary rushed over to see if we were all right. From the upstairs window, he had seen a hole in our frozen pond. Sure enough, we could see where Ritzy had broken through and thankfully made a U-turn up to the bank. Had he fallen asleep and become disoriented? Though seeming to come through it unscathed, within a few weeks, he lost interest in eating, completely out of character for him. In spite of the very best care offered in holistic and traditional methods, he grew weaker. Chasta reversed the roles and became his guardian, mindful of his dignity.

The emotions that surface when faced with making decisions about the quality of life for someone we love can challenge us to our core. I had been dealing with this situation with Ritzy for some time. Most horses spend multiple hours and times during the day and night resting and sleeping on the ground. The legendary racehorse, Seabiscuit, loved nothing more than taking long naps flat out. He must have known that it gave him the power and energy to run flat out, too. Sadly, over the years, Ritzy did not allow himself to rest on the ground—he spent far too much time being vigilant. That extended hypervigilance let to his early demise. He spent far too much time *going*, and less time *relaxing. What a life lesson that has been for me to observe.*

He was a senior horse, a true elder—but oh!—that we might have his gentle countenance and throaty knickers a little longer. But I heard a clear message: *It's time.* Though he tried to stay on his feet, it was not long before he would fold down again, exhausted.

I called Gary, Evan, our vet, Dr. Greg Ingman, and my good friend, Joanne, Ritzy's former owner. Joanne arrived earlier than we had agreed upon. She had a knowing, and when I reached for my phone to call her and ask that she come now, she pulled up our driveway. She took one look and said, *"Oh, Ritzy"* and then to me, *"It's time."* It was the same words that I had heard distinctly that morning.

I had made a bed with fresh shavings in an attempt to keep him warmer and more comfortable under one of the remaining cedar trees. We were lying down with him, Chasta standing nearby, when Evan pulled up the driveway in his truck. *"Mom?!"* he hollered, not seeing us behind the stable. I had told the school secretary to tell him his mother and Ritzy needed him—*he knew.* Ritzy, calm but lying with his head on the ground, pricked his ears to the sound of Evan's voice and staggered to his feet for the last time. *"Oh Ritz,"* was Evan's greeting, too, as he buried his face in the neck of his devoted friend. Rolling waves of sadness surrounded us as we shared our feelings of love for this incredibly sweet animal.

Evan helped Ritzy back to his final resting spot on the ground. Dr. Ingman arrived and though Chasta has great affection for him, she hid herself from sight. *She knew.* Dr. Ingman agreed that Ritzy's end was very near and that in spite of his peaceful appearance, he was suffering greatly. We all said our final goodbyes and thanked him for all he had so generously given us. He seemed to soak up all the love with great dignity and peace. Ritzy's final breath was quiet and then he was still.

After everyone left, I asked Evan if he would help me make a cross for his grave. "I can't now, Mama," he said. "I have to *run.*" He and Ritzy used to run on the ground to the river down the farm fields, in perfect harmony, connected by an invisible thread, with the lead rope folded across his withers at the base of his neck. *The invisible rope is the strongest kind.*

Gary called our wonderful neighbor, Doyle, who agreed to bring his backhoe and bury Ritzy on our land. As I laid there by myself crying over Ritzy's body, I saw Chasta peeking out at us from the always open door of her stall.

"It's OK girl, everything is all right," I offered. And *in that instant* I recognized the complete incongruence of that utterance. It was *not* OK! It was awful, sad, painful – anything but OK – I was being as clear as mud to the mare that meant so much to me. It can be a mother's natural instinct to help others feel better and that is beautiful. But as women, we have also been conditioned to help others to their peril if we immediately pretend not to feel what is *really* going on, *and not allow the full range of emotional response*. When I tell Chasta, or anyone else, that it's OK, I want her to know *that* is what it truly means. If the horses are teaching me anything – or better yet, *if I am learning, it is to know and speak my truth in that moment.*

So I apologized to her and said, "actually Chasta, I feel just awful. Ritzy is dead and my heart hurts so badly that I can hardly bear it, but we are here when you are ready." She looked at me for a long time with soft eyes, recognizing my return to my core. She walked over slowly, ears forward, and went to his head. Evan had covered it with a small wool saddle blanket after he passed over because it made him so sad. I was stretched out over his body, sobbing, in reaction to the reverence she had for her dearest friend. She sniffed the blanket, then carefully took it in her teeth and pulled it away.

When she saw his stilled face, she cocked her head and looked confused. Not unlike humans facing the finality of death, it seemed as hard for her to accept that his life was over. She leaned over to his nostril to exchange breath, as horses greet each other, and when there was no response, she yelped shrilly, like a dog, and jumped back, startled. Then she started to nibble at his nostrils and blew, slowly and deliberately, then more frantically. She sniffed down the area to his neck where it was shaved to the lesion where a plum-sized abscess had been drained a week before. It was deflated and leathery and she licked it furiously, going between the lesion and his nose, as if she were attempting to resuscitate a slow-to-thrive or stillborn foal. She worked diligently for most of an hour, while I watched in awe and wonder. It was one of the saddest and most beautiful experiences that I have ever had. *To be a sacred witness to love is one of the greatest privileges we can have in life.*

Finally, she hung her head in resignation all the way to the ground. Then she looked slowly and painfully at me. "We both did all we could for him, Girl—we have to trust that," I told her. Then she raised her head slowly to the sky and blasted the loudest trumpet sound I have every heard from a horse. It was as if she was proclaiming his passage to all life.

A few minutes later, Gary and Evan appeared to say goodbye. Evan had to attend a science lecture at the college that he needed to receive credit for in his high school chemistry class. Gary did not want his son to drive alone in the emotional state he was in, so he decided to go with him and chose to remember Ritzy alive and on his feet, as he had seen him that morning when he said goodbye.

We stood together a short distance from where Chasta hung her head over Ritzy's body and hugged, releasing our grief in a wet, collective embrace. In that moment, in Evan's words, "the largest, lowest, most perfect V-formation of Trumpeter Swans" flew directly over us all, then made a sharp ascent. "They are taking Ritzy's spirit to Heaven, Mama," Evan smiled through his tears. "V for Victory," I smiled back. *Trumpeter* Swans. It was as if they had heard and responded to Chasta's own blast.

As Gary and Evan left, my dear friend, Kathy, drove up our driveway toward the stable. I introduced her in earlier chapters as my horsewoman mentor. She has taught me so much and I was intending to call her *in that moment* to see if she wanted to say a final goodbye. I didn't have to. She pulled up and opened her car door. "It's over, isn't it?" She had been at her daughter's when she jumped up, attending to *her* inner knowing. She had a meaningful time with Chasta and Ritzy where he lay and her timing was perfect as Doyle arrived with his backhoe and it allowed me to be with Chasta while she opened gates for him. It was getting dark and very cold and started to rain. Kathy needed to leave to tend to her own horses, so I said a prayer of gratitude again for the rich friendships these magnificent animals encourage.

Chasta and I watched Doyle, an artist with heavy equipment, maneuver his huge machine by the headlights. He dug the enormous hole and lowered the body. He turned off the motor and stood down in the hole next to Ritzy, who now looked like a sweet, sleeping colt. Then he said tenderly to Chasta, "This is where we will all be one day, Girl. Now I will step back so you can say goodbye to your best friend."

She looked softly at her lifemate for a while, then she lowered her head and stepped back. Doyle covered Ritzy's body with a wool blanket I gave him and then started to fill in the hole. I wanted Chasta to know where his body was to help her cope with her loss. She and Ritzy shared an *unusually* close pair bond. Doyle had unearthed a huge rock in the digging process and I asked him to please put it on top as a grave marker. He told me that he knew I would want it, so that is why he had set it aside. *Yet another knowing without spoken words.* I told him I would get my checkbook and he shook his head, saying "That is what neighbors are for." I tried to insist, but he just smiled and got into his big rig. More tears of gratitude.

After he left, Chasta and I walked to the gravesite and I sat upon the big rock and cried anew. Chasta sniffed the ground, then ran to the place close by where his body had laid, and trumpeted a shrill blast. Then to the grave and back again, with her head up, and released another plaintive cry. She called out into the night many times.

The next morning, our friends Robert Eagle Bear and Mary Snowdown called to say that they had been prayerfully gathering white feathers on the beach the day before and had thought strongly of us and asked if we were all right. I told them about Ritzy and Chasta and the swans, knowing that we had been connected in spirit. They said in their Native American traditions that the swan means help in sorrow and that the ascending birds were symbolic of Ritzy's "Swan Song"—his loving goodbye.

In the days immediately following his death, I felt cloaked in the presence of our mutual love. I had a deep sense that his final gift for me was for his death to be a gateway to *feel* and truly *embody* my long held sorrow. To really grieve my pain and loss, not just for him, but for all the emotions frozen in my soul. He had crashed through the ice, freeing me to plunge into the icy waters of deep forgiveness that lead to the warmth of true love.

To let go.

Partners Evan and Ritzy stand tall

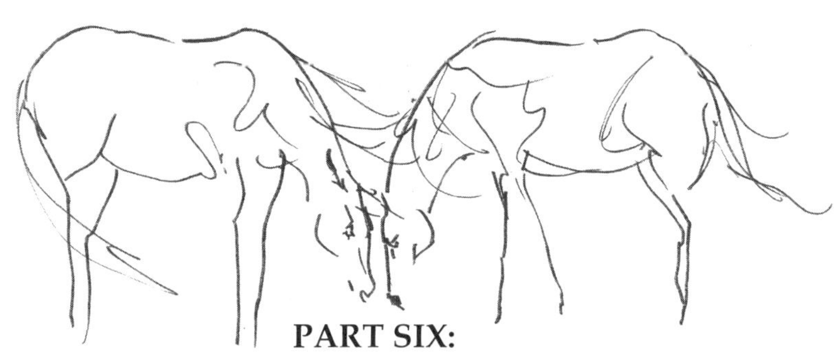

PART SIX:

Life On Life's Terms

Chapter Twenty Two

Acceptance

Horses are models for forgiveness. But forgive and forget? Maybe not. Horses have incredible memories. They don't forget, but they do forgive us our weaknesses and accept us where we are. They may struggle against us mightily, but it is an attempt to get us to see the light.

I have heard it said: Learn to "accept life on life's terms." *Until we can accept the gift from God that is our own life, we will struggle to accept all else.* And what we resist, persists. No *wonder* Chasta has had so much resistance to help me recognize my own.

I thank Ritzy for helping me realize my beautiful swan is within by letting go of my fear of being an ugly duckling. And what *is* beauty? Beauty and the Beast. We are both. We need to allow the light to reveal our shadows so that we can embrace and heal them. Finding our true inner peace is our greatest gift to the universe. It is the essence of world peace, one soul at a time. Finding our inner light and shining it will illuminate the path for others.

One day I stopped at the local mall to get a Hoola Hoop for my horseplay in the obstacle course. Having horses step into the hoop or allow it over their heads helps them to be relaxed about movement, sound from the trickling sand inside the cylinder, and where they put their feet. Who could imagine Chasta and I in our early days running together in relaxation while she has a big blue necklace on?! It may sound crazy, but it builds trust. And building trust is always a good thing.

As I zoomed through the mall to get to the toy store, I noticed my reflection in a mirror. Instantly, I saw myself as having a bad hair day, at the very least. Judgment, which is the opposite of acceptance, came rearing its ugly head. Suddenly I realized I was doing it again! See how these words of judgment permeate our thoughts, our speech, our beliefs, our actions and therefore our destiny? With much respect to Ghandi and his oft quoted words, do you see a pattern here?

Just then I passed a hair salon that accepted walk-ins. "Go do something about your silver hair, you look old and unattractive," came the voice of the inner critic. Not to be outdone, the part of me who had begun healing said, "You are just fine, relax, it's about working on the inside." My inner voice took another tactic. "You'll feel better if you look better...." It was just starting to sound rational when the guilt kicked in. "It's too expensive; give it to charity where there is a greater need and don't be so shallow."

Geez! What a tremendous amount of energy, just for the internal debate! Finally, I remembered to *breathe*! I could feel myself relax as I headed for the Hoola Hoop display in the corner of the toy store that was open to the mall. In that moment, I felt the presence of someone behind me literally to the point of touch. I turned around, fully expecting it to be someone I knew. I was startled to look *directly* into the round and luminous blue eyes of a man who looked like a cross between Andy Warhol and a leprechaun. He leaned toward me, enlarging his already big eyes as he smiled and said, "Your hair is *so* beautiful *just the way it is.*" As you might imagine, I am rarely speechless, but I finally squeaked out, *"Thank you,* I *really* needed to hear that in this moment." He smiled, and replied, "I know. God bless you!" And in the blink of an eye, he disappeared. I scanned the passersby but he was nowhere in sight. Angels in the mall? For a girl who prefers the natural world, it was a very important message.

Shortly after that experience, I was reading master horseman and clinician Chris Irwin's incredible book, *Dancing with Your Dark Horse.* I was at a restaurant alone and used the restroom while I waited for my meal. As I washed my hands, I saw my reflection in the antique oval mirror. "The beauty is in the shades of gray," came the distinct voice as if it were coming from the "mirror, mirror on the wall." Hmmm, I thought. At least I am moving forward here, hearing an authentic voice. A rush of peace and comfort came over me. I returned to my table and once again opened by book and started to read. "Thrill bumps" (Barbara Rector's description of gooseflesh) came over me. Chris was talking about a meditation he had about shades of gray and the *realization* and *acceptance* of our nature of both dark and light. My mirror on the wall, truly my own reflection, had said the beauty was in the shades of gray. The synchronicity was amazing. I felt that every shade of gray in my hair and in my spirit had been earned. Badges of courage. Beauty marks. *Beauty from brokenness.*

I was finally coming into my *mareness.* Loving the child within so that I could be the woman I came to be. The woman *I am.*

Chapter Twenty-Three

The Peace that Surpasses All Understanding

And that's it. The peace that *surpasses* all understanding. We don't *have* to understand it all. Trust in the process. Pick yourself up and dust yourself off. Give yourself a hug. Go back to God. Once we get to a level of self love, the way He first loved us, we are delivered with a sense of peace so that we can truly offer service to others.

Chasta had awakened my awareness of our mutual needs for wellness on every level and exposed me to the great big world of equine therapy for "wholeness healing." Our first horse, Chad, knew I was nowhere near ready, so he had simply made it his mission to just take really good care of me and our young son. We went for long rides to the river with only a lead rope tied off on a halter because he was so kind and willing and I didn't know any better.

But Chasta became my mentor, and a real taskmaster at that. She is my *anam cara*, Gaelic for soul friend. Our dear friend, Father William Treacy gave me a beautiful book of that title years ago, written by John O'Donohue, and it is referred to in *Horses and the Mystical Path: The Celtic Way of Expanding the Human Soul,* an enchanting, life affirming book by Drs. Adele, Marlena and Thomas McCormick that had my heart beating faster with every sentence the way horses can. The McCormicks have an equine therapy practice as well as teaching the art of classical horsemanship skills. It thrills me to think that I have descended from the Celts on both sides of my family and that I am connected to the horses and my ancestors in an ancient way that has contributed to my journey in the present. The Celtic people are well known for being aware of the interconnectedness of all of nature and with their horses as a way of life.

Early on in my adventures with Chasta, I had a knowing that this portion of my life had become a calling to commit to sharing this healing journey with others. One day I went to a traveling charismatic mass at a local church with the intention of finding peace in prayer about a family situation that was distressing me. This was not a format that I was familiar with. People were crying out to Jesus. The music was fresh and alive. Tears were flowing. The power of the Holy Spirit was palpable. I was deeply into my prayers when I heard the priest who was celebrating announce the end of the service. He was advising us that there were prayer groups in the corners to aid anyone in need of special requests. I looked at my watch and realized that two hours had gone by. It also registered in various parts of my body that I was tired, hungry and needed to find the restroom. I made a decision to skip all extra prayers and get the heck out of there.

As I headed for the exit, a woman's kind gaze was riveted on me. I smiled back and racked my brain for where I knew her from. Her look was one of *total* recognition. The harder I thought, the more it eluded me. As I walked closer, I intended to extend my hand in a greeting of peace and walk on. Instead, she leaned forward as I approached and asked, *"May we pray with you?"*

Suddenly I realized she was sitting with two other women and they were one of the prayer groups the priest had spoken of. My face flushed as I sat down. "Of course, thank you." She took my hand and asked, "What is on your heart, my dear?" Instantly forgetting what I had come specifically to pray about, I blurted, "I am feeling called to help people heal with horses and horses heal with people and ..." Although garbled, it felt completely sincere yet totally out of context. How could these three women possible know what I was mumbling about? What felt like a very pregnant pause (the most fertile kind for a mare, rich with meaning and significance) she said, "I know *exactly* what you mean! My family raised Quarter Horses on the island of Hawaii. Our children have taken over in our retirement. You are indeed being called to this healing ministry. Follow your heart and go in peace to love and serve."

Our beloved Chad was a Quarter Horse—solid, stable and full of quiet strength. By now, all four of us were holding hands and crying when the woman in the center said, "My favorite meditation is a vision of riding through the clouds with Jesus on white Arabian horses. I had Arabians while growing up. My prayers are with you!" Ritzy was an Egyptian Arabian. Oh, how I knew their springy, floating gaits!

The third woman was just as tender. She said, "I don't know much about horses, but I am a social worker and am involved with families. I have participated in therapy with children and horses and the love and healing is magical. This is a path to God that I can understand."

To say that I felt validated to follow my heart would not be adequate—I was wobbly, but euphoric! What are the chances of three women older than me sharing *exactly* what I needed to hear about something somewhat unconventional for their generation? That is because God always knows our hearts and guides us to our next step. And just like the horse, one foot follows the other. Horses are masters of forward motion and always know the way home—*home to our hearts.*

I am confidently moving in the direction of my dreams, as philosopher Henry David Thoreau advised. In doing so, *I am living my dream in this moment.* As a student of the horse and all life, I have a long, *long* way to go. But when I turn around and look back down the trail, I am amazed at how far I have come. I am also in complete awe of the view at the top of the mountain from the back of a horse. Valleys and mountain peaks, all a part of the journey.

I love having children's groups from schools and Boys and Girls Clubs come to our farm to share a day of learning about compassionate animal care, recycling, organic gardening and composting, and all of the life lessons that come with it. It is *vital* for children living in this world of technology to connect with the rhythms of the natural world. *Children of all ages need to go outside to discover what is inside.*

My friend Marylin Power rolls out of her specialized van in her wheelchair and tacks up her miniature horses to give the children cart rides, much to everyone's delight. We horse-sat the mini mares while Marylin vacationed in Arizona. Gary wanted to keep them forever, not only because they are adorable animals, but for the fact that they were equine powered weed-eaters and systematically chewed the higher grass around the fences that they could reach by hanging their heads over the lower rail. They didn't miss a patch over the entire acreage! We felt like children, longing for their very own pony, watching them.

Marylin is a powerful example for the children about how we make choices in life to give up or to live life to the fullest. She was a horse owner and lover when she had an accident that left her paralyzed from the chest down and became dependent on a wheelchair at an age when she was retired. Rather than give up her dream of being with horses, she modified it and now has her mini mares, who stand right at her level.

God continues to put wonderful people and horses in my path, and in the case of Marylin and Rosie and Goodie, that was the situation, literally, when one day I drove down a country road near my home and came up behind them, the foursome including her little dog, Newman, out for a bit of exercise and fresh air. I pulled over to talk with this remarkable woman and commented on her delightful little horses. She said she was just pulling into her driveway and she would be pleased to visit with me. We have been great friends ever since and when she comes over, she drives her wheelchair up the ramp in her van, and the miniature horses jump in behind her. She pulls the carts in a trailer behind the van. When she arrives at our place, I assist her in tacking up the girls with their harnesses and she lifts herself out of her wheelchair onto a board and then slides into the seat of the cart, using her upper body that she still has control over.

Then we take off behind the sturdy little mares and head for the tractor roads on the farm field below us, the wind blowing in our faces as we pick up speed, and I feel like a happy seven year old like the children who we have

Marylin and her horse, Goodie, and dog, Newman

come to visit our farm. Marylin has a smile for everyone and chooses to focus on what she *can* do rather than what she cannot. Her joy is contagious and she has been a tremendous source of inspiration to me. All this while she also takes care of her 94-year-old mother!

So there we are together, putting on a horse and mini show (not to mention the dogs and other wild and domestic critters) for the children, and Chasta takes it all in, bowing to them after she jumps over the picnic table and they cheer wildly. I never taught her to bow, she just does. She does it for *fun*, sensing the joy it gives the children. Rediscovering my child within in the company of the horses has reconnected me to that sense of fun. When we relax, laugh and allow ourselves joy, the whole world benefits. When we play games together, children and animals, the feeling of their innocent joy is contagious. It leaves me giddy and reminds me that healing, like anything else, *can be fun*! Plan and allow for fun every day!

My sister and I took her daughter and grandson to the local Fourth of July parade last year and I felt complete delight as I watched Marylin roll by, pulled by her little mare, Goodie, while Rosie ran along side them. Marylin got up that morning, and made a decision to go to a lot of work, especially for her, to spread a tremendous amount of joy for others. I watched the beaming faces of the children of all ages in the parade crowd as they cheered as she went by in her fanciest helmet, a smile from ear to ear on the face of my friend, with her devoted dog, Newman, perched in her lap, as happy as she was to participate. She is one of my (s)heros for sure, and I often reflect on the dignity and strength she has modeled for me, and I feel profoundly grateful.

The children will miss Ritzy this season when they arrive on the big yellow bus. But how rich it will be, to learn more about the circle of life and death, when they see his grave. *To learn that the more we love, the more we grow and the stronger we become.*

And I can hardly wait to introduce them to Remoe, our big, beautiful new sorrel chestnut horse. He is love on four legs. Remoe was his "barn name," on the dental record in the envelope with his registration papers, when he arrived. I asked his former owner how he acquired the name. She had no idea. As unlikely as it sounds, I looked it up on a search engine on the computer and I just had to stare in amazement at the significance of the meaning. If you have a remote-controlled toy boat, car or plane, the device that affects it is the remote and what is being affected is the remoe.

"Remoe!" It is my heart's desire to have relationships with my horses, and all life, *wherever I am*. That is what praying without ceasing is: *Remote love.*

I will continue to study with my many mentors and friends, two and four legged. I am living large and dreaming big, as Wyatt Webb, author of *It's not About the Horse* would say. He facilitates healing sessions with humans and horses and also opened my eyes, heart and mind to the possibilities of this work. I intend to create our Woodylane Farm to be a place where hearts can learn, heal and grow, like the magical *Crystal Peaks Youth Ranch – The Ranch of Rescued Dreams*, as described by Kim Meeder in her exquisite books, *Hope Rising* and *Bridge Called Hope*. Kim and her husband, Troy, are inspiring people the world over with their dedication to this path. I have a piece of tiny Victorian paper scrap that says, *"Hope is my star."* How true.

I have big dreams to create more curriculum for schools and Boys and Girls Clubs and other groups that incorporate learning, growing and healing with animals and all of nature. This work is already being done with many individuals and groups, including the corporate level with much success. I intend to be a part of the expansion. Like Oprah Winfrey's *Leadership Academy for Girls* in South Africa, the fruit of this work is *finding the leader within.* Oprah realized we must go from *root to fruit* if we are to make lasting change. *We must teach our children to fish.*

Another remarkable synchronicity followed the arrival of Remoe. Shortly after we brought him home and bonded with him, I opened a copy of the Oprah magazine, *O*™, one of the few I read besides horse publications. It fell open to a page that had a beautiful image of a horse that looked exactly like Remoe with an excerpt of a poem called: *For What Binds Us,* which is about the beauty and strength created by our wounds—precisely the theme of my book! It was written by Jane Hirschfield, an extraordinary poet who has read her work at the Skagit River Poetry Project here in LaConner, friend to the superintendent and curriculum director who can help me to write programs for children! *For What Binds Us* is my most favorite of all of her poems.

My greatest dream is for Gary to retire and become the gentleman farmer and horseman that I believe he has the heart for. He *loves* animals and children and has life experiences that are so very rich to share. And for Evan, who dreams of racing cars professionally, a sanctuary to come home to. He may love going fast and turning left on a racetrack, but inside, he is my true "Nature Boy" companion. And like his parents, he has a heart for children and animals.

Shortly after I got off to my rocky start with Chasta, my horse crazy cousin, Lorean, sent me an article about another Connie. Connie Douglas Reeves. She rode her horses every day until a few weeks before her 102nd birthday when she died peacefully in her sleep! She taught *36,000 girls* how to be with horses, which is a lifetime gift. Talk about inspiration! *One very tiny woman can make such a difference!* I have a framed photo of her in my tack room which I nod reverently to and smile over often. Connie is one of the subjects of a project called *American Cowgirl,* created by Jamie Williams and Lisa Dee to honor the spirit of women and horses and how they have shaped our culture.

Part of realizing my dream is to share my stories in hopes of expanding this vision. True stories are the best stories, I believe. Jesus taught His truth in stories as do all of the world's sacred faith traditions. What the world needs now is love, sweet love, and the horses—and indeed all of creation, are *calling us to love.*

Chapter Twenty-Four

Passion

Do what makes your heart sing. Do what you love. Follow your heart's desire. Live your passion. Here is an example of the synchronicities that I *live* because I am passionate about children and horses. I was at the school district office using the computer after hours to go online and request donations for our Boys and Girls Club auction fundraiser as a volunteer. I could hear the children's voices below playing outside. The club is located on the school campus so the children can go safely from class to their after school programs. School was out of session for the afternoon and I was the only person left in the office.

The phone rang. I answered to hear a young boy's voice say urgently, "Help! We are on the playground and someone is injured!" Just as I started to reply, I heard giggling. I asked, *"Where are you?"* looking for a specific location. "On the playground!" More giggling. Though I had the sense that this could be a prank, I ran down the stairs as fast as I could to the largest area of the playground. As I approached at a run, I saw a group of boys scatter, turning around and milling nervously.

The horses are teaching me to be a student of body language and it seemed clear to me that I was in the midst of the pranksters that I had been upstairs trying to raise money for! "Everyone OK?" I hollered. More shuffling, then a muffled, "Uh huh." I slowed down to a jog and looked at all of the other pockets of children playing happily. I headed back upstairs to finish my inquiries, and as I entered the office, the phone rang again. I answered and heard the same voice, "*Uh*, I just called to say we are sorry. We didn't know that was *your* number! We were making a prank call." Kids and cell phones!

"Well," I said. "That took a lot of courage for you to call and apologize. Please remember that your choice to make the first call really worried me—you guys need to know that there are a lot of people like me who truly care about you. I am proud of you for your decision to call back. Please keep making good choices." Pause. "Uh, OK. *Sorry*. Bye."

I smiled and renewed my efforts to raise money to keep these kids aware of the community of people who care and provide their programs. The phone rang again. This time it was the director of the Boys and Girls Club, my good pal, Marlene. The kids call her "Queen Marlene." "Hi," she said, I just called to see if you were all right." She knew I was at the district office working. "I just looked up and saw you running outside my window. *It was the strangest thing,"* she said. I was *just* thinking about you and had gone to look for the DVD of Ritzy and Chasta running with you at liberty from our field trip to your farm, and from all of the boxes we have, I opened one and the *first case* I put my hand on was the one with you running with Ritzy! I felt so thrilled to find it and I looked up and saw you running by outside my window! It was *amazing* and it is giving me goose bumps again just telling you! We will make you a copy!"

Two weeks before I had told Marlene how I had regretted not filming my progress with Ritzy on video to have my training levels assessed and especially to remember his great beauty and grace. I had lots of still shots of us together, but she had the only real video footage. She had assured me she would look for it....

As I shared my successes about procuring items for the

auction (one positive response came over the computer while we were talking!), I told her of her young Boys and Girls Club member's idea of a joke, remembering my own forays into prank phone calls while my siblings held pillows up to their faces to suppress the giggling. Just then I looked up at the big colored photo of a young, strong Ritzy hanging over my computer, just like those children playing outside with their whole lives ahead of them, and realized *Marlene is living her passion for youth.*

My own Evan has a passion for racing cars. He loves his animals, baseball and he plays the cello, but he is passionate for his faith and racing. *Everything* about the sport of auto racing is out of my comfort zone. Now I *love* dirty, sweaty horses and find them intoxicating. I like nothing better than digging lustily in my garden, but the dirt at the race track seems, well, so *dirty!* The methanol fumes that I find offensive make my son's heart beat faster the way horses do mine. The roar of the engines make me reach for my earplugs and he was quoted in an interview about them "resonating in my chest." *That is where his heart is!*

Recently, we saw David Copperfield, the famous magician, appear (as opposed to disappear!) for our first time. Midway through his *amazing* performance, he told a very poignant story about how his father received a full scholarship to a theatre for the performing arts, but that his grandfather had forbidden him to attend. *"No son of mine will be in show business,"* he threatened. David had no idea of this until his grandfather told him the same thing when he wanted to pursue a career in magic. He was devastated when his grandfather told him he would disown him if he proceeded. David shared with the rapt crowd that he had known his life's path from a very early age so he held strong. Sadly, he did not see his grandfather for the final years of his life because he refused to acknowledge David's passion—his true path.

He then went on to create one of the most mind-boggling "illusions" I have ever seen. Call it what you will, but it *sure* looked like magic to me! God is the true magician, but *David is aligning himself with his creator to be living in the mystery*. Plus he is having *a lot of fun*, and so are his audiences! At the end of this amazing act, which involved conjuring up an enormous green Lincoln automobile from the 40s, his grandfather's dream car that he had never acquired, the audience responded with a collective gasp. Gary is a collector car dealer so he and Evan were cheering wildly.

Then David, somehow climbing aboard some invisible scaffolding to get to this enormous car that seemed suspended from *nowhere,* looked up with pure love and forgiveness and said, *"I hope you are proud of me, Grandfather, because this is who I am."*

There was not a dry eye in the house. I reached over and hugged Evan tightly. "Go for it, Son!" I whispered, tears streaming down my face, *"Race for your dreams!"*

Evan Funk in his element at a pre-race meeting
Photo: www.johnsracingphotos.com

Chapter Twenty-Five

The Family Sandwich

As I write this, I am a midlife Baby Boomer. I am at the age where my son is preparing to go out into the world and both of my parents are facing an adjustment to a sharp decline in health and the changes that situation creates. Feeling unprepared to cope with new territory seems like my life's theme some days. *Remember to breathe.*

Evan has graduated from high school a year early so that he can take the opportunities coming his way to develop his racing career. It is a very steep learning curve, but we are encouraging him to follow his heart, trusting the path of the heart is guided by God. My parents seem much too young and vital to lose such basic forms of independence, to have their health challenges limit their choices so profoundly. Gary is working much too hard to support us all. After making good healing progress in the area of his workaholic tendencies, the challenging economy has influenced him back into full time plus business management at a time in his life where he would like to be more available to help support Evan's career goals and dreams in racing, something they love together.

Daily I make choices of how I can best serve all of them, our animals and the community, while remaining focused on my own health and well being. If this is a family sandwich and I am the filling, sometimes I feel like a fried egg! Or even scrambled!

Humor. Thank God He invented it. I count my blessings daily and feel grateful for a family who has been gifted with a healthy sense of humor. Gary and Evan both have humor as a way of being in the world and have done *so much* for me to lighten up over the years. And Chasta? Though she has become quite the wise sage over time, she still cracks me up regularly with her mischievous nature. I believe that she works at making me smile, and sometimes belly laugh. After all, the lighter I am, the better partner I make for her. All of us could lose perspective easily if it were not for the built in relief valve of laughter.

Alone. We are *never* alone! So often we feel unique in our challenges but just look around and you will see others facing similar circumstances in every corner of the globe. Back to that all important community of support. And faith. *Focusing on blessings expands them.*

Even though I have savored every day of Evan's young life, it has raced by—no pun intended! And I am sure that all children feel that their parents will live forever, or that we can somehow avoid the painful realities that are a natural part of life. This point in time has given me pause to reflect on what I want to do with the rest of my time in this form on the planet.

As I look at my life today, it feels like a rich and beautiful mosaic. In learning to create mosaic art over the years, fitting the bits and pieces together is somewhat like crafting a complex puzzle. And for whatever reason He had in mind, God apparently made my particular personal puzzle a pretty darned rich adventure, though not a script I would ever have written myself. It was Helen Keller, the courageous author and inspirational speaker who said, "Life is either a grand adventure, or nothing at all." She was never defined by her disabilities, but by her enormous heart and spirit.

And that is the Mystery! A little color from this experience, a border or boundary from this one, and a whole new dimension emerges when you see something in a new way.

Today, I am *finally* grateful for all the bits and pieces of my life. Donald Nichols summed it up nicely when he said, "We cannot lose once we realize everything that happens is designed to teach us holiness." So my desire to achieve wholeness is really a path to holiness. *In all things, give thanks.*

What I have experienced on my healing path with horses rings so true for me that I feel a missionary zeal to share it with others. Pat and Linda Parelli refer to themselves as "shareaholics" because they have such a profound depth of understanding about horses that they want to leave as a legacy. And they are, *because they are willing to share it.*

With all due respect, "my name is Connie, and I am a shareaholic." When I applied to college, my mentor, dentist Robert Murray, wrote me a letter of recommendation for the dental hygiene program. He referred to me as "wildly enthusiastic." It was intended as a compliment and I was accepted into the program and after graduation I went back to practice with him for many years. His daughters were our flower girls when I threw my bridal bouquet off the balcony of the building that was originally a livery stable for horses. The word enthusiasm comes from the roots, *En Theos,* translated to mean "of God." So now I realize through an inner knowing that I have always been wild for what I believe to be the truth of God.

All of this accelerated change in my life has given me a new sense of my own value and power and my own humility. Like Dorothy Gale in the story of *The Wizard of Oz,* I feel meek. Humble. Humble was the perfect word for Templeton the rat to find for Charlotte the spider to spin in her web to save Wilbur the pig in the children's classic, *Charlotte's Web,* by E. B. White. Charlotte helped Wilbur find his worth, and he returned the favor, and in doing so they remained humble together.

Horses help you find your worth and they sure keep you humble!

Chapter Twenty Six

The Wonder of it All

Always be on the lookout for the miracles that are everywhere! One day my horse pal Amelia was working around her stable when she noticed a distinct image of a horse head on the outside wall of the building. She called her husband Erich to ask him if he had painted it. "What are you talking about?" he replied. As they examined it closely together, it appeared to be dried mud that clearly made a "painting" of what appeared to be a wise and knowing horse head.

Apparently, the artists were their own equines, Mariner and Jewel. Many of us have seen artwork created by KoKo the gorilla, who uses her hand to paint, and I have seen a video of an elephant artist who does watercolors with her trunk holding a brush—*amazing!* I have even seen incredible artwork done by an Arabian horse, who held the paintbrush with his teeth! While all of this is truly astonishing, Mariner and Jewel created their expression with either their dirty noses or rumps or a combination! I have a framed copy of the photo Amelia took of it on my bookshelf, which I pass daily. Sometimes it feels like looking at the Mona Lisa and the eye seems to follow me! Mostly, it makes me smile and shake my head over the wonder of it all! It always delights me to share it with others and see the look of wonder and amazement on their faces. Can we even begin to understand the possibilities? That is the very nature of beauty—that often it is beyond our wildest imaginings!

And speaking of miracles, another fascinating example

that will boggle your mind and expand your heart is a book called: *Beautiful Jim Key: The Story of a Man and His Horse Who Changed The World*, by Mim Eichler Rivas. It is the riveting true story of a relationship between a man and his horse that affected many thousands of people by touching hearts and breaking down stereotypes by the love that bonded them. The extraordinary intelligence of the horse, Jim, who Dr. Key had raised from a colt caused continuous questioning about his training techniques. His response was always: *"love, love and love."* People who witnessed their incredible connection at the touring performances at World's Fairs in the 1800s changed history by creating the groups to prevent cruelty to animals and the Humane Society at a time when this awareness was desperately needed.

Life is in the moments. It is so easy to miss them. So much chaos and confusion. Hustle and bustle. Frenetic schedules. But if we just take a deep breath and focus on being aware, it's there. Quietly waiting for us to notice.

The little things that seem to make time stand still and stop you in your tracks. Like the one and only time I had ever needed to close the door to Chad's stall during what was to us, in Washington State, a blizzard. The wall that had been concealed behind the sliding door was hosting hundreds, if not thousands, of ladybugs for their winter home. The red sea of shiny, round insects was a sight to behold. Right out of *National Geographic*.

Or the time we were cooking a summer dinner outside when then five-year-old Evan ran to me, eyes aglow. He led me to a rhododendron, ablaze in hot pink blooms, that had *baby* hummingbirds, zooming for nectar, the size of my thumbnail, emerald green in contrast. Evan's thrilling discovery had us in complete awe.

The year we went to Minnesota to visit Evan's God-family and we saw lightening bugs for the first time on a walk at night. Not knowing what they were until we were told, they looked like dancing fairy flashlights to me. The native Midwesterners got a pretty good chuckle out of the fact that I felt giddy with delight as an adult over an insect!

Another summer reverie was at the home of Evan's cello teacher. While they played duets in their cozy waterfront cedar dwelling, I sat outside on the deck overlooking the bay with his teacher's husband, sipping lemonade. I heard the eerie barking call of a wild blue heron and suddenly the sky was filled with them. Every time I tell this story, the numbers grow, but *I know* there was a flock of at least a dozen! The primitive silhouette of those majestic birds in flight is still etched into my soul. We see heron daily in the magnificent countryside where we live, but usually solo. There was a rookery in the old growth trees above where we were sitting and it seemed as though the world stopped revolving in that moment as I took in the magical sight and sound, cool glass in my hand and the warmth of the sun on my face. With the tangy, sweet lemon taste still lingering, I heard the gloriously mellow resonance of the cellos in the background.

Recently I was heading home on my country road when I saw a sedan pulled over to the side and a distinguished looking gentleman walking a distance ahead of it. I slowed down to offer help when I saw him bend down and with gloved hands, pick up a dead raccoon and place it carefully in the ditch. When I got closer, and rolled down my window, he offered that he had kept gloves in his car for many years for that reason, choosing to take the time to give the body the softer cushion of the earth rather than leave it on asphalt, perhaps to be run over again by rushing humans. I blessed him and drove off, mindful of his special contribution, his choice to be present.

A half mile later, in a field at the turn to our home, were four longhorn cattle, nestled on the ground at rest in the lush spring grass. Arranged with their rumps nearly touching, each body lay at an angle like some amazing bovine pinwheel, their huge horns at the corners facing outward. The pastoral scene with the valley and mountains behind them couldn't have been more beautiful if it had been choreographed. And actually, it had—with God's paintbrush! They looked completely serene and passed it on to me.

We got a big ride-on stuffed horse for my nephew's baby son, Rylan. I lifted him up onto the plush back of the chestnut horse that looks like Remoe for the first time, smiled and started to "cluck, cluck," (the traditional sound for asking a horse to move forward) and said, "Go, horsey!" as he bounced and giggled. Thirty minutes later, we went outside so he could meet the *real* Remoe, also for the first time. Remoe approached, and Rylan studied the big horse, cocked his head, then leaned in and "cluck, clucked" at him! *Thirteen months old!*

The sight of spring lambs cavorting after a long winter. Endless acres of tulips and daffodils that host a flurry of tourists every season. Among the visitors are babes in strollers, couples walking hand in hand, tour busses of seniors with floppy hats and name tags, and families licking the immodest ice cream cones that the local organic produce stand is famous for.

The Snow Geese and Trumpeter Swans. Thousands and thousands of them returning from their winged migration dotting the vast and fertile farm fields. Frog song from our pond. Fortunately, we love the sound, because it's *loud*. Gary getting out of bed in the morning, opening the window and calling, *"Duuuucks!"* and having them quack back in response. Flowers growing up through the cracks in the brick walkways and stone walls, and seeding themselves in the gutters, not to mention their blaze of glory in the gardens. And the list goes on.

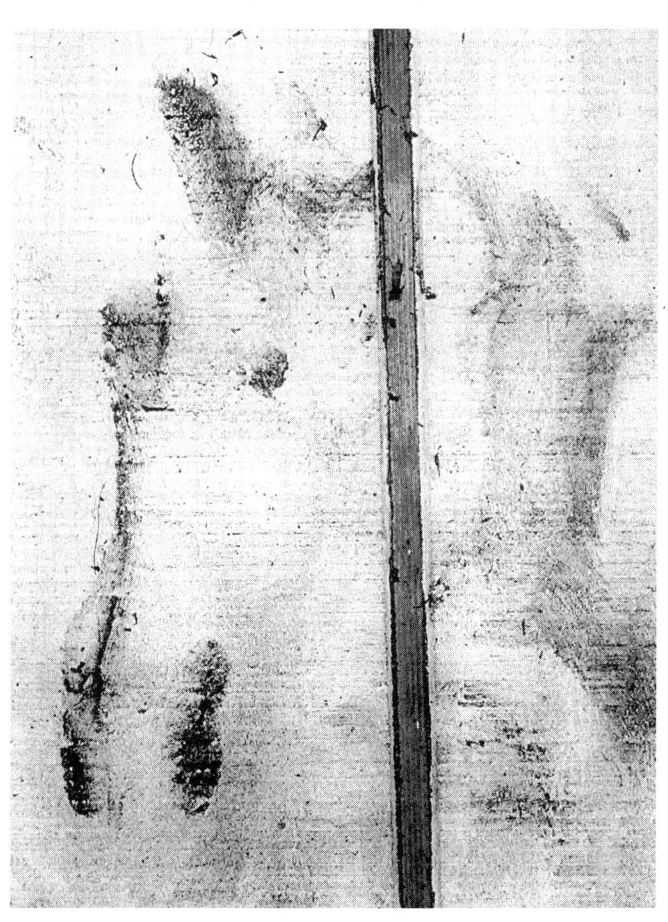

The Horse Sage by Mariner and Jewel

And then, I walked down the hall in our home, and looked through the square pane of an inside French door, in a telescopic view, through a window to the outdoors, and framed by the wind-ruffled spring green leaves of a weeping birch tree was Chasta, grazing peacefully in the distance. There she was, resplendent, an equine sculpture, looking contented and completely at home. I wonder, does she realize after her challenging beginnings of being moved from place to place, exchanged from human to human, that this is where she belongs? That she is home?

Albert Einstein, truly one of my greatest heroes said, "There are two ways to live your life. As if nothing is a miracle or as if everything is a miracle." You know which camp I choose.

Louis Armstrong reminds us in his lovely, distinctive voice, "It's a wonderful world." Take time each day to notice.

God is in the details.

Chapter Twenty Seven

Diamond in the Rough

We had been horse sitting for our friend Marylin's miniature mares when Ritzy's health failed. The four horses had been in a herd together comfortably, finding mutual respect for each other. Ritzy was the leader, but as he grew weaker, I separated them so that he could be alone with his beloved partner, Chasta, to give him the most comfort and peace possible. Chasta was his perfect nursemaid.

The mini mares, Rosie and Goodie, seemed to be very aware of the situation and stayed close to the fence line of whatever area I kept the big horses. They approached to offer equine moral support for Ritzy and Chasta and nickered to me soft greetings that felt like acknowledgement for my concern.

The night Ritzy died and Chasta trumpeted shrill blasts long into the night, they stood vigil at the gate that faced her, heads down.

I was in and out with Chasta most of that night, and in the morning, she was waiting for me at the gate, facing her tiny friends, who were doing the same at theirs across our long driveway. I asked Chasta to walk with me at liberty back to Ritzy's grave, but she planted herself firmly where she stood and nodded to her diminutive companions. It was apparent that she was ready for their equine company. I took her over and fed them together as they reunited happily.

We had another week before Marylin returned from her

winter holiday in Arizona and had generous offers from several friends to "borrow" one of their horses to keep Chasta company until we could find her a permanent herd mate. We accepted the lovely gesture from Amelia and Erich to have their Arab gelding, Mariner, join us. He had stayed here before and we all love him. Mariner has a gentleman's disposition like Ritzy and it seemed fitting that his best pal would step in to comfort his best girl. Evan and I made plans to go pick him up the night before the minis were to go home.

Then fate stepped in. The "everything happens for a reason" scenario. More lessons needing to be learned. A family friend, one of Evan's school teachers, "bumped into me" and told me that he had been meaning to contact us to see if I could help his college-aged daughter find a good home for her young horse. She was returning to school and felt heartbroken that she couldn't afford to board or keep him. This teacher's bright and pretty daughter had been a favorite of ours over the years, and in the small town where we live, Evan had crushes on a number of the high school girls back when he was in classes at the middle school which was across the street on a common campus, and she was one of them!

The situation immediately touched my heart. A sweet young lady needed a loving home for her sweet young horse, and Chasta needed a pal. I contacted her and offered her a free care situation for an indefinite period with my main criteria that he be a healthy match for Chasta. That way it may make it possible for our friend to keep her beloved horse. She agreed, relieved, knowing that we would love and care for her horse, but told us that she was very hopeful that we would commit to buying him as soon as possible so that she could finance her studies.

I had to be gone overnight that weekend and told Evan and Gary where her horse was being boarded and suggested that they try to get out and take a look at him.

They did. They liked what they saw. He was big, friendly and handsome, and his young owner was there, very sad and distraught in having to sell him. Gary gave her a check and called to tell me what a great horse Remoe was. *"What?!"* I questioned after my budding horsemen husband told me how easily he had picked up his feet, and allowed them to touch him all over. *Shades of another gifthorse who I had yet to even see!*

When Evan and I went to get him a few days later, he was indeed friendly, and walked into the trailer like a champ. He was *much* bigger than I would have chosen, his enormous hindquarters at my eye level. I have a determined dream to become a natural and fluid rider and plan to enjoy time on horseback into my golden years, eager to savor my newfound health and vigor that horses have helped me to realize.

I had expressed numerous times to family and friends that my next horse would be *my* choice, small and probably gaited for a comfortable ride. Remoe, in all of his huge, sturdy male glory, did not fit my mental *physical* picture. Yet he walked backwards out of the trailer as easily at our farm as he had walked in. He approached Chasta, who seemed delighted to see a horse her size, she being a big and sturdy girl herself.

They did a lovely equine dance of exchanging breath, necks arched, with their silhouettes backlit by the setting sun. After it appeared that they were on amiable terms, I upped the ante by tossing out two flakes of grass hay about thirty feet apart. They both started munching simultaneously from their respective piles, watching each other intently. They moved each other back and forth between the two, and seemed to be happily engaged in their musical hay piles game. So far, so good. No squealing, biting or kicking or even posturing to do so.

Well, how could I argue with such a nice, young horse? It

was more important that he provide Chasta with comfort than be my personal ideal in a horse. After all, he was to be *her* 24/7 companion, not mine.

I could picture him enjoying time with the young school children when they came out for field trips. Determined to continue to improve my horsemanship skills, I spent time with him daily playing ground games where he seemed to be a quiet and easy study.

But the honeymoon period seemed as if it was waning as I started noticing him moving Chasta aggressively. She refused to turn and face him, but he drove her constantly, nipping her as she moved. Soon I observed that the nipping had turned to bites, breaking her skin repeatedly. He moved her off her food if I was not there to supervise and out of both her stall and loafing shed. Then I saw a large hole in the wall of her stall where they had struggled over her territory. She would squeal and kick out, but not where she would make contact. She would go into flight, but not fight back.

It is so important to a horse's confidence in us, when we are in a position of leadership with them, to protect them from threats. So whenever I was interacting with them, my focus was in running interference for Chasta from Remoe. I made points with *her*, but *he* became increasingly wary of me, although I was attempting to be horselike and matter of fact. He respected me, for the most part, but watched me carefully. The willing attraction that he had for me in the beginning became guarded. I attempted to counter it with lots of friendly "hang out" time reassuring him that all was well between us, but that I expected him to be kind to Chasta. Leadership was fine, but not aggressive dominance. I played games with him whenever he started to bully her and he began nipping at me, too, asking if I was his leader, *or not*.

Then our neighbor remarked over the fence that he did not

realize that Remoe was a stallion. "He isn't," I answered. "He's a young gelding."

"*Really?!*" He seemed surprised. "He's been mounting her repeatedly and she *sure* doesn't seem to appreciate it!" *Oh, my!* How would I explain *that* to my first grade visitors?! Ritzy used to spend a lot of time at Chasta's tail looking wistful when she was in her heat cycle, but their relationship was loving and platonic.

I moved them to pastures that I could more readily watch during the days ahead, and sure enough, he mounted her clumsily and repeatedly daily until I had to separate them for periods to give her a break. After seeming initially relieved, within a few hours, they would stand and look at each other over the fence line, appearing to be pining for a reunion. Sheesh.

I contacted a talented equine homeopath, Leta Titus, and she came and tested Chasta and Remoe and gave them both herbal blends and flower essences to balance their wildly fluctuating hormones. Wow. Literally overnight, the mounting behavior stopped, and they both seemed to return to the way they were in their early weeks together, quiet and close.

Daily I noticed Remoe trying to advance on Chasta, seeming to want her affection. "Take my advice, pal, from someone who has been there," I started talking out loud to Remoe. "You cannot force affection on Chasta. She appears to be very aloof, yet you and I both know that she has a soft and gentle heart, and wants very much to be in a close relationship. But she needs to have a lot of space. Go gentle. Go easy. Allow her to *offer* herself to you, and then, when she does, be careful not to get greedy!"

Back to those space issues again. Whether they are between horses or people, until we can learn to respect the boundaries of others, and ask them to return the respect, there will be issues of violation that create problems. Chasta was not able to stand up for herself well, nor was Remoe able to control his desires in a healthy way.

Pat Parelli asks his students one of his classic questions in discussing the horse/human relationship: "Does your horse want to dance with Fred Astaire or Fred Flintstone?!" Ritzy had offered Chasta the Astaire touch, but the young and eager Remoe was more like an equine version of Fred Flintstone.

But he seemed to be getting the message! He appeared to be more deliberate in how he approached her. Chasta is lovely and voluptuous and he would look at her almost shyly and start nibbling on her withers in an attempt to be affectionate. Intrigued, she would arch her neck and return the favor.

"Perfect!" I coached from the sidelines, careful to keep my distance and feeling a bit voyeuristic. Chasta was melting into pure pleasure when Remoe suddenly resembled Gomez on the Addams Family television show when he could not resist his beautiful wife, Morticia, as he began kissing her up her arm, especially when she spoke French, excitedly exclaiming, *"Cara Mia!"* The next thing I knew, Remoe nibbled down Chasta's back with increasing pressure, and just as she was undulating with waves of pleasure, he was overcome and bit her rump lustily, *hard*! Squeal-kick! And off she ran, more affronted than ever.

This became a routine—arrgggh! Remoe needed a job! A purpose. He had *way* too much youthful energy and Chasta was his unwilling plaything. *Now what?* Most every lifetime horse caregiver I know, whether professional or backyard horseperson like me, has had horses come and go over the years. It seems to be the nature of the consuming passion of keeping equines. But for people like my family who become so attached to our animal companions and their unique ways, this situation between Chasta and Remoe felt very distressing.

There are many reasons that horses move on. People change physical locations. Horse crazy girls grow up and develop new interests. Illness. Divorce. And in this case, a wonderful young horse we had all bonded with who needed more time and training than I was able to give him. And my first allegiance was for Chasta's well-being. Daily, whenever Chasta saw me, she whinnied and approached, but as soon as Remoe saw us, he barreled up and cut her off, unless I could get there in time to prevent it. I no longer had the same access to my girl unless I separated them. And it is not my desire to have horses and to have to keep them apart. That is why we brought him home in the first place.

After much prayerful consideration, I started focusing on trusting that there was a perfect solution. Every challenge has a gift for us to realize—sometimes many. Relationships often change as part of the human experience I mentioned my situation to a good friend from a horse loving family and she suggested that I call a mutual friend who also had a college graduate daughter who was looking for a young horse. She was *another* one of the high school girls who Evan had a crush on in his budding adolescence!

When the young woman saw Remoe, it was love at first sight for both of them. Her name is Tamsyn, and she is a tall, long-legged beauty who adores his enormous hindquarters that she looks *down* on and she is also a student of natural horsemanship, and thrilled with the games I had started with him. She has the time, freedom, youth and desire to develop this beautiful and willing boy into a happy and well-balanced partner. When I delivered Remoe at their lovely farm, the lead horse in their herd made it clear from the get go that he was in charge and that their mare was *his*. Humbled immediately, it just increased Remoe's bond with his eager and caring new human.

"What is his registered name?" she asked me. "Rowdy Jack Diamond," I answered. "And as I have described to you," I started, "I realize that it appears to suit him because he *does* seem to be a true diamond in the rough." She smiled and looked at Remoe adoringly. And in that bittersweet moment, I realized that she was better suited than I was to polish him into his exquisite clarity and brilliance. I gave an emotion packed nod of thanks to Remoe for the time he had given to helping *me* polish *my* inner diamond. I had shed my tears at home and knew that I had made the best decision for all involved.

Hoping that our friendship and close proximity and shared interests with horses would allow us to continue to know and love Remoe, I offered quietly, "Goodbye for now, 'Moe." He pricked his ears from the top of the pasture and came down to the fence to offer his goodwill.

Everything happens for a reason. All part of the grand and glorious adventure that is life. I found out later that these two young women had been roommates at college! All of us united and touched by the love for a diamond in the rough. *Remoe.*

Here was my chance to practice remote love and affect Remoe from afar, sending affection out on my thought waves from my heart to a farm down the road....

PART SEVEN:

The Adventure Continues

Chapter Twenty Eight

Will you be Mine?

Kim McElroy called me to see if I would meet her at a beautiful horse facility near my home called *Wildwood Farm* where she was to visit with the owner, Heather Carder, who also owns a beautiful store in Seattle called *The Noble Horse* that features Kim's artwork. "I'd love to!" I replied. We set the date and planned to go to dinner afterward and catch up on our lives with horses.

She took the ferry up and I crossed the bridge to get to the beautiful island location. The acreage was gorgeous: hilly pastures dotted with healthy and contented horses overlooking a tranquil pond. The property is framed by wooded forests which give it a magical aura of privacy and seclusion. A bevy of tail-wagging farm dogs greeted me, while I drove slowly up to the main boarding stable. Seeing the office, I parked and got out to knock on the door. I introduced myself to the trainer, who was just finishing talking with a student, who happened to be a friend of mine! The horse world, like the entire planet, so often seems very small! She told me to make myself at home and that she would join us in a short while. Feeling welcomed and relaxed, I walked past the well-kept paddocks and saw clean water troughs and nicely stocked mangers. What a joy to see such carefully tended horses! The atmosphere felt very peaceful and healthy.

My reverie was quietly interrupted when I heard what I thought was a voice coming from outside my head. "*Will you be mine?*" Just like a greeting on an old-fashioned Valentine. I turned to see a small, lovely paint horse looking intently at me. "*Me?!*" *I* wondered aloud. "Hello, girl," I said. "You are just the beautiful little Indian Paint Pony of my dreams!" and then, without thinking, peered under her belly to confirm her plumbing. She seemed to roll her eyes at me for being such an amateur, and I flushed, feeling awkward, when I heard, *"Will you take me home?"* It did not sound at all distressed, just matter-of-fact. My heart started beating fast and I stared at her tricolor markings and large brown eyes and the shock of black forelock over a cocoa brown face falling into one of the longest and silkiest manes I had ever seen.

I fell to my knees like a seven year old and started picking up the grass hay that had fallen through the fence and started to feed it to her through the holes in the wire, while she nibbled daintily, watching my every move. The trainer had told me to make myself at home, but horse etiquette told me that did not mean personal access to the horses without permission, especially since I felt that this little beauty must be boarded there. Standing back up, I flushed again, startled by my giddiness in response to this little animal.

She then turned around slowly and deliberately to reveal the huge brown perfect heart-shaped spot over her left flank. It looked like it was made of milk chocolate. *Was she my heart horse?!* This facility is well known for its high level dressage horses and jumpers and this little probable boarder did not fit that description and likely had an adoring owner. Standing at the fence, we exchanged breath and I scratched her quietly for a long time. Finally, I sighed and walked down the hill, feeling like I was in a dream.

At the bottom of the hill I saw the lovely owner's barn and their beautiful horses in the distance in a nearby pasture. Putting down the drive came a little farm rig driven by an attractive woman with a chic haircut. She pulled up and stopped. "You must be Connie," she offered. "Yes, Hello!" I replied. It was the owner, Heather Carder. "Kim just called from the ferry landing and she is on her way." "Terrific," I answered, and then followed with "What a lovely place you have! I am very impressed with the high level of care the horses are given here. If only all equine facilities were of this quality. The horses are all so content and I felt very connected to them, one in particular."

She looked at me carefully and said, "Well, since you are a friend of Kim's, I'll go ahead and tell you that I thought I saw a horse walking at liberty next to you when I was coming down the hill!" "Really?! What kind?" I asked. "We don't know—we just call her a little Indian Paint Pony," she smiled in reply.

"*Oh, my*!" I responded incredulously. "That is the horse I just had an amazing connection with! I felt as if I heard her ask me to take her home! Who does she belong to?" I continued. *"Me!"* she beamed. "I almost never go to auctions and for some reason found myself there and she was little orphan Annie, a rescue, basically. Isn't she sweet?!" "Yes!!" I exclaimed. "What are your plans for her?" "She is being trained using Parelli™ techniques for resale." My jaw dropped.

By the time Kim arrived, I was standing in the paddock with the little horse, Heather, and trainer, Sarah Cassatt, completely convinced that I had found my next equine teacher. Kim beamed with delight, snapping our photo with her high quality camera, the one she uses to capture the exquisite beauty of the horses she paints.

Chasta is not through with me*! Not by a long shot*. But this little mare can join my big mare in my guided development, and prayerfully I can offer them the same in return.

"What was her name when you bought her?" I inquired. "We have no idea," Sarah replied, so I named her Gayla —it just came to me and seemed to be right." "I like it—it suits her!" I smiled.

The next day I went to lunch with Evan at our wonderful rural goldmine, *The Rexville Grocery and Café,* a combination gourmet grocery store and eatery that also sells corn based biodiesel for our tractor. It's a place where the locals, farmers and fishermen mix with the tourists who have discovered our beautiful valley on the way to the islands. We enjoyed a conversation about the little paint pony and I told Evan about the amazing connection that I felt for her. *"Go for it, it, Mom!"* was his recommendation. He had to buzz back to classes, and I chose to walk home.

I was still trying to sort out how I had committed to a horse without handling or riding her. Walking along the country road at a brisk clip, I asked God for a sign when something slowed me down and turned my head sharply to the right. I looked directly at a small *handmade painted sign* that was crooked from the winds that whip up the valley from the bay. It read: *Gala.* It named an apple variety sold there at the Pleasant Ridge Farm. Every season we buy Gala apples for the horses there, leaving money at the honor stand in an antique oak telephone that has a slot to deposit it. I smiled, thanking God for my sign, *literally. Gala, the horse!* I resumed my walking and had gotten about forty feet when a woman slowed her car down and through the open window pointed and said, "You dropped something back there!" as she smiled and drove away. I turned and walked back to a white image on the ground that was just adjacent to where I had abruptly turned to look at the sign—*my checkbook!* Buy Her?!! Good Heavens!

In the weeks ahead, I was preoccupied with thoughts and dreams of this special horse by day and night as I went back and forth to observe her excellent play/work sessions. She followed Sarah's gentle suggestions and was very attentive, but kept an eye on me and checked regularly to see if I was noting and appreciating her progress. *I was!*

I knew her name was meant to be Gayla, but the way they spelled it seemed to be incorrect. Was it Gala, like the apple? Hmmm.... Maybe it was Gaila, the French spelling, I wondered, which means merriment and pleasure. That's nice, I thought, but it still did not seem to ring true.

The lesson that day was inside a huge covered arena on a windy, rainy afternoon. The little horse followed Sarah confidently through all of her suggestions, and they had a wonderfully productive session, while I watched from my perch on a barrel at the other end of the arena. Ready to finish for the day, when they found the perfect high note to end on, Sarah praised the little mare and gave her time to soak it in, and then took off her halter and sent her out at liberty with a pointed finger onto a large circle. She trotted purposefully in a wide arc, directly into me and put her nose onto my heart!

Not daring to breathe, I quietly said to Sarah, "This would be the perfect response if she had been playing the Parelli game of "Put Your Nose on Something"—in this case, Me!" "*That* was my focus!" she beamed. I felt myself melt onto the barrel as if I was made of jelly! I stroked her face and neck quietly, thanked her and walked her at liberty over to take the tack off. She stayed in sync with my stride at my side without a rope like she had forever!

While driving on the way home in the rain in my reverie, it clicked. Her name is *Gaela*! The Gaelic spelling, according to my family heritage. When I got home, I typed "the meaning of the name Gaela" into a search engine on the computer and the first offering I read had a quote that told of historic nomadic horse tribes coming up from the Normandy region of France into the British Isles, precisely the lineage of my family tree! It gave me goose bumps. I clicked onto the site for the significance of the name. *It means calm healer. Whew!*

While Gaela was in training, I was given the privilege of

spending time with her at Wildwood Farm. One warm, sunny evening I arrived and when she saw me turn the corner she sounded a hearty nicker that made my day. I took lots of quiet time to groom her sweaty body and even gave her a tepid hose down before our walk in hand on a lead line. It was important for me to establish a friendly foundation for our relationship that was not too demanding. Joined by her dog buddies, we headed for the wooded trails, still warmed by the sun. We entered the woods and walked together eye to eye along the trails. We crunched over branches in our path and stepped over fallen logs, Cody the spotted dog keeping pace with the spotted horse. We emerged from a long and invigorating walk onto a beautiful meadow under a canopy of trees where the summer grass was still lush.

A perfect spot to stop and reward her for her delightful companionship, I laid down on my back on the ground and suggested she help herself to the grassy perfection. As she stretched her neck to the ground to graze, her long, silky mane was backlit by the setting sun and glowed like coral neon. From my vantage point looking up, I noticed the brown spot on her chest had a distinctive scalloped design across the bottom which formed the top line for a white heart that had curlicues of swirling hair in all directions like a lacy valentine *directly* over her actual horse heart! It occurred to me that I have loved and collected antique Valentines for many years, and here was the most beautiful one of all in three dimensions with a heart of gold! I was mesmerized and wondered why anyone would ever want an artificial high when the natural world provides more intricate beauty than I can ever wrap my mind and heart around!

Ahhh, bliss. The clothes on the floor in my laundry room at home and all my other various piles would just have to wait. *This* was a moment in time to be savored. By taking the time to be present in that moment to nourish myself allows me to be able to help others when they need my support. *Such an important balance to remember!* Ask yourself each day what you do to nourish yourself—to recharge your batteries—to make deposits in your own energy and well-being accounts. It needs to be at the top of the list. *Trust that if it is, the rest will follow.*

Jane Savoie, an expert horsewoman who has represented the United States Olympic ReserveTeam as a Dressage rider and coach and is a wonderful motivational speaker, loves sharing stories about the horses she has loved and trained over the years. I have heard horses who are docile and tractable described as: honest, willing, and even "a trouper." But I really love what Jane calls her favorite horses: volunteers. The heart of a volunteer is a being who wants to serve from their heart—to give of themselves for the benefit of others. *Gaela is a volunteer.*

I believe this diminutive creature (by horse standards) is the stuff of dreams. I borrow that description from William Shakespeare since he was a well respected horse lover.

Not just for me, but for all children at heart. I know that she has the special quality to help others access the child within. And it is my intention to make certain in the years ahead that people who may need her most of all will have the chance to look into her eyes and feel the silkiness of her long mane, as I have. To see her heart-shaped spots on the outside and feel her heart on the inside.

A dream is a wish your heart makes, and Gaela is a horse of my dreams.

Chapter Twenty Nine

A Residue of Love

What is it about these horses anyway? What is this mysterious power and fascination they seem to hold for humans over time, culture and geography? When people have a passion for something, I have heard it described by the expressions that *"it gets under their skin,"* or *"it is in their blood."*

I had the pleasure of spending lots of time with my high school boyfriend's Italian grandmother many years ago. She had come from "the old country" as numerous immigrants from this island community had, and kept a charming home and gardens that looked like a transplant from the Italian countryside. She made her own wine, salami, pasta and goat cheese, and baked crusty bread that was possibly where the "slice of heaven" expression originated. Hungry or not, when you went to visit Maria, you were *fed*. I learned to come on an empty stomach! She had the gift of being fully present and helping you to feel as if the time spent together was of great importance to her.

I can still picture her vividly now. She had dancing eyes and a body that was familiar with hard work. Her aprons were dusted with whatever she was working with at the moment, from baking to tending her glorious gardens. She spoke very little English, and at that time, I knew zero Italian. But we communicated. *Well*! We smiled, nodded, hugged, pointed, touched and occasionally both said our own versions of 'ahhhh', 'ohhhh' and 'hmmm'.... *We spoke with our eyes and our hearts and our bodies.*

Maria had the most heady aroma that surrounded her like an ever present cloud – she smelled of the earth, of salami and wine and fennel and rosemary from her gardens. It was the most delightful feeling to be hugged by her and go home smelling like the powerful sweet, musky scent that literally came out of her pores. Her passion for life was actually "under her skin" and "in her blood." She sent a trace of herself home with me every visit. I will remember our time together forever.

And that is what horses do for me. They leave a trace of themselves. They communicate with their dancing eyes, their bodies, and their hearts. And if we are aware, we can do the same for them. And after a grooming session or a ride through the forest, their scent lingers. The earthy sweet, musky smell that comes from within.

I thought of Maria's dancing eyes the other day when I saw a tee-shirt that said, "He who smiles first, wins." Sometimes when there seemed to be a lull in our "conversation" where we shared such a primitive yet remarkable language, she would simply beam at me with delight. And she won my heart.

I want to remember those moments in my daily life. To be the person who smiles first. And last. Not to win a contest, but to win a heart. I want to ooze love from my pores like Maria and the horses.

I want the love that is in my blood and under my skin to leave a residue.

Chapter Thirty

Girdled, Cinched and Otherwise Strangled

Life continues to offer lessons that are right under our noses. Just as Dorothy Gale shared in her famous line at the end of the film classic, *The Wizard of Oz,* they are often no further than our own back yard. She gained this wisdom from her dream journey of her adventures in the fanciful land of Oz, interwoven with her own real life on a farm in Kansas, as the story goes.

Mine is a life of dreams, stories and farms as well. Many years ago, Kelli, a dear friend of mine from high school, gifted us with a topiary giraffe form for our wedding anniversary. This was no table top ivy giraffe—it arrived full-sized, shaped in chicken wire with four Catoneaster starts to plant under each leg. Kelli knew that giraffes were Gary's favorite wild animal, and that this would be a fun gift for all of us, especially her little charge, Evan.

She had become an honorary auntie to him at birth, never having married or had children of her own, and she had such amazing love to share. When I was the new girl from Seattle at the little rural island school that we attended in those awkward years known then as "junior high," Kelli went out of her way to be kind to me and helped me to feel included in the close knit groups of kids who had grown up together. She had a soft spot for Gary, having known him all of her life. Every visit to see Evan was like Christmas for him, with gifts she had made or purchased, and she played with him with special joy. Evan adored her. She loved to treat us to the monstrous hand dipped ice cream in the homemade waffle cones that produced a scent that called to you over the breeze from the *Snow Goose Produce* stand near our home every summer after a romp around our property. Kelli had endless patience with pushing Evan on the swings and running under him while yelling "Underdoggie!" much to his giggling delight. He enjoyed it when I did it, but it was something that *she* had taught him, and mine were never quite the same, which was just fine with me. *There is no greater gift for a parent than for others to truly love your child.*

I decided that the chicken wire structure could use the extra strength of an iron armature, and asked my friend, Mary Taylor, owner and garden designer of *Rosebar,* to make one for us. Evan, young and full of good ideas, thought it would look great to have the giraffe reaching up to "eat" the leaves of the apple trees in the orchard. We agreed and planted the Catoneasters against the iron of the "legs" within the chicken wire. It was fun to watch the progress of the fast growing plants as they twined up the legs over time to form the back, fill in the tail and start the long ascent up the neck to the ears and finally the soft horns characteristic of the stately giraffe. The evergreen plants with small leaves blossom white in the spring, attracting bees and butterflies, and later berry in the autumn when the birds feast upon them. Every year our giraffe received several "haircuts," as the form took shape to completion.

This year, in the heat of summer, I noticed that the leaves were turning brown in areas of the body of the giraffe and made a mental note to myself to give it extra water. It is easy to get complacent about plants like Catoneaster since they are so hardy and do well in most all conditions, including neglect. Fred, a friend who helps me prune the hedges, trees and vines here, thought maybe it had some kind of insect infestation.

He knows that I do not use chemical sprays, so we talked about dousing it with some kind of soapy bath once he identified the problem from a master gardener. He had to go no further than John Christianson, a renowned nurseryman down the road, who made the diagnosis.

Fred returned with the branch in hand and said, "it is being girdled by the chicken wire and dying." *"Huh?!"* was my response. I either did not know that the chicken wire would become a problem over time as the plants grew or I had forgotten. I looked the giraffe form over carefully and saw for the first time that as the caliper of the woody plants had increased over the years, the bark was literally being cut as it came into contact with the wire. These hardy plants had survived my lack of attention, though I had given them the advantage of good soil, water and trims, *because I had not looked on the inside.*

It took a deep freeze to make the difference. The same deep freeze that changed our pond to solid ice. It put severe stress on plants that were already under siege by the invasive wires, putting them over the top in a state of increased vulnerability. The wires were strangling the plants from receiving the oxygen from the water that nourished them from within. The combination was too much and now they were starting to die from the inside out.

Girdled. Corseted. Cinched. Forms of slow strangulation. It gave me true pause to think of the women throughout history who have been corseted by the whims and expectations of the culture and fashion dictates, though it has been proven that their internal organs were misshapen and damaged. Often beyond repair. Even pregnant women were often not spared this dangerous ritual. And the horses? Cinched tight and cruelly around their bellies that gave them terrible soreness in their backs and then expected to ride into battle and serve man? Thinking about these horrors really had me aware of my emotional juices and how I needed to let them bubble to the surface, to be felt and released.

Gary and Evan went to a collector car show out of state to sell some inventory a few days before our thirty-first wedding anniversary. Before they left, we brought Gaela home, a new member of our family, as a gift to each other. I set out to save the giraffe on the day of our wedding those many years before when *we* were young and "green."

By now, the heat of summer following the freeze that set it up to die around the wires had the entire form of green leaves turning brown and dying off. Little did I know what a task it would be! Now I know how a surgeon must feel, trying to get all of a tumor removed. As I cut away the dying branches, I had to make sure that no small wires were remaining to cut into future new growth again, and carefully pull those away where they had embedded into the bark. I am not comparing human life to a topiary form, *but this was life, too!* Life that represented things that were very dear to us. Our marriage, that had looked good on the outside when it was dying on the inside. What are the things that strangle relationships? Neglect? Complacency? Self-doubt and fear? Addictions? Overwhelming debt? Unresolved conflicts and anger? Bitterness and resentments?

Deadwood. *Was there ever deadwood*! How important it is for us to work at pruning ourselves regularly with self exploration and letting go of that which we do not need—that which will damage us from within. The hurt and anger that needs to be released by true forgiveness. The critical judgement, whether directed at ourselves or others. The iron armature and the large inner branches represented my faith in a God who will always support me with a strength I must tap into. *Consciously. And constantly.*

I read a wonderful book written by Nikki Mackay called

Spoken in Whispers: The Autobiography of a Horse Whisperer. One of the stories that I enjoyed the most was of an adventure in Kenya where she was exercising some young race horses for the wealthy owners who were watching her from the nearby veranda of their stately home. As she galloped a lovely young colt, she noticed a wild herd of giraffes nearby and watched as a young member of another species ran over to join them in their frolic.

She described beautifully how as the giraffe ran along beside them, the horse and giraffe exchanged relaxed glances and then her horse found another gear, followed by a burst of speed from the young giraffe. After entering an incredible state of unity that seemed to make time stand still, they finally had enough of the high speed romp, when she slowed her horse down and they made a large circle back to the area where she started. The young giraffe looked over and she said he seemed to smile and thank them for the pleasure as he trotted back to his herd. She recalled being in a state of complete awe from what she considered one of the greatest thrills of her entire life.

When she returned, the owners started to ask her opinion of the performance of their promising racehorse, and she was literally still breathless, not only from the ride, but from the total wonder of what she had experienced with a wild animal and the domestic one that she had only just met.

Knowing that she and the horse and giraffe had been in plain view, she asked incredulously, *"Did you see that giraffe?!"* The response was, "Oh, goodness, yes, they do that *all the time,*" as if it was something very ordinary. Nikki vowed then and there that she would never regard any encounter with any animal or living thing with complacency, but with wonder. I have thought of that incredible story so many times since I first read and was inspired by it, and now her experience gave me the resolve to keep going with my arduous snipping, and I felt stronger with every discovery of the woody shape within. Nature had made perfect loopy giraffe shaped ears and a tail and little horns in the branching skeleton that had a beauty all it's own after being stripped of the damaged greenery.

Not only did I want to save this living shape as a symbol of our marriage that had needed healing from the inside out, but I had a deep need to save it for Kelli and her kind and loving heart.

She had developed a rare lung disease that took her life when Evan was still small. On her last few trips out here for ice cream, she was attached to an oxygen machine, her lungs starved for it as the branches of the giraffe had been. Evan was big enough to sail through the air on his huge swings on his own, as she watched from the sidelines, knowing that his days of "underdoggie" were behind him, but that the memories would remain. I look at Evan now, big and strong, and know that one day if he is blessed with a child, *he will remember*.

The last time that I talked with Kelli, we had agreed to meet at a baseball game nearby that both of our nephews were playing in. Evan and I looked forward to the date when we got the call that Kelli had died that evening. We were stunned and saddened deeply. At the funeral, her beautiful mother bravely announced that a man was seeing that day from Kelli's eyes, a gift that meant a great deal to all of them because it had been their generous daughter's final wish.

Seeing with new eyes. I was reminded that I have that gift every day.

There were more gifts. I had to get the mounting block that we use for the sake of our horses' backs when we swing a leg over to ride them to stand on to snip away at the neck of the giraffe. There nestled in the inner branches was a beautiful and intricate abandoned nest where a bird family at one time had a remarkable sanctuary from the elements. The nest, like all of those found on our property, was carefully lined with hair from our horses that had fallen to the ground during our grooming sessions. This intricately woven masterpiece represented the family to me and the importance to tending to the health of ours, above all else. It is our gift to each other and the world to love ourselves and one another.

The giraffe as an animal has almost a mystical appeal. They have always seemed otherworldly to me with their lacy eyelashes and long amazing necks covered with the unique patterns that actually reminded me of the hexagon shape of the chicken wire that seemed so innocuous and had provided support until it became a threat. We need to be loving, but aware and vigilant in healthy ways. Horses teach us to do just that. The soft horns of the giraffe on each side of the head also include one in the center of the forehead, like a third eye, which represents intuition. Horses help us to find that sense within us, too. From their vantage point of extra height, the giraffe sees the horizon and gains wisdom in the seeking of what is there. Horses possess the larger outlook as well, and pass it on to us.

In the wake up call of the freeze that was the beginning of the end for the topiary giraffe because of it's state of vulnerability, can we look at other challenges as blessings? The loss of a job, the diagnosis of an illness? The state of world affairs that we do not understand? How can we see these as life lessons and opportunities to find our faith and strength within and offer it to others?

Gary and Evan returned from their trip and I took Gary out into the garden to see the giraffe, stripped of it's bulk down to it's botanical bones. He was startled and became very quiet as I shared with him how this discovery and process of cutting away of what was dead and dying had meant to me. The experience felt like a metaphor for this entire collection of stories from our lives in three dimensions, which I felt had brought us full circle.

"I am willing to do whatever it takes to preserve the beauty of our marriage and the gift of Kelli's love!" I proclaimed. "I have cut all of the chicken wire and dead branches out and now only the legs remain," I continued. "Since there are four, here are gloves and clippers. You do yours as a metaphor for standing up on your own two legs for yourself and I will for mine." It was all I could do to keep from standing on top of the mounting block as a soapbox or pulpit for what I felt was a powerful homily in our lives!

He smiled through tears in his eyes and sat down on the top of the mounting block and started to snip. I, the gardener, resisted the temptation to tell him how to do the job, and only offered suggestions when he *asked* for help! *Honest!*

One of the saving graces of this wake-up call of the giraffe was that it also rescued all of the trees in our orchard! Years ago when our cats were small, they were using the young trees as scratching posts, damaging the delicate bark. I was told to make loose cylinder "cages" of chicken wire around the trunks and they would discourage the cats. It worked great and for some unknown reason, in my attention, when pruning the trees or enjoying their harvest (especially the apples and pears for the horses), I had failed to notice that the caliper of the trunks had increased so much that they were also completely girdled by the chicken wire! I spent the time that Gary and Evan were away removing the very thing that I had put on to protect the trees in the first place!

Lessons, always lessons to be learned! Acknowledging and appreciating the energy of our faith, our combined tenacity (which is almost as strong as a team of horses!), our unwillingness to give up, and sheer endurance, gave us both a healing balm for our hearts.

And now, with careful attention to watering and the application of organic fertilizer, we have what we earned by being willing to go to any length to look within and lookout for each other—*new growth.*

Chapter Thirty One

Remember

"If you look into the eye of a horse,
there lies the wisdom which is deeper
than a thousand prose contained in books ...
The knowledge, which is so innate it is a heritage ...
And if you look far enough, and are very lucky,
you will see a reflection which
Is the best of you ... ***and is the image of God!"***

~ *Alice Trindle*

There is nothing I have shared on these pages that hasn't already been said many times, many ways. I have been affected and impacted by human interpretations of God all of my life. We all have. The gift to understand and resonate with truth is the Holy Spirit within—a gift we have all been given. The ability to align with that inner knowing simply takes practice. We just forget sometimes. Less often with repetition. Author Marianne Williamson refers to "The Holy Instant" of our remembering. That moment when we recognize we are in fear and protection rather than love and growth. The chance to be aware of our own breath, take it in deeply, blow it out slowly, and choose peace. Choose the way back to God. Make a U-turn on the trail back to love.

In an equine facilitated self discovery session, Adventures in Awareness™, Barbara Rector, creator of the process, told me to "Always remember what you already know." Once in the light and love of God, we know. In the stillness, you will know. Awakened from our deep sleep, we see with different eyes and feel from an expanded heart.

With Chasta and with life, it has sometimes been a wild ride. *Remembering,* I chose to get back on.

It is my hope that my words give you a leg up to fully experience the ride that is *your* life....

My Warmest Wishes,

Connie

Constance Funk
Woodylane Farm

P.S. I invite you to read on...

Epilogue

There is no beginning and there is no end. That does not make an author's task easier when it comes to finishing a book, especially a first book. Birthing anything this personal and significant must get easier each time. Like birthing babies, I'm told. Being the mother of only one child, I can relate to the feeling of trying to get it right the first time, still in new territory.

When I sat down to recall and record my stories, they literally poured out of me. More than once, fatigue and writer's cramp tempted me to end a session, when my hand continued to twitch, telling me there was more. The bones of it came out in four days time, and in the weeks and months ahead, I began to flesh it out. It had gestated for exactly the right period: half a century! I felt like I just needed to connect the dots, the outline already there by my intentions, prayers and memories. Remember those cardboard pictures from your childhood that you stitched? God of the universe supplied the card, all I needed to do was thread the yarn and loop it through the holes. To *become whole*.

I was typing the first draft when Evan came into the room, holding the wishbone that had been drying in the kitchen windowsill since Thanksgiving. *"Make a wish!"* he said. I closed my eyes and felt the bone break between my fingers. I got the big piece, so I closed my eyes and made my wish. "Guess what I wished for?" I asked him. "You can't tell me or it won't come true!" he cautioned, "What if I telepath it to you?" I teased, knowing how often Evan and I are on the same wavelength. He looked at me and said, "You hope to publish your book to benefit many." *My thought verbatim.*

And if that were not enough, an hour later when I finished the typing, I closed my eyes and asked God to give me a sign that I was on the right track, feeling gratitude for the privilege of being a scribe. Immediately, a very powerful visual image of an engraving of a hand and a feather pen came into my mind—naturally, the first manuscripts were done with quills and it occurred to me how many feather symbols and sightings I have had in the past few years—Chasta has, in fact, put her hoof on more than one! It was time to pen my stories. *Our* stories. Because stories are universal, and speak for all of us. And I feel this is only the beginning.

Then I walked through the entry to our home and a book lying there caught my eye. It was a book I bought for my mother. I have been reading aloud to her and we enjoy our time together very much. The words across the top of the page said *"New York Times Runaway Best Seller."* My story started with a runaway horse, so why not?!

I sent copies of the first draft to my friends and family who gave me support and encouragement and helped me to find the seemingly endless typos that I thought I had corrected.

When I felt the manuscript was finished, I had a strong feeling that there would be something to add from the pilgrimage trip to Italy that we were scheduled to take as chaperones with Evan's youth group, made possible by our church family. After all, we would be retracing the steps of Saint Francis and Saint Clare in Assisi. Gary's passport needed to be updated and Evan had never had one. The weeks were winding down and we had yet to receive them. I went online and the message said that you could not get any information on tracking them for four weeks. Our trip departure was scheduled before then! I called the automated number and could not get through. *Those are always fun calls!* I went to bed with anxiety and spent a restless night. In the morning, Evan asked me what was wrong. As I shared my concern with him, he said, *"You know what to do."* Evan has been one of my greatest spiritual advisors since the day he was born—and even before! I must have looked blank because he continued, "Say the serenity prayer." I did. Attributed to Reinhold Niebuhr, this sentence has the power to transform. *"God, grant me the serenity to accept the things I cannot change, the courage to change the things I can, and the wisdom to know the difference."* I closed my eyes and thought of Saint Francis and how his words had always given me comfort. I said another prayer. I could not change the dates or the system, but I could change my attitude from one of anxiety and fear to one of trust and confidence. Lately, this was one of those times when Gary and Evan would point me in the direction of my book and suggest that I read it! Sheesh! *Walk the talk.*

I took action. Change what you can. I called back to the office where we had filed, and explained our dilemma again to a woman and told her that I had tried everything and that we still had a time crunch challenge. She started out a bit on the defense, and the softer and kinder I became, the more helpful she was. She gave me another e-mail address, and I immediately sent a message, followed up by a copy of it plus our itinerary sent by fax. Feeling better, I envisioned it all working out just fine. That night when I checked my e-mail, hoping for a response, it was there, from the customer service manager from the passport center. He had traced our passports all the way across the country, and made the staff there aware of the need to expedite them. The passports arrived a few days later. Our benefactor's name was *Francisco*! Saint Francis was also known and loved as Francisco, and in his native Italian, Francesco. What more could I learn from my trip than to put my faith and trust in God? *And keep it there!*

It turns out that the trip to Italy was, indeed, a pilgrimage. Do you remember my intention in the introduction of this book that I am working on the awareness of traveling light? First, I focused on packing for the trip as minimally as possible before we left and then the airline lost our luggage when we changed planes so it was not at our destination when we arrived in Rome!

Our delightful and inspiring Italian-American guide, Anthony, a postgraduate college student in Rome, reminded us in Assisi of Saint Francis renouncing his worldly goods in the public square and focusing his hands and heart to service. Of all of the grand and glorious art and architecture I witnessed on the trip, one of the relics that most touched my heart was the aged and tattered robe worn by Saint Francis, repaired with dozens of patches by hundreds and probably thousands of careful stitches. Seeing it while wearing my travel clothes for the third day in a row was *extremely* humbling. Visiting the sacred sites where Saint Francis and Saint Clare and their brothers and sisters lived and loved, the feeling of *Pax et Bonum,* the familiar greeting of Saint Francis to all life, translated as "Peace and All Good," was palpable.

Anthony, incredibly knowledgeable and wise far beyond his years, shared the story of the miracle of the pair of white doves who have kept a vigil at a statue of Saint Francis for centuries. With no food left to attract them, one is always resting on or near the image of the Saint while the other perches nearby. How can we understand this mystery of communication between these lovely winged messengers who have responded to this call to love? Generation after generation. I watched the teenaged students, Evan among them, ponder what they were witnessing, jaws dropped and eyes wide with wonder. God's symbolic messenger of the Holy Spirit, the dove, small and fragile, but looking completely serene and at peace amongst the constant throng of tourists and seekers.

Several days later in Rome, there I was again in my sweaty travel clothes, the pants that had served me well on the flight over from Seattle, Washington, were rolled up past my knees and sticking to me in the humid Roman heat. We were touring the Colosseum while Anthony described the history that had occurred there. The architecture is mind boggling—the sheer size and structure hard to comprehend in it's scale. He recounted the events that crowded the stadium-like building. Battles against man and beast. Beast against beast. Dramas and re-enactments that resulted in death. But these were not simulations to the extent that everyone involved walked away following the performances. People and animals actually died. By the numbers. The blood shed was that of slaves and others like the animals who had no voice. Saints and saints in progress, children among them, martyred for proclaiming their faith—executed for entertainment.

Although I had knowledge of this history from textbooks, it was quite another thing for me to be there physically, my mind picturing the brutality in vivid detail while my gut was wrenching. I have heard and read of similar responses by people touring places like the battlefields of the Civil War or the sacred ground at Wounded Knee.

The group split up to walk through the facility, agreeing to return to a designated meeting place. Already uncomfortably hot, I was now experiencing nausea and constriction of breath. I focused on deep belly breathing, finding a granite wall to lean on in a small area of shade. I wanted to experience this feeling deeply throughout my body in order to release it. By the time the group reassembled, I felt calmer and lighter and very much aware of healing love all around me.

We walked out as a group toward the ruins that surround the area and found ourselves looking back at the gigantic Colosseum. Two men, apparently street vendors, rushed by us with their goods rolled up in sheets in order to avoid the local "polizia," either because their merchandise was illegal or that they had no permits—or maybe both.

We parted as they ran through us, and I had a beckoning sense to step into the shade of a nearby path. I was at the back of the group and something that felt like angelic presence cause me to turn my head around and look down. There camouflaged against the light colored pebbles was a tiny image that drew me in. I bent down to pick it up as it fluttered slightly to distinguish it from the rock.

It was a pair of die-cut white doves barely more than an inch across made of *tissue paper!* I held it up carefully, trying not to tear it in my heat dampened hands in total amazement while the enormity of the stone Colosseum loomed in the distance as a backdrop for this delicate image. *The doves!* Serene and at peace. Always there. *Always everywhere.*

I stood up straighter, realizing that I felt strong and invigorated and that my group was moving off without me as I was contemplating this miracle!

The feeling of peace and utter serenity was offered again as we viewed Michaelangelo's masterpiece in marble, *The Pieta.* Anthony's description of what the youthful yet master sculptor was intending to convey moved me so deeply as to transform me. He explained that Mary's devotion to and trust in God allowed her to remain serene and at peace in both the joy at the birth and sorrow at the death of her son, Jesus. The statue represents both, and her right hand embraces the baby Christ while her left hand releases the crucified Savior. As Anthony described the subtle nuances of this exquisitely beautiful chiseled marble many centuries later, I experienced the full range of emotions that the young Michaelangelo hoped to convey. The agony and the ecstasy, and everything in between, fully felt and embodied, leading to a true and lasting peace. The silhouette of Mary's accepting gaze in the stone and the memory of the soft eyes of the doves keeping vigil for the statue of Saint Francis back in Assisi seemed to merge as I stood in the enormous Basilica of Saint Peter, feeling truly unaware of the mass of humanity all around me and at the same time feeling deeply connected to every soul who had stood in the same spot over the centuries. I felt as one with all life in the company of family, friends, strangers, Saints, and the pair of watchful doves. I am confident that a mother from any faith tradition would understand and share my response and I felt as if I was embracing them all.

Acceptance. Humility. Joy, love and laughter. The perspective we gained over losing our luggage added a great deal to the depth of our experience. And it wasn't just my family. The entire group had parted company with the carefully packed contents of their luggage, wandering the cobblestone streets with little more than the clothes on our backs. After the initial frustration individually and as a group, we felt liberated and humbled by our newly imposed simplicity. We shared freely and supported each other with what we had. Our basic needs were more than met as we gained greater appreciation for the tremendous abundance in our lives. Gary and I received our luggage by courier on the final day of our trip, just in time to lug it home!

Home. We have a loafing shed for the horses in the lower pasture below the pond. As I have described, Ritzy and Chasta were unusually close in their bond as best friends—true mates. Like an old married couple who have their own sides of the bed, they stood inside it against the wall, backed into it in the same configuration each time they entered, whether to get out of the sun or rain. Though Ritzy was clearly a lover, not a fighter, he was fiercely protective of Chasta until he could be satisfied that whoever approached was not a threat to her, especially with other horses. I will always remember how he reacted when a young, handsome horse half again his size entered the pasture where he stood guarding his girl. Ritzy was wearing a fly mask with especially long, pointy ear covers that he pinned back in warning like two mailbox flags. It made his head look like a giant light bulb and you could see his eyes bugged out through the transparent web of the mask. We thought he resembled Barney Fife, the nervous deputy character on the old Andy Griffith show from the fifties, when he got worked up over his girlfriend, Thelma Lou. Old Ritz was *besotted*.

Chasta still grieves for him, as I do. We wander together to our old familiar places and though she never stands in his spot in the loafing shed, she often walks into it and sniffs against the wall and lingers, hanging her head quietly. We walked in together recently and I stood next to her, remembering. That is when I saw the little blue flowers in full bloom, seeded by the wind in the most unlikely spot in the deepest corner where he stood, his hair still on the wall where he liked to scratch his itchy spots: *Forget-me-nots.*

Scanned image of tissue paper doves found on a path in Rome

Recommended Resources

Equine Art:

Kim McElroy
(360) 297-7736
www.spiritofhorse.com

Diane Williams
(604) 542-2664
www.dianewilliamsart.com

Liz Mitten Ryan
www.onewiththeherd.com
(250) 377-3884

James Montgomery/Nature's Steel Sculptures
(503) 661-8738

Marion Cox
(604) 463-1191
www.catinthebathtubpress.com

Favorite Books from my Library:

The Tao of Equus
Riding Between the Worlds
The Way of the Horse
All by Linda Kohanov

Horse Sense and the Human Heart
Horses and the Mystical Path:
The Celtic Way of Expanding the Human Soul
Both by Drs. Thomas, Marlena and Deborah Mc Cormick

Horses Never Lie
Life Lessons from a Ranch Horse
A Good Horse is Never a Bad Color
Horsemanship Through Life
All by Mark Rashid

Natural Horse-Man-Ship by Pat Parelli

Horsemanship Principles: The Art of Developing a Willing Partnership by Alice Trindle

Horses Don't Lie
Dancing With Your Dark Horse
Both by Chris Irwin

Adventures in Awareness: Learning With The Help of Horses
by Barbara Rector

Molecules of Emotion
What to do to Feel Go(o)d
Both by Dr. Candace Pert

Kindred Spirits, How the Remarkable Bond Between Humans and Animal Can Change the Way We Live
Love, Medicine and Animal Healing
Both by Dr. Allen Schoen

All Creatures Great and Small (series) by James Herriott

Inspiration: Your Ultimate Calling by Dr. Wayne Dyer

Everyday Grace by Marianne Williamson

The Biology of Belief by Dr. Bruce Lipton

The Missing Piece/Peace in Your Life by Rob Williams

Soul Medicine by Dr. Norman Shealy and Dawson Church

The Tellington TTouch: A Revolutionary Natural Method to Care for and Train Your Animal by Linda Tellington-Jones

From Heart to Art by Kim McElroy

Naked Liberty by Carolyn Resnick

BioSpirituality by Drs. Peter Campbell and Ed McMahon

Focusing by Dr. Eugene Gendlin

Hope Rising
Bridge Called Hope
Both by Kim Meeder

Beautiful Jim Key by Mim Eichler Rivas

Seabiscuit by Laura Hildebrand

Move Closer, Stay Longer by Dr. Stephanie Burns

The Lives of the Heart: Poems by Jane Hirschfield

Codependent No More by Melodie Beattie

Charlotte's Web by E.B. White

Believe
The Faraway Horses
Both by Buck Brannaman

Kinship with all Life by J. Allen Boone

A Winning Attitude! by Jane Savoie

Power VS Force by David Hawkins, MD, Phd.

Other Areas of Interest for Inspiration and Wellness:

Touch Drawing
Creator: Deborah Koff-Chapin
(360) 221-5745
touchdrawing.com

Psych-K Centre
Psych-K.com
Psych-K Practictioners:
Dhebi DeWitz Jensen, empoweredtransformations.com
Larry Valmore, sacredmind.net

Camp Brotherhood
(866) 344-CAMP (2267)
(360) 445-5061
www.campbrotherhood.com

Bowenwork
Bowenwork Health Center
Nancy Clark, LMT, RBT
(360) 658-6071

Watsu
Liz Bart, M.Ed.
www.soothingwaters.net

Rejuvenetics
(360) 466-1856
www.rejuvenetics.com

Tai Chi
www.americantaichi.net
contact@americantaichi.net

Morter Health System
(800) 874-1478
www.morterhealthsystem.com

Native Artwork
Mary Snowdown and Robert Eagle Bear Lawrence
(360) 293-3761

Equine and Human Natural Horsemanship Training:

Pat & Linda Parelli
Parelli Natural Horse-Man-Ship
(800) 642-3335
www.parelli.com

Jonathan Field
Field Horse Centre
(604) 857-1831
www.jonathanfield.net

Kathy Yaeger
(360) 708-1151

Wildwood Farm
Owner: Heather Carder
(360) 679-3474
www.wildwoodfarm.com

Sarah Cassatt, Trainer
(360) 320-8215

Carolyn Resnick
www.beyondthewhisper.com
(760) 743-3377

Bryan Smith, Equine Ethnologist
(206) 229-6922
www.libertytraining.net

Alice Trindle
T & T Horsemanship
(541) 856-3356
www.tnthorsemanship.com

Amelia Tritz
(360) 592-9008

Equine Facilitated Therapy/Experiential Learning and Development:

Sandra Wallin, MA, RCC
Chiron's Way Centre for Equine Guided Development
(604) 462-9182
www.chironsway.com

Linda Kohanov
Epona International Study Center
(520) 455-5908
www.thetaoofequus.com

Barbara Rector
Adventures In Awareness
(520) 247-3383
www.adventuresinawareness.com

Bonnie Treece
Horses Way Equestrian Arts
(970) 931-2278
www.horsesway.com

Equine Inspiration:

The Way of the Horse cards and book set
Text by Linda Kohanov and artwork by Kim McElroy

One With The Herd by Liz Mitten Ryan
www.onewiththeherd.com

American Cowgirl, a Documentary film by Jamie Williams and Lisa Dee

Seabiscuit, the film, based on the book by Laura Hillenbrand

Hidalgo, the film, based on the life of Frank Hawkins

The Tapestry Institute
Jo Belasco, Director
The Study of the Horse Human Bond
(575) 387-6855
www.tapestryinstitute.com

Cloud, Wild Stallion of the Rockies, a film by Ginger Kathrens
www.thecloudfoundation.org

Any book or film or CD by Robert Vavra,
www.robertvavra.com

Cavalia
(514) 879-9002
cavalia.com

Lorenzo of Provence
International Horse Show
showlorenzo@aol.com

Dancing with Horses
Book & film by Klaus Ferdinand Hempfling

Equine inspired music by Mary Ann Kennedy
www.maryannkennedy.com

Tony Stromberg, Equine Photographer
www.tonystromberg.com

Davina Andree Long
Arrowhead Graphics
www.arrowheadgraphics.com

Leah Juarez, Equesse, Inc.
www.equesseinc.com

The Path of the Horse, a film by Stormy May
www.stormymay.com

Equine Health and Wellness:

Allen Schoen, D.V. M., M. S.
Integrative Holistic Animal Health Care
(860) 354-2287
schoenoffice@gmail.com

Riva's Remedies, Ltd.
Marijke van de Water
(800) 405-6643
www.rivasremedies.com

Leta Titus, M. A.
Herbs and Flower Essences
(206) 384-5697
(360) 939-0253

Dolores Elliason
Naturally Balanced Hoofcare and Bodywork
(604) 290-2014

Dr. Nels Rasmussen
Chiropractic and B.E.S.T.
(306) 436-1663
(425) 238-2668

Debra Thiesen, Energy Practicioner
(360) 778-1227

Acknowledgments

I try to start and finish everything with gratitude to God. When I do, everything feels so much better. When I forget, thanks to those of you who help by reminding me. Including my horses. So thank you to Chad, Chasta, Ritzy, Gaela and for my time with Remoe and Sonny (aka Lefty), Mariner and Moussie, Rosie and Goodie, my equine teachers. Where do I begin to thank everyone for all they have been and done for me in my life to help create the opportunity to share my heart? I feel as if I should list them as "The Cast of Characters" because they are a rich and varied group!

The best place to start is with the family who gave me life — my parents, Glen and Kay Bartlett, for encouraging me to love language and beauty wherever I experienced it. Your initial response to my book was a profound healing for me. My siblings, Debbie, Craig and Wendy, and the extended family who has had the most impact on my life: my maternal grandmother, Helen, my uncle Rob, my paternal grandfather, Percy, my great aunt Gertrude, my aunt and uncle Loren and Jean Bartlett, and their children, Lorean, Glen and Brent. For the next generations of horse lovers: Callie, Tynan, Matt, Katie, Hunter, Rylan, Ashley and Sydney. For those of us alive in this form on the planet, let's all know and love each other the best we can!

To my husband Gary and my son Evan. I love you both to the moon and back. *We are the Funks*. Whatever motivated you to bring Chasta home for me, it was a great decision. She is a gift that keeps on giving!

For my wonderful friends — there is no way to include you all, or to put you in any order of importance, so I trust that you all know who you are and how much your contribution has meant to me, on this book project, and in my life. Kim McElroy — for your countless hours of editorial suggestions, for knowing my heart and believing in me and for saying that I possessed courage. The root of the word courage means heart, and that is what I have attempted to share. I believe courage is not the absence of fear, but the willingness to walk into that fear (or in my case ride at lightening speed when I least expected it) to come through the other side stronger. You and your incredible art have helped me to do that. Your Spirit Sketches® and print of *Silent Night* make the text come alive! And to Kim's beloved husband, Rod, for your patience and kindness in sharing Kim and loving the animals the way you do. You are a man amongst men. For Lisa Dee, who looked me straight in the eye, and told me, "the time is now." Your spark lit my fire, and I am truly grateful. For Dhebi and Phil Jensen, who were there at that defining moment, and who have shared so much on a soul level. For Kathy Yaeger, who shared my heart for Chasta from the beginning, and has taught me so much. For Amelia and Erich, the sweetest couple on the planet—you are family! For my dear friend and mentor, Sandra Wallin—you have accepted me into your home and heart by seeing into mine. You are my guide and inspiration, and I am forever grateful for who you are and what you have done for me. For Greg, for taking in the Funkster at all hours! For Jonathan and Angie Field, for welcoming me into your extended family of students of the horse, and for all of the life lessons I have learned because of our time together. For Pat and Linda Parelli for their amazing program that has provided my family and me so much opportunity for growth. For all of my Parelli pals all over the world—you know who you are! Especially Joanne Carrigan, for sharing Ritzy with us. And Aurora Wright, always a bright spot of support. For Diane Williams—your brilliant equine photographs and paintings are an inspiration, as you are!

For Marella Dubuque for professional typing and Kate Morgan for your expertise with photographs. Many thanks to Jeremy Townsend of PublishingWorks for your patience and expertise.

For Barbara Rector, with my complete admiration. Thank you for helping me to remember what I already know. For Linda Kohanov, whose brilliant writing and research about the horse/human bond that caused my heart to dance and sing, and for your personal and heartfelt guidance. For my friend and graphic designer, Davina Andrée, whose creative and loving spirit is just what my heart needs to move forward in my dreams. For Bonnie Treece for seeing into my dreams.

For Elke Macartney and James Montgomery for being living examples of the power of "paying it forward." And for Liz Mitten Ryan and her amazing herd, for showing us the possibilities that love creates.

For all of the "healing artists and scientists" who have helped me to regain my health: My nurse practitioner, Dolly Joern, who has been with me through it all. My massage therapy angels, Rebecca Vest, Joanne Mitchelle, and my sister, Debbie. For my pal and physical therapist, Lynette Cram. Dr. Nels Rasmussen for helping me to lighten my spirit and strengthen my body. To Liz Bart for the transformative bliss of Watsu and our cherished friendship. For Melinda Burghduff, for biofeedback sessions. For the crew at Rejuvenetics, for energy healing. For Nancy Clark for your mastery of Bowenwork, and for Joanell Tylor, the most amazing medical detective/intuitive ever—you epitomize the art and science of healing as a person and a practitioner. For Barbara Paul, Jayne DeFelice and Kristin Fernald for your expertise. For Dr. Mark Backman, for your kindness and support for my healing journey. For the Psych-K teachings of Rob Williams, Dhebi Dewitz-Jensen and Larry Valmore. For Camille and June, my Tai Chi teachers. And for my teacher/healer/friend from moment one, Debra Thiesen. There have been many others along the way, and to each of you, my gratitude.

For the amazing group of equine healers who have

worked directly with my horses—bravo! Thank you to Kathy Yeager, Amelia Tritz, Dr. Nels Rasmussen, Marijke van de Water, Vita Lobelle, Leta Titus, John Lala, Jr., Alexa Linton, Debra Thiesen, Dr. Greg Ingman and my buddy Dolores Elliason. Dolores has a way with horses based on her admiration for them, plus she makes me laugh. If I were ever tempted to do stand up comedy, I would have Dolores help me write my stuff!

To Heather Carder of Wildwood Farm and trainer Sarah Cassatt—Gaela is the stuff of dreams—thanks for witnessing our heart connection, and for making it happen! To Jannae Hammer and Kathy Yeager for animal care when we are away—what a gift! For Anette Vos, for tending the gardens and keeping the home fires burning, not to mention your computer savvy and patience with my current skills! And to all my neighbors for loving our animals, especially to our dear Nonie, who at eighty years young is Chasta's number one cheerleader!

To the outstanding authors who have inspired me, too numerous to mention here—you will find them in the resource section for recommended reading. But I must thank those of you who have personally supported me in this endeavor: Kim McElroy, Barbara Rector, Linda Kohanov, Dr. Candace Pert, Dr. Allen Schoen, Jane Hirschfield, Patricia Kelley, Helen Lescheid, Elisabeth Bart, Jane Savoie, Alice Trindle and Liz Mitten Ryan.

And always, my gratitude for my many special friends over the years—you all know who you are whether you knew I was writing a book or not! I truly love and appreciate each of you. And finally, to the people who I was sure I had challenges with in any way. Thanks for your help in awakening my spirit. All is forgiven, I trust.

I will never be finished with feeling grateful, for it is an attitude of gratitude that keeps me balanced and well. I saw a message on a reader board once that said: "I am too blessed to be stressed." Cliché as it may sound, *that* is the secret to living well in these times. So thank you, God, for the great opportunity to practice my emotional fitness with this experience! I pray that as you continue to communicate with me that I heed the call!

~ Connie Funk

About the Author

Constance Funk has been a lifelong lover of animals and nature and their connection with the human family.

After graduating from college with a degree in dental hygiene, she was in private practice until the birth of her son, Evan, in 1990.

Her interests have created pursuits in landscape design, antique sales and appraisals, multi media artwork, and the committed study of the horse. She teaches mosaic design and offers field trips for local school children to learn about compassionate animal care, recycling, and organic gardening and composting. She has been an ardent volunteer to support organizations that benefit children and families, animals and the environment, and the arts.

A lifelong interest in writing has resulted in publications in magazines and newspapers, and this is her first book.

Connie lives on Pleasant Ridge in rural Washington State with her husband, son and extended animal family.

Photo (on left) of Chasta and Connie by Evan Funk

INDEX

All of the horses and other animals' names in the text are listed in the index to honor them equally.